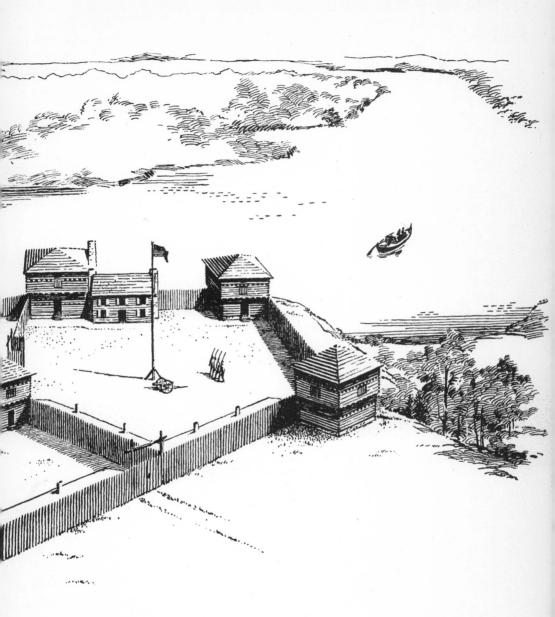

FORT OSAGE ON THE MISSOURI, 1808–1825

Westernmost U. S. military outpost until 1819 and
farthest west of the goverⁿ
factory

Guns on the Early Frontiers

GUNS

On The Early
Frontiers

A HISTORY OF FIREARMS FROM COLONIAL
TIMES THROUGH THE YEARS OF THE
WESTERN FUR TRADE

By Carl P. Russell

BONANZA BOOKS · NEW YORK

© MCMLVII
By The Regents of the University of California
Library of Congress Catalog Card Number: 57-6042
Designed by Rita Carroll
Printed in the United States of America

This edition published by Bonanza Books,
a division of Crown Publishers, Inc.,
by arrangement with University of California Press
A B C D E F G H

DEDICATED

TO THE MEMORY OF MY FATHER

Alonzo Hartwell Russell
1834–1906

Captain, Company C, 19th Wisconsin
Volunteers, 1861–1865

Preface

The gun had a greater influence in changing the primitive ways of the Indian than any other object brought to America by the white man. It is true also that firearms became the decisive factor in subduing the Indian and in settling the quarrels between white men during their early occupation of the New World. By the beginning of the seventeenth century the gun had become an institution in America and there were definite patterns of procedures in procuring and distributing arms and ammunition. Traditions in design and manufacture of guns were recognizable very early in the American trade, and pronounced preferences for certain types and models were shown by both the Indian and the invading white man. In this regard the military in the earlier periods were less selective than the private citizenry. Efforts were made by several governments to prohibit the trading of guns to Indians, but for the most part the prohibitions had little effect; statistics on guns imported are impressive even in the present day of astronomical figures.

As the gun frontier moved westward, the native tribes discarded their primitive weapons and lost their aboriginal traits. This process of change moved across the continent during a two-hundred-year period. In the early years of the nineteenth century it reached the Pacific slope. Contrary to popular belief, the Indian of the Colonial period was not a skillful user of guns. As a matter of fact, he was abusive of his weapon and rather heedless of its powers and limitations; yet he made his simple musket function importantly in hunt-

ing and warfare. The gun-carrying Indian played a notable role in
the economic scheme of the white man and in the tragic contests
for empire everywhere north of Mexico. White politicians of the
day made all-out efforts to keep the gun and its powder and ball
always available to the tribesmen.

It is the purpose of this book to identify the guns that were used
in America during the era of eastern settlement and the westward
advance of the frontier. Because the fur trade provided much of the
initial *modus operandi* in westward expansion, the earliest armament on all frontiers consisted chiefly of the guns of traders and
trappers. Since the military sometimes went along with or ahead
of the traders, military arms had a notable influence upon the westward movement; the guns of the soldier therefore find place in the
story. Ammunition, which formed a large and important part of the
frontiersman's property, also receives some attention.

Guns on the Early Frontiers is concerned particularly with the
arms used in the West during the first half of the nineteenth century,
but since the guns used in the earlier settlement of the eastern half
of the continent were the antecedents of the western arms, these too
are discussed. And in order that the story of guns in the West may
be better understood, the roots of the gun trade are traced to their
seventeenth-century origins on the eastern seaboard and on the
St. Lawrence. Dutch, French, and English traders, especially, laid
the groundwork for the gun trade in the New World two hundred
years before the Americans started to trade in guns. Consequently,
European arms and European influences are given some attention.

The commercial and political aspects of the earlier story of the
Indian and the gun are highly dramatic subjects; yet the better-
known annals of the American West have few true tales of the gun
trade. This book accords the subject a popular treatment which
should lead to further exploration in this field. The illustrations and
the analytical text related to them will enable the reader to recognize
the guns themselves. Some sections of the book are addressed particularly to the fraternity of gun collectors, to museum curators, and
to those archaeologist-historians who precede the curators in han-

dling guns and parts of guns as they are dug up in the course of excavation of historic sites. It is my hope that the interpretation of the progressive advance in mechanics and models of arms will appeal to the general reader of American lore and that it will perform a practical service to the widespread program of analysis of gun fragments which are being brought to light in the course of archaeological work on sites that once were the haunts of Indians. The book should be useful to curators who are organizing firearms material for publication or display, and interesting to private arms collectors everywhere. Especially do I desire that this gun story bring before the public eye the mountain man and his role in history and give to that "reckless breed" its just due.

Many individuals and institutions have been of assistance to me in the preparation of the book. In the Acknowledgments I have expressed my indebtedness to them in some detail, but at this point I want to express my appreciation of encouragement given by the several Directors of the National Park Service since I began work on the project. I am grateful to the Service, too, for permission to use as illustrations a large number of pen-and-ink drawings prepared for display at the Jefferson National Expansion Memorial in St. Louis. I am indebted to the American Association of Museums and the Carl Schurz Memorial Foundation for opportunities to study some European gun collections, and to the John Simon Guggenheim Memorial Foundation for financial support necessary to the completion of the writing. The several authors and publishers who have permitted use of certain copyrighted pictures and explanatory text matter have been gracious in coöperating, and I am indebted to them for their help in covering some important spots which otherwise would have remained as gaps in my story. I want here to express my thanks to my publisher, the University of California Press, its manager, Mr. August Frugé, and his staff for much assistance and coöperation. I am particularly grateful for the guidance given by Mr. Emlen Littell and the other editors who collaborated in organizing my material. To Miss Dorothy H. Huggins, especially, I am greatly indebted for expert editing, patient counseling, and sympathetic handling of many problems of presentation. A great many curators, librarians, and archivists also have extended helping hands. The guns and parts of guns upon which the book depends for its substance are preserved in the repositories listed in the Finding List. With the possible exception of some guns in European museums that may have been destroyed in World War II, the specimens cited are still available for study.

In eliminating errors in the manuscript and drawings, I have had the help of experts in several fields of history, ethnology, and firearms specialties. A good deal of manuscript and printed source material has been drawn upon, and possibly some factual mistakes still persist. I do not hold any of my collaborators and critics responsible for errors that remain. The gun pictures, with a few exceptions, as indicated in the legends, are based upon specimens which I have examined, and I assume responsibility for interpretations of mechanical features represented in the drawings.

Finally, I acknowledge an indebtedness to my wife, who during the long period that this book has been in preparation has made sacrifices and put up with my whims. Her patience, encouragement, and secretarial assistance have been of prime importance to the completion of the work.

CARL P. RUSSELL

Berkeley, California

Contents

Illustrations

FIGURES

FIGURES

I

Arming the American Indian

"Having gone about eight leagues, the Indians [Montagnais and their allies], towards evening, took one of the prisoners [Iroquois] to whom they made a harangue on the cruelties which he and his friends without any restraint had practised upon them, and that similarly he should resign himself to receive as much, and they ordered him to sing, if he had the heart. He did so, but it was a very sad song to hear.

"Meanwhile our Indians kindled a fire, and when it was well lighted, each took a brand and burned this poor wretch a little at a time in order to make him suffer the greater torment. Sometimes they would leave off, throwing water on his back. Then they tore out his nails and applied fire to the ends of his fingers and to his *membrum virile*. Afterwards they scalped him and caused a certain kind of gum to drop very hot upon the crown of his head. Then they pierced his arms near the wrists and with sticks pulled and tore out his sinews by main force, and when they saw they could not get them out, they cut them off. This poor wretch uttered strange cries, and I felt pity at seeing him treated this way. Still he bore it so firmly that sometimes one would have said he felt scarcely any pain. They begged me repeatedly to take fire and do like them. I pointed out to them that we did not commit such cruelties, but that we killed people outright, and that if they wished me to shoot him with the arquebus, I should be glad to do so. They said no; for he would not feel any pain. I went away from them as if angry at seeing them practise so much cruelty . . . When they saw that I was not pleased, they called me back and told me to give him a shot with the arquebus. I did so, without his perceiving anything, and with one shot caused him to escape all [further] tortures . . ." [1]

So wrote Samuel de Champlain after his first punitive expedition into the land of the Iroquois. The date was July 30, 1609, and the locale Lake Champlain, so named on this occasion by Champlain himself. The Indians who perpetrated the atrocities upon their Iroquois victim were Algonkin, Huron, and Montagnais, the more substantial allies of New France at this time. This was the occasion of Champlain's famous shot which won a battle but engendered the fury of the Iroquois that was to be visited upon New France for a century and a half.

The fight which had yielded the unlucky prisoner had taken place that same day, and Champlain's account of it is quite as lucid as his description of the torture. He and two volunteer Frenchmen, armed with arquebuses, had accompanied the war party from the St. Lawrence for the express purpose of demonstrating to their savage allies the superiority of guns over Indian weapons. On the evening of July 29, the invaders, traveling in canoes at the south end of Lake Champlain, had encountered a war party of Iroquois, also in canoes. Obligingly, the leaders of the opposing parties had agreed to await a new day before waging their fight. All combatants of both sides had spent the night at quarters close enough to permit the hurling of insults back and forth, and the Iroquois had taken advantage of the opportunity to throw up a small fortification. Of the events of the next morning, Champlain wrote:

> After we were armed with light weapons, we took, each of us [three Frenchmen], an arquebus and went ashore. I saw the enemy come out of their barricade to the number of two hundred, in appearance strong, robust men. They came slowly to meet us with a gravity and calm which I admired; and at their head were three chiefs. Our Indians likewise advanced in similar order, and told me that those who had three big plumes were the chiefs, and that there were only these three, whom you recognize by these plumes, which were larger than those of their companions; and I was to do what I could to kill them. . . .

[The enemy] . . . stood firm and had not yet noticed my white companions who went into the woods with some Indians. Our Indians . . .
put me ahead some twenty yards, and I marched on until I was within
thirty yards of the enemy, who as soon as they caught sight of me halted
and gazed at me and I at them. When I saw them make a move to draw
their bows upon us, I took aim with my arquebus and shot straight at
one of the three chiefs, and with this shot two fell to the ground and one
of their companions was wounded who died thereof a little later. I had
put four bullets [balls] into my arquebus. . . . The Iroquois were much
astonished that two men should have been killed so quickly, although
they were provided with shields made of cotton thread woven together
and wood, which were proof against their arrows. As I was reloading
my arquebus, one of my companions fired a shot from within the woods,
which astonished them again so much that, seeing their chiefs dead, they
lost courage and took flight, abandoning the field and their fort . . . I
[pursuing them into the woods] laid low still more of them. Our Indians also killed several and took ten or twelve prisoners.[2]

Champlain's account was published in Paris a few years after
the events. He embellished his text with illustrations which leave
no doubt about the type of gun used. It was a matchlock, light
enough to be fired from the shoulder without a rest. Whether the
"four balls" fired with that momentous shot at the Iroquois
amounted to a buckshot load, or whether four standard musket balls
were placed one upon another has not been explained, but there is
no reason to question the ability of a seventeenth-century gun barrel
to withstand the pressure of such a load of musket balls. Probably
the "light armor" helped to protect the gunner from the full strength
of the resulting kick.

In Champlain's accounts of his forays both before and after this
incident of 1609, there are repeated references to the "match," which
was all-important to the guns of his day. In his *Voyages, 1604–1618*,
he depicts French musketeers firing the heavier and longer weapon,
which did require the gun rest. Champlain and his contemporary
Lescarbot have handed down a number of rather illuminating accounts of the Frenchman's demonstration of guns to the seventeenth-
century Indians of the north Atlantic Coast and the St. Lawrence.
About the still earlier French firearms brought to America by

Jacques Cartier, Sieur de Roberval, Jean Ribaut, René de Laudonnière, and the many unnamed navigators who brought French
merchandise to the Newfoundland fishing banks in the sixteenth
century, little was recorded by the participants in these expeditions,
with one notable exception, which will be mentioned farther on in
this chapter.

Actually, the dependable personal weapon of the period of American discovery was the arbalest, or crossbow, which with a lingering
representation of the longbow gave the first adventurers from Spain,
France, and England only a slight advantage in armament over any
Indians who might be resentful of invasion. Generally, during the
earliest contacts, curiosity, superstition, and covetousness of iron ex-
cluded from the Indian's mind the hatred and justified hostility
which later marked so much of his intercourse with Europeans. One
of the factors in establishing the white man as "manitou" was his
possession of cannon and a comparatively few small guns which were
but little advanced beyond the ancient hand-cannon stage.[3]

The gun first to be demonstrated to the native American in the fif-
teenth and early sixteenth centuries was a cruder arm than Champlain's matchlock, little more than a tube of iron, mounted upon a
wooden stock and provided with a touchhole, a flashpan brazed to the
barrel, and a means of applying fire to the priming charge. In its
earlier form this gun had no lock. At the moment of firing, the gunner applied the burning end of a slow match to the priming in the pan
and this ignited the charge. By this method it was impossible for the
gunner, if he had no assistant, to keep his piece aligned upon his
target at the crucial moment of discharge. However, by the time the
matchlock was brought to the North American mainland, there had
been developed a firing mechanism which employed a serpentine, or
"cock," in which the slow match was held. The cock was operated
by a lever installed under or at the side of the grip in a position that
enabled the gunner to manipulate it as a trigger and at the same time
keep the barrel "sighted" upon his target; this improved the chances
that the ball might find its mark.

The musketry sergeants of the day placed a good deal of emphasis upon the importance of using only very fine powder in the flashpan. Wallhausen in 1615 directed:

> Let every soldier take well care of this. The priming powder must be ground up fine, be completely dry and mixed with a little sulphur in order that no misfire may occur, because the finer the powder the more easily it can be ignited and the better it can enter the vent [touchhole], and occasionally when the serpentine [in this case the priming powder] burns off the flash-pan without firing the charge, this is the reason. In order to be certain of the shot, the musket should be slightly turned and tapped after the priming powder is placed upon the flash-pan so that the priming may fill the entire vent.[4]

Upon his person the soldier carried a number of accessories for the care of his piece, including a cleaning needle with which to "prick" the touchhole when it became clogged with coarse powder or fouled with burnt-powder residue. These large-bore weapons ordinarily were loaded with a ball which was enough smaller than the bore to permit the gunner to seat the bullet upon the powder charge by the simple expedient of jarring the butt of the gun upon the ground; only the corporal possessed a ramrod, which was carried separately and was made available to any soldier who believed that a ball required ramming home. Later it was decided that every loading was occasion to make sure that the ball was seated properly; forestocks were manufactured with a longitudinal channel and ram pipes which made it possible to equip each gun with its own ramrod carried neatly on the underside of the forestock.

Powder, balls, a reserve of slow match, and various accouterments for the gun commonly were carried on a broad strap, or bandolier, slung over the gunner's left shoulder. The weight and clumsiness of this inflammable equipment, combined with the troubles of loading and firing the piece, made the weapon oppressive to the soldier. In effectiveness also, the gun in its early stages of development did not compare favorably with either the long bow or the crossbow. A practiced bowman could discharge twelve arrows a minute, and each would fly to a mark two hundred yards distant and there strike with such force as to penetrate two inches of oak. The loosely fitting ball from a matchlock could do no better, and the musketeer was at disadvantage because of the difficulties he encountered in loading and the resulting slow rate of fire. In heavy rain his match was likely to be extinguished, and his priming powder became wet in the pan. Under such conditions misfires were the rule, not the exception. Even under favorable weather conditions the gunner's burning match "gave him away" when he attempted surprise attacks, because of the smoke, fumes, and the glow of fire. Actually, about the only superiority that could be claimed for the early matchlock was the psychological effect it had upon an uninitiated and superstitious foe who quailed before the roar and flame of exploding gunpowder.

However, at the beginning of the sixteenth century characteristics of the matchlock began to change for the better. The flashpan was equipped with a hinged cover, the burning end of the long match was protected by a perforated cylindrical case of brass, and the lock was improved by the invention of a snapping cock geared to a sear and propelled by a spring. The cock was released for its downward thrust by the pull of a conventional trigger, and the trigger was protected by a trigger guard. The guns used by Champlain were of this type. The wheel-lock mechanism and flint guns also began to be used at this time, but the matchlock was less costly to manufacture, and most European governments ruled that it should be the arm of their ordinary soldiers.

When the Spaniards arrived in America early in the sixteenth century, they brought with them some of the heavy matchlock muskets which for a hundred years had been the prescribed arm of the Spanish military. The standard musket weighed fifteen to twenty pounds, and it was quite customary for the soldier to equip himself with a pad or pillow to be placed on his right shoulder to ease the weight of the gun as he marched. In firing, the barrel was supported on a forked rest, and the butt was held against the shoulder. This ten-gauge weapon was loaded with more than an ounce of gunpowder and a loosely fitting ball weighing about twelve to the pound. Its normal range is said to have been three hundred paces, but there is no testimony in regard to its accuracy at this distance. Before the Spanish conquests in America, the Duke of Alba had ordered that there should be one musketeer to two pikemen in the military forces under his command. Although evidence of the proportionate distribution of matchlocks in the expeditionary forces of the early sixteenth century is incomplete, contemporary accounts reveal that the heavy musket was used by the expeditions in Mexico in 1519 and in Peru in the 1530's. Both the wheel lock and the matchlock are identifiable in the records of the armaments of Coronado (1540–1542) and Oñate (1598–1608) in New Mexico.[5] Exploration and assault upon the natives was the typical procedure wherever the Spaniard forayed during this period, and the introduction of the gun in these southern precincts of Spain had murderous consequences. The repeated attacks upon Florida and the Gulf Coast also made during the first half of the sixteenth century were the works of musket-armed Spaniards who searched in vain for the wealth of another Mexico City. Relics of their edged weapons and armor occasionally come to light, and it is reasonable to expect that gun parts will someday be discovered along the trails of Narváez, Cabeza de Vaca, or Hernando de Soto.

The French, who laid their first determined claim to empire in America in the 1530's, brought the matchlock to the St. Lawrence. Both the heavy musket and a lighter gun, the arquebus, which required no forked rest when fired, were used by these explorers of the north country. No documentary evidence has been found upon which to base detailed descriptions of the French matchlocks carried on the expeditions of Jacques Cartier (1534) and Sieur de Pontgravé (1603), but there are numerous references to the use of guns in saluting the friendly Indians met by these parties, and there is the account already given of Champlain's encounter with the Iroquois in 1609.

Among the relics left by sixteenth-century Frenchmen in America are excellent pictures made by Jacques Lemoyne, a member of the ill-fated Huguenot party which attempted to establish a French colony in Florida in 1564–1565. Spaniards already established in the West Indies wiped out the rival colony, but the artist, Lemoyne, escaped the massacre and preserved a precious record of some of the affairs of the Protestant colonists. Fortunately, he gave attention to guns as well as to gunners. Figure 1 shows a French arquebusier as depicted by Lemoyne in Florida. This fellow and his trappings may be accepted as representative of any and all Europeans who brought the first guns to America. The weapon shown is an arquebus which weighed ten or eleven pounds and was fired with the broad, flat butt against the gunner's chest. No forked rest was required. The

Fig. 1. A sixteenth-century French arquebusier and his matchlock in Florida. After Lemoyne *ca.* 1564; reproduced by Lorant, 1946, p. 105.

bullet (.66 caliber) weighed about an ounce, and the bore of the barrel was approximately .72 of an inch. The range was two hundred yards, but the expectation of hits at this distance must have been small indeed. The flask for coarse powder, the smaller flask for priming powder, and the burning end of the slow match are conspicuous in the drawing. The match was a rope of twisted cord which had been soaked in a solution of saltpeter. It burned at the rate of four or five inches an hour and was carried, always lighted, in the soldier's right hand. When there was occasion to fire, a short piece of match

was placed in the serpentine, or cock—which appears near the arquebusier's chin as seen in the drawing—and lighted from the long
match. The small match was replaced after each shot. Some troop
units of the day, instead of using the short match, regularly placed
one end of the long match in the serpentine and kept both ends
burning at all times. Under such circumstances, the flashpan and its
content of priming powder were enclosed under a hinged cover
which had to be opened manually before the gun could be fired.
Pressure on the long and awkward lever which served as a trigger
moved the sear and the link within the lock to bring the serpentine
and its fire to the powder in the open pan. After the resulting
ignition, a spring forced the serpentine back into its upright position.

The usual bandolier and its capsules for individual powder charges
do not appear in Lemoyne's pictures. Bullets ordinarily were carried
in a leather pouch, but in time of action a number were held in the
mouth ready for quick loading. This practice, which was borrowed
by many Indian tribes, persisted all through the period of the muzzle
loaders. The noncommissioned officers of the French Army commonly accompanied the arquebusier and carried a ramrod.[6]

English colonists carried matchlocks to Jamestown (1607), to
Plymouth (1620), and to Boston (1630). Crossbows, long bows,
wheel locks, and flint guns also came from England at this time, but
the matchlock predominated. The first flint gun, the snaphance, was
a great improvement upon the matchlock and, because it was attain-
able by any industrious colonist, eventually became the popular firearm in New England. Many matchlocks were converted to the flint
system, new flint guns were imported in ever-increasing numbers,
and soon after the Pequot War in 1637 the snaphance was in the
hands of ordinary men as well as in those of the aristocrats and
military leaders. The matchlock was cast aside in Virginia in the
1630's, and Massachusetts and Connecticut outlawed the obsolete
mechanism in the last half of the seventeenth century, although the
mother country did not attain this degree of progress until twenty-
five years later.[7]

The Dutch who arrived on the Hudson in 1613 brought match-locks which by law had been standardized for military use. The sixteen-pound musket shot a ball weighing ten to the pound, and the ten-pound arquebus used a twenty-to-the-pound bullet. Boxel, a con-temporary writer, described the Dutch matchlock musket as measur-ing 4 feet 9 inches over all and having a bore of .69 inch. The bullet was .66 caliber.[8] The proportions of this arm were quite similar to those of the later Dutch flintlock muskets discussed in chapter ii. Because many Dutch civilians were prone to sell their guns to Indians, the Dutch government in 1656 ruled rather futilely that only match-locks could be owned by immigrants. The order was no more effective than was the law imposing death upon the Dutchman who supplied guns to Indians. When English forces under the Duke of York brought about the downfall of New Netherland in 1664, the New England law banning all matchlocks was enforced on the Hudson.

The Swedes who in 1638 essayed to occupy the Delaware Valley introduced their particular brand of matchlock. Gustavus Adolphus, just before the Swedish colonization in America, had equipped Sweden's victorious army with an eleven-pound matchlock which could be fired without a rest. It shot a ball which weighed a trifle more than one ounce, from a barrel the bore of which was .72 inch. Two-thirds of the Swedish infantry in Europe carried this weapon. It came to America with the small contingents of troops assigned to Fort Christina, at the site of present Wilmington, and Fort Gothen-burg, near the site of present Philadelphia. It did not suffice, however, to win arguments with the Dutch in 1651 and 1655, and New Sweden fell to the New Netherlanders. In turn, New Netherland, as previously mentioned, was seized by New England in 1664, and in accordance with the law of the new proprietors all matchlocks on the Delaware were discarded.[9]

So far as I have been able to learn, French authorities did not legis-late against the matchlock, and it is possible that the arm found some use in New France even in the closing years of the seventeenth century, but there was little reason for the Frenchman to cling to it. Flint guns were shipped from France in some numbers during the

1640's, and soon thereafter so many reached America that the French traders were able to do a wholesale business in supplying flintlocks to tribes deep in the interior. By 1675 the matchlock as a military arm was in use nowhere in America. In its day of predominance— the first half of the seventeenth century—it had of course been of value in fighting against the Indians, and sometimes it had served importantly in winning Indian allies, but it never was an important item for trade with Indians.

Fig. 2. A short, light fusil (snaphance) made in Italy in 1650. This gun type was the forerunner of the Indian trade fusil. The specimen is preserved in the Victoria and Albert Museum, London.

The flint gun, on the other hand, quickly became a prime factor in the Indian trade. The snaphance with its sliding pan cover (fig. 2) was quite common in western Europe during the last half of the sixteenth century. No doubt it came to America along with its contemporaries the matchlock and the wheel lock, but its great significance in the story of the evolution of the gun is found in the role it played as intermediary between the wheel lock and the true flintlock. One of the weaknesses of the early snaphance was the arrangement of the cock; the gunner found it necessary always to carry his primed piece at full cock. If the cock was lowered, the pan cover slid open and the priming powder spilled out. Spain, just before 1650, seems to have led the way in obviating this disadvantage by using the half cock. By cutting an additional notch in the tumbler of the snaphance lock, the gunsmith was able to combine the pan cover with the frizzen in a solid unit. This improvement made it possible to lower the cock, yet keep the pan cover closed. The same result was attained by some manufacturers by providing a "dog-catch" on the back of the cock itself, so that it could be held in half-cock position. It was the feature of pan cover and frizzen in one piece which particularly distinguished the true flintlock—a lock mechanism which persisted with very little change for more than two hundred years. With the general adoption of the flintlock by the armies of Europe in the middle of the seventeenth century, civilians also insisted upon having this improved gun. England, France, and Holland all shipped flintlocks to their military forces and to their colonists and merchants in America. By 1650, in spite of laws to the contrary, an extensive trade in guns and ammunition was conducted with Indians by all Europeans in the New World except the Spanish.

Even before 1650, Dutch agents at Fort Nassau (in what is now Gloucester County, N.J.) and at Fort Orange (Albany, N.Y.) had set the pattern for this trade. Their customers were the Iroquois, particularly, and the Dutch stronghold at Orange was in effect the seat of the Iroquois confederacy. Many of the Dutchmen were engaged in the beaver trade, and the Dutch establishments, including New Amsterdam, were for a time sustained by traffic in peltries. Up the Hudson, up the Connecticut, and down the Delaware rivers the Dutch went, forming liaisons with the natives. Unlike most of the French traders to the north, the Dutchmen on the Hudson consigned their guns, with powder and lead, to the Indians, with no qualms of conscience and with little regard for the day when these weapons would be turned upon their countrymen at New Amsterdam and elsewhere in New Netherland.[10]

During the first half of the seventeenth century, the British had supplied the Mohawk, a unit of the Iroquois, with just enough guns to cause that entire Indian nation to crave firearms. The Dutchmen of Rensselaerwick on the Hudson, sensing the opportunity to conduct a lively business, and knowing that their special charter was quite independent of the States-General, ignored the New Netherland law which imposed the death penalty for supplying guns to Indians. They sold "firelocks" to these Indians at the price of twenty beavers for one gun; they also got ten or twelve guilders a pound for gunpowder. A guilder was equal to about four dollars in modern United States currency. This highly profitable trade made traders out of the greater part of the population of Rensselaerwick. It continued until some four hundred Indians had guns and knew how to use them. In 1643, some of the Mohawk supplied guns to the Mahican who went to war against New Netherland. However, they spared the white men up the Hudson, who afforded a source of guns and ammunition. This war continued for two years. The States-General then obtained a peace agreement and thereafter attempted to enforce a more lenient regulation of the trade in guns. In 1650, the Dutch government ruled that all sales of firearms in New Netherland were to be limited by means of permits issued to traders by the Council; guns were to be priced at six guilders, pistols at four guilders; powder was to be sold at six stivers the pound. The trade was to be terminated by the Council as soon as it might appear feasible to withhold guns from the Indians. The Chamber of the West India Company was not slow in remonstrating to the States-General. This commercial agency pointed out that the Indian could and would pay twenty times the prices set by the Council. Under Peter Stuyvesant, 1647–1664, some further attempts were made by the New Netherland government to enforce fair trade practices and to keep on friendly terms with the Indians. Three Indian wars were fought, nevertheless, and it was not until May, 1664, that peaceful relations were again established.

By that time even a more determined foe was upon Stuyvesant. Rivalry for the fur trade and covetousness of land seekers from New England stirred ill feeling between the British and the Dutch. Rebellion among his followers made it difficult for Stuyvesant to prepare military defenses, and when an English fleet sailed into his harbor in August, 1664, he was forced to surrender. His Dutch province passed to the Duke of York, and New Amsterdam became New York.

The Dutch merchants on the Hudson continued to operate long after the British took over, and the British traders who established themselves in the former New Netherland settlements adhered quite closely to the prevailing Dutch methods of trade. The rate of return to the New York Indians continued to be high in comparison with that accorded by the French to their Indian allies at Montreal. In

1689 at Orange (Albany) the Mohawk could obtain a gun for two beavers; at Montreal the French demanded five beavers for a similar weapon. One beaver at Orange paid for eight pounds of gunpowder; it took four beavers at Montreal to buy the same amount of powder. Similarly, one beaver was exchanged for forty pounds of lead at Orange; the French demanded three beavers for the same amount of lead. To add to the disparity in prices, the Orange traders were indifferent to the quality of the fur; "they take it all at the same rate." [11]

In 1693, the English governor, Benjamin Fletcher, attempted to present to the leaders of the Iroquois some of the heavy British muskets of the military type used in King Philip's War. They spurned the gift, and Fletcher appealed to the British Committee of Trade to "procure 200 light fuzees for a present from their Majesties to the Five Nations of Indians; they will not carry the heavy firelocks I did bring over with me, being accustomed to light, small fuzees in their hunting." [12] The two hundred flintlocks asked for by Fletcher, and more, were forthcoming. [13]

Something further regarding the characteristics of the guns destined for distribution among the Iroquois by the British may be gleaned from the 1694 "List of goods proper to be presented to the Five Nations of Mohaques, Onedes, Onondages, Cayouges, and Senekes within the River Indian at Albany": "50 guns as the Traders have from Liege, the barrel of 4½ foot long which used to cost at Amsterdam about eight stivers the foot, and the lock with all that belongs to its use to cost there twelve stivers. The stocks are better made at New York or Albany at 4ˢ a peece." [14]

The idea here expressed that guns lacking stocks were regularly imported by the English is corroborated by an item in the tariff rate on firearms shipped up the Hudson in 1687: "For every gun or gun-baril with a lock six shillings." [15]

Governor Fletcher's request of 1693 makes clear that the long-barreled musket referred to above, and described in more detail in chapter ii, did not stand alone as *the* gun of the day. During the first half of the seventeenth century there had come into vogue snaphance and flintlock "carbines"—short, lightweight guns devised for cavalry use in Europe. By 1650, these were being manufactured in Germany, Belgium, Italy, France, and Spain. England was not slow in recognizing the advantages of this weapon in the hands of mounted troops, and some of the "carbines" of English make were supplied to American colonists before King Philip's War. In 1673, the Massachusetts soldiers were ordered to "equip with flint firearms if possible, those of mounted troopers to be carbines." [16]

Figure 2 shows one of the early "carbines" (more properly musketoons) of Italian make. The snaphance lock is marked "Lazarino Cominazzo 1650." This gun is a fair example of the earliest short-barreled arms which became popular in America before the end of the seventeenth century and which, in general design, set the style for Indian guns during two hundred years of trade throughout the continent north of Mexico. The snaphance mechanism here shown was the first to use the flint; it was used to some extent in western Europe during the last half of the sixteenth century and throughout much of the seventeenth, but it was short-lived in America. References to the snaphance are numerous in Colonial American documents, but, as Peterson has explained, the word was used loosely in the seventeenth century in designating any flintlock, and its frequent appearance in Colonial literature is not a good indicator of the number of guns in America which were equipped with locks having a sliding pan cover. The early French *fusil-court* and the English smoothbore carbine, in popular demand among American Indians after 1675, were similar in general style to the Italian gun here pictured, but they had the conventional flintlock firing mechanism, not the snaphance lock.

The long-barreled musket, which had been distributed by the Dutch throughout the greater part of the first half of the seventeenth century, did not go entirely out of vogue among the Iroquois; but even among these Indians the demand grew for the shorter guns during the 1690's. Elsewhere in the realm of the British trader, the light musket was preferred, and by the end of the seventeenth century the gun that has become known as the Hudson's Bay fuke, or fusee (fig. 18), was a distinct entity so far as its essential characteristics were concerned.

The French importers found it necessary to meet the competition offered by the English fusee, and soon after the beginning of the eighteenth century the words *carabine, mousqeton,* and *fusil-court* became conspicuous on the invoices of the French traders. Like the short musket of English origin, the *fusil-court* had many of the characteristics of the later Hudson's Bay fuke.[17] In keeping with the light structure of the arm, the price was low. A record of the "expenses incurred by the French in the war with Fox Indians," Butte des Morts, Wisconsin (1715–1716), reveals that even in the wilderness the *fusil-court* was valued at no more than 30 livres each, or about $6.00. A hundred years later the American Fur Company invoiced to the trader James Kinzie, in approximately the same locality, North West guns (the flintlock Hudson's Bay fuke) at $6.00 each.[18]

With the wide acceptance of the short and light musket, the eighteenth-century Indian gun became fairly well stabilized so far as the design and mechanical characteristics of the arm are concerned. The rifle made a bid for attention as a trade weapon early in that century, but with few exceptions [19] it was not sought by the tribes until a hundred years later. Some long-barreled fowling pieces and a few regulation military muskets and pistols, both French and English, fell into Indian hands; but throughout the land the gun commonly used by the Indians in the eighteenth century was the short musket, the forerunner of the arm discussed in chapter iii. Our present concern, then, is with the distribution of this gun and with its effect upon the way of life of the American Indian.

THE FRENCH TRADE IN GUNS

In the opening years of the seventeenth century, the region about the Gulf of St. Lawrence became the center of French enterprise in the New World. Tadoussac, Quebec, and Montreal successively became capitals of trade, to which traveled not only local Indians but also delegations from tribes far to the west. Approximately 150,000 Indians of the St. Lawrence–Great Lakes axis [20] looked to the French establishments for their trade. Of this number some 33,000 were warriors—potential buyers of guns and ammunition. During the first half of the seventeenth century the numerous Huron lived in the immediate precincts of the French on the St. Lawrence, and their allegiance was so great that every Indian was virtually an added Frenchman. Similarly, the Montagnais, Algonkin, and Ottawa were at home in the region first occupied by the French, and they also maintained the friendliest of relations. The Ottawa particularly— their very name signifies "to trade"—promoted the distribution of French merchandise among tribes to the west. Within a comparatively few years the coveted guns filtered into wilderness country to which a white man had never traveled.

The favorable system of distribution through middlemen did not persist, however. The Iroquois south of the St. Lawrence, traditional foes of the Huron, looked with hate upon the prosperity brought about by the trade in French goods. In 1618, the Iroquois formed an alliance with the Dutch on the Hudson (see chap. ii), proceeded to buy guns, and became adept in their use. By 1646, the French in Quebec were told that all groups in the Iroquois league were fully armed. Subsequent events proved this to be true. The Iroquois rampaged through the Great Lakes region and along the St. Lawrence, to become the scourge of New France. The Frenchman's reliable partners, the Huron, were the first to be destroyed, and other nations that had befriended the French were harassed into incompetency.

To meet the disastrous conditions brought about by the loss of Indian middlemen, an increasing number of French traders traveled westward to obtain furs close to the virgin country where beaver were abundant. In 1663, Louis XIV took personal interest in the problems of New France, and within a decade, under the drive of Louis de Buade, Count de Frontenac, Governor at Quebec, trading establishments and missions were established on the shores of Lake Michigan and on the Mississippi in the country of the Illinois. In this new territory resided 100,000 savages,[21] all desirous of obtaining the white man's trade goods. Included in this Indian population were 30,000 warriors craving muskets. The St. Lawrence route between Lake Ontario and Montreal, made perilous by the marauding Iroquois, was replaced by the Ottawa River route, Lake Huron to Montreal, and canoes laden with guns again moved westward as the rich fur fields north of the Great Lakes were made to yield their bounty. Thus, in spite of the fierce and far-ranging Iroquois, French parties succeeded in harvesting enormous crops of beaver and other fine furs and in extending the boundaries of New France. Further, augmented French military forces struck avenging blows against the Iroquois. Among the goods imported from France, guns and ammunition came in steadily increasing quantities, and the march of French imperialism into the American West seemed uncontested.

However, in 1670, British interests founded the Hudson's Bay Company upon a plan projected by two embittered Frenchmen. This company even in its infancy traded guns [22] and in the new-found fields of the beaver trade offered competition that was felt by the French throughout their northern border to the western limits of their domain. The Assiniboin and the Cree, especially, turned to the new English trading posts in their territories, and the French in self-defense built three forts north of Lake Superior. When the mother countries engaged in King William's War (1689–1697), French troops from these places and from Quebec moved upon the British forts which had threatened French trade in the West. The roar of musketry and cannon became commonplace in the remote northern wilderness where gunpowder had never before been used in warfare.[23]

At this time the aging but redoubtable Louis, Count de Frontenac, came back to New France as governor. He entered into the business of rebuilding and expanding Indian alliances, and the distribution of guns to Indians became a major factor in his strategy. His earlier plan to build a city at the mouth of the Mississippi was revived, and renewed attention was given to exploitation of Louisiana, the entire valley of the Mississippi. Biloxi on the Gulf of Mexico came into existence, and pirogues burdened with merchandise ascended the streams of the Gulf Plain. In the North, trusted leaders took flotillas of canoes loaded with guns from Montreal to the existing posts and to new establishments in the country that today is Michigan, Wisconsin, Minnesota, Indiana, and Illinois. Ships from Rochelle, Bordeaux, and Bayonne came in increasing numbers laden with powder, ball, and fusees. For the first time, the Frenchman made determined efforts to put plenty of guns in the hands of all their Indian allies. In the last decade of the seventeenth century, French muskets were in use by natives everywhere from Lake Winnipeg to Lake Champlain and south to the mouth of the Mississippi.

Of the gun trade, La Salle wrote: "The savages take better care of us French than of their own children. From us only can they get guns." [24] That the French muskets were not always regarded with favor, however, is evident from Lahontan's report. He tells of the sale of fusees to the Huron and Ottawa in 1685 and quotes a Huron as complaining, "The French give us fusees that burst and lame us." [25]

Before the seventeenth century ended, Frenchmen had explored the entire course of the Mississippi River and had had a look at many of its tributaries. In the Southwest they had visited much of what is now Texas and Arkansas, and after the beginning of the eighteenth century they penetrated repeatedly into the southern lowlands and the plains region of the Southwest. Approximately 60,000 Indians resided in these southern precincts which the Frenchmen hoped to govern.[26] Here, in round numbers, were 18,000 warriors in need of guns—a need which the French authorities determined should be met from the armories of France.

As the eighteenth century advanced, French traders pushed ever deeper into the southwestern country within or neighboring upon the Spanish holdings in Texas and New Mexico. In the North, advances were made upon the Missouri and Great Plains regions, where British guns from Cree and Assiniboin sources already were in use. Conspicuous among the leaders of the French expeditions during this period were Etienne Veniard de Bourgmond, Louis Juchereau, St. Denis, Bernard de la Harpe, Claude Charles du Tisne, the Mallet brothers, Pierre and Paul, Celeron de Bienville, Pierre Gaultier de Varennes de la Vérendrye, and Charles de Langlade (whose silver-mounted pistols are described in chapter ii). Most of these men enjoyed the advantages of good breeding, the prestige accorded to representatives of government or of the large trading companies, and wealth with which to purchase personal equipment befitting their stations. As might be expected, their guns were out of the ordinary.

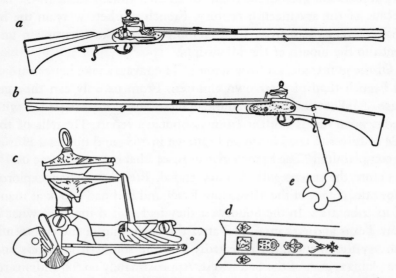

Fig. 3. A Pigrav-Gabiola fusil. A fine gun of the type carried by gentlemen leaders of the eighteenth-century fur brigades. The specimen is shown here by permission of the Chicago Historical Society.

Some account of their arms is given in chapter ii. By way of comparison with the trade gun, a description of a fine fusil of the day—a fair example of the mid-eighteenth-century gun carried through the American wilds by French army officers and by commanders of exploring expeditions and trading parties during this period of French expansion—is given here.

Figure 3 shows such a weapon. It is a Spanish-French fusil with a miquelet lock bearing the punch mark of Pigral (Pigrav), a Spanish armorer who was active in the 1730's. The Damascus barrel and the trigger guard have the marks of one of the Gabiolas of Eibar, in Navarre, artisans recorded for the periods of 1725–1750 and 1790–1800.[27] Among the gold-inlay ornamentations on the arm is the date 1676, a circumstance not readily explained considering the evidences of eighteenth-century workmanship on barrel and lock. Quite possibly parts were taken from an earlier high-grade weapon and built into this one, a common practice in the construction of fine guns. The forestock is pin-fastened; the ramrod is wood.

The French incursions west of the Mississippi River enraged the Spaniards and bothered the English, but the chief conflict of this period occurred on the Ohio. Since the days of La Salle's explorations in 1682, the French had laid claim to the entire drainage of the Ohio. In their view, the western boundary of the English colonies was the crest of the Alleghenies, and they pointed to treaties of 1697, 1713, and 1748 in defending their contention. The Virginia Company relied upon its Charter of 1609 and the provisions of the Treaty of 1748 (giving to the British jurisdiction over all lands of the empire of the Iroquois) in claiming lands west of the mountains. When in 1749 a group of Virginians organized as the Ohio Company began exploration of their Ohio grant, the surveyors found Pennsylvania traders already ensconced in trading posts which they had built on the upper Ohio. The French resisted this invasion by erecting a line of forts extending from Presque Isle, at the site of present Erie, Pennsylvania, southward along the Allegheny River to the site of Pittsburgh at the Forks of the Ohio. When Virginians commanded by George Washington attempted in 1754 to build fortifications at the Forks, they found French forces in possession of the site. The fight put up by the Virginia militiamen near Great Meadows on this occasion (May 28, 1754) is regarded to be the opening engagement of the French and Indian War, a conflict which raged for seven years.

Immediately the French made of the water route from Lake Erie to the Forks of the Ohio an artery of supply. Fort Duquesne at the Forks of the Ohio became an arsenal from which French muskets in unprecedented numbers passed to Indians. Lavish distribution of guns and ammunition took place also on the Great Lakes and on the Mississippi. For four years the French and their musket-shooting Indians withstood British thrusts along the middle colony frontier and in the Lake Champlain corridor; not only did they withstand attacks, but they won some brilliant victories. The French successes served to turn against the English some of their one-time Indian allies. Conspicuous among the allies of the French in the North were the Abnaki, Chippewa, Delaware, Huron (then called Wyandot), Ottawa, and the Pennsylvania-Ohio Shawnee. In the South, the western Choctaw and the Cherokee (belatedly) sided with the French.

The doling out of armament and other presents was done at great expense to the French government, but expenditures for this purpose were regarded by officials to be necessary at all times and especially necessary during this period of all-out war.[28] According to François Bigot, four hundred million francs were expended in making presents to American Indians in 1759,[29] yet the cry was for more and bigger gifts. The blockade established by British men-of-war and the threat to the homeland posed by England and her ally Prussia made it increasingly difficult for France to maintain her shipping. The shortage of French goods for Indians and for the general military supply in America became acute, a circumstance which of course affected the progress of French campaigns and interrupted intertribal trade in guns and ammunition among some Indians of the West; for example, the Sioux and the Missouri tribes far from the scenes of battles between the French and the English.[30] On the other hand, England increased her armament,[31] added to her forces, and placed the American problem in the hands of a new minister, William Pitt. In August, 1758, the French line of supply between Lake Erie and the Ohio was broken by a British attack; Fort Duquesne was then burned and abandoned by its defenders. Quebec fell to the British in September, 1759, and a year later the English general, Amherst, demanded and received from Governor de Vaudreuil the surrender of Montreal and with it all of Canada.

New France as an entity had ceased to exist; the flow of French guns to the Indians of America was ended. Conservatively it may be estimated that 200,000 muskets had come from the French factories [32] to America during the slightly more than a hundred years that France had traded guns. Many of the old-time traders were still alive when in 1776 the French government again sent guns to America; approximately 80,000 French military muskets were supplied to the colonists during the Revolution.[33] The various military models are well represented today in collections in the United States, but French trade guns are as scarce as the proverbial hen's teeth.

THE DUTCH AND THE SWEDES

Characteristics of the Dutch trade have already been described, and the Dutch guns will receive attention in chapter ii. At this point it is necessary only to identify the Indians with whom the Dutch dealt, and to reëmphasize the importance of the Dutch trade in establishing the Iroquois as the bane of the French.

The Delaware, Montauk, Mahican, Susquehanna, Honniasont, Wappinger, and Iroquois were the principal peoples within the zone of Dutch influence, a combined population of some forty thousand Indians. The Honniasont were destroyed by the Susquehanna in the early years of the Dutch trade, and remnants of the tribe joined the Iroquois, who were at war with the Susquehanna. The Mahican also warred with the Iroquois, and the Wappinger developed a great hatred for the Dutch. New Netherland was not a calm and peaceful colony. In 1643, William Kieft, the director general, instigated a brutal massacre of friendly Indians who had taken refuge from the Iroquois with Dutch farmers on the site of present Jersey City. Most of the tribes of New Netherland except the Iroquois arose in fury to retaliate. From 1643 to 1645, a war raged which brought devastation to the entire countryside from the Raritan River to the Connecticut. Long Island, Westchester, and Manhattan were laid waste. Only Fort Orange and Rensselaerwyck, far up the Hudson, and Fort Amsterdam on Manhattan Island escaped destruction. Dutch reinforcements came in 1644; and in August, 1645, a general peace was attained. The record indicates, however, that Dutch traders continued to supply guns to the tribes. At about this time, Beauchamp Plantagenet wrote that a wholesale business in guns and ammunition was being conducted by the Dutch and that the savages were being instructed in the use of guns. He reported that to his knowledge 2,000 Mohawk and Delaware Indians had been armed by Dutchmen.[34]

Kieft was replaced by Peter Stuyvesant in 1647. The new director made earnest efforts to make up for the evil ways of his predecessor and to establish friendship with the tribes; but in 1655 there was an uprising of the Delaware Indians in New Amsterdam, and the Montauk went on the warpath on Long Island. Four years later, other units of the Delaware at Esopus (now Kingston) and in what is now Ulster County, New York, were goaded into war by a few Dutch settlers who made an unprovoked attack upon one of the Indian villages. Sporadically, this "Esopus war" continued until the spring of 1664. Approximately a thousand Indians—mostly Delaware, Mahican, Wappinger, and Montauk—were killed in this strife.

Unquestionably, the New Netherlanders led the way in establishing the gun trade among Indians, but it cannot be said that the Dutchmen pioneered in developing favorable relationships with the natives. Quite the contrary. Rapine and murder characterized the relations between the Dutch and the Indians.

The outstanding result of Dutch merchandising in Colonial America was, of course, the arming of the Iroquois. The immediate area served by the New Netherlanders was very small and their period of activity was brief, but by placing guns and ammunition in the hands of the Iroquois they started the chain of events which brought about the ascendancy of the most remarkable confederation of red men north of Mexico and influenced the history of all that part of America from the St. Lawrence south to the Tennessee and from the Mississippi east to the Appalachians. The Dutch, as colonists, were eliminated by the English in August, 1664, but the effects of Iroquois predominance which the Dutch had engendered persisted until after the Revolutionary War. It is an interesting fact that Dutch guns contributed to American successes in the Revolution. Arms from Amsterdam were shipped to St. Eustatius, the Dutch island in the Caribbean, as early as 1775, and were picked up there by American ships and used against the British.[35]

The long-barreled Indian muskets traded by the Dutch dropped out of favor about the same time as New Netherland was wiped off the map. Probably not more than twenty thousand of these guns came to America, but it is noteworthy that even though three centuries have passed since the last of them were traded, many specimens of the guns are still extant.

The New Sweden Company, which in 1638 established its first colony where Wilmington, Delaware, now stands, was supported equally by Swedes and Hollanders. A tract of land extending from the site of present Trenton, New Jersey, to the mouth of Delaware Bay was purchased from the Delaware Indians (Unalachtigo), and small forts were built near the sites of present Philadelphia and Chester, Pennsylvania, and at the mouth of the Schuylkill River. The principal contacts with Indians were with the Delaware, the Susquehanna, and the Mahican. During the regime of Governor Johan Printz, 1643–1652, the Swedes competed for the Indian trade on the Delaware, contending with both the English and the Dutch. There is evidence that they supplied Swedish powder and ball to the Indians, but the guns which they traded appear to have been of Dutch or English manufacture. They treated the Indians well; there were no Indian uprisings or raids.

When the Dutch built Fort Casimir a few miles from the Swedish stronghold Fort Christina (Wilmington), the Swedes seized it. In retaliation, Peter Stuyvesant in 1655 took seven Dutch ships and three hundred Dutch soldiers from New Amsterdam to the Delaware and in a bloodless attack took over all of New Sweden.[36] The resulting extension of New Netherland to the Delaware River lasted ten years. These holdings, together with the rest of the Dutch colonies in America, were seized by the English in 1664.

If any Swedish guns from New Sweden still exist, I have not heard of them. Records which I have searched reveal that a good deal of ammunition was imported, but the inventories show no trade guns, and only a comparatively few military arms are known to have been

brought from Sweden during the two decades that the Swedes held
sway on the Delaware.

THE BID MADE BY SPAIN

From 1513, when Ponce de Leon discovered Florida, until 1565, when
Pedro Menéndez de Avilés founded St. Augustine, the story of Spaniards in what is now the United States is a succession of episodes in
which slave-hunting expeditions,[37] deaths of the explorers, Indian
attacks, and martyrdom of missionaries figure prominently. The
matchlocks of the invaders receive some notice in the record of events
of this half century, especially as they pertain to the Caribbean area,
the Gulf of Mexico, and the Carolina-Florida coastal strip. Some
seventy thousand Indians [38] occupied the mainland in what are now
the Gulf States from the lower Mississippi River to the Atlantic and
along the coast northward to the Carolinas. Approximately eighteen
thousand warriors were to be contended with. A number of the tribes
were furiously resentful of their dominating white visitors. They
made short shrift of careless explorers and hampered attempts at
settlements on the Peedee River (in what is now South Carolina)
in 1526, and at Pensacola Bay in 1559–1561. Luis de Cancer, a Domin-
ican missionary, was murdered by Indians in Florida in 1549. These
incidents were prognostic of the trend of Spanish affairs in the next
two hundred years.

Having "put Jean Ribaut and all the rest of them [the French
Huguenots] to the knife" on the St. John River, Menéndez in the
period 1565–1573 laid the groundwork for the defense of Florida
and the expansion of "service of the Lord Our God and of Philip,
King of Spain." Trade with Indians did not figure in this program,
but the enslavement of rebellious natives and attempted conversion
of the tribes to Christianity involved a great deal of coercion. Numerous presidios and some missions were built in Florida and along
the Atlantic Coast as far north as Parris Island, St. Helena Sound,
South Carolina. Indians were forced to perform the heavy labor
and they were held in subjection as far as possible. It behooved the

Spaniard to withhold guns from his native victims,[39] for even without guns the outraged Indians kept Florida in a state of turmoil. To make matters worse, Frenchmen from ships in the Caribbean fomented further trouble, in some instances actually joining the Indians in their warfare. Due to the threat of attacks, the activities of the Spanish settlers were very much limited to the protected zones immediately adjacent to the forts and presidios. Reasonably enough, guns and ammunition figured prominently in the personal equipment of sixteenth-century Spaniards in America.

Contemporary accounts of this equipment and its use are disappointingly few, but the record is sufficiently clear to permit us to recapture some details. One instance in which Spanish matchlocks passed from white owners into the hands of Indians is well worth recording here. In 1576, a Captain Solis, commander of the Garrison at San Felipe, in the vicinity of what had been the Port Royal of the French Huguenots, executed two Indians, one a chief. Also, Solis had demanded that the neighboring Cusabo bring to the garrison a quantity of corn and other provisions. Because the food was not promptly forthcoming, the Captain dispatched Moyano and twenty-two soldiers to the Indian villages to seize the needed corn. As the party approached one of the towns, some of the natives came out to meet it. They explained that their women and children were terrified by the burning slow match carried with every gun, and they indicated that they would coöperate if the soldiers would extinguish their matches. Moyano complied with this request, whereupon the Indians immediately killed all but one of the Spaniards and took the captured matchlocks to the Cusabo town.[40]

After this incident, the Indians of Guale, Uscamacu, and Oristan all arose in revolt, ambushed the punitive expeditions sent out by the Spaniards, and besieged the fort at San Felipe. In the course of the fighting, more Spaniards were killed, and more matchlocks were acquired by the Indians. Later it was revealed that the Indian villages harbored a number of Frenchmen. Undoubtedly, these white men encouraged the rebellion, and they may have coached the Indians in the use of their stolen guns. But if they did so, history does not record that fact. It is a matter of record, however, that a number of Frenchmen were captured eventually and were executed by the Spaniards.

In 1580, there was another revolt, and San Felipe, by this time rebuilt and renamed San Marcos, suffered additional attacks, which resulted in its abandonment in 1587 or 1588.[41]

During the last decade of the century, Spanish missionaries expanded their efforts in Florida and in what is now South Carolina, and through a system of mission provinces made a bid for peace in the land, which was quite successful except for another outbreak of the Guale tribe in 1597. Militant action by the Spaniards broke this particular rebellion in 1598, and for half a century thereafter it appeared that the Franciscans had won southeastern North America for Spain.

By 1663, however, the Englishmen of Virginia had pushed southward until they were dangerously close to the Spanish settlements. Charles Town was founded on the Ashley River about one hundred miles north of the Spanish mission province Guale and within the fringe of Indian country over which the Spaniards tried to exercise control. Unlike the Spaniards, the Englishmen sent out trading parties to serve not only their near neighbors but also large tribes at the headwaters of the Carolina rivers. Their pack trains even crossed the mountains to deal with peoples on the upper Chattahoochee River and the Tennessee, an innovation which was to change the entire complexion of the relationship between Indians and whites in the Southeast.

To stem the tide of British expansion, the Spaniards in 1680 encouraged the Westos (probably a division of the Yuchi) to attack the English traders and some of their Indian allies. This attack precipitated a war which took the Carolina militia, armed with flintlocks, to the very doors of the Spaniards in Guale. The resulting fighting drove the missionaries and small contingents of Spanish troops out of Guale and at the same time wo.. over to the English some of the Indians regarded by the Spanish as safely fixed within their empire. Among these were approximately two thousand Yamasee, who had made their camps about the outskirts of the strongly fortified St. Augustine. Most of the Yamasee abandoned their Florida homes and removed to South Carolina, where the English established them in a sort of protectorate near the mouth of the Savannah River. Into their hands went British muskets.

Spanish officials, thoroughly alarmed by the turn of events, tried desperately in 1681 to counteract British influence in the back country by establishing a station among the Lower Creek Indians at the confluence of the Flint and Chattahoochee rivers. This particular band of Creeks had voluntarily removed from strife-torn Guale, and their allegiance to Spanish interests seemed secure. With their help the Spaniards hoped to put an end to the trading activities in which English interests were engaged on the upper Chattahoochee and Ocmulgee rivers, but there is no evidence that they supplied guns to these friends. It was a vain hope. When the Spanish policing of the upper country was well started, the Creek Indians along the Chattahoochee spurned the Spaniards and moved eastward in order that they might be nearer the English and thus more easily obtain trade guns.

This was the beginning of a long period of ignominy for the Spanish in the Southeast. Before the end of the century, French forces occupied Biloxi, Mobile, and the mouth of the Mississippi. Spain held Pensacola. When Queen Anne's War broke out in 1702, Spain sided with France against England, but this alliance was of little help to Spaniards in Florida. The invasion of Florida by Carolina troops in 1702 brought about a general collapse of the colony. Many mission stations, including the important establishment at Apalache, were destroyed, and the defection of Indian tribes followed. The town of St. Augustine surrendered, but the fort proved to be impregnable. The few Indians that fought faithfully in behalf of the Spanish—the Apalache notable among them—seem to have had no guns. The victorious Indian allies of the English, however, had firearms and became the envy of all unarmed tribes, neutrals and belligerents alike.

French traders pushing northward from the Gulf and eastward from the Mississippi complicated the situation. By 1714, the French-

men were firmly entrenched among the Upper Creeks and the Alabama tribe. Fort Toulouse, a strong post built by the French near
the confluence of the Alabama and Tallapoosa rivers just north of
the site of present Montgomery, became an important distribution
point for French arms and ammunition. English traders aroused to
desperate action by the favor accorded the French by the tribes of the
Gulf Plain flooded the towns of the Chickasaw, the Upper Creeks,
and the Lower Creeks with gifts, including guns. This technique won
the friendship of the favored tribes and contributed to the ill feeling
among some slighted groups which brought on the war between the
Natchez and the French in the 1730's and undoubtedly had an influence upon the Yamasee, who in 1728 went to war for the second
time against the British.

Spaniards in Florida may have taken some satisfaction in these
troubles that beset the French and the English along their boundaries,
but if so, their amusement was poorly timed. Oglethorpe, who by
this time had made his Georgia colony safe for British settlement
and trade, was well prepared to descend upon Florida when in 1739
England declared war on Spain. Creeks, Chickasaw, and Cherokee,
carrying both French and English guns, supported the Georgians in
their four years of seesaw war against the Spaniards (1739–1742), a
conflict which was a prelude to the cession of Florida to England in
1763.

So ended the first episode in the story of Florida under Spain. For
two hundred and fifty years the Spaniard had barely hung on in the
Southeast. Spain's narrow and repressive colonial policy consistently
included rule of the natives by the sword,[42] and of course up to this
time there had been no relaxation of the regulation which outlawed
the sale of guns to Indians.

In the Southwest the story was somewhat the same but with variations peculiar to the vastness of the land and the ferocity and strength
of the natives. After the Niza explorations of 1539, a succession of expeditions from Mexico entered the country that is now Texas, New
Mexico, and Arizona, and toward the end of the century one lone
Spanish settlement existed on the upper Rio Grande north of the
site of present Santa Fe. A few years later, Santa Fe was established

as the capital of the New Mexican missionary field, and the business of settlement, coöperative farming, church building, and conversion of infidels went on without interference from European rivals or any other notable incident for eighty years. By 1680, three thousand Spanish settlers were in New Mexico, and the Pueblo Indians had become restive under the pressure exerted by these settlers. Under the leadership of a Tewa Indian who had been abusively treated by Spaniards, the tribes joined in a general revolt which, in the period 1680–1696, cost the lives of several hundred white settlers and twenty-one Franciscan missionaries. This war caused a general exodus of the settlers, who took refuge near the presidio (which had been established in 1683) at El Paso.

The policy of "no guns for Indians" had prevailed from the beginning of the New Mexico settlements, but through the years there had been some "leaks." About Spanish arms in the hands of Indians at the time of the Pueblo revolt, Curtis writes:

> There can be little doubt that a large part of the determination to revolt came from the gradual acquisition, piece by piece, of such small store of weapons as gave ground for the feeling that the advantage held by the Spaniard was at least reduced to the point where a favorable outcome could reasonably be expected. The early results [of the revolt], moreover, were quite in accordance with expectations, and the hearts of the Pueblos, as well as their hands, must have been strengthened by the first tide of success, which overwhelmed every settlement in New Mexico except Ysleta and Santa Fe as well as placing in the hands of the Indians a supply of nearly 300 hackbusses not to mention swords, lances and other steel weapons.[43]

In 1692, Governor Pedro de Vargas, with Mexican troops armed with flintlock muskets, began the reconquest of New Mexico. Figure 4 shows the guns of that day. This type of flintlock was narrowly limited in its use and distribution to the realm of the Spaniard in America. From the time of the Pueblo revolt it persisted in the southwestern United States until well into the nineteenth century. Josiah Gregg found it in the hands of Mexican militia in New Mexico in 1839, and Albert Brackett witnessed its use by Mexican guerrillas in the Mexican War in 1847. It was never openly traded to Indians; but the red man sometimes acquired it as he had acquired the earlier arquebus—surreptitiously through trade, or through murder or theft. After the siege of Santa Fe in 1694, when the conquering Spaniards approached the Hopi pueblos, they were met by eight hundred Indians, some of whom carried these flintlocks. The lack of ammuni-

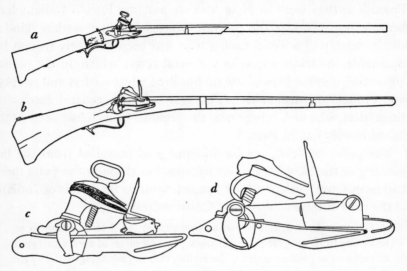

Fig. 4. The Spanish *escopeta* of the seventeenth and eighteenth centuries. After photographs by Nat Dodge. Details of the lock of *a* are given in *c*. The guns are in the collections of the Historical Society of New Mexico, Santa Fe.

tion, however, prevented the Indians from realizing any great advantage at that critical moment, and through the following century the Spaniards were very conscientious in withholding both guns and ammunition from their Indian subjects in the Southwest.[44] The French traders who entered the Southwest in the early eighteenth century did everything possible to distribute their particular brand of flintlock among the nomadic tribes in the southern Great Plains. The *escopeta de arzon* with its distinctive miquelet lock, even in its home territory and during its period of fashion, was but little known to the Indians, because to them a musket was the French or English product. Today it is almost impossible to acquire specimens of the old Spanish guns. The several ancient pieces in the Museum of New Mexico, Santa Fe, are unique in the United States.

The Pueblo revolt was still raging when the first hint of French meddling in the Spanish Southwest reached the ears of Mexican officials. The initial French approach was made accidentally by La Salle, when he landed at Matagorda Bay, Texas, in 1685. This invasion of Spanish territory incited no vengeful attack by Spanish forces, but it was a prelude to the establishment of French Louisiana on the lower Mississippi. The colony built there by the French in 1699 quickly demonstrated its threat to Spanish claims west of the Mississippi River, yet nothing effective was done by Spain to forestall the approaching troubles. In succession, beginning in 1706 and continuing through the 1740's, St. Denis, Du Tisne, La Harpe, Bourgmond, the Mallet brothers, and others sampled the trade possibilities in Spanish-held Texas and New Mexico and in much of that extensive country south of the Platte River which the Spaniards had intended at least to control. Very satisfying records of each of the French expeditions and of the several western trading posts are extant. Here it is enough to state that guns and ammunition were among the principal items of trade, and that the supplying of guns to the Apache, Comanche, Kadohadacho, Kansa, Omaha, Osage, Pawnee, Ponca, Shuman (Jumano), and Wichita altered the old pattern of intertribal wars, completely upset the economy of intertribal trade, and, generally, placed a hornet's nest in the laps of Texas and New Mexico officials. Even English traders in South Carolina and their Chickasaw middlemen were affected when the Pawnee and other Caddoan tribes obtained French guns, for the trading Chickasaw had been accustomed to carry a few English arms and other merchandise into the country that today is eastern Oklahoma.[45]

The effect of the excitement occasioned by the French encroachments was not limited to denouncements voiced in government houses in Santa Fe, Los Adaes, Monterrey, and Mexico City. The inhabitants of Texas and New Mexico towns had the awful import of their loss in prestige brought home to them by the raiding Comanche, who came to their very gates. The two notable Spanish attempts to strike back [46] resulted in heavy losses, and in 1758 all of northern Texas was abandoned by settlers and missionaries alike in fear of the gun-carrying tribes allied with the French frontiersmen. At this crucial moment New Spain got a reprieve by way of Paris in the form of an alliance with France. The mother countries joined forces in 1761 for the purpose of fighting the English during the last stages of the Seven Years' War. In November, 1762, France ceded Louisiana west of the Mississippi to Spain as an inducement to agree to peace terms, and the negotiations culminated in the Treaty of Paris in 1763. This pact also deprived Spain of the Floridas.

Here begins a third episode in the history of Spanish policy toward the Indians. In 1766, troops and civil officials established a seat of government in New Orleans. This government was at first beset by revolution staged by some of the French inhabitants of the city. By 1769 the disturbances had been quelled, and attention was given to the management of affairs in parts of the great expanse of country which constituted Louisiana. Trade with hostile Indian tribes was forbidden, unlicensed traders were removed from Indian villages in the southern sections, and all Frenchmen were warned to stay away from Texas Indians, under threat of death. The old law prohibiting the supplying of guns to Indians was given new emphasis,[47] but there is no evidence that the hard-bitten French traders still on the southern plains heeded the pronouncements.

In the North, the gun trade which had flourished for almost a century continued, the traders taking no cognizance whatever of the political changes in lower Louisiana. In the last decade of the seventeenth century, Englishmen on Hudson Bay and Frenchmen on the Assiniboine River and along the upper tributaries of the Mississippi had brought guns and ammunition to the western Indian middlemen, especially the Cree, Assiniboin, Chippewa, and Sioux. Almost from the beginning of this trade the Cree and the Assiniboin carried guns to the Missouri, where they were bought by eager Plains peoples trading at the Mandan villages. By 1750 the Sioux, also, were supplying guns to trade centers on the Missouri.

Ewers identifies this intercourse as a continuation of an intertribal trade pattern originally based primarily upon the corn grown by the Mandan. He develops the interesting thesis that the ancient Mandan-Hidatsa trade center became a focal point for the early distribution of both horses and guns, and he recognizes the Crow, Cheyenne, Arapaho, Comanche, Kiowa Apache, and Kiowa as the principal tribes that brought in horses and carried back to the West and Southwest the guns and ammunition sought by their remote tribesmen. The Arikara, another agricultural tribe residing on the Missouri near the mouth of the Grand River, not far from the site of present Mobridge, South Dakota, had also produced corn, beans, squash, tobacco, and similar products in aboriginal times, and the nomadic tribes converged upon this trade center very much as they did upon the Mandan villages farther north.[48] (See fig. 5.) Before 1763 most of the guns traded by the Sioux were of French origin. After the fall of New France, the Sioux in Minnesota arranged with British interests for a traders' rendezvous on St. Peter's River (the Minnesota). Here and at the old post, Prairie du Chien, they obtained English guns and ammunition, which they delivered to tribes on the Missouri by the same routes as they had previously used in supplying French arms.[49] In the 1780's, Americans, Frenchmen, and Englishmen, all traders and exploiters, penetrated to the Missouri in ever-increasing numbers. There a few of them took up residence in this land which belonged to Spain. Only a very few of these men were regularly authorized by the Louisiana government to engage in trade, and these few limited their activities to the lower part of the Missouri Valley.

The Indians' possession of guns affected intertribal relationships in the northern plains–Rocky Mountain area very much as it had in the Southwest. The Ute and the Pawnee joined the Comanche in incessant war upon the Apache and at the same time made devastating raids upon Spanish settlements in Texas and New Mexico. The tribes of the high plains—the Blackfeet, Atsina, and Sarsi, as well as the Assiniboin and Plains Cree—now owning plenty of guns, extended the range of their forays against old enemies to the west and southwest. The Snakes (Shoshoni), traditional foes of the Blackfeet, for the first time bowed before the northwestern plains tribes. Formerly the Snakes had enslaved and sold Blackfeet captives; now the Blackfeet captured Snake slaves and sold them to Canadians. In the warfare between these peoples, which started about 1770 and

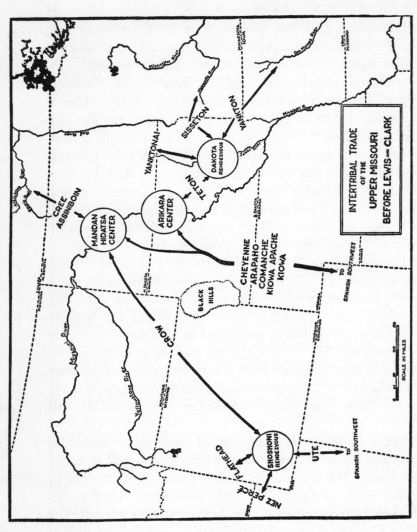

Fig. 5. The early gun trade on the Missouri River and the northwest plains. From the late seventeenth century until the time of Lewis and Clark certain tribes functioned as middlemen in trading both French (until 1763) and English guns. Chart from Ewers, 1954, p. 441, used by permission of John C. Ewers and the Missouri Historical Society.

became more intense after the North West Company [50] entered their territory, the Kutenai and Flatheads (Salish), both lacking guns, were cowed and displaced. The strife, however, was not restricted wholly to the tribes of the far-western areas. The Sioux, with increased armament supplied by the North West Company, began to push into the plains country from the east side of the Mississippi. They challenged the Omaha, Ponca, Cheyenne, Kiowa, and Crow upon their home grounds, and as a result these tribes redoubled their efforts to obtain more guns. Trade on the upper Missouri was brisk during practically all years of the American Revolution.

After the treaty of 1783, Spain took steps to combat the encroachments of English traders in the Missouri River country. Beginning in 1790, Spanish governmental parties from St. Louis made regular trips up the Missouri to the Arikara and Mandan villages to obtain information in regard to poaching by British intruders. Their observations of the volume of business done in the importation of guns led them to view with great concern not only the safety of the upper Missouri country but also the security of their establishments around St. Louis and in the Southwest, which were open to attack by gun-carrying Osage, Oto, Pawnee, and Kansa, as well as from their traditional foe, the Comanche. When, in 1791, Spanish traders on the Missouri were challenged in their own territory by armed Indians who declared that Englishmen supplied all their wants and that Spaniards were unwelcome, the authorities in St. Louis decided to remedy the humiliating situation. Recommendations were made to the senior statesmen in New Orleans that a method be devised for cementing some friendships among the Indians in preparation for the making of a buffer state in upper Louisiana. To this Carondelet, Governor General of Louisiana, assented; on July 12, 1794, he approved articles of incorporation for a trading company, "The Company of Explorers of the Upper Missouri." [51] Jean Baptiste Truteau led the company's first party of traders out of St. Louis and up the Missouri. Included in the merchandise with which Truteau's boats were loaded was a consignment of trade muskets obtained from the transplanted English firm of Don Andrés Todd.[52] Spaniards were now in the Indian gun business on the Missouri. These arms, of course, were identical with other English trade muskets of the day and will be described under the section "The English Trade." The tribes to which the Spanish company gave particular attention during its several years of activity were the Arikara, Mandan, Omaha, Oto, Pawnee, and Ponca. In serving those tribes the traders often had to contend with the Kansa, Missouri, Osage, and a division of the Sioux. Most of the tribes were avid in their demand for guns, and the supply afforded by the Spanish company was much too scanty to satisfy them even when the shipments were distributed in a planned manner. On a number of occasions the tribesmen simply accosted the traders and helped themselves to the armament.

In the course of their field work in 1795, the Spaniards found that "the [English] company called the North [West] Company has just taken a bold step in building a fort this year on the Missouri [Jusseaume's establishment] about a half league distant from the Mandans and in the midst of Spanish possessions." [53] Jacques Clamorgan wrote to Governor Carondelet about the fort, on April 30, 1796:

> By the journal of Mackay you will see that the English were on the point of building a fort among the Mahas [Omaha] and that their traders have had the impudence to cross the Missouri in order to go to the Panis [Pawnee] who inhabit the Platte River, a few leagues above the Otos. It is time to close the doors to this nation if we do not wish them to kick us out.[54]

The Spaniards did not "close the doors" to the English on the Missouri; British traders and their trade muskets were still there when, in 1803, the United States acquired Louisiana.

The account of the Spanish trade with the Indians cannot be concluded without reference to another locality where the old law "no guns to Indians" was revoked by government decree. At the end of the American Revolution, Spain recovered the Floridas. Arguments in regard to boundaries created tense feeling between the United States officials and Spanish diplomats until a settlement was reached in 1795. During the thirteen years of official bickering and frontier conspiracy it was the policy of Spain to see to it that the Indians of the Gulf Plain were well supplied with guns and ammunition. When in 1785 the Georgia legislature opened a portion of the disputed territory to American settlement, the Indians of the powerful Creek confederation, allies of the Spaniards, went to war against the Americans. In the city of Pensacola was the English house Panton, Leslie and Company, which the Spaniards tolerated after the Floridas passed from English ownership. To this firm, Louisiana's Governor Miro turned for help in sustaining the Indians in their fighting. The Creeks had signed a treaty which bound them to engage in only such trade as might be conducted under Spanish authority. Governor Miro turned this trade over to Panton, Leslie and Company and authorized the firm to import from England guns, munitions, and other merchandise, duty free. In 1788, Spanish authorities included the Choctaw and Chickasaw among the peoples to be served by the English firm.

Thus, English guns, at this time as always preferred by the Indian, continued to come from English factories to the Florida ports and thence to the tribesmen on the Gulf Plain and the lower Mississippi. It seems probable that some Spanish arms also reached the Indians in the South, either by trade or gift, but neither documentary sources nor archaeological finds seem to present any proof of this. Peter A. Brannon gives a rather thorough account of the southern Indian trade for the seventeenth and eighteenth centuries. In his study of artifacts from southern Indian sites he failed to find remains of Spanish guns, and the metal objects he did find were of non-Spanish origin. He observes, "Even though there were Spanish subsidized firms, there is no question that their Spanish-sold goods must have been obtained in Great Britain." [55]

In the fall of 1795, Spain softened. At San Lorenzo, Thomas Pinckney, acting for the United States, signed a treaty which met the American demands regarding boundaries, trade, navigation of the Mississippi, and the right to deposit properties at New Orleans. This right was granted for a period of only three years, but it could be renewed. By the time that this settlement was reached, the Indian strife in the South had subsided. Governor Carondelet, in a report to the Spanish ministry, stated that the arms, presents, and monetary remunerations to his Indian friends north of Florida had cost Louisiana $55,000.00 a year.[56] Pinckney's treaty put an end to this Spanish supply of munitions except those the Indians were able to obtain by visiting authorized trading posts and the Florida towns. Panton, Leslie and Company persisted at least until 1818. The continued private supply of English guns was one of the factors that brought about the American-Creek war of 1813–1814; it also had much to do with the troubles the Americans had later with the Seminole. General Andrew Jackson attacked the Seminole at St. Marks, Florida, in 1818, burned one of the Panton, Leslie and Company stores, and executed two British subjects for their collaboration with the hostile tribes.[57] Thereafter, Spanish statesmen harbored some fear that the United States might take Florida by force, and in 1819 Spain signed away her ownership to both East and West Florida. The cession was not officially proclaimed until 1821.

Henceforth any concern we have with Spanish arms is related to the story of Texas and to the Mexican War. The guns used in these episodes receive some attention in chapter iv.

THE ENGLISH TRADE

The extensive and very complicated story of Great Britain's muzzle-loading muskets for Indians began with a record for 1623.[58] It ended in the years this book has been in preparation.[59] The London and Plymouth companies, whose colonists settled in Virginia, Maryland, and Massachusetts early in the seventeenth century, had little opportunity at first to engage in trading guns to Indians, yet as the colonies and settlements multiplied there was some ill-advised arming of the tribes, even in the face of such troubles as the Powhatan confederacy war, 1622–1636, and the Pequot war, 1637. At Plymouth and Boston, particularly, many men turned to the beaver trade. Irresponsible traders were so numerous that in 1641 the British Crown felt it necessary to issue the following order: "In trucking or trading with the Indians no man shall give them for any commodity of theirs,

Fig. 6. Distribution of guns as of 1754. Historical data superimposed upon Goode Base Map No. 202; copyright 1937 by the University of Chicago; used by permission of the University of Chicago Press.

silver or gold, or any weapons of war, either guns or gunpowder, nor sword, nor any other Munition, which might come to be used against ourselves." [60] Nevertheless, guns were traded. "The Journal of New Netherland, 1641–1646," records that the Mohawk obtained "firelocks" from the English as well as from the Dutch,[61] and there is clear evidence that by 1664 English guns were in the hands of the Mohegan, Narraganset, and Wampanoag, as well as in those of most of the Indian neighbors of the New Netherlanders.

In the New England, New York, Connecticut, and Pennsylvania sector were some sixty thousand Indians who had relationships with the English colonists. This grouping includes the tribes that once dealt with the Swedes and the Dutch, nationalities which were removed from the American scene in 1655 and 1665, respectively; it excludes those who were on the fringe of English territory but gave allegiance to the French. In the country held by the southern English colonies and in the Appalachians were approximately eighty thousand Indians exclusive of the marginal groups that were more or less linked with Spanish Florida.[62]

In the South, the English established a brisk trade in guns and other merchandise which took their agents deep into the interior along the ancient trails that skirted the southern tip of the Appalachians. This commerce, conducted by pack-train methods, won over the powerful Choctaw, the Chickasaw, and the Upper Creeks, all eager to own guns, which the Spaniards would not supply. The Chickasaw extended the trade system of the South Carolinians far into the country west of the Mississippi. There is evidence that their intertribal trade prevailed as early as 1719. While the French trader La Harpe was visiting a Caddoan town in the eastern part of what is now Oklahoma, a Chickasaw trader arrived with a load of English merchandise. According to La Harpe, this Indian displayed great annoyance when he discovered that French goods were to offer competition.[63]

In the latter part of the seventeenth century the Carolinians had placed their guns with the Cherokee and Catawba of the highlands, as well as with the Gulf Plain peoples, and by the end of the century

England's hold on the country north of Florida was quite secure. Throughout the English colonies, in both North and South, the increasing number of whites and the extension of settlements brought pressure upon the natives which by 1675 caused widespread hostilities and the ultimate destruction of several tribes.

King Philip's War, 1675–1676, cleared the way for the occupation of New England by white men. The Dutch already had thinned the Indian population in New York, Connecticut, and New Jersey. Hard on the heels of the New England slaughter came the destruction of the Susquehanna of Maryland, initiated by the Iroquois and completed by the Virginia and Maryland settlers. In the South, the Westos were driven from their Savannah River territory in 1680, and before the end of the century a succession of lesser whippings quieted all tribes of the tidewater country clear to Florida. Even Florida was invaded, and the tribes showing allegiance to Spain were chastised by Carolina forces in 1702 and several times thereafter. In the Gulf Plain area English parties bearing gifts won over all the principal tribes except the Choctaw. Subsequently (1711–1715), the Tuscarora and the Yamasee turned their English-made muskets upon the English settlers and traders among them, but South Carolina mustered the strength to win these wars. In 1729, English interests helped to stir the Yazoo and Natchez to make war on the French on the Mississippi, and in the ten-year struggle the English-allied Chickasaw participated on the side of the Natchez. English prestige was thereby increased among the tribes of the South. After Georgia was founded in 1732, James Edward Oglethorpe intensified the earlier efforts of the Carolinians to conduct trade north of Florida and continued the attacks on Florida Indians.[64]

Thus, at last, the country east of the mountains was cleared for settlement. Small groups of Indians were tolerated on lands set aside for them, but with the exception of the Iroquois, who had adapted themselves to life with the whites, the stronger nations had been exterminated or driven westward all along the coastal lowlands of New England and the tidewater and piedmont provinces of the middle and southern colonies. In the first half of the eighteenth century, hundreds of thousands of German, Welsh, and Scotch-Irish immigrants poured into the "pacified" back country of the colonies. To these newcomers was added the overflow of Yankees and Southerners who by this time constituted surplus populations on the eastern seaboard. All the high valleys and upland regions from Maine, New Hampshire, and Vermont south through the Berkshires and the piedmont of Virginia and the Carolinas received an influx of settlers. By the 1720's these had become true frontiersmen, rugged, versatile, and independent. Their institutions were conditioned by the American wilderness, and their mental attitude was strongly affected by their almost complete isolation from the influences of the populous centers along the coast. These people were not traders, they were not speculators, and the majority of them were not dependent tenant farmers. They were free American backwoodsmen intent upon making homes in the rich virgin country that had recently been wrested from the Indian. One of the backwoodsman's notable institutions was the long-barreled rifle derived from the heavy sixteenth-century rifled arm that had been brought to America by the German and Swiss immigrants. Every man and boy, and more than a few of the women on the "western" frontier mastered this phenomenally accurate weapon, which was first produced by the skillful back-country gunsmiths in the 1720's. As mentioned previously, the rifle in its early days was not an arm for the Indian; however, maurading red men sometimes snatched one from a luckless settler, and in some localities civilized remnants of tribes adopted the rifle at a very early date (see note 19). It was, however, in universal use among the settlers in the back country by the middle of the eighteenth century; and although it was popularly called the "Kentucky rifle" as early as 1780, it is more fittingly identified with Pennsylvania, where in the western towns its makers were fairly well concentrated. Today it is known as the "Pennsylvania-Kentucky Rifle." During the approximately one hundred years of its use this rifle won for itself a reputation for ruggedness, ease of loading, accuracy, and all-round efficiency. An aura of romance surrounds it to this day.

There was sufficient real merit in the arm and its tactical use in warfare to bring about a new era of world armament (see chap. iv, note 38), but the fact remains that the rifle, at first, was a weapon to be turned against the red man and not a gun for the Indian trade. Not until the opening of the nineteenth century was there any notable arming of the tribes with rifles. The story of this arming is told in chapter iii.

Moving westward ahead of the tide of settlement were a few English traders who maintained contact with certain Indian groups that had been forced to migrate. The Delaware and Shawnee, for example, had withdrawn from their hunting grounds along the Susquehanna and Delaware rivers and in the 1730's were occupying the country about the Forks of the Ohio. George Croghan, a trader from the Susquehanna, catered to the needs of these tribes at a time when the French were unable to supply trade goods to the upper Ohio area. Croghan established posts on the upper Ohio, and from these new centers of trade he pushed westward and northwestward with pack outfits laden with British merchandise. His traders went to the upper Miami (Pickawillany), where they threatened the French hold on the Maumee-Miami portage. They also penetrated to the shores of Lake Erie, where they dealt with close friends of the French, the Huron, at the site of present Sandusky, and they even moved down the Ohio to trade with the Illinois Indians in country that had been French territory for half a century. In 1748 Croghan gave further insult to the French when he built a fort and warehouses at the new Miami town, Pickawillany, a village inhabited by Miami, who had deserted the French at Fort Wayne. Croghan was not alone in exploiting the trade in the Ohio Valley; other English traders entered the region, and by 1748 it was possible for the English to obtain treaties of friendship with the Miami, Delaware, Shawnee, Wyandot, and contingents of the Iroquois residing on the Monongahela and Allegheny rivers and at the confluence of those streams.

Croghan and Christopher Gist of the Ohio Company assisted the Virginia commissioners in distributing guns to these Indians as gifts

from the Crown. They also arranged for the construction of two fortified trading posts: one on the Monongahela and one designated for
the Forks of the Ohio.

In January, 1754, Governor Dinwiddie of Virginia sent a construction crew to the Forks of the Ohio to build the English fort.
George Washington, then twenty-two years old, led a force of 150
Virginians in the wake of the builders, with the expectation of gar-
risoning the new establishment; but near the confluence of Wills
Creek and the Potomac (where Cumberland, Maryland, now stands)
he learned that the French were already constructing Fort Duquesne
on the site at the Forks selected by the English, and that Dinwiddie's
fort builders were returning to their homes. Proceeding westward
with his militiamen, Washington on May 28, 1754, surprised and
defeated a small French force near Great Meadows on the Cumberland Road, in a fight which is regarded as the opening engagement
of the French and Indian War. At Great Meadows, a few miles east
of the site of present Uniontown, Pennsylvania, Washington entrenched his small army and awaited attack by forces from Fort
Duquesne. To his earthworks he gave the name Fort Necessity. On
July 3 the expected attack came when some five hundred Frenchmen and four hundred Indians besieged the position. The open
meadows around the fortification precluded close approach by the
enemy, and the fight was largely one of long-range firing of muskets.
The ammunition and food of the English were exhausted at the end
of the day; Washington gave up the fight, but only on terms that
permitted his men to retain their muskets and march back to Virginia. This retreat of the Virginians marked the evacuation of the
Ohio country by English civilians and the beginning of seven years
of war, 1754–1763.[65] Much larger armies were in the French and
Indian War than had ever before fought on American battlefields.
A score of Indian tribes were embroiled in it, some of whom were
opportunists who readily changed allegiance to meet changes in the
tides of war—changes which after 1758, when Lord Pitt reorganized
the British plan, led to the rapid crumbling of French strength. On
September 8, 1760, Amherst, the English general, demanded and

received from Governor de Vaudreuil the surrender of Montreal and with it all of Canada.

New France as an entity ceased to exist, and the flow of French guns to the Indians of America came to an end. This was a circumstance which the many French traders still in the western wilds could hardly accept as true. Among their Indian friends they engendered hatred for the English, and, because the lavish gifts of wartime were no longer forthcoming from the new rulers of the land, reaction among the Indians was sharp and immediate. In the Old Northwest, particularly, the tribesmen wanted guns and ammunition; but English officials said, "No guns." In response to the edict, Chief Pontiac of the Ottawa brought about a confederation of the Ottawa, Ojibway, Potawatomi, Seneca, Wyandot, Miami, Kickapoo, Shawnee, Delaware, and Chippewa for the purpose of annihilating the English in the Northwest. The year 1763 witnessed repeated Indian attacks and the collapse of the frontier posts, with the exception of Detroit, Fort Pitt, and Niagara. Fort Pitt had been built by the English in 1758–1761 at the Forks of the Ohio, close to the site of the destroyed Fort Duquesne of the French. Massacres throughout the northwestern wilderness brought the death lists of 1763 to totals which exceeded the casualties suffered by the British in any one year of the French and Indian War. But Pontiac was incapable of the sustained management of campaigns and the disciplined, persistent fighting necessary to win a large-scale war. When relief expeditions brought reinforcements and supplies to the remaining Englishmen in the West, the Indians became discouraged and Pontiac scurried to the Illinois country for safety.

In 1765 a government expedition entered the Illinois country to take over the French towns which had not been touched during the French and Indian War. Fort de Chartres, between Cahokia and Kaskaskia, became the seat of English rule in the country of the Illinois. Unregulated traders then swarmed into the West, and by 1769 private interests were erecting trading posts at several favorable places in the Old Northwest and were extending their expeditions to the Sioux west of the Mississippi, to the Lake Superior country, and to the vicinity of present Winnipeg. The English guns which these far-ranging white traders supplied mingled in the Indian camps with the French firearms which for half a century had filtered into the Great Plains country from La Vérendrye's posts on the Assiniboine and from Michilimackinac, Prairie du Chien, Green Bay, the Illinois River, New Orleans, and Mobile. Also, in the North, they competed with the arms then being supplied by the Hudson's Bay Company[66] from its posts served by ships on Hudson Bay. By this time the Hudson's Bay Company was energetically extending its influence to Indian tribes far distant from the forts. In the period 1754–1774, sixty expeditions from Hudson Bay penetrated to the Arctic Ocean, to the Rocky Mountains, and southward to the Missouri.

After the fall of New France, French traders from Montreal, then British subjects, regarded themselves as rightful successors to La Vérendrye and in the region once exploited by La Vérendrye proceeded to divert the trade from Hudson Bay to the St. Lawrence. The resulting clashes between "the English," as the Hudson's Bay Company people were termed, and "the Canadian peddlers" became steadily more violent. By 1784, nine different companies among the Canadians had combined to form the North West Company.[67] Competing posts were built by "the partners" side by side with the "English" establishments, and bloody combats, kidnapping, arrests, and legal actions became the order of the day.

The tremendous country north, west, and south of Hudson Bay in which the British rivals staged their contest held more than three hundred thousand natives [68] and provided the best furs to be found in America. The prize was indeed worth the effort.

To round out the picture of intense competition and widespread activity of the English fur traders in the 1770's, it is only necessary to examine the government records of the traders' credentials for the period. Grace Lee Nute reveals that she found 2,431 *voyageurs* represented in the formal licenses issued at Montreal and Detroit for the one year 1777. She estimates that these men, together with the traders who already were working the interior, "the employees of the Hudson's Bay Company, and the American traders from the new United States," would bring the total of traders to "5000 men sprinkled from Montreal to the Rocky Mountains and from Hudson Bay to the Gulf of Mexico." [69] Guns and ammunition were highly important items of trade throughout the enormous area worked by the traders, and English arms predominated—in spite of the fact that Great Britain had a war on her hands which by this time she could recognize as a grave threat to her empire in America. Generally, the British system for the distribution of guns to Indians was regarded by her leaders to be a contribution to her war effort.

The King declared that the Old Northwest was to be left without political organization, reserved as Crown lands, exempt from purchase and settlement. Thus did the English government attempt to adopt an aspect of the western policy of the French. In the 1772 report of the Lords Commissioners for Trade and Plantations, it was asserted:

> The great object of colonization upon the Continent of North America has been to improve and extend the commerce and manufactures of this Kingdom. . . . It does appear to us that the extension of the fur trade depends entirely upon the Indians being undisturbed in the possession of their hunting grounds, and that all colonization [settlement] does in its nature and must in its consequence operate to the prejudice of that branch of commerce . . . Let the savages enjoy their deserts in quiet. Were they driven from their forests the peltry trade would decrease.[70]

It has been recognized by historians that (1) the Proclamation of 1763, which prohibited settlement west of the Province of Quebec and the Appalachian Mountains, and (2) the Quebec Act of 1774, which propagandists declared "established the doctrines of Royal absolution and Roman Catholicism throughout the Colonies," estranged the American West from the Crown and guaranteed that the frontiersmen would join the Revolutionary movement as that ideology spread during the winter of 1774–1775. The story of the Indian and the gun during the Revolutionary War has to do almost entirely with these frontiersmen who revolted and their war on the western borders.

EFFECTS OF THE AMERICAN REVOLUTION
UPON THE DISTRIBUTION OF GUNS TO INDIANS

When, in April, 1775, the first shot of the Revolution was fired on the Lexington green, the British already had the advantage of assured friendship and support of Indian allies. Not less than thirty thousand warriors were on the side of the redcoats.[71] Most of these Indians already had muskets of either French or English make, but the new war was occasion to acquire new guns. In 1776–1778, the British sent heavily loaded pack trains carrying arms and ammunition to the Cherokee in the western Carolinas and Tennessee, a section which for a hundred years had received English guns from Charlestown and Virginia trade centers. The shipments included the "Brown Bess" military musket.[72] The Choctaw, Creeks, and Chickasaw received guns by the Mobile-Tombigbee and Mobile-Alabama river routes. Probably the most important aid rendered by the southern Indians who served Great Britain was their defense of the seaport Mobile, which continued to be an important distribution point until it was captured by the Spaniards in 1780.[73]

In Kentucky and the Old Northwest, the Indian population was almost solidly aligned with the British, who encountered little or no difficulty in delivering guns from the St. Lawrence to the Indian towns. The arms were sent up the river to Lakes Ontario and Erie and thence over the several well-established and adequately protected portages which gave access to the Mississippi and Ohio river systems. It was the purpose of the British leaders working out of their headquarters at Detroit to prevent defection of any tribes which might possibly aid the enemy, to embarrass American shipping on the Ohio, and to prevent further settlement in Kentucky—all of which, it was thought, would assure eventually an Indian state "exempt from purchase and settlement." To accomplish these objectives it was deemed necessary to provide the Indians with an abundance of supplies of all kinds, especially armament, and to devise raids which would give outlet to the Indians' proclivity to pillage and kill. In these endeavors the British attained only partial success; in the face of spasmodic, flaming, frontier warfare the Kentucky settlements became more firmly rooted, grew larger, and extended ever westward. The remarkable campaigns of George Rogers Clark and his rifle-shooting backwoodsmen [74] did not result in decisive American victory in the West, nor did they ever give Americans full control of Kentucky, Illinois, or Ohio; yet they played a significant part in thwarting certain British drives, in encouraging the Kentucky settlers, and in obtaining the Old Northwest for the United States at the end of the war.[75]

In the Northeast, the frontier was still east of the mountains during the years of the Revolution. Most of the Iroquois confederacy elected to sustain the British cause, and the greater part of their fighting was done at no great distance from the eastern front. The Iroquois, the first tribe of Indians in which every man carried a gun, were adroit in the use of arms, and because some of their leaders were educated and thoroughly indoctrinated in the ways of the white man, they were especially capable of fitting into the British war plan. As might be expected, they were fully equipped with the best armament that England could supply. The American settlements in the Wyoming, Mohawk, and Schoharie valleys, particularly, felt the impact of Iroquois attacks; the Indians sometimes succeeded in destroying the settlements and as many times were repulsed. By the summer of 1781, nearly all Americans had evacuated the New York frontier; yet it was in the Mohawk Valley that an army of Americans in the late summer of 1781 won a decisive and final victory over the Iroquois and Tories at West Canada Creek.

By the time that Cornwallis surrendered in October, 1781, practically all Indian tribes in the eastern half of what is now the United States were thoroughly familiar with guns and gunpowder. It cannot be said that cultural traits were suddenly affected by the arming and rearming of the warriors during the Revolution, for most of the tribes that sided with the British had dropped their primitive weapons in favor of firearms long before the war. However, close contacts with Tory comrades in bivouac and in the heat of battle made a new generation of Indians wise to the white man's ways with a gun.

Whether or not the tribesmen could be classed as good soldiers in the white man's sense of the term is beside the point.[76] The gun did increase the Indian's capacity to hunt, and from this standpoint its expanded use as engendered by the Revolution was significant in the later wilderness commercial enterprises in which the Indian was to continue to play a leading role.

The Treaty of Paris, September 3, 1783, ended the Revolution, but it did not put an end to the hostilities of Indians either in the South or in the Old Northwest. The Indian trade continued to be a transcendent interest in Great Britain's plans in America. Her aspirations in the North included visions of an Indian barrier state in the Great Lakes area south of the boundary agreed upon in 1783. Here, Great Britain proposed, should be a reservation which would assuage the disappointment of the former British Indian allies and assure permanence of the fur trade. It would be open to traders of both countries, England and the United States, but closed to all settlers.

British agents worked among the Indians of the northern boundary country during the period 1785–1787 to form a confederation of tribes that might be equal to the task of forcing the United States to set up the proposed Indian state. The Iroquois, Shawnee, Delaware, Wyandot, Kickapoo, Sauk, Miami, Ottawa, Chippewa, Mingo, and Potawatomi took formal tribal action in joining the confederation and in repudiating treaties which earlier had ceded their claims to much of the country that is now within the state of Ohio. To these Indians within the new United States the British again sent guns and ammunition, and with the supplies went advice; the tribes were urged to demand immediate and exclusive Indian occupancy of the Ohio country. By the fall of 1790, a new war was raging. It brought into the Old Northwest a succession of United States military expeditions which after a number of failures finally brought victory at the Battle of Fallen Timbers, in 1794, and the collapse of the Northwest Indian confederation.

However, the breakdown did not terminate the sale of English guns to Indians in the United States. John Jay's treaty negotiated in England in 1794 gave to the traders from Canada the right to enter the United States to trade with the former allies of Great Britain. Their trade goods were to be taxed at the same rate as the goods traded by Americans, and they were free to carry furs from the United States back to Canada without paying any tax whatever, advantages which perpetuated the sale of English guns to Indians and brought sharp protests from American traders.

All along the northern border and well into the interior in the upper Missouri region,[77] English guns were supplied to United States Indians quite as freely as before the Revolution. In the Old Northwest, the British trade felt the pinch occasioned by the influx of American settlers into the Ohio country, and again an agent of the Crown counseled the Indians to resist the United States treaty makers who were bringing about land cessions. Tecumseh, the Shawnee chief, and his brother, "the Prophet," at this time launched their crusade of tribal reforms and organized another Indian confederacy designed to stay the flood of white settlement. To encourage the Indian resistance, the British set up a base at Fort Malden on the Canadian side of the Detroit River and issued arms to Indians from the United States. Some of the Shawnee warriors, rejoicing in their new guns and itching to use them, raided border farms and villages. A punitive expedition led by General William Henry Harrison and composed of United States regulars and militia descended upon the Shawnee center, Prophetstown on the Wabash. On November 7, 1811, the Indians attempted a surprise attack upon this small army, but it backfired. The troops broke up the attack, scattered the Indians far and wide, and burned their town. This, the Battle of Tippecanoe, was no great military victory, but it provided a springboard for popular sentiment favoring war with Great Britain. Of Britain's part in the Indian disturbance, Harrison on December 2, 1811, wrote:

> Within the last three months the whole of the Indians on this frontier have been completely armed and equipped out of the King's stores at Malden. . . . The Indians had, moreover, an ample supply of British glazed powder. Some of their guns had been sent to them so short a time before the action, that they were not divested of the list covering in which they are imported.[78]

In 1812, six thousand Indians from the United States visited Malden and Drummond Island, near Mackinac, to obtain English guns. American frontiersmen, faced with the threat of annihilation by the hostile tribes, clamored the louder for the conquest of Canada and the destruction of Fort Malden. Provoked by this situation and by Britain's maritime policy in her war with France, the United States Congress declared war on England on June 18, 1812. The fighting during the next two and a half years included much action in the Great Lakes region, in the Old Northwest, in Georgia and Florida, and on the Lake Champlain frontier. American victory in a battle on the Thames near the offending British arsenal, Fort Malden, on October 5, 1813, restored American dominance in the Old Northwest. The destruction of the British fleet on Lake Champlain on September 11, 1814, ended the threat of invasion via the vulnerable Lake Champlain corridor. Englishmen at the peace table in Ghent thereupon decided that there were obstructions to victory which would be too costly to remove. They surrendered Great Britain's long-established interest in an Indian state in the Great Lakes–Ohio region and agreed that the fur trade no longer could be the prime consideration in planning the future for the Old Northwest. The treaty of peace, signed on December 24, 1814, gave to the United States none of the objectives that had been set forth when war was declared; yet the war was not a failure. The matter of westward expansion of settlements was disposed of favorably; and the bogy of an Indian state with British control was laid to rest. In the eyes of American frontiersman this was victory enough.[79]

The British government made some final gifts of guns to Indians in the United States in 1815,[80] and English traders on the Missouri and at the headwaters of the Mississippi quietly continued to trade in guns for a few years after the signing of the Treaty of Ghent. Policing by the U. S. Army in 1816–1818 curtailed this trespassing [81] and probably influenced England in 1818 to agree to the forty-ninth parallel as Canada's southern boundary from the Great Lakes to the Rocky Mountains.

On the Columbia and elsewhere in the disputed Oregon country

English traders continued to sell guns in accordance with the "joint occupancy" agreed upon in the Convention of 1818, a commerce that did not end until 1846. Everywhere, from the Arctic Ocean to the Gulf of Mexico and from the Atlantic to the Pacific, English trade muskets were the Indians' first choice, "light guns, small in the hand and well shaped, with locks that will not freeze in winter." Figure 7 shows the trade gun in the hands of Indians at the northern and southern extremes of its range of use. At the left is a Kootchin Indian as sketched on the Yukon River in 1847 by Alexander Hunter Murray. In the North, it was the regular practice of English traders to supply red woolen slip covers with the guns they traded. When these cloth covers wore out, the Indian owner commonly made a buckskin case for his weapon, like that shown by Murray.

The Indian on the right (in fig. 7) is Tokos Tmathla, the Seminole chief, as represented in a painting made early in the nineteenth century. When the Seminole waged war against the United States in 1816–1818, most of them were armed with this type of British gun. In their bitter fighting with the U. S. Army in 1834–1842, they used some rifles, but the trade musket was still their principal arm.

As the country settled down to the even tenor of peace time, English trade guns continued to be sold to Indians in the United States, but the vendors were Americans. In Canada, of course, there was no interruption of the trade except as strife occurred between men of the North West Company and the Hudson's Bay Company. These ruptures ended when the two rival organizations joined forces in 1821. Throughout the realms of Indian traders the English trade musket maintained its place as the superior gun for Indians. Sales continued wherever there were Indians and whenever the guns could be imported. Details of the story of the "fuke" and the history of its distribution are presented in chapter iii.

INDIAN GUNS IN THE UNITED STATES

Immediately after the Revolution, frontiersmen and speculators swarmed into country west of the Appalachians which was still

Fig. 7. The Indian gun in the North and in the South. After contemporary drawings. *Left,* a Kutchin Indian with encased musket, 1847, drawn by A. H. Murray (*The Beaver,* June, 1947, p. 43), first published by the Canadian Government, Archives Publication No. 4, 1910; used by permission of the Hudson's Bay Company. *Right,* a Seminole chief, from McKenney and Hall, 1836.

claimed by Indians. Land companies in Georgia, Tennessee, New York, Pennsylvania, and elsewhere waited scarcely long enough for ink to dry on the Treaty of Paris before making demands upon Indian lands. The resulting tension and, in places, bloody warfare became a political problem which the U. S. Congress attempted to meet by enacting ordinances "for the disposal of lands in the western territory" and by creating an Office of Indian Affairs within the War Department.

The Treaty of Fort Greenville, 1795, at the conclusion of Anthony Wayne's successful campaign in Ohio, encouraged settlement of some of the most desirable—and most bitterly contested—land where Indians were still in occupancy. The government desired to assuage, as far as possible, the tribal hatreds engendered by its seizure of the Indian domain and so facilitate settlement. Almost coincident with the ratification of the Treaty of Fort Greenville was the establishment of the United States Indian factory system.[82] George Washington, in 1793, had advocated this system, a chain of government-operated stores on the frontier where Indians could secure goods at cost. One of the first stores to be installed was at Tellico, Tennessee, where in 1798 the Cherokee were required to cede three tracts of land. Other more important government stores were built at Chickasaw Bluffs, Natchitoches, Fort Wayne, Detroit, Chicago, Prairie du Chien, Green Bay, and Mackinac. Twenty-eight factories were established, but not more than a dozen existed simultaneously. Only one, Fort Osage,[83] was west of the Mississippi. (See end papers.)

It was intended that the factory system should aid the military units dealing with Indians, prevent exploitation of the Indians by renegade traders, and terminate the meddling of British and Spanish interests in Indian affairs in the United States. Philadelphia was headquarters for the system until 1808, when the offices were moved to Georgetown, D.C. Trade goods went to the trading posts by way of Detroit, St. Louis, or New Orleans. At the outposts the tribes exchanged furs and hides for the merchandise afforded by the nonprofit organization.

Here, as everywhere in the Indian trade, guns and ammunition were highly important items on the inventories. There was not a tribe served by the factory system that had not become thoroughly familiar with guns and gunpowder through contact with Spanish, French, or English traders. The American government factors discovered very quickly that the Indian was a discerning customer who knew one gun from another and who would accept only a good quality of ammunition. He demanded the English trade gun (see chap. iii). That the government traders did succeed in bringing about some change in the red man's views in regard to firearms is evident in the record of rifles sold at the Indian factories. This innovation which took place during the opening years of the nineteenth century was the first change worthy of mention in a trade pattern which had prevailed for two hundred years. An account of it is given in the section "Rifles to Indians" in chapter iii.

About the time that the rifle was first passed out to the tribesmen, forced treaties took from the Creeks, Cherokee, Choctaw, and Chickasaw millions of acres of land in central Georgia, southern Tennessee, and Mississippi Territory. In 1802, further cessions were exacted from the Delaware, Miami, and Kickapoo in the Old Northwest. The Kaskaskia were required to surrender title to their Illinois lands in 1803, and immediately thereafter the Sauk and Foxes gave up some fifteen million acres south of the Wisconsin River. The southeastern corner of what is now the state of Michigan and three million acres in Indiana were taken from the Delaware and Potawatomi. These were events leading up to the formation of Tecumseh's confederation, the Battle of Tippecanoe, and the outbreak of the War of 1812. During the war, the Indian factories and the Indian trade, generally, fared badly. The government posts at Fort Mackinac, Detroit, and Chicago were captured by the British, and a number of others, including Fort Osage, were abandoned.

After the war, Congress enacted a law which limited the Indian trade to American citizens and placed fourteen hundred troops in the Great Lakes area and on the Mississippi. Fort Osage on the Missouri was reoccupied. John Jacob Astor, whose fur-trading enterprise on the Columbia (1810–1813) had been wrecked by English interests,[84] made a new start at this time and proceeded in 1816 to establish trading posts on the upper Mississippi and in the Great Lakes region. Throughout the greater period of his activity, Astor's connections with Canadian firms had been such as to assure him of a supply of English-made trade goods; but during the War of 1812 this supply was curtailed, if not completely interrupted. He resorted to substitutes. When he offered Belgian and German muskets to his northern Indian customers, they rejected the arms. Presumably, it was on this occasion that Astor persuaded certain American manufacturers to produce fusees of the English type. At any rate, Astor's American Fur Company and a number of other firms and independent traders found that the demands of the tribesmen at last could be satisfied with American muskets.[85]

The stabilizing influence of the military in the West resulted in a general revival of Indian trade in the country along the lower Missouri drainage. By 1819, the Missouri Fur Company was serving the Pawnee, Oto, Omaha, Iowa, and some divisions of the Sioux; the traders Robidoux, Papin, Chouteau, and Berthold overlapped upon the field of the Missouri Fur Company; Pratte and Vasquez traded with the Omaha. The more important posts maintained by these companies were at Council Bluffs (Nebraska), Chouteau's post on the Kansas, Nishuabotna near what is now the Missouri-Nebraska boundary, and the Pratte-Vasquez house just north of Council Bluffs.[86] St. Louis was the headquarters for these concerns. In the spring of 1822, Ramsay Crooks, agent for the American Fur Company, established a St. Louis headquarters for the western department of his company. It was at this time that the political drive, launched by Astor and other private interests, against the government's twenty-six-year-old factory system of Indian trade culminated in the overthrow of that system. Thus in 1822 the way was opened wider for the American Fur Company's march to monopoly.

The upper Missouri and Rocky Mountain fur trade now entered upon that phase of its history in which the "mountain man" attained a stature which overshadowed and to a great degree displaced the *voyageur* of the earlier day. Present in the field or about to enter it when

Astor's men came to the Missouri were the Missouri Fur Company, the Columbia Fur Company, the Rocky Mountain Fur Company, Stone-Bostwick and Company, Bernard Pratt and Company, the French Fur Company, Sublette and Campbell, Nathaniel J. Wyeth, Captain B. L. E. Bonneville, Gant and Blackwell, and a number of lesser lights, all of whom left some imprint upon the record of the gun trade in the West.[87]

As the volume of the gun trade increased, problems of arms production and supply multiplied, but manufacturers in the East and transportation companies in the West found no great difficulty in meeting the situation. Guns and ammunition poured to the West. The ruthless competition between American trading interests seldom brought true benefits to the Indian, but a shortage of armament usually was not one of his handicaps.

The policy of Indian removal was put into effect by President Monroe in 1825, and by the time Andrew Jackson entered the White House, the Congress had become relentless in ejecting most of the tribes from their homes east of the Mississippi River. The uprooted Indians were to be transplanted to a "permanent Indian Country" west of Arkansas and Missouri. These emigrant tribes were supplied with firearms, as were the "wild" tribes indigenous to the western lands allotted to the emigrants. The impact of the newcomers upon the western tribes was accompanied by sniping, ambuscade, and pitched battle, which required years of interventiton by the United States Army. In the South, especially, the Army also was occupied in enforcing the orders for removal of the Indians. The "Five Civilized Tribes"—Cherokee, Creek, Chickasaw, Choctaw, and Seminole—had adopted many of the white man's ways. They resisted the order to move, which if obeyed would have resulted in the loss of their farms, herds, schools, and towns. The futility of rebellion was recognized, eventually, by most of these Indians, but the well-armed Seminole went to war against the United States and put up a bitter fight, which lasted from 1835 to 1842.

The tragedy of Indian removal was but one of the facets of the story of guns in the West from the 1820's to the 1840's. The penetration by Americans into the country west of the Rocky Mountains and the related conflict with British interests in Old Oregon, the overland trade with the Spanish in the Southwest, the expanded missionary activity among Indians in the Far West, the beginnings of emigration to the Pacific slope, and the winning of Oregon and Texas introduce additional aspects of firearms history. In part, they are the themes which underlie the accounts which follow.

Fig. 8. Indians receiving guns.

II

Personal Weapons of the Traders and Trappers

In choosing his personal weapons the trader was influenced in no small measure by his judgment of what would best aid him in preserving his own life. But this selection was dictated also by the weapons available. Many traders carried the same kinds of arms as were used in trade. Some fortunate members of the fraternity were able to obtain specially made sporting weapons from England and the Continent. Others favored the military models, and a few carried the Kentucky rifle.

As better weapons were developed, the far-ranging traders and mountain men were quick to adopt the improved arms. Indeed, their needs stimulated the manufacture of guns of advanced design, such as the Hawken rifle. The records indicate that the superiority of the revolving rifles and pistols was recognized by civilians on the frontier long before the new devices were accepted by the military. From the time of the earliest American trade in the Far West to the appearance of the repeating rifle, the traders' reports exercised a substantial influence on the development of effective weapons.

MUSKETS

A satisfying analysis of the earliest trade muskets is that of Mayer,[1] who assembled a mass of seventeenth-century gun parts from one-time Iroquois village sites near Rochester, New York. He writes:

Judging from a careful examination of recovered fragments, we venture to say that the average musket used by the New York redman was a light, sturdy weapon, serviceable both in war and in the chase. It is recalled that the Jesuits remarked that the Iroquois were supplied with "good arquebuses." They were long (around 50″), slender and octagonal or circular at the breech. Brass sights were common. Calibers varied, but .50 or .60 seems to have been popular. Attachment to stock

Fig. 9. A Mohawk chief with a seventeenth-century musket. In England in 1709, portraits were made of four Mohawk chiefs who had come to visit Queen Anne. The weapon depicted by J. Simon, who made the original mezzotint from which this drawing was prepared, seems to be a Continental or an American weapon, probably a Dutch musket that had been acquired by the Indian in New Netherland. Comparison of this Mohawk's musket with the seventeenth-century flintlock piece shown in fig. 10, *b*, reveals striking similarities. After Mayer, 1943*b*.

was made by a tang screw coming up from below and by three pins engaging lugs on the under surface of the barrel. . . . The stocks were
full length and customarily strengthened in front by a simple band-
like finial of iron or brass. The butt was protected either by a small
triangular plate of brass nailed to its heel or by a full buttplate of
metal. Iron or brass was used for such furniture as trigger guards,
ram thimbles, name plates, etc. Not until late in the century did screw
plates appear.[2]

Except for the length of the piece and the lack of the screw plate,
the seventeenth-century musket described by Dr. Mayer approxi-
mates the gun which two hundred years later was put into the hands
of most of the American tribes, under the names "Hudson's Bay
fuke," "North West gun," and "Mackinaw gun"—the musket treated
in some detail in chapter iii (see fig. 18).

A few of the seventeenth-century guns from New Netherland were
handed down intact and can today be examined in collections. For
the most part, these relics of early gunning in America have been
preserved because of the distinctive art work on them, or because
they were owned and used in families in which succeeding generations attached sentimental value to them and treasured them as heir-
looms.

The Dutch guns presented in figure 10, *a* and *b,* are specimens of
good workmanship but with no unusual ornamentation. In all likelihood they were owned by important New Netherlanders, or perhaps by favored chiefs of the Indians. They did not receive the abuse
regularly given to trade guns, and they are almost intact after some
three hundred years in the homes of transplanted Dutchmen and in
present-day gun collections.[3] They serve quite well to represent the
type of personal long arm carried by the New Netherlanders who
shaped the early methods of the beaver trade—methods which became traditional.

Figure 10, *a,* is a good example of a seventeenth-century Dutch
flintlock musket which displays the characteristic long barrel with
massive breech (in this specimen, circular in section),[4] the recurved
trigger, half stock, and three brass ram thimbles with a wooden ram-

rod. Other characteristics of guns of this period, which are not apparent in the drawing, are a tang screw which comes up from below to hold the breech upon the stock, and pins which engage lugs in the undersurface of the barrel and thus attach the forestock to the barrel. The caliber of this piece is .80. The forestock has been splintered, and

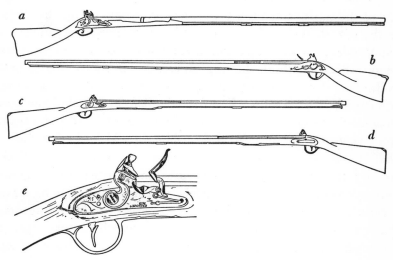

Fig. 10. Long arms—muskets—of the traders and trappers. *a* and *b*, guns from the Iroquois country in New York State representative of the seventeenth-century arms used in the early Dutch trade: *a* is illustrated in U. S. Cartridge Co., n.d., pp. 96–97. *b*, from the collection of William J. Young, is pictured in Mayer, 1943, p. 34. *c* and *d*, an American gun made more than one hundred years after *a* and *b* arrived in the New World, is reputed to have been carried overland by the Astorians from St. Louis to the mouth of the Columbia in 1811; it is in Milwaukee Public Museum (no. 21238). *e*, detail of the lock of *c* and *d*.

since longitudinal parts of it are missing, the swell of the well-proportioned heavy breech is exposed. The specimen is fairly typical of the arms carried by the Dutch traders who entered the country of the Iroquois and started a chain of bloody events which continued through American colonial times. The musket is illustrated in the catalogue of the collection formerly owned by the U. S. Cartridge Company,[5] but its present whereabouts is unknown.

Another seventeenth-century musket from the Iroquois country of New York State is shown in figure 10, *b.* The barrel is 53⅛ inches long and is about .70 caliber. The breech is octagonal except for a short section which is sixteen-sided. On the underside of the barrel are the initials "I C." The barrel is attached to the stock by pins. There are four fluted ram pipes. The full stock is of curly maple, one of the signs of its probably American origin. In this musket, as in the one shown in figure 10, *a,* the stock proper is clublike, or "mutton-leg," as were most continental stocks of the period, a style adopted occasionally in the English colonies but somewhat unusual in England. Inside the lock plate are the initials "B.H.S." The chased and chiseled steel scrollwork of the side plate is typical of the times. In general, the characteristics of the piece indicate that it is from the late seventeenth century. In all probability it was stocked and assembled in the colonies; the barrel and lock were made in the mother country. It is interesting to note in how many particulars the gun resembles the musket held by the Mohawk chief pictured in figure 9.[6]

Most of the arms carried by the leaders of French contingents in the American hinterland during the seventeenth century were not notably different from the Dutch guns just described. However, some English commanders of the fur-hunting parties on the American frontier even in the late seventeenth century carried firearms which, generally, resembled the specimen pictured in figure 10, *c* and *d.* Streamlining and a fair balance marked many of these English guns. By the end of the century, British flintlock arms for civilian use had advanced to a stage of good workmanship and good design, characteristics which changed but little in the succeeding century.

Figure 10, *c, d,* and *e,* depicts a weapon assembled in America in the early nineteenth century. The barrel, however, is of London make; in design it follows closely the specifications long standard in England for sporting arms. The lock bears the inscription "McKim and Brother." This firm was a manufactory which was active in Baltimore, Maryland, "prior to 1825," according to Sawyer [7] and Metschl.[8] The caliber of this gun is .68. A section of the barrel is hexagonal, and stamped on it is the word "London." Details of the lock are given in figure 10, *e*. Apparently, the imported barrel was assembled with other parts having an American origin, by McKim and Brother—such assembling of guns was a common practice among gunmakers in America in the eighteenth and first half of the nineteenth centuries. The specimen is owned by the Milwaukee Public Museum, in which it is exhibited as a "voyageur's gun." Records show that the piece made the overland trip to Oregon with the Astorians in 1811; it is thus the oldest far-western firearm considered in this study. In the inventories of Astor's goods at Astoria seventy-two muskets are accounted for; twenty-two of them were the military type complete with bayonets.[9] These were undoubtedly company-owned, not personal arms.

Brown Bess.—Dillin shows a "Brown Bess" English musket made in 1740 which he states was carried up the Missouri by Manuel Lisa in 1807.[10] Where the old gun is now he does not say. In the Milwaukee Museum (no. L1468) is Solomon Juneau's "Brown Bess" musket with the "Tower" impress.[11] It also bears the London proof marks and the monogram of King George III (1760–1820). Juneau was the first permanent trader in the Milwaukee area, and like some other frontiersmen he carried a retired British army gun, which he considered to be the best personal arm that he could take into the wilds. These British military guns came into use at the opening of the eighteenth century. During the reigns of Queen Anne (1702–1714) and George I (1714–1727) the barrel was 46 inches long and the bore was eleven-gauge. There was no bridle to the pan cover, and the lock plate had a pronounced upward curve to its underside. Mountings were of heavy brass. There were four ramrod pipes. The butt plate had an ornamental tang extending well up on the comb of the stock, and the side plate had a "tail." The ramrod was wood. The total weight was about fourteen pounds. This musket and its various features seem to have persisted without change throughout the first quarter of the eighteenth century. During the reign of George II (1727–1759) the lock was improved by adding a bridle to the pan cover, and the steel ramrod was introduced. There was no change in stock, barrel, or mounts.[12] Manuel Lisa's "Brown Bess" is of this type. Under George III (1760–1820) the barrel was shortened, but the bore remained unchanged. The curve of the underedge of the lock plate was straightened out. The stock and the mounts were made lighter, and the total weight of the musket was reduced to about twelve pounds.[13] Solomon Juneau's "Brown Bess" is of this type. This arm was used by both British and American soldiers during the Revolutionary War. At the end of the war, many guns of this type which had been carried by British soldiers became the private possessions of Americans. Subsequently the British government invested in the "India pattern musket," a lighter and cheaper version of the "Brown Bess." The bore remained eleven-gauge, but rather consistently the barrel length was reduced to thirty-nine inches. There were three instead of four ram pipes, and the side plate was a simple S-shaped plate without the ornamental tail. This type of gun, formerly made and used by the East India Company, became the standard service arm. It was brought to America during the War of 1812,[14] but examples of its use in the western fur fields have not come to my attention.

Some of the traders preferred sporting shotguns of their day to the standard light trade musket or the heavier military musket. Charles P. Chouteau carried such a weapon on his snowshoe journey from Mackinac, Michigan, to St. Louis in 1832. This gun can be seen among the exhibits of fur-trade materials in the Museum of the Missouri Historical Society, St. Louis. It has a 54-inch barrel, and closely resembles the Astorian's musket shown in figure 10, *c* and *d*.

Certain criteria were used in the selection of these smoothbores, whatever the type or origin of the piece carried; these were durability, ease of loading and cleaning, reasonable accuracy at short range, and effectiveness. It was also important that they have the capacity to fire a heavy ball at Indian enemies or at big game and to scatter fine shot in hunting small game. The fact that the musket did not shoot a ball with accuracy had little weight in the trader's selection of a gun, for most of his encounters with man and beast were at very short range. Zenas Leonard, clerk of the Joseph Walker party, which came to California in 1833, describes an experience of this kind. One of his companions had "a good gun carrying an ounce ball, which he called KNOCK-HIM-STIFF." When charged by a grizzly, this man discharged the gun "with the muzzle in her mouth . . . gave her a very bad cough." [15]

Rudolph Friederich Kurz provides a satisfying account of the use of a musket by mounted hunters of the 1850's:

> When running buffaloes the hunters do not use rifle-patches but take along several balls in their mouths; the projectile thus moistened sticks to the powder when put into the gun. In the first place on buffalo hunts, they do not carry rifles, for the reason that they think the care required in loading them takes too much time unnecessarily when shooting at close range and, furthermore, they find rifle balls too small. The hunter chases buffaloes at full gallop, discharges his gun, and reloads without slackening speed. To accomplish this he holds the weapon close within the bend of his left arm and, taking the powder horn in his right hand, draws out with his teeth the stopper, which is fastened to the horn to prevent its being lost, shakes the requisite amount of powder into his left palm, and again closes the powder horn. Then he grasps the gun with his right hand, holding it in a vertical position, pours the powder down the barrel, and gives the gun a sidelong thrust with the left hand, in order to shake the powder well through the priming hole into the touchpan. (Hunters at this place [Fort Union near the mouth of the Yellowstone] discard percussion caps as not practical.)
>
> Now he takes a bullet from his mouth and with his left hand puts it into the barrel, where, having been moistened by spittle, it adheres to the powder . . . Hunters approach the buffaloes so closely that they do not take aim but, lifting the gun lightly with both hands, point in the direction of the animal's heart and fire.[16]

Had Kurz made his observations anywhere else in the buffalo country in the first half of the nineteenth century he might have noted the same procedure as that described above.[17]

Peter Rindisbacher in the early 1820's made an excellent water-color painting of a Canadian prairie Indian firing a musket at a buffalo from the back of a horse.[18] This hunt took place in the vicinity of the Red River settlement sometime between 1821 and 1826. The manipulation of the gun, as shown in the painting, seems to be the same as that described by Kurz.

BLUNDERBUSSES

The bell-mouthed type of scattergun which was rather widely used in the eighteenth century and the first years of the nineteenth century might reasonably be classed here as a military arm, or even as a swivel gun (see chap. vi). In its various sizes it was employed on the frontier in a number of capacities during the first few years of the western fur trade, but for the sake of convenience it is classed here as a personal weapon.

Quite possibly, as tradition would have us believe, the light blunderbuss was the preferred shoulder arm of the Pilgrims in what is now the state of Massachusetts, but there is no evidence that it was widely used in America until a hundred years after Plymouth was founded. Probably the effectiveness of this gun in boarding actions during naval encounters early in the eighteenth century gave to it some status the world around as a weapon for warfare. However, blunderbusses had been used by mounted troops at a much earlier time. Riling quotes from Samual Rush Meyrick:

> The troops called Dragoons have been most absurdly said to have been so denominated from the Draconarii of the Romans. They [dragoons] were raised about the year 1600 by the Mareschal de Brisac, in order to be superior to the German Reiters, who used the pistol to so much advantage. On this account they had a more formidable weapon like a small blunderbuss, the muzzle of which being ornamented with the head of a dragon, gave it its denomination, and from this weapon those who used it were called dragoneers and dragoons.[19]

In 1748, the French had a military carabine, or *fusil-court,* "Mousqueton-Obusier-Traboneu," [20] which was characterized by a muzzle with wide horizontal flare. Perhaps it was his knowledge of these French military arms used by land forces which prompted George Washington in 1799 to suggest to the American Board of War that American cavalry be armed with light blunderbusses, which "on account of the quantity of shot they will carry" would be "preferable to carbines for Dragoons . . . especially in case of close action." However, the Board did not follow the recommendation of the former President on this particular detail.

Several years before Washington made his recommendation, the blunderbuss already was known on the upper Missouri. Spanish preparations for possible conflict with their English rivals in the late eighteenth century included the arming of the Spanish Missouri Company party then among the Omaha with both swivel guns and blunderbusses.[21]

That the United States Navy was using the blunderbuss at the time Washington made his suggestion is shown by James McHenry's instructions of June 17, 1797, to John Harris: "Deliver to Tench Francis, Purveyor, Naval Service . . . 42 Blunderbusses . . . to be repaired and then returned to the store." Some were in use by the U. S. Army, also, and Lewis and Clark took a few with them on their journey to the Pacific. Lewis' journal entry for June 26, 1805, refers to "2 blunderbushes" which were left by the westbound explorers in a cache near Whitebear Islands above the Great Falls of the Missouri in what is now the state of Montana. Clark refers to these same guns as "2 blunderbuts." There are other references to the Lewis and Clark blunderbusses in connection with preparations for defense when the fortified quarters where the expedition spent the winter of 1804–1805 were built opposite the mouth of Knife River in North Dakota.[22]

John Jacob Astor included at least twelve blunderbusses in the armament which he shipped round the Horn to his fur-trading establishment at the mouth of the Columbia in 1810 and 1811. In the inventory of Astor's goods turned over to the British North West Company at Astoria, Oregon, in October, 1813, are "5 brass blunderbusses and 7 iron blunderbusses" valued by the appropriating company at $7.85 each, an evaluation which by Astor's personal testimony was but one fifth of the worth.[23]

On April 2, 1811, Manuel Lisa's second expedition set out from St. Charles, Missouri, on its 1,600-mile trip up the Missouri River.

H. M. Brackenridge, a young member of the crew of twenty-five men on the twenty-ton "barge," described the armament on the deck and added, "we have also two brass blunderbusses in the cabin. . . . These precautions are absolutely necessary from the hostility of the Sioux bands who of late have committed several murders and robberies on the whites, and manifested such a disposition that it was believed impossible for us to pass through their country." [24]

The published records of the United States Ordnance Bureau fail to throw much light on the manufacture or procurement of blunderbusses for military use, but occasional specimens bearing marks of national armories have been found by arms collectors. The Milwaukee Museum has a specimen (no. N7-14) with a 26½-inch barrel with an elliptical muzzle arranged with the long dimension horizontal so as to distribute its entire discharge into the bodies of massed victims before it. It is marked with the anchor, indicating Navy property, and its lock is stamped "Harpers Ferry 1810." Recently, Colonel B. R. Lewis found an unusual U. S. blunderbuss in Venezuela, which is but 20¾ inches in total length. It is marked on the lock plate behind the cock, "Harpers Ferry 1814." Presumably, it was designed to enable a sailor to hold it with the butt in the crook of his arm while he clung to the rigging during a boarding action and fired upon the enemy ship alongside. "Col. [B. R.] Lewis has found no records of sale of weapons of this type to Venezuela, but he theorizes that because the United States was much interested in the affairs of that country in the era of the gun's manufacture sales may have been made, but records destroyed for political reasons." [25]

In its report of March 4, 1822, the Congressional Committee on U. S. Naval Affairs lists seventy-six blunderbusses "in bad condition" or "unfit for service." Most of these were in Washington, D.C. Seven serviceable blunderbusses were stored in New Orleans, apparently at that time the entire supply for the Navy.[26] The blunderbuss obviously was obsolete so far as the U. S. Armed Forces were concerned, but there is plenty of evidence that this type of arm continued in use for many years after 1822 in some parts of the world. In Mexico the blunderbuss was still being made as a percussion arm in the 1870's.

In the Orient, especially, it persisted. Even in the period when metallic cartridges were in general use, gunmakers in Belgium were supplying the Oriental trade with short blunderbusses, somewhat like the Venezuelan specimen previously mentioned, which were provided with a tip-down barrel chambered for pin-fire twelve-gauge shells to be loaded at the breech.[27]

Most of the blunderbusses in American collections are of English origin, but the gunmakers of Arabia, Belgium, France, Germany, India, Mexico, Scotland, Spain, and Turkey are all represented by specimens in museums. Among them are very few having a recorded history of use in the American fur fields.

For illustration of the blunderbuss, see figure 48 in the section on swivel guns in chapter vi.

RIFLES

Very few pioneers in the Far West clung to the long-barreled Kentucky rifle used by their forebears and contemporaries in the East. The reasons for this are given in chapter iii. However, along with the ubiquitous musket, some Kentucky rifles were for a time used in the West. No less a person than General William Clark had one that was made by Rogers and Brothers in Valley Forge, Pennsylvania, in the early nineteenth century. This percussion specimen, which originally was a flintlock, is now exhibited with materials pertaining to the Lewis and Clark expedition in the collections of the Missouri Historical Society, St. Louis.[28] The usual rifle of the trapper and trader on the Plains and in the Rockies, however, was a modification of the Kentucky rifle, which made its appearance in the 1830's after a great many practical mountain men had determined just what it was that made the Kentucky rifle unfit for their use.

Plains rifles.—Figure 11 depicts representative rifles of this "Plains" type which was used by many mountain men. The maker of the Meek rifle (see fig. 11, *a*) has not been identified, but the piece displays the earliest deviations which marked the beginnings of a new rifle type. It retains the full forestock and the sharp drop to the butt which characterize the Kentucky rifle, but it has been decidedly shortened. It was brought to the Willamette Valley, Oregon, in 1840 by the noted trapper Joseph L. Meek, and is typical of the modified Kentucky rifle first manufactured for use in the West in the early 1830's.

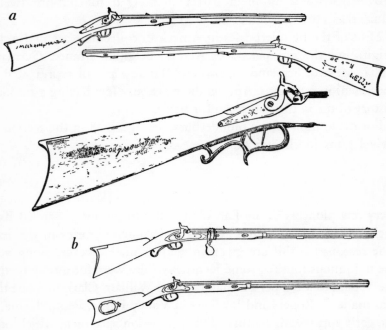

Fig. 11. Long arms—rifles—of the traders and trappers in the West. *a* and *b*, percussion rifles of the "Plains" type once owned by Joe Meek and Jim Bridger. *a*, three views of the Meek rifle, now owned by the Oregon Historical Society (no. N. 419), which obtained it from Grace M. Fleckenstein in 1932. *b*, Hawken rifles. The upper one was bought from Jim Bridger in 1866 for $65.00 by Pierre Chien, interpreter for the Crow Indians. In 1877 the rifle was presented to J. J. Allen at the Crow Agency on East Rosebud Creek, Carbon Co., Mont., who gave it to the Montana Historical Society in 1910. The lower piece is owned by the Los Angeles County Museum (no. A-827).

On the barrel behind the rear sight is the inscription, inlaid with silver, *Verein zum Schutze Deutscher Einwanderer in Texas,* which may be translated as "Organization for the protection of German immigrants in Texas." [29] Crudely carved on the right side of the stock are the words "J. Meek, Rocky Mountains." On the left side of the stock are similarly carved the word "Death," followed by the figure of a running deer, and the signature "A. Kelly." Three notches have been filed in the right edge of the trigger guard. The lock is percussion, and as was usual during the period of the Plains rifle there are double triggers.

Jim Bridger's Hawken rifle, shown in figure 11, *b* (upper), is a half-stock rifle typical of the early percussion period. It is so similar in general design to the U. S. rifle, Model 1803 (see chap. iv), as to arouse the belief that arms makers of the 1830's and some of their customers admired that particular military model. Actually, this convenient and durable type of weapon was not limited for long to western use. In the 1840's its superior qualities were known throughout the country. The one-time Plains rifle became the American sporting rifle—"Merely a Plains rifle adapted for use anywhere by anybody." [30] Barrel lengths ranged from 26 to 38 inches and weights were from 6½ to 10 pounds. Calibers ran from .28 to .48. The double set or hair trigger was quite regularly provided on these rifles. By the time the Plains rifle appeared (in the 1830's) the percussion system was in general use except in the Army. Only when some old-timer insisted on having a flintlock was the Plains rifle equipped with the antiquated mechanism.

Of the Plains rifles known to have been used by mountain men, those made by Hawken [31] are especially well represented in collections. Jacob Hawken established himself in 1820 at St. Louis, where his brother Samuel later joined him in partnership. Their rifles became famous throughout the West during the later years of the western fur trade. Kit Carson [32] owned one, and so did Jim Bridger, James Clyman, William H. Ashley, Edwin T. Denig of the American Fur Company,[33] and many other leaders of the fur brigades.

A fine specimen of these later guns is shown in figure 11, *b*, (bottom). The rifle is 4 feet 3 inches long, with a 33⅞-inch barrel of ½-inch bore. Like the Bridger piece directly above it, the barrel has seven lands and seven grooves. The barrel weighs 7⅛ pounds, and the total weight of the arm is 10⅛ pounds. The barrel is fastened to the stock by two flat metal slugs which pass through loops under the barrel. In all particulars it is as nearly a counterpart of the Bridger and Carson arms as could be made by hand workmanship, the method by which these weapons were produced.

Repeating rifles.—Repeating rifles of the revolver type were brought into the Far West just in time to be used by the mountain man before he left the scene. Josiah Gregg, in his *Commerce of the Prairies,* writing of the late 1830's, states:

> The repeating arms have lately been brought into use upon the prairies and they are certainly very formidable weapons, particularly when used against an ignorant, savage foe . . . If, according to an old story told on the frontier, an Indian supposed that a white man fired both with his tomahawk and scalping knife, to account for the execution done by a brace of pistols, thirty-six shots discharged [from revolving cylinders] in quick succession would certainly overawe them as being the effect of some great medicine.[34]

Kit Carson had high respect for the new fire power. According to Oliver Wiggins, "he [Carson] plainly warned Fremont that although he was not a government officer, his word was supreme with his men, and that a few men armed with repeating rifles were more dangerous than a small army with old-fashioned guns and government authority." [35] The repeaters referred to were Colt's percussion repeating rifles made in Paterson, New Jersey. An 1836 model had the operating mechanism geared to the hammer. Other models made in 1836–1842 had mechanisms which caused the cylinders to revolve through the operation of a ringed lever in front of the trigger, or of a sturdy but clumsy lever which extended through a slot in the trigger guard. These phenomenal guns have been the subject of much study recently and are well described by a number of authorities.[36]

The Colt repeating rifle and carbine "cut quite a swath." In spite of the inconvenience, even serious danger, resulting from the sideways blast of hot gases emerging between the cylinder and the barrel and the occasional explosion of two or more charges simultaneously, which caused injury to the shooter and the gun, the Colt rifle quickly gained a reputation for accuracy and effectiveness. Extra loaded cylinders could be carried by the rifleman, which made it possible for him to fire a score or more shots in quick succession. No other weapon of the day could compete with the Colt in this respect. At Paterson the earliest of these rifles—1836–1842—were made in .34, .44, .47, .52, and .69 calibers. The cylinders for the two larger calibers were six-shot and seven-shot; the .34, .44, and .47 were eight-shot. As previously stated, in some specimens the cylinder was revolved by pulling back the hammer. Others were cocked and revolved by a ring lever in front of the trigger, and those of a third type were operated by a lever which extends downward through a slot in the trigger guard. In all three types the revolving cylinders had a locking device at the rear which assured that each loaded chamber would be held in exact alignment with the barrel when fired. Some were equipped with loading levers and some were not. Some were made with a forestock extending along the full length of the barrel; others had half stocks. A few shotguns similar in mechanism to the rifles and carbines were also manufactured at Paterson. Longer cylinders and longer barrels characterize the shotguns. They have no loading lever.

Figure 12, *a,* illustrates one model of the rifle manufactured in Paterson between 1836 and 1842. In this model the cylinder was revolved by means of the ringed lever in front of the trigger guard. It was made both with and without the built-in loading lever. Before 1843 the number of carbines, shotguns, and rifles used by mountain men was enough to create a stir of interest throughout the West.[37]

. No sooner were the Colt revolving firearms on the market than countermoves were made by competing manufacturers of guns, not only in America but in England as well. Determined efforts were made to infringe upon the Colt patents. Samuel Colt's path to riches and glory was so beset by political interference, technical rivalry, and economic hostility that it came to an abrupt, though temporary, end in 1842. The interruption was of short duration, but it was long enough to place the period of Sam's second start outside the scope of this book.

Some further account of the Paterson Colt revolving weapons and their eventual great success is given in this chapter under "Pistols" and in chapter iv.

Another repeating rifle which had a very short life was the 1837 Cochran rifle, which had a turret mounted on a vertical axis. Because this revolving device permitted some of the loaded chambers to point into the face of the user of the gun it was soon classed as dangerous. There was good reason for this disrepute. As the model

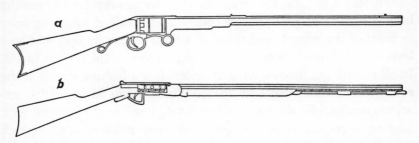

Fig. 12. Repeating rifles with revolving mechanism. *a*, Colt Paterson rifle of 1836, after Serven, 1952, fig. 820. *b*, Cochran rifle of 1837, from a specimen in the Stephen Van Rensselaer collection. The invention of the percussion system gave quick impetus to the manufacture of effective multishot weapons. In the western fur fields the early rifles with revolving mechanism made a deeper impression upon traders and trappers than the first repeating handguns, or "revolvers." The types pictured above were used in the western fur trade before 1843.

began to be used, shocking accidents occurred, which indicated the rifleman might be subject to more damage from his weapon than it inflicted on his adversary. The Cochran was made with cylinders in the form of turrets holding seven, eight, and nine chambers. In 1840, Gregg was returning from a Mexican trip armed with a nine-chambered Cochran. On one of his hunts he found it possible to approach within forty yards of a herd of buffalo. He writes:

> I took aim at one that stood broad-side and "blazed away." The buffalo threw up their heads and looked about but went on grazing . . . They were no sooner quiet than I took another more deliberate aim at the first victim . . . Believing him mortally wounded I fired at four others . . . Yet there stood my buffalo, some of them still quietly feeding.

Three animals proved to be wounded; one of them fell eventually, but the others got away.[38]

The model of which Gregg speaks is that shown in figure 12, *b,* which was patented in 1837 by John Webster Cochran of New York City.[39] This model was also manufactured by H. and C. Daniels, Chester, Connecticut, by C. B. Allen, Springfield, Massachusetts, and by W. Berry, Poughkeepsie, New York. It was made in calibers .36 and .44. The Monitor-type cylinder of these weapons is bored radially to take eight loads and revolves on a vertical axis. Nipples for the percussion caps are on the underside of the cylinder. A top strap over the turret lifts to permit the removal of the cylinder for loading and priming. The identifying markings are on this top strap. Serial numbers are stamped on the barrel, frame, top strap, and turret. The trigger guard is also the hammer.

Even the heavier Cochran arms could not be loaded with more than eighty grains of powder, which was probably a fortunate circumstance. The board of Army officers which investigated certain breech-loading arms for possible military use had this to say of the Cochran:

> Of all the arms submitted to the Board that of Cochran is deemed the most unsafe when subjected to rapid discharges with cylinders fully loaded. The slightest defect in the metal of the receiver would render it highly dangerous both to the bearer and to others in contiguous positions, and that such defects will frequently exist will not be doubted by mechanics whose experience every day convinces them of the many circumstances that serve to prevent a perfect union of parts [chamber and barrel]; and even admitting original perfection in this important limb it is nevertheless liable from the effects of constant and severe service to receive fractures or other injuries sufficient to destroy its character for safety and render it more dangerous to the ranks it is intended to support than to those of the enemy. One accident of the kind that occurred in our practice of the 19th of June [Cochran's musket, 77 grains powder, one ball, fired 16 times in 10 minutes, blew out laterally] would alone not only impair the confidence of the troops in the ability and power of these arms, but would infuse such a degree of dread of their dangerous qualities as to render them an unpopular, and consequently almost powerless weapon . . . However ingenious in design, therefore,

and creditable to the mechanical skill of the inventor the Board is of the opinion that the arm is unsafe and unsuited to use of men acting in masses.[40]

Needless to say, this appraisal by the U. S. Army did not promote sales, yet a few of the arms were bought and used by civilians. Promotional literature produced by J. Webster Cochran (see Bibliography) indicates that his arms were still being manufactured and sold in 1866.

The Cochran rifle is now a much-sought relic owned by comparatively few collectors of old firearms, though in the early days of the American West the gun was of no great importance to frontiersmen.

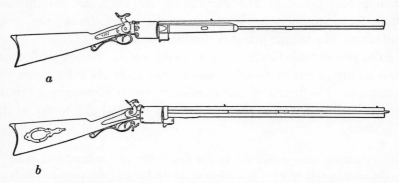

Fig. 13. William Billinghurst's revolving rifles made in Rochester, N.Y. *a,* seven-shot, pill-lock rifle; in Milwaukee Museum (no. N3709). *b,* revolving rifle with auxiliary smoothbore barrel. Drawing used by permission of The Stackpole Company, Harrisburg, Pa., owner of the 1952 ed. of *The Muzzle-loading Cap-Lock Rifle,* by N. H. Roberts.

A little-known but decidedly ingenious revolving arm of this period was the Billinghurst rifle shown in figure 13. According to Gluckman and Satterlee (1953), Billinghurst was in business in Rochester, New York, in the early 1830's. One of his most notable products was the revolving rifle. The earliest examples of this gun employed the pill lock; later pieces had the cap-lock ignition. Billinghurst really gave Rochester a world-wide reputation as a gun-manufacturing center; in the 1830's and 1840's his revolving weapons were purchased by Indian potentates, the Emperor of Brazil, and several dignitaries, noblemen, and wealthy sportsmen in Scotland, England, France, and Norway. Contemporary newspaper accounts announced:

> Our friend William Billinghurst, who made a repeating rifle for the Emperor of Brazil a year or two ago, has just completed one for the Maharaja of Bombay, India. It is designed for the demolition of tigers, and carries but 16 balls to a pound [.68 caliber], probably the largest ever made in this city. It is a beautiful piece of workmanship with remarkable engraving; and it is highly creditable to Mr. Billinghurst and this city that orders for work of this description should be received from so great a distance.

And nearly ten years later, from the same newspaper:

> Yesterday we were shown a revolving rifle made by Mr. William Billinghurst, a veteran gun manufacturer whose fame is only hindered by a modesty which equals his genius. The complete and beautiful firearm is constructed upon a principle long well known here. A cylinder about 4 inches long contains 7 barrels which receive the charge through the long barrel like other guns, the cylinder being turned by hand as each charge is deposited. When loaded and primed the gun may be carried safely for any length of time. The whole 7 can be fired in ¼ of a minute by an expert shot. Attached to the gun below the rifle barrel is another barrel for shot, which extends to the breech through the cylinder and is entirely disconnected. It operates separately and may be fired at the same time as the rifle or afterwards. Such guns, excepting the shot gun part, are not very novel in this region where Mr. Billinghurst has made them for some time. This rifle was patented by Mr. Miller, the inventor, but the patent expired and the patentee died and it was not renewed. The principle was subsequently adopted by Colt and others in making revolving pistols and rifles.[41]

Roberts observes:

> . . . it appears that Mr. Miller (whose first name I was unable to learn) invented the revolving rifle some years before Colonel Samuel Colt invented his revolver and that Mr. Miller had taken out a patent on his invention at that time. However, when Mr. Miller died his heirs did not renew the patent, which allowed anyone to adopt as much of Miller's invention as desired. It is very doubtful if any of the other old-time makers of muzzle-loading rifles were so noted that their fame extended to foreign countries, as was the case with William Billinghurst.[42]

Figure 13, *a,* shows a .38 caliber, seven-shot, pill-lock Billinghurst revolving rifle in the Milwaukee Museum. The 29¼-inch barrel, stamped "W. Billinghurst, Rochester, N.Y.," is octagonal at the breech and is rifled with six grooves. The cylinder, which is manually operated, has seven chambers, each with a receptable for detonating pills. The cock is curved laterally, to give it an offset that permits it to strike into the central receptacle.

Another Billinghurst rifle, owned by Mr. C. Stuart Martin of Webster, New York, has a 25⅛-inch barrel stamped with the same words as the Milwaukee Museum specimen referred to above. It is rifled with six grooves, is of .40 caliber, and is equipped with a ramrod of wood and a peep sight. The cylinder is fluted and has six chambers for detonating pills. The half stock is walnut with brass mounts and is tipped with a white-metal finial. The total length of the piece is 44 inches.

Harold's Club, in Reno, Nevada, exhibits a "Billinghurst" pill-lock revolving rifle which was made by a one-time Billinghurst craftsman, B. Bigelow, who established his own shop in Marysville, California. This specimen is eight-shot, .50 caliber, and in all particulars of design similar to the Milwaukee specimen figured here, except that it has a pinlike projection on the cock like that on the over-and-under gun shown in figure 13, *b,* which represents a specimen having an auxiliary smoothbore barrel and two cocks and triggers.[43] In this, too, the detonating system is pill-lock. The ramrod is carried between the barrels.

PISTOLS

The handgun, darling of every American frontiersman, the weapon of the last-ditch stand, and the sure resort of reckless men everywhere during five hundred years of gun-toting, comes in for remarkably little notice in the written or published record of the American fur trade. It should not be concluded, however, that the single-shot pistol and later the multishot pistol were the least important of the firearms used in the days of the fur trade. As trade items, pistols did not figure importantly, but as personal side arms the trader and trapper found them indispensable, and their ubiquitousness in the fur fields—at least as far back as the mid-eighteenth century—can be proved.

During the French and Indian War, most of the pistols in the hands of military officers were owned by the officers themselves. However, there were prescribed government-model flintlock pistols which were regularly issued to British troops as early as 1648, when the British government standardized its military handguns.[44] All over the civilized world both military pistols and those for civilian or sporting purposes were made to be carried in holsters hooked on the belt, or in pockets. They ranged from diminutive ones which could be concealed in small pockets to formidable horse pistols of great weight. At this time they had only one thing in common— all were flintlocks. Outside the Army and Navy there were few standards of size, shape, ornamentation, material, or mechanism; and manufacturers in many parts of Europe contributed to the supply. Pistols, generally, were a mixed lot indeed.

Flintlock, percussion, single-shot pistols.—A few representative types from the variety of weapons used by traders and travelers on the eastern seaboard, on the Ohio, and inland as far as the Great Lakes and the Mississippi in the late 1700's are shown in figure 14. The "cannon-barrel" pistol in figure 14, *a,* has a stout cylindrical brass barrel about seven inches long, of .60 caliber, and turned at the muzzle to resemble the rings at the muzzle of a cannon barrel. On the top of the barrel is the word "Clarkson"; on the underside, "London." It bears the London proof marks of an eighteenth-century weapon. Near the breech on the undersurface of the barrel is a projection of metal over which can be fitted a cylindrical key, or spanner, having a slot to engage the projection. With the leverage provided by the wrench, the user of the weapon can unscrew the barrel from its mounting in the breech. Within the breech is a thick-walled chamber of smaller bore than the barrel. Into this chamber, exposed when the barrel is unscrewed, the powder charge of a dram or two is loaded. The rear of the barrel also has a small chamber, very slightly larger than the bore, into which the half-ounce ball is inserted. Thus, in effect, this pistol is a breechloader. The lock is an integral part of the breech member. A continuation of the breech toward the butt provides a tang to which the wooden grip is fastened. The butt is covered by the embossed silver plate usual in pistols of the type and referred to as a "mask butt." Such ramrodless cannon-barreled pistols are of British origin; they are of expensive design and workmanship, belong to the first half of the eighteenth century, and are often called "Queen Anne" pistols. They were well made and were popular in their day. To a limited extent their use extended into the nineteenth century, although by the middle of the eighteenth century improved locks had been devised.[45] Both English and French traders and adventurers sometimes carried these screw-barrel pistols and their improved successors into the Hudson's Bay country and the Mississippi Basin.

The small flintlock in figure 14, *b,* is a Belgian pocket model of about .50 caliber. The brass barrel and body are cast in one piece. The lock is within the body, and the cock and frizzen are central and in the line of sight. There is a safety device in the form of a slide behind the cock. The Liége proof mark is stamped on the barrel. The wooden grip is checkered.[46]

The convenience and "insurance" provided by a small pocket weapon were sought even by men on the frontier. This was true in the days of the first occupation of the Missouri River country and continued to be so in the percussion period and the later days of the western fur trade.[47] Some of these small weapons of the cap-lock system, though short of barrel, were rifled and of relatively large caliber. At close quarters they packed a man-stopping wallop, and certain manufacturers, of whom Deringer was the most noted, lavished care and real pride on their production.[48]

Figure 14, *c,* is one of a pair of English flintlock pistols formerly owned by Charles de Langlade in Wisconsin.[49] This moderately decorated piece is of excellent workmanship and beautiful balance, and is in good taste throughout. It and its mate were made by Bate of London, presumably about 1775. This pistol is a fair example of

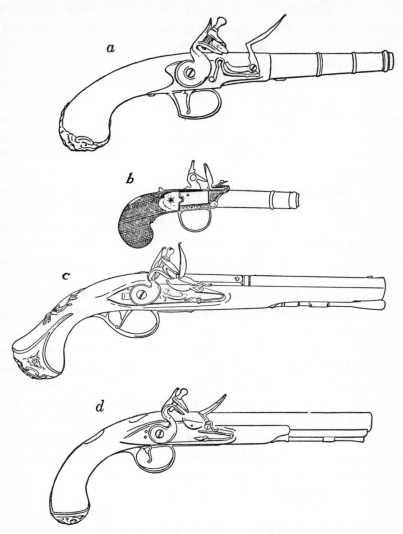

Fig. 14. Personal pistols of frontiersmen, late eighteenth and early nineteenth centuries. *a*, cannon-barrel or "Queen Anne" pistol carried by Capt. Hugh Waddell in the French and Indian War and in the American Revolution; North Carolina Hall of History, Raleigh, N.C. (no. 14 152 1–2). *b*, pocket pistol carried by A. Darby on the Allegheny frontier; museum of the Missouri Historical Society, St. Louis, Mo. (no. 61). *c*, one of a pair of pistols by Bate of London owned by Charles de Langlade in Wisconsin in the late 1700's; Wisconsin State Historical Society. *d*, Ketland pistol once owned by John Haywood, State Treasurer of North Carolina in 1800; North Carolina Hall of History (no. 14 144.8 GC).

the hand weapons of the aristocrats of the period.[50] Behind the cock is a safety bolt which permits the piece to be locked in half-cock position, a safety provision which came into general use in the last half of the eighteenth century. Nicely worked silver ornaments the grip. The half-octagon barrel and the lock plate of iron are marked with modest decorations. The smooth bore of approximately .60 caliber permits a load with real stopping power. The weapon is at once befitting the dignity of a leader and equal to practical demands that might be placed upon it.

Figure 14, *d,* shows a Ketland flintlock pistol of the eighteenth century. Ketland flintlock "horse" pistols appear rather commonly in gun collections. Factories using the Ketland mark were active both in London and in Birmingham in the eighteenth century, and large exportations were made to America. The specimen illustrated is stamped LONDON and has the London proof marks on barrel and grip. The barrel is 8 inches long, the caliber .65. This flintlock pistol is a fair example of the type of civilian's handgun which was used on the midwestern frontier in the period following the Revolution.

These types were carried westward as the Missouri country was occupied. At the time of the Lewis and Clark expedition and for some forty years thereafter, pistols of the character shown were to be found in trapper camps and at trading posts from Taos to the northern Rockies—everywhere that American and British fur companies penetrated. Some of the finer specimens were cherished by their owners and later by the descendants of the owners; a few of these can be seen today in private collections and in museums. A far greater number of the flintlock pistols of the mountain men were "used up" and discarded as the improved percussion models came into general use. Even those that are preserved, with a very few exceptions, have lost their identity, and it is difficult to find specimens known to have been used by mountain men.

When Osborne Russell was in Pierre's Hole, west of what is now Grand Teton National Park, in 1835, his party was attacked by Indians. He records: "I kept a large German horse-pistol loaded by me in case they should make a charge when my gun was empty." [51]

So far as I know, Russell's horse pistol has not been preserved. German flintlock pistols were brought to America in some numbers by the thirty thousand Germans who were hired by King George to fight some of his battles during the American Revolution. After the Revolution, several hundred pistols for civilian use were imported from Germany each year.[52] These weapons were very similar to the British specimen shown in figure 14, *d*. A good illustration of a regulation German flintlock horse pistol of the same period appears in Sawyer,[53] and an impressive specimen is exhibited by Harold's Club in Reno, Nevada.

Another one of the rare contemporary references to the mountain man's use of the pistol is in Samuel Parker's *Journal* and pertains to the 1835 rendezvous on the Green River. In it Parker introduced to the world a man who was destined to become famous:

> A hunter who goes technically by the name of the "great bully of the mountains" mounted his horse and with a loaded rifle challenged any Frenchman, American, Spaniard, or Dutchman to fight him in single combat. Kit Carson, an American, told him if he wished to die he would accept the challenge. Shunar defied him. Carson mounted his horse, and with a loaded pistol, rushed into close contact, and both almost at the same instant fired. Shunar's ball passed over the head of Carson; and while he went for another pistol, Shunar begged that his life be spared.[54]

During the early years of the nineteenth century the U. S. government manufactured regulation Army pistols at its Harpers Ferry and Springfield arsenals. Since production in these government factories failed to meet demands, pattern weapons from Harpers Ferry were placed in the hands of contractors, and reproductions of the government models were made by several private manufacturers. The purpose of the government of course was to supply its military units with these pistols; some of the pistols, however, were put up for private sale while in new condition. As improvements were made and new models were adopted, guns of earlier issues, especially worn-out or damaged pieces, were discarded by the Army, and some of these discarded weapons also reached private hands. Figure 15 shows two of these Army pistols which were found in Montana and New

Mexico right where they were dropped, presumably by their early nineteenth-century users.

The Harpers Ferry flintlock pistol (fig. 15, *a*) was picked up with

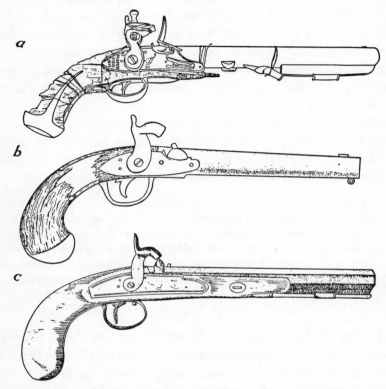

Fig. 15. More personal pistols of traders and trappers. *a,* Harpers Ferry Model of 1806, a U. S. Army pistol picked up from the ground in Montana; Everson Collection, Bozeman, Mont. *b,* U. S. pistol, Model 1826, made by Simeon North, found on top of Guadalupe Mountains, N.M.; Livingston Collection, Carlsbad, N.M. *c,* weapon of the dueling type taken from the body of Jedediah Smith after he was killed by Comanche Indians on the Cimarron in 1831. The drawing is from a photograph reproduced by Dawson's Book Store, Los Angeles, 1926.

a hayrake on a Montana ranch about 1910. The role it played in frontier affairs can only be conjectured; however, there is no reason to believe that it was carried to the upper Missouri country by a military unit. On the contrary, it is well known that military pistols of this type had some distribution among civilians after the War of 1812, and it is likely that this particular specimen was lost by a member of one of the fur brigades. It has a 9½-inch smoothbore barrel which is round throughout its length. The caliber is .54. The lock plate is stamped with the United States spread eagle above the letters "U.S." Behind the cock are the words "Harpers Ferry 1806." Only the wooden parts show disintegration after many years of weathering. This model was made at the government arsenal at Harpers Ferry, Virginia, during the years 1806, 1807, and 1808. (See chapter iv for a more detailed description of the Model 1806.)

The U. S. pistol, Model 1826, shown in figure 15, *b,* which was converted from a flintlock, was found in 1883 by Morgan Livingston near the summit of the Guadalupe Mountains, New Mexico. The 8½-inch round barrel is .54 caliber and of smooth bore. The ring near the muzzle was once used for attachment of the swivel-type link which held the ramrod to the barrel. The lock plate is stamped: us / 1828 s NORTH. This is one of the last pistols made by the famous contractor Simeon North, who began his program of pistol making for the U. S. Army in 1799. For the model represented by the weather-beaten specimen here figured, North had three contracts—1826, 1827, and 1828—for a total of three thousand pistols. In the 1840's, a large number of flintlock U. S. arms, both handguns and long arms, were converted to the percussion system. One method of conversion entailed the brazing of a bolster lug upon the barrel, to cover the original touchhole; the cone was then screwed into a hole bored in the bolster. This method was employed in converting the specimen illustrated. Since the conversion apparently was made in a United States armory, it is probable that this weapon was used in New Mexico very late in the fur-trade period.

Other weathered specimens of U. S. pistols of various models have been found in the western fur region, where they were dropped in the course of battle or were otherwise lost by their soldier or civilian owners. One Army flintlock pistol was found on Signal Mountain, Jackson Hole, Wyoming, in 1932. This piece, representative of the last flintlock model, was made by R. Johnson of Middletown, Connecticut, who contracted to manufacture Army pistols, Model 1836, in the late 1830's and continued production of them well into the 1840's. Excellently designed and well made, the pistol was in demand for civilian use in the later days of the fur brigades. The smoothbore iron barrel is of .54 caliber and is 8¼ inches long. The fore sight and pan are made of brass, but other metallic parts are iron. Metschl observes that in fine finish and shooting qualities the Model 1836 "was nearly the equal of the old-time dueling pistols." [55]

It is not surprising that trappers would adopt the Army guns, especially if they could be acquired at little cost from soldiers who carried pieces for which they were not personally accountable.

The personal pistol of Jedediah Smith, one of the most famous of the mountain men, is shown in figure 15, *c*. In 1831 Smith, Jackson, and Sublette, with Fitzpatrick as a "passenger," went to Santa Fe for a consignment of goods.

> Near the present Ulysses, Kansas, while riding ahead of the train to search for water, Smith was lost from view (May 31), and though carefully searched for could not be found. On the arrival of the caravan at Santa Fé, on July 4, it was learned that he had been waylaid by Comanches and killed. His rifle and a brace of pistols had been bought from the Indians by some Mexican traders, who told the story of his death.[56]

The Indians presumably had found it difficult to obtain percussion caps for the weapons and for that reason were willing to part with them. Sabin [57] records that one of Smith's nieces obtained the pistol here illustrated. Dawson's *Catalogue,* 1926, reproduces a photograph of the weapon and reports that it was then the property of Walter Bacon of Los Angeles, Smith's grandnephew.[58]

Smith was a prominent man in the fur brigades, and this pistol would indicate that he armed himself in a manner befitting his station. It is marked by evidences of skilled workmanship, elegance of form, proper balance, and fine finish. The arm is the English duelling-pistol type, well made and, for its time, the *ne plus ultra* in handguns. The percussion system was just coming into general use in the more civilized parts of the world at the time of Smith's death, and even then his more conservative contemporaries in the fur fields of Western America clung to the flintlock, which they regarded as the most dependable type of weapon. Other characteristics of this half-stocked pistol mark it as up-to-date for its day. The duelling pistol of 1800 was usually full-stocked, the wood reaching to the muzzle. In the period 1800–1810 the half stock with a rib under the barrel to carry the ramrod came into vogue,[59] and barrels were invariably octagonal throughout, as in the specimen shown in the illustration. About 1820, English gunmakers began to convert the earlier flintlock duellers to percussion and to manufacture new percussion pistols of the same lines and dimension. During the second quarter of the nineteenth century the duelling pistol fell into disuse.[60]

Multishot pistols.—The acceptance of the percussion system hurried the development of multishot pistols. Flintlock revolving pistols had been given trials and some practical use very early in the nineteenth century,[61] but the loose priming powder in the pan of each cylinder constituted a hazard which was never eliminated. Inventors of revolvers were quick to take advantage of the relatively safe percussion system, and both the pepperbox (multiple barrels) and the conventional revolver featuring a series of revolving chambers which discharged into a single fixed barrel were patented in England, France, and the United States in the 1830's. Ethan Allen in 1834 patented the double-action mechanism for pepperbox revolvers in the United States, and the system was well established in Europe at least as early as 1830.[62] The pepperboxes ranged from .26 to .50 caliber and had barrels from two inches to about six inches in length. If these guns were of caliber large enough to do any notable damage to an adversary they were of necessity big and extremely heavy. Even the small-caliber pepperboxes were clumsy, and yet they were far from sturdy in construction. However, they were taken into the West in the heyday of the fur trade, and there was some demand for the peculiar guns right up to the time of the Civil War.

The Allen-Thurber pepperbox as made from 1837 to 1842 is illustrated in figure 16, *a*. It has six chambers and is of .32 caliber. Stamped on the left side of the flat top-hammer is "Allen and Thurber, Grafton, Mass."; on the left side of the body, "Allen's Patent." This is one of the first of Allen's double-action pepperboxes. Guns of carbine proportions were made with this same type of mechanism; Jim Baker, a mountain man, owned one.[63] In 1842 the Allen factory was moved to Norwich.

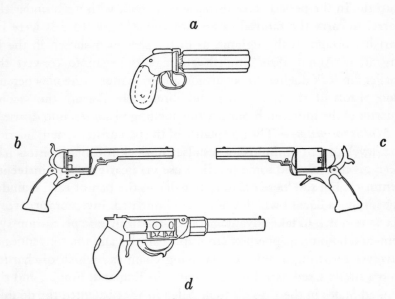

Fig. 16. Revolving pistols of the late fur-trade period. *a*, Allen and Thurber pepperbox revolver of 1837–1842, one of the first with a double-action mechanism; Nunnemacher Collection, Milwaukee Museum (no. N4465). *b*, Colt's first revolver, the 1836 belt model; Harold Smith Collection, Harold's Club, Reno, Nev. *c*, another view of the 1836 Colt, cocked and with trigger extended. *d*, The 7-shot Cochran revolver of 1837; Harold Smith Collection. Details of its operating mechanism are given in the section on the Cochran rifle.

A pepperbox revolver was found at Rocky Crossing of the Big Sandy on the fur traders' route to Green River. It has 4-inch barrels of .31 caliber, two of which contain the loads which were in it when it was dropped by the owner. Now in the Fort Bridger Museum, Wyoming, this piece is one of many which are exhibited in western museums. For all their unpredictability, the multibarrel guns were rather widely distributed before the true revolver came into use.

Some of the Allen-Thurber-Wheelock pepperboxes have exposed nipples, a mechanical feature which sometimes resulted in unexpected excitement for its user:

> A further source of trouble was the arrangement of the nipples, which projected at right angles to the axis of the barrels, and which were not, at first, separated by any form of partition to prevent the flash of the exploding cap from communicating with those on either side of it. The consequence was that . . . [sometimes] the weapon would go off like a fire-cracker, the flash from one nipple firing the cap upon the next, and so on round the cylinder in a sputtering "feu-de-joie" which was, as the writer [J. M. George] can testify from his personal experience, most disconcerting for the user of the weapon but which must have been even more so for any unfortunate standing in the line of fire.[64]

American manufacturers produced a substantial number of the weapons during the period of the California gold rush, and European makers continued to get new patents on guns of this type even after metallic cartridges had come into use. The specimens described above are representative of the early members of this group, which included even some pepperbox rifles.[65]

Contemporary in America with the popular but temperamental pepperbox was the pioneer among true revolvers, the Colt.

Young Sam Colt, whose repeating rifles have already been described, is especially and justly famous for his revolving handguns. Colt launched his invention and factory just early enough to place his guns in the hands of the fur traders at the end of the period with which this book is concerned. In 1830, Colt was apprenticed by his father to the captain of the brig *Carlo*. While he was aboard this ship bound for India he whittled a wooden model of the revolver which was to become one of the most famous weapons in the world.

Upon his return, Colt obtained in 1835 a patent on the mechanism, claiming as his particular innovation the ratchet which rotated and locked the cylinder of his pistol so as to bring each chamber successively and exactly in line with the barrel. On February 25, 1836, he obtained other patents. In the same year, the twenty-one-year-old Colt was able to rouse the interest of his father and others and form his company, the Patent Arms Manufacturing Company, which began operations in an unoccupied section of a silk mill in Paterson, New Jersey.

Colt attempted to interest President Jackson in his project, without success, but finally Congress authorized a government test of the weapons. Ordnance testing boards rejected the weapons for use by the Army and the Navy. South Carolina Militia officers did buy seventy-five Colts, and Sam placed a few guns in the hands of Army officers who accepted them as gifts or bought them as personal weapons. Purchasing agents from the new Republic of Texas acquired a small store of the arms from dealers in Baltimore, in 1839, a purchase which contributed to the later success of the advanced models.

The first pistols manufactured in 1836 were for the most part five-shot belt models of .28, .31, .34, and .36 caliber. They were single-action, with a disappearing trigger and no trigger guard (fig. 16, *b* and *c*). These early Colts were made both with and without the loading lever. Some two thousand of these weapons, bearing the mark "Patent Arms Mfg. Co., Patterson, N. J. Colt's Pt.," were made in the period 1836–1842.[66]

One heavier model was made in 1839, of .36 caliber with a 9-inch barrel, which like its predecessors lacked a trigger guard.[67] In the hands of the Texas Rangers the Models 1836 and 1839 proved to be mighty weapons. It was this use which provided the turning point in Colt's struggle to market his revolver, but the evidence of success was not immediately apparent. Mass orders were not forthcoming, and the Colt factory at Paterson went into bankruptcy. Manufacturing of the revolvers ceased in 1842. There is a stirring sequel to this depressing part of the Colt story, which is outlined in chapter iv.

References to the 1836 and other Paterson Colts are not numerous in contemporary literature of the fur trade, but enough was printed to show that these pistols deserve a definite and important place in the story of the trader's armament. Josiah Gregg went from the Arkansas to Santa Fe and Chihuahua with a wagon train in 1839. He wrote,

"My brother and myself were each provided with Colt's repeating rifles and a pair of pistols of the same—36 ready loaded shots apiece; capacity rarely matched on the prairies." [68] In his diary and letters Gregg made subsequent entries regarding the effect of the Colt rifles upon Indian warfare and the general progress of the Mexican War. Quotations bearing on this subject are contained in chapter iv.

The reaction of the Kiowa and Comanche to their first encounter with the increased fire power provided by the Colt is given by Sabin in his account of the experience of a caravan which was beleaguered on the Santa Fe Trail 175 miles east of Taos in the fall of 1841:

> The Carson men distributed themselves among the wagons, to await the Indian charge. At daybreak, down swooped the reds—to be lured on by a feeble round of a few muskets and pistols. But when they were well inside point-blank range, the whites delivered the first volley; nevertheless, still the charge continued, for to the Indian mind the defenders now had only empty guns.
>
> Abruptly and disastrously the galloping warriors were made acquainted with an evolution of firearms. The Kit Carson company, according to Oliver Wiggins, was maintained in the highest state of efficiency; the revolving pistol had lately been adopted; and springing from cover to the backs of their animals, the trappers met the Indian charge with a countercharge, shooting right and left *without reloading*. Saddle pads were emptied, the Indians broke and fled, with that accusation which has become historic: "White man shoot one time with rifle and six times with butcher knife!"
>
> . . . More than a hundred Indians were killed, while the whites lost but one man.
>
> . . . According to Oliver Wiggins, Carson was alert and his men were alert to secure the most advanced ideas in offensive and defensive weapons; and so his party in the fight of 1841 . . . were armed with the new revolving pistols of Sam'l. Colt. [69]

The Colts referred to by Josiah Gregg and Oliver Wiggins undoubtedly included the 1836 model, but in the 1841 affray the larger 1839 model was also represented. Although fewer than two thousand of all sizes were manufactured before the collapse of the Colt factory, the reputation made by the few guns that were issued contributed greatly to the later success of the heavier models. The Paterson Colts proved to be the answer to the horseman's prayer in the troubled Southwest; for the first time the white men could battle the Plains Indians on an equal or a superior basis.

John Cochran adapted his patented action (described in the section "Repeating rifles") to a revolver, which is shown in figure 16, *d*. It is a seven-shot, .36 caliber piece with a 5-inch rifled barrel. On the top strap is the inscription "Cochran Patent. C. B. Allen, Springfield, Mass." The metal parts behind the turret and the disk in the varnished wood grip are of German silver. The gun has an underhammer but no trigger guard. A metal shield projects over the rear-pointing chambers. The objections to the Cochran rifle apply also to the revolver.

Wesson, Stevens, and Miller produced a revolver at Hartford, Connecticut, on the prescription of a patent granted to D. Leavitt on April 29, 1837; but the date of its earliest manufacture is in doubt, and no reference or other evidence of the use of this revolver in the Far West at the time of the fur brigades has been found.[70] One Leavitt revolver has been described as a .40 caliber, six-shot, single-action piece with a tip-up action controlled by a lever inside the front end of the trigger guard. The total length of the gun is 13⅞ inches.[71]

Other revolving arms were manufactured by such gunmakers as Nichols and Childs, Conway, Massachusetts, and James Warner, Springfield, Massachusetts, but only the Colt is strongly in evidence as the arm which marked the turning point in Indian warfare in the Far West by giving the white man superiority.[72]

GUNSMITHS AND GUNSMITHING

In order that the firearms of the trappers might be kept in some state of repair, the western fur companies employed gunsmiths or blacksmiths in shops established in the larger and more permanent posts in the back country. The larger expeditions into the wilds also included blacksmiths among the hired personnel. St. Louis, of course, as the emporium of the trade in the West, attracted a number of gunsmiths, the most famous among whom were Jacob and Samuel Hawken, who have been given some attention earlier in this chapter.

Thanks to the research of Kauffman, we have good evidence of the importance of gunmaking and gun repairing to the trade of the period. Twenty or more established gunsmiths was a large number for a town with a population of 10,000 or 15,000 in the 1830's.[73]

A very few of the early gunsmiths set out from St. Louis for settlements in California, Oregon, and the Southwest. James O. Pattie tells of meeting an American gunsmith in the El Paso area in 1827.[74] This man had gone to the Far West with Major Andrew Henry of the Rocky Mountain Fur Company in the early 1820's.

Thomas R. Garth of the National Park Service, in the course of his archaeological work on the site of the Whitman Mission at Waiilatpu near Walla Walla, Washington, uncovered interesting relics of a migrant gunsmith. Garth reports:

> Probably the most spectacular of our finds occurred on the cellar floor. This was a large pile of gun hammers, springs, triggers, dies, and other tools for gunsmithing. The following words from a letter sent by W. J. Berry, a gunsmith, to Gov. Joseph Lane explains how it, the cache, came to be at the Mission:
>
> "Besides the usual outfit I had with me a full and valuable set of tools and implements for the manufacture of rifles and other firearms; together with a large and valuable assortment of materials used in said business you know is my trade." [75]

Garth explains that Berry had deposited his gunsmith's outfit with the Reverend W. Rodgers at Waiilatpu in the fall of 1847 just before he, loaded lightly, journeyed down the Columbia. The outfit was to have been shipped to him the next spring, but the Whitman massacre occurred a month after he left, and the mission was destroyed. Garth states further, "The majority of the pieces found are gun hammers for percussion-type (cap-and-ball) guns of the period. These hammers were cast iron and in use they frequently broke. Consequently, a gunsmith would have a large number in stock." Berry placed a value of $5,000.00 on his lost outfit.

In the journals of the traders and in the official records of the fur companies there are more than a few references to the employment of gunsmiths. Only two will be cited here. In November, 1827, when

Jedediah Smith's party was at Mission San Jose, California, Smith wrote, "I made an arrangement with the Priest by which I was to have the use of the smith shop for one week for the purpose of repairing my guns." [76] The journal of Nathaniel J. Wyeth records a bit of the alfresco gunsmithing which the early practitioners of the trade were prepared to undertake. On December 9, 1834, when he was near the Deschutes River, Wyeth made the following entry: "During this time [the five preceding days] we percussioned 3 rifles, our powder being so badly damaged as to render flintlocks useless." [77]

The U. S. government assumed some responsibility for the repair of guns used by its Indian wards, but dependable references to such gunsmithing are scattered. Fragmentary notes on this business can be found in the annual reports submitted by the superintendents, agents, and subagents concerned with Indian affairs. During the 1820's and 1830's the United States maintained government agencies at St. Louis, Council Bluffs, Fort Clark, Fort Armstrong, Prairie du Chien, Green Bay, Fort Mackinac, Fort Wayne, and Fort Dearborn. Ordinarily, the mending of guns at these places was classed as black-smithing and the workmen were hired as blacksmiths at the rate of $500.00 a year. It does not follow, however, that the employment was always a year-round job. For example, William Clark, Superintendent of Indian Affairs at St. Louis, submitted accounts for 1823 and 1824 which include several items for "mending Indian guns." "Jacob Hawkins" (*sic*), the name of a blacksmith employed at the rate of $500.00 per annum, appears three times in records of the period September 1, 1823, to September 1, 1824; yet the man's earnings were but $32.75. Solomon Migueron and John Leabeani also were paid for gunsmithing within the same period.[78]

As might be expected, Indians appreciated the services of gunsmiths as much as the white trappers. Charles Mackenzie, North West Company leader on the Missouri during the early years of the nineteenth century, tells a story which reveals that the gunsmith was held in high esteem by the Plains Indian of his day. He quotes a Hidatsa chief as saying of the Lewis and Clark party then on the Missouri: "Had I these white warriors in the upper plains . . . my men on horseback would soon do for them as they would for so many wolves, for . . . there are only two sensible men amongst them, the worker of iron and the mender of guns." [79]

Although the gunmakers of the frontier were usually able to get along with remarkably simple tools, the work of the more highly skilled artisans was of high quality. The Hawken brothers were noted for the perfection of their arms. One of their more elaborate tools was the rifling machine shown in figure 17. This machine was by no means an original development of the Hawkens, but their careful work with it earned for them a great reputation. They were able to produce arms which for their time were remarkably uniform in accuracy and reliable in performance. The rifling machine was quite simple in principle, as the illustration shows, but skill was required to operate it.

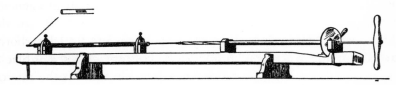

Fig. 17. Rifling machine used by the Hawken brothers in their St. Louis factory. This valuable relic of the Hawkens' craftsmanship is in the museum of the Missouri Historical Society, St. Louis.

At the left is the barrel to be rifled. It is aligned with the rifle guide or spiral-grooved cylinder (shown in the center of the picture), and then clamped firmly in place. A rifling rod is fastened to and extended from the rifle guide through the bore of the barrel. Near the end of the rifling rod is a cutterhead which holds the saw. This cutterhead consists of a plug of lead slightly smaller than the bore. It is cast to the rifling rod. Embedded in it to a depth of $\frac{1}{16}$ inch is a toothed device, or saw, of hardest steel. By means of the handgrips at the extreme right in the illustration, the spiral-cut grooves in the rifle guide are forced through corresponding reversed grooves, or threads, in the elongated tubelike head block shown immediately to the left of the handgrips. The head block bears the same relation to the rifle guide as a nut does to a bolt. When the rifle guide is forced through the head block by a push or a pull upon the handgrips, it revolves in such a manner as to rotate the rifling rod as it passes into the barrel. The saw thus makes a spiral cut in the bore each time it is forced through the barrel when the operator pushes or pulls on the handgrips. The spiral grooves of the rifle guide and the head block were cut in such a way as to cause the rifling rod to make one complete turn in a space of 48 inches. When the saw had cut the first groove as deeply as its adjustment permitted, the rifling guide was withdrawn from the head block and inserted again, one groove to the right. The cutting process was then repeated until seven spiral cuts had been made in the barrel. The saw was then removed from the lead plug, or cutterhead, and a strip of paper was placed at the bottom of the slot in which the saw had been seated. The saw was reseated upon the paper shim; this time it stood slightly higher above the surface of the lead. The grooving of the barrel was then resumed and the several parts of the process repeated until the seven grooves in the rifle barrel were "ten to fourteen papers deep." This left the lands of the barrel standing high enough above the bottoms of the grooves to impart the desired spin to the bullet when the rifle was fired. Approximately seven hundred cuts were necessary to rifle a barrel.

A "dressing out" followed the rifling process. This was for the purpose of smoothing the grooves and the lands. A hickory rod smaller in diameter than the bore of the rifle was tightly wrapped with twine at a point several inches from one end, to make a band about the diameter of the bore. This rod was pushed into the barrel until the end with the wrapping was flush with the end of the barrel. Molten lead was then run into that end of the barrel. The twine wrapping retained it, making a lead plug several inches long cast upon the end of the hickory rod. This plug conformed to the grooves and lands of the rifled barrel. The hickory rod and its leaden end were then withdrawn from the bore, and a small, fine saw was mounted midway in the lead plug in alignment with one of the rifle grooves. A second saw just the width of the lands was inserted in the lead plug in exact alignment with one of the lands. These fine steel saws were carefully adjusted for height above the lead, and then the stick, well greased, was drawn back and forth through the barrel until all grooves and all lands were uniform and very smooth.

With the placing of the breech plug, boring of the touchhole, or placing of the nipple, the brazing on of metal tabs, loops, or pins with which to fasten the barrel to the stock, and the addition of front and rear sights, the rifle maker's work on the barrel was complete. Still to be done, however, were the important tasks of manufacturing the lock, making the stock, and mounting both the barrel and the firing mechanism upon the stock.[80]

The techniques of the western rifle makers were essentially the same as those of the eastern manufacturers of the time, yet changes in method were contributed by successive generations of western workmen. It is now well known that the American rifle did not suddenly spring full-blown from the bench of some unnamed Pennsylvania gunsmith of the early eighteenth century. Experiments with spiral-grooved barrels had been conducted by Spanish artisans at least a hundred years before the first trials in America. Swiss and German gunsmiths also made their contributions at about the same time. Even greased felt wads and patches were used in Europe long before they were tried in Pennsylvania. However, the European experimenter seems to have adhered to the idea that the diameter of his rifle ball must always exceed the diameter of the bore, and that it should be forced into the barrel in such a manner as to press the lead into the grooves of the rifling, a procedure which involved the use of a mallet in loading. The success of the rifle in America grew out of the discovery that a ball should be no larger than the bore, and that a soft, greased patch surrounding the lead could be depended upon to take the rifling and so impart a spin to the bullet. To push home such patched balls, it was necessary to exert no more than twenty pounds pressure upon the ramrod, a factor that made for rapidity in loading. With this great advantage, the American gunsmith devoted his attention to improvements in the accuracy and efficiency of his product.

What size should the bullet be? What proportion of powder to lead? How many grooves and how deep should they be? What rapidity of twist in rifling? And what length of barrel would give greatest range and shocking power yet retain accuracy?

Many of the basic questions had been answered to the satisfaction of easterners while all the centers of rifle manufacture were still east of the Alleghenies, and the gunsmiths, when they did move to the West, tended to adhere to proven procedures. Yet, some individuals varied the established methods in accordance with their own ideas for improvement, and new discoveries resulted from their work. The big and very significant change in the traditions of the American rifle grew out of the special needs of the westerner who spent much of his time on the back of a horse. Here, indeed, came an upset to the accepted answers to the questions regarding bore and length of barrel. The sympathetic and very effective response of western gunmakers to the demand for a better saddle arm has been referred to in the section "Plains rifles," and it will receive further attention in chapter iii.

III

Trade Muskets and Rifles Supplied to the Indians

Before the end of the eighteenth century no gun had been designed specifically for the Indian trade, nor had any been designated as a trade gun. The earlier trade guns were substantially the same as those used by the settlers and traders themselves (see chap. ii). The prototypes of the true trade gun were cheap, light fowling pieces which could be had in quantity from England and the Continent. Not until the first years of the nineteenth century were rigid specifications established deliberately by the great trading companies, although there was ample empirical knowledge of what the Indians would and would not accept. The tradition of the short and light fusil had been well established; English makers had been supplying weapons of the general dimensions the Indian customers had been insisting upon since the late seventeenth century. But a hundred years elapsed before the type became so standardized as to be known as the "trade gun." The earliest recorded specimen of the "Hudson's Bay fuke" with its distinctive dragon ornament is dated 1805. Probably earlier specimens will be reported.

Long before the mountain man came to the upper Missouri, Indians in the East and South were using rifles. Dillin reminds us of Auguste Chouteau's statement, "In 1736 the Chickasaws were not only armed with rifles but were generally good shots." [1] At first the Indian rifle was nothing but the Kentucky rifle snatched from the hand of the white man. The western Indians in general, however, showed little interest in it. Not until the early nineteenth century was there a demand for the Indian rifle, and at that time a fairly distinct weapon was developed for trade purposes.

THE TRADE GUN

Of all the properties on the inventories of the Indian traders none is more interesting to the antiquarian than the "Hudson's Bay fuke," the "North West gun," or the "Mackinaw gun." All three of these names were applied to the same weapon. Until recently the fraternity of gun collectors had not identified the trade gun as an entity, and dealers and museum officials also allowed the distinctive old "fusee" to be submerged in the welter of musket types of all classes and periods. Even the writers of firearms history have slighted this very significant musket type; yet the story of its manufacture, importation, distribution, and use constitutes a rather important chapter in Americana. It is a fact, also, that from the standpoint of numbers made and traded this gun should be accorded a respectable place in the record of firearms used in America.

The trade gun came from many different factories in Europe and the United States. Regardless of its point of origin, certain characteristics were constant. First of all, it was light in weight, often short of barrel, and cheaply constructed. Commonly it was gauged to shoot a one-ounce ball; that is, it was sixteen-gauge, or about .66 caliber, although some were smaller. The trigger guard was clumsy in appearance and was large enough to permit access to the trigger even though the trigger finger was enclosed in glove or mitten. It was a gun made for the north country. Certain other characteristics of structure were constant, as detailed in the pages which follow.

Just why the design and specifications of the first Hudson's Bay fuke were what they were we do not know, but there is evidence that representatives of the British government brought the type to America during Revolutionary times for presentation to tribes which the government wished to conciliate and win to its cause (see section on Whately trade gun). Present-day officials of the Hudson's Bay Company are decidedly conscious of the distinctive weapon type which their company featured in the Indian trade of the nineteenth century, but they know nothing of its history. Clifford P. Wilson, Curator of the Hudson's Bay Company Museum, states:

> We have a number of the old trade guns such as you describe in our collections, most of them made by Barnett or Bond. It appears that most if not all that were traded at one time had this brass dragon, but we have never been able to discover why. You may find also on your lock plate and possibly on the barrel of these guns the initials "EB" surmounted by a fox similar to the crest of this Company. A search in our archives has not explained the reason for this either.[2]

The Montreal interests known as the "North West Company," which after the American Revolution had opposed the Hudson's Bay Company in its operations in the fur fields of the Great Lakes region, appropriated the fuke as their own. In the realm into which this company traded, the gun was known as the "North West gun." Similarly, around the shores of Lake Michigan and westward to the Mississippi and in Canada east of Lake Huron another British concern, the "Mackinaw Company," dispensed the same gun to trappers, who knew the weapon as the "Mackinaw gun." These competing companies all turned to the same European manufacturers for their supplies of trade guns.

When John Jacob Astor formed the American Fur Company in 1808 he wasted no time in adding the popular fuke to his stock in trade. It is said, however, that at first he attempted to introduce substitutes, which the Indians rejected. Later (1811), when he entered into agreement with the North West and Mackinaw companies, it is probable that he found it easy to obtain the British guns. There is evidence also that he contracted with J. Henry, a Pennsylvania firm, to supply him with American-made muskets.

About this time (1809) the U. S. government also recognized the established trade gun as a necessary adjunct to its factory system of Indian trade. The Superintendent of the Indian Trade Office wrote to Thomas Waterman, of Philadelphia, on March 21, 1809, as follows:

"I want 100 of the real North West guns by Barnett or Ketland. I beg you will inquire if they can be had in your city; perhaps they may have been imported since last year. I pray you particularly inquire and that you may buy and send me one hundred if on tolerable good terms." [3]

Apparently Waterman complied with this request, though his reply is not preserved among the archival materials that contain the letter books of the Indian Trade Office. However, the Superintendent acknowledged the receipt of his letter and sent him a detailed description of the desired guns:

> I have this moment received your letter of the Ninth. I fear from the description and price that the guns you have bought are not as described by me,—the real North West Gun. They cost in England 21 shillings to 22 shillings 6 pence, Sterling; they are to be known by the large guard of iron, by three screw pins to the lock, by one screw only (which passes quite through the stock) being used to secure the upper part of the guard and the lower part of the barrel; and above all by a brass mounting opposite to the lock, exactly as per sketch enclosed [undoubtedly the dragon ornament] be they from Barnett or Ketland, they are uniformly this way and such exactly were those (some forty or fifty) on hand and inventory to me by General Shee.
>
> If those bought by you are not of this kind they will not answer any purpose and need not be sent. [4]

Many subsequent entries in the records of the Indian Trade Office testify to the acquisition of the "real North West guns" and their distribution to the factories maintained by the government. [5]

Records of many kinds and evidence in gun collections have provided substantial information about the makers of trade guns in England. Occasional references indicate that manufacturers in Holland, Belgium, and Germany also shipped trade guns to the United States; but their names have not been found, and I have seen only one specimen. [6] Considering the period as a whole, England produced the greater number of the pieces. Barnett, whose history goes back to the seventeenth century, Bond, W. Chance and Son, J. Hollis and Son, Ketland, Lacy and Company, Parker Field and Company, Robbins and Martin, Sargent Brothers, and Wilson are known to have contributed guns for use in America. Barnett, W. Chance and Son, J. Hollis and Son, and Parker Field and Company usually are listed as London firms. All the others were in Birmingham. W. Chance and Son also maintained a factory in Birmingham: stationery bearing the firm's printed address is preserved in the papers of the American Fur Company.

Some of the makers of finer guns in England, especially those established in London, looked with disdain upon the Birmingham contractors who turned out "park paling muskets" for the American trade.[7] They sometimes referred to the manufacturers of trade guns as "blood merchants" and called their factories "blood houses." It is a fact that many of these contractors cut down the costs of production by using inferior charcoal iron [8] for the barrels of their trade guns—"sham damn scelp, too bad even for our general dealers, used solely for the guns made for exportation." [9]

Not all trade guns were booby traps, however, and it is to be remembered, as one reads of the numerous instances of fusee barrels bursting, that even superior guns might be expected to blow up under careless handling by Indians. W. W. Greener of Birmingham took exception to the disparaging remarks of some of his London contemporaries: "The indefatigable exertion of some of the leading gun makers have served to remove in a decided manner the stigma which, until a few years ago rested upon all Birmingham-made guns; and it is now a well recognized fact that guns are made in Birmingham fully equal in every respect to the best guns the world can produce." [10]

During and immediately after the War of 1812 there was a dearth of English-made trade muskets on the market in the United States. When John Jacob Astor bought out his partners in Canada in 1817 he sought American-made fusils. To just what extent Astor was responsible for initiating the manufacture of the trade gun in the United States is uncertain, but there is no question regarding his use of American-made fusils in the Northern Department of his American

Fur Company. (See section "Other trade guns" in this chapter.) It is clear also that he was distributing the American product after 1822 from the trading posts of his Western Department.

Among the American gunmakers known to have produced the cheap trade musket that was a facsimile of the English "fuke" are "C H & S Co.," New York; Deringer of Philadelphia; the famous Henry works of Philadelphia and Boulton, Pennsylvania; Leman of Lancaster; and Tryon of Philadelphia. Eli Whitney, in New Haven, also made a bid for some trade-gun business, but evidence that he actually produced these muskets is lacking.[11]

Barnett muskets.—For more than three hundred years the name Barnett was prominent among gunmakers in England. Hudson's Bay Company records show no purchases of Barnett guns by the company until 1821, at which time the firm of Barnett and Sons is included in the list of manufacturers with whom the company dealt. The North West Company, the Mackinaw Company, the American Fur Company, and the U. S. Indian Trade Office all distributed Barnett trade guns in the early nineteenth century. The descendants of the American Indians affected by this trade continued to demand the fuke long after most of the above-mentioned organizations had ceased to exist. After the perfection of the percussion system in the early nineteenth century, Barnett produced cap-and-ball trade guns and converted some of the earlier flintlock fukes to the percussion system; but many Indians still preferred the flintlock.[12]

The details of the lock and the "dragon ornament" of the earliest specimen of Barnett trade musket—made in 1805—which has come to light in this survey are shown in figure 18. Note the "large guard of iron, the three screw pins to the lock, and one screw only (which passes through the stock) used to secure the upper part of the guard to the lower part of the barrel; and above all the brass mounting opposite to the lock," as specified by the United States Indian Trade Office in 1809 (see note 4).

Many of the fusils which have escaped the junk piles are sawed off in the manner of the one shown in figure 19. Some muskets were cut down so that the gun could be more conveniently handled by

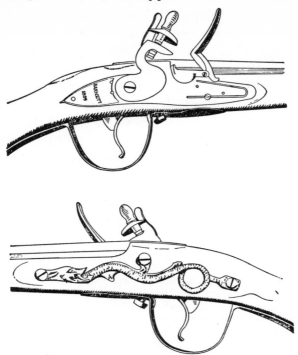

Fig. 18. Barnett trade musket, 1805; detail of the lock. The earliest trade gun (the "North West gun") that has been positively dated; it is owned by Mr. Irving Tier of Cheshire, Conn. Photographs supplied by Dr. Alfred F. Hopkins of the Chicago Historical Society.

the Indian owner as he rode his horse. More frequently, however, the barrels were sawed after the gun had burst—and this type of accident was common. The accounts of the western fur traders contain innumerable reports of the bursting of fusils. When it is considered that the Indian habitually hunted the buffalo from the back of a charging steed, and that he reloaded his musket as he ran, it is readily understood that little care was exercised in seating the musket ball upon the powder charge.

Often, in loading and pointing, the ball would roll away from the powder charge and lodge somewhere in the barrel far from its proper place. When the gun was fired under such circumstances, there was great likelihood that the explosion would cause the light iron cylinder to rip wide open at a point just below the ball. It was not at all un-common for the hunter to lose a hand as a result of such an accident.

It is impossible to state whether the specimen shown was sawed off in accordance with an Indian's whim, or whether the shortness of barrel is due to an accident; but, like many another trade gun now in collections, it certainly was shortened after it left the factory. The barrel is octagonal, at the rear end, for 7½ inches of its length—a char-acteristic of most trade guns. The total length of the barrel is 20 inches, and the over-all length of the gun is 35¾ inches. There is a

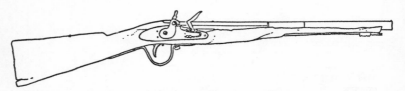

Fig. 19. Barnett trade gun, flintlock, 1868. Most of the trade guns picked up from the ground at points in the Far West where they were dropped by their owners resemble this badly weathered specimen. A few fusils in similar condition have been taken from Indian burials. This gun was acquired by the National Park Service for the Jefferson National Expan-sion Memorial, St. Louis, Mo., as a gift from the Chicago Historical Society. Its history is not known.

simple, notched rear sight and a small burr of metal which is turned up to form a front sight. On one of the plane surfaces on the left side of the octagonal part of the barrel appears (1) the mark of the Lon-don first proof, and below it (toward the breech) in the order given: (2) the figure 24, meaning 24 balls to the pound, or caliber .577; (3) the mark of the London second proof; (4) the initials "J.E.B." sur-mounted by a crown; and (5) a pennant-like insignia. On the top of the barrel, 1½ inches from the breech, is the usual seated fox super-imposed upon the initials "E.B." The same mark and the name "Barnett" and date "1868" are on the lock. Opposite the lock is the always-present dragon ornament.

Figure 20 shows top, bottom, and side views of the Barnett trade musket of 1833. The iron ramrod may be a replacement, as are the upper jaw and the screw of the flint vise. A light brass band on the forearm close to the muzzle seems to have been improvised by some owner of the piece. The wood around the lock has been repaired. All other parts of the gun seem to be the original ones. The barrel is 31 inches long including an octagonal section 9 inches long. There is a front sight but no suggestion of there ever having been a rear sight. On the lock appears the name "Barnett" and date "1833." The usual sitting fox appears on the lock just in fro_nt of the hammer. Initials

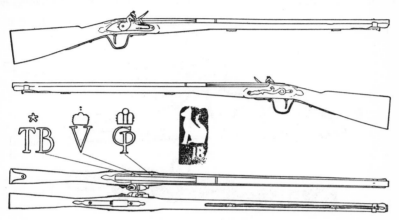

Fig. 20. Barnett trade musket of 1833. This specimen has undergone some restoration and repair, but in its major parts it is essentially as it came from the factory. The four figures show right and left sides, details of top and undersides, and the marks (enlarged) on the barrel. The gun is in the Jefferson National Expansion Memorial.

were stamped into the metal under the seated animal, but the job was so poor that they are not distinguishable. Details of the lock and the dragon ornament are given in figure 21. On one of the plane surfaces of the octagonal part of the barrel are the following marks in the order given: (1) the initials "TB" surmounted by a small star (Thomas Barnett headed the Barnett organization for many years before 1850), (2) the London second proof mark, (3) the London first proof mark, and (4) the seated fox. Like those on the lock, the initials under the fox are not clearly discernible. The apparently defective reproduction of this mark in figure 20 is actually a fair representation of the mark itself as it appears on the gun.

The Barnett of 1822 formerly owned by the late J. D. Kimmel bears the same marks on the barrel as those shown, except that there is no fox. That animal is on the lock, however, and under it are the initials "HB." An 1848 Barnett owned by Mr. Ned Frost has on the barrel the seated fox over the the initials "GR." Clinton A. Russell's specimen (1869) lacks the fox on the barrel; in its place is a crown superimposed on the initials "JEB." (John Edward Barnett operated the Barnett establishment from 1850 to 1875). A Barnett gun of 1883

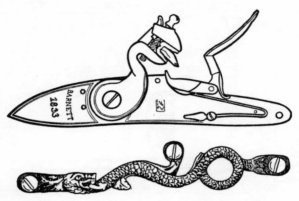

Fig. 21. Details of lock and dragon ornament, Barnett trade gun, 1833. The bronze ornament shaped like a dragon or sea serpent is a never-failing insignia on nineteenth-century trade muskets of whatever make or origin. Some of the antecedents of this ornament are shown in fig. 27.

(percussion) owned by Mr. D. A. Reynolds also has the crown and "JEB." Probably there are still other variations in the markings used by the factory, but the great majority of Barnett trade guns have been stamped with the fox and the initials "EB" on the lock. Not all of them have these marks on the barrel.

In 1637 a member of the Barnett family became president of the Gunmakers' Guild. Charles I granted a charter to him and his organization and recognized the mark "G P," which stands for "Gunmakers Proof." Whether or not Barnett manufactured the first of the distinctive trade muskets discussed here has not been determined, but it is known that for at least eighty years the Barnett factory made these

guns for the American Indian trade. More Barnett trade guns have
been preserved by collectors than any other make.

Bond muskets.—The name Bond is prominent in the lists of London gunmakers from 1768 through 1879. It does not appear on the
list of those who supplied trade guns to the Hudson's Bay Company
before 1821, but many of the later muskets imported by that company are reported to have been made by Bond (see note 2). In the
company's collection there is a Bond flintlock fusil which bears the

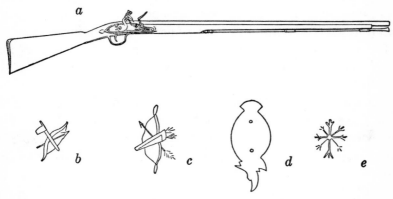

Fig. 22. P. Bond trade musket, early nineteenth century. An exceptionally light, graceful musket obtained by the Museum of Natural History,
University of Kansas, in 1952 from a dealer in West Hurley, N.Y.

date 1858. Pollard's list of British gunmakers indicates that Edward
and William Bond were making guns in London from 1850 through
1861.[13] Other lists locate "E. and W. Bond" at 45 Cornhill, London,
the same address as that given for the Philip Bond who is reported
to have manufactured arms during the approximate period 1776–
1815.[14]

The gun shown in figure 22 is one of only two trade guns by Bond
known to me. It is marked "P. Bond" on the lock plate below the
pan, and "Cornhill, London" on the top flat of the barrel. On the left
flat of the barrel are the London first proof mark and the London
second proof, or "viewed," mark. Between the two proof marks are

the initials "E B," surmounted by a crown. On the undersurface of the forestock is impressed the figure of a foxlike animal within an oval enclosure. Some rather unusual decorations (fig. 22, *b–e*) on this gun give the impression that it may have been a special offering of the fur company. The two decorations of Indian motif (*b* and *c*) appear on the cock behind the lock and on the 3¾-inch tang of the butt plate, respectively. The fancy escutcheon (*d*) is mounted flush on the left side of the stock, and the curious eight-armed marking (*e*) appears on the 2¼-inch bow of the trigger guard. All the mountings—including the usual dragon ornament—are of brass and are well finished. The ramrod is wood, tipped with black horn.

The piece is 49⅞ inches long, with a smoothbore twenty-four-gauge barrel 34⅛ inches long. The weight of the gun is only 5½ pounds.[15]

Trade musket with a Belgian barrel.—The gun illustrated in figure 23, *a–d,* is one obtained from the Pawnee by Samuel Allis, the first Presbyterian missionary among these Indians in Nebraska. The maker is unknown. The barrel is 30 inches long; an 8½-inch section at the breech is octagonal. On the top of the barrel is a seated fox surrounded by a circle (fig. 23, *d*), but it is not the conventional animal used by Barnett. Also on the top of the barrel is the Belgian mark— E [above] L $_*$ G—stamped in the Liége Proof House. The stock at the grip is cracked, and the damage has been repaired by a sleeve of zinc or tin applied to the wood with screws. On the lock behind the hammer is the date, "1834." Just in front of the hammer (see fig. 23, *b*) is an encircled fox like that on the top of the barrel. The dragon ornament (fig. 23, *c*) is identical with those on all other trade guns.

W. Chance and Son trade musket.—The Montana Historical Society owns the sawed-off Chance trade gun shown in figure 23, *e.* The barrel is about 12½ inches long, no doubt having been cut off below the point of rupture after it had burst in the hands of some luckless hunter. The maker's name, W. Chance and Son, is on the lock behind the hammer. In front of the hammer is the seated fox that appears on the Barnett guns, and under this animal are two initials which are illegible.

In the collections of the Missouri Historical Society, St. Louis, is a W. Chance and Son trade gun with a complete barrel bearing front (blade) and rear (V-notch) sights. The greater part of the fore-stock has been broken away, exposing two of the loops, or eyes, through which formerly passed pins which held barrel and wood to-gether. The gun has been repaired by rounding off the end of the

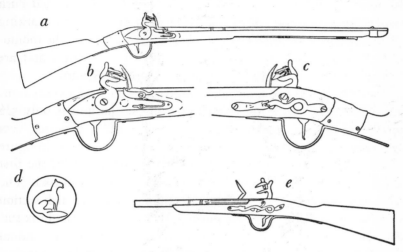

Fig. 23. European trade muskets. The Belgian piece (*a, b, c,* and *d*) is unique among the specimens reviewed in this book. No maker's name is on it, but the Belgian mark, "E" above "L * G" (Liége Proof House), is plainly stamped on the top of the barrel. The gun was presented by Mr. Otis E. Allis to the Nebraska State Historical Society (no. 2460). The W. Chance & Son gun (*e*) is preserved in the Montana Historical Society Museum.

remaining forestock and binding this end to the barrel by means of a metal sleeve from a military piece. The lock, like those of other trade guns by this maker, bears no date. Mr. L. C. Winant of East Orange, New Jersey, reports that he has a W. Chance and Son trade gun from which most of the forestock has been broken and the broken part has been replaced by a piece of a forestock from a Civil War Springfield. The original wooden ramrod has been replaced by a steel rod. Mr. Ben L. Meibergen of Salinas, California, writes that he has a trade gun made by W. Chance and Son upon the barrel of which is stamped not only the word "London" but also the first and second Birmingham proof marks. The seated fox is on both lock and barrel. Mr. Meibergen believes that the initials under the fox are "IA." In the Deadwood Museum, Deadwood, North Dakota, is a badly weathered W. Chance and Son trade gun which, like those already described, lacks the forestock. When the gun was found in the open in 1877, decay of wooden parts was well advanced, but the small remaining section of the forestock seems to have been rounded off and repaired before this disintegration took place. The Yellowstone National Park Museums have a W. Chance and Son trade gun which was found in the mountains near Bozeman, Montana, in 1895. The barrel had been sawed off to 16½ inches by some previous owner. The very badly weathered wooden parts have been restored; the original stock and part of the forestock, however, have been preserved and are exhibited with the gun.

Collectors commonly speak of the distribution of the W. Chance and Son guns by the Hudson's Bay Company. That company's list of firms which supplied its trade goods before 1821 does not include W. Chance and Son, but it is possible that this manufacturer dealt with the Hudson's Bay Company after 1821. Among the papers of the American Fur Company, now preserved in the manuscript collections of the New York Historical Society, is a letter of 1841, on a printed letterhead, "Wm. Chance Son & Co. Merchants, Birmingham." The letter, addressed to Ramsay Crooks, explains, "The extra 3^d charged on each of the lowest priced guns is what we have had to pay the workmen for the additional work ordered to be put on the stocks." It is signed "W. Chance Son and Co." [16]

Trade muskets by Leman.—Henry E. Leman learned gunmaking under the tutelage of Melchior Fordney about 1828–1831. From 1831 to 1834 he was with George W. Tryon, the noted rifle maker of Philadelphia. In 1834 he established his own factory in Lancaster at East Walnut and North Duke streets, "manufacturing largely for the Indian trade." His first government contract, in 1837, is said to have been for 500 Indian rifles at $14.00 each. In 1842 he made 500 trade guns for the U. S. Indian Department at $7.00 each. [17]

In 1843 Leman wrote to Ramsay Crooks, head of the American Fur Company, a letter in which he referred to his experience in making trade guns for the government and asked that his efficient plant devised for this special purpose be maintained. "It would be doing the Indians justice and it will be a credit to the Department to continue with me as the manufacturer," he wrote, and pleaded for Crooks's endorsement "to lay [the matter] before the Commission of Indian Affairs at the next letting of Indian goods." [18] Crooks's response to this request is not on record.

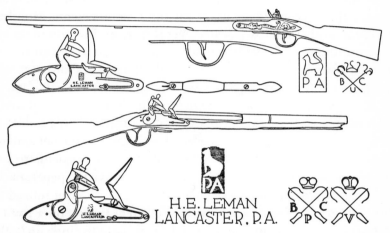

Fig. 24. Trade muskets by H. E. Leman. The full-length specimen shown in the upper figure is a nearly perfect gun exhibited at the Kit Carson Museum, Trinidad, Colo. Except for the missing ramrod, it is intact. The lower sketch shows a sawed-off, weathered fusil now owned by Mr. E. A. Hawks of Concord, Mass.

A nearly perfect specimen of the Leman musket is represented in figure 24. The barrel is 36¼ inches long, including an octagonal section 9 inches long. It has never been equipped with sights. The total length of the gun is 51 inches. On the lock plate in front of the hammer is a foxlike animal superimposed upon the initials "PA," and beneath this emblem are the word "H. E. Leman Lancaster." On the left side of the barrel, in the octagonal section, is a mark which resembles the Birmingham first proof mark and a small edition of the emblem that appears on the lock (see the figures under the stock in fig. 24). The dragon ornament mounted opposite the lock is the same as that on all other trade guns.

The sawed-off specimen of Leman trade gun represented in the lower drawing of figure 24 is owned by Mr. E. A. Hawks of Concord, Massachusetts, who in a letter written in 1944 explains: "This old gun was picked up on the prairies of South Dakota by a relative some 50 years ago—picked up out of the prairie grass where it had lain for many years. Its wooden stock is weather-worn and decayed, but its metal due to the dry prairie air is still almost bright." On the lock are the same marks as those on the Colorado piece described above, except that the fox is seated. Yet this seated fox differs noticeably from the animal that was used as a mark by the British manufacturers of trade guns, and it is also unlike the seated fox that marks the Belgian gun, figure 23, *a–d.* Mr. Hawks describes his weapon in one of the very few articles in which the trade gun has been given a definite place in the history of American firearms.[19] He points to the fact that H. E. Leman imported British gun barrels and incorporated them in muskets of his own manufacture. On the barrel of his Leman gun both the first and second Birmingham proof marks have been stamped, as shown in figure 24.

At the time that I examined the gun shown at the top of figure 24, the Kit Carson Museum had a second H. E. Leman fusil. This one had been cut down to a 14-inch barrel. On the left side of the octagonal section of the barrel was stamped: "H.E.L." with an asterisk underneath; above the initials was the name H. E. LEMAN surmounted by the Birmingham first proof mark and LANCASTER, PA. Stamped in the wood on the left side of the stock 2½ inches from the butt was a foxlike animal like that in the second row of figure 24. An indented circle enclosed the animal.

Mr. Herman P. Dean of Huntington, West Virginia, writes that he has a Leman trade gun in exceptionally good condition, on the barrel of which are stamped both Birmingham proof marks.

Trade guns by Sargent Brothers and by Whately.—The Sargent gun shown in figure 25, *a, b, c,* and *d,* was for sale in the Southwest

Arts and Crafts Curio Store, Santa Fe, New Mexico at the time I examined it. Except for the thongs of rawhide which bind the barrel to the forestock at a point seven inches from the muzzle, the specimen is sound and complete as made—unless the ornamental brass tacks on the forestock are the handiwork of an Indian.

The barrel is 32 inches long, with an octagonal section 9 inches long. There is a front sight but no rear sight. The total length of the gun is 46 inches. On the lock in front of the hammer is a foxlike figure similar to the animal in the emblem used by Leman (see fig. 24, second row). The initials with the animal are illegible. Behind

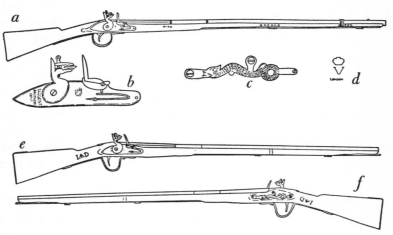

Fig. 25, *a, b, c,* and *d,* trade musket by Sargent Brothers, Birmingham, England, 1850. *e* and *f,* trade musket by Whateley, of undetermined date. The Sargent gun was examined in the Julius Gans collection, Santa Fe, N.M. The Whateley piece, one of the most significant guns in the series here described, was the property of Mr. Benton Kidwell of South Charleston, Ohio, who sold it to the Museum Association of the American Frontier, Loomis, Neb., in 1954.

the hammer are the words SARGENT BROTHERS 1850 (see fig. 25, *b*). On the barrel near the breech is stamped the London second-proof mark (fig. 25, *d*). The dragon ornament opposite the lock (fig. 25, *c*) is typical of all such ornaments on trade guns.

But one other Sargent Brothers trade gun has come to my attention. Mr. James E. Serven, Santa Ana, California, writes that he has one of 1849 vintage which has been converted to percussion. On March 31, 1838, Ramsay Crooks of the American Fur Company wrote to C. M. Lampson, London, England:

> The gun you sent us from the agent of Messrs. Sargent of Birmingham is a better article than our usual supply this year and cheaper than those of your London friends. The danger of changing is the great uncertainty of the goods being equal to the sample which is always sure to be first rate. If we could be certain that Sargent would give us guns every way equal to the one we have we would be tempted to give them next seasons order. . . . Our guns are so important an article and the sample seems by comparison so much better than either Jacks or Lacy and Co. that I am inclined to give them a trial. . . . Satisfy yourself that we can definitely rely upon the quality of the goods, for bad guns are dear at any price. If the reputation of Messrs. Sargent does not afford a positive guarantee for their work you need not take any further trouble in the matter.[20]

On April 14, 1840, Sargent Brothers of Birmingham acknowledged payment by the American Fur Company of a bill for guns, adding: "We are very anxious of increasing our sales of these guns and we are disposed to use every caution to make them to the wishes of those concerned. We hope therefore to receive an increased order this year."

The Whately gun (fig. 25, *e* and *f*) was owned by Mr. Benton Kidwell of South Charleston, Ohio. Mr. Kidwell writes that the relic is reported to have been owned by a Mr. Walker who settled near the Shawnee Indian village (Tecumseh's) on the Mad River early in the nineteenth century. The barrel is 36½ inches long, with an octagonal section 8 inches long. The bore is ⁹⁄₁₆ inch, or about .69 caliber. The butt plate is brass. The total weight of the gun is 5½ pounds. On the lock in front of the hammer is a seated fox like the emblem on the Belgian gun shown in figure 23, *d*. Behind the hammer is the name WHATELEY, but no date. The mark of the "broad arrow" and the Indian Department, "I⋀D," which occasionally is found on axes and other equipment distributed in times past through British government channels, here appears prominently on both sides of the grip. On the barrel, two crowns and "GR" superimposed on the horizontal broad arrow indicate that the gun was once classed as British government property. Since the mark "GR" (George Rex, first adopted during the reign of George I, 1714–1727) was used continuously between 1714 and 1830, and because for an even longer period the broad arrow was stamped on a variety of merchandise destined for use among American Indians, it is not possible on the evidence of marks alone to date this gun very closely. It is a fact, however, that during the Revolution Great Britain gave Kirtland and other muskets as presents to several Indian tribes, and that the custom of annual gift making was continued until after the end of the War of 1812.[21] Although it cannot be asserted flatly that this Whately fusil was a gift piece of this period, its characteristics suggest that it probably was. Its reported association with the Shawnee early in the nineteenth century lends credence to the idea. It is well known that British agents in Canada favored Tecumseh and that the Shawnee Indians received British arms and ammunition.[22] Tecumseh was killed while commanding a force of Indians fighting on the British side in the Battle of the Thames, October 5, 1813.

J. Hollis and Son percussion trade musket of 1886.—The entire Hollis gun shown in figure 26 seems to be as it came from the factory except for the ornamental design in brass tacks on stock and forestock.

The barrel is 33 inches long, with an octagonal section 7½ inches long. A double deeply incised ring divides the octagonal from the round part, and 4½ inches forward from this ring is a second similar ring. There is a blade front sight integral with the barrel. A crude rear sight of copper is inserted in a slot in the barrel 5¼ inches from the breech. The caliber is .56. The trigger guard and butt plate appear to be of German silver; the rod guides are also of this material. The total length of the gun is 49 inches; the weight is 6 pounds.

The hammer in size and shape resembles that of a Civil War Springfield musket. The nipple socket seems to have been welded to the barrel. On the lock plate behind the hammer is the monogram "IHS" encircled by the finely lettered words "Makers to Her Majesty's

War Department." In front of the hammer is "J. Hollis and Son London 1886." On the left side of the barrel in the octagonal section are the two unusual marks shown in figure 26. Between them is the number 26, meaning twenty-six gauge, or twenty-six balls to the pound. This gun is further distinguished by the checkered grip and forestock. Apparently the wood is cherry.

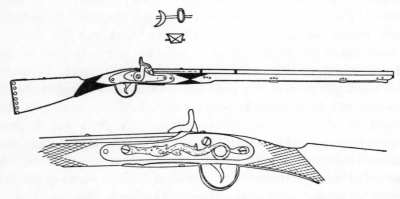

Fig. 26. J. Hollis and Son (percussion) trade musket of 1886. The most recent trade gun considered in this study; it is owned by Mr. Robert H. Wilcox. The Hollis trade guns are marked on the lock, "Makers to Her Majesty's War Department," and have several unusual features, which are described in the accompanying text.

Other trade guns.—In addition to the established manufacturers of trade muskets, many gunmakers aspired to enter the business and solicited the patronage of the great fur companies. Some kinds of guns were made in only small quantities; others were assembled from imported barrels and domestic parts. Of some varieties only one specimen is known to have survived, and some are known only through the reports and correspondence of the commission houses and traders.

Charles E. Hanson, Jr., of Loomis, Nebraska, has provided me with photographs and a description of a flintlock trade gun which has "C H & S Co./ N.Y." stamped on the lock in front of the hammer. The barrel is 28⅜ inches long and is marked with the London proof marks and the name "J. Clive." Greener states: "The manufacture of barrels from scrap iron with tilt hammers was in its prime about 1845, when John Clive, the noted barrel maker, kept a mill in Birmingham, turning out large quantities of barrels weekly, by which he achieved a good reputation and a considerable fortune." [23] Like Leman of Lancaster, the C. H. & S. Company seems to have imported parts from which a hybrid was produced. Mr. Hanson bought the gun in Iowa from a man who stated that his grandfather had obtained it from an Indian in a Sauk and Foxes village in the late 1840's.

Some years ago a Deringer flintlock musket was advertised by Theodore Dexter: "Deringer-Phila., 1814 flintlock musket. Probably a U. S. contract musket. Marked Deringer-Phila., U. S. and the eagle on lock. On barrel: Deringer-Phila. Brass snake [dragon ornament] on left side of stock. Large loop trigger guard." [24] Obviously this is a musket built in the trade-gun design. In the Invoice Book of the Indian Trade Office are the entries "8 Philadelphia guns" and "7 guns—Deringer." [25] Henry Deringer, Jr., working in Philadelphia from 1820 to 1840, upheld his father's reputation as a gunmaker and won laurels for himself as well; his contracts with the U. S. government for rifles are a matter of record.[26] The gun referred to by Dexter as an 1814 product is some evidence that Henry Deringer, Sr., also supplied the Trade Office with some fusils.

Mr. Charles E. Hanson, Jr., of Loomis, Nebraska, owns a flintlock fusil from the factory of J. Henry, the well-known Pennsylvania gunmaker. The gun was obtained by Mr. Hanson in Missouri. The barrel is 30⅜ inches long, with the usual octagonal section at the breech. It is marked J. HENRY and is embellished with two stars in lieu of proof marks, and with the seated fox similar to the one in figure 20. The small initials under the fox are illegible. The caliber is .65. On the lock in front of the hammer is stamped J. HENRY, but no date. The butt plate is brass. The trigger guard, dragon ornament, ramrod, and details of stock and forestock (partially restored) are typical of all trade guns.

A voluminous correspondence was carried on between the Henrys and the American Fur Company. Most of the letters pertain to Henry rifles, but occasionally James Henry would broach the subject of trade muskets. The answer from Crooks was always the same: "We cannot hold out any encouragement for North West guns. Our people will not take any but the English."

The existence of the specimen discussed here is evidence that the Henry establishment did make trade guns for someone. Dillin refers to Henry's contracts with John Jacob Astor in 1816 for light flintlocks—quite likely the trade gun—and Captain Bonneville testifies to the fact that American-made fusils were supplied to the Blackfeet by the American Fur Company in the 1830's.[27]

As mentioned earlier in this chapter, the Ketland "North West gun" was held up as a model by the U. S. Indian Trade Office in 1809. It was described to the agents of American manufacturers who aspired to supply the U. S. government as "the real North West gun."

Larocque in 1805 noted in the hands of the Big Bellies (Hidatsa), who lived just north of the Mandan, "one musket by Ketland and one gun by Barnett," [28] and he regarded this particular circumstance as evidence that white men had been robbed and killed. Journals and reports written in the West in the half century following Larocque's pioneer observations on the Missouri and the Yellowstone make occasional reference to Ketland muskets, but in the course of my search for details of the story of the trade gun only one Ketland specimen has come to light. It is owned by the Museum Association of the American Frontier, Loomis, Nebraska. Seven different Ketland firms are listed as in Birmingham in the period 1750–1829. Sawyer credits all of them with "specializing on the American trade." [29] It is interesting to note that Ketland's private mark (crossed scepters and the crown) became the basis for the Birmingham proof marks in 1813.[30]

The Hudson's Bay Company does not identify any of the Ketlands among the firms that supplied the company with trade goods before 1821, but an invoice of merchandise taken from the Indian annuity stocks of the U. S. Indian Trade Office, Georgetown, July, 1812, included "19 Ketland guns @ $7.50; 23 Ketland guns @ $6.50." Obviously the "real North West gun" sought by the Indian Superintendent in 1809 was acquired finally for the government's trading system.

Dr. Carlyle Smith has provided me with a full-scale drawing of a musket lock which obviously was made for a flintlock trade gun. It was fastened by two screws, and, like the Barnett lock shown in figure 21, it has the figure of the seated fox stamped on the plate in front of the cock. On this lock, the letters under the fox are "L R." Behind the cock in two lines is the inscription "Lacy & Co. 1837." A Lacy of London is known to have made superposed brass-barreled pistols with a spring bayonet attachment during the flintlock period, but I have no specific information regarding the factory, and no complete trade musket by Lacy has come to light. However, there is evidence that at least a few Lacy trade guns were shipped to America. On March 31, 1838, Ramsay Crooks wrote to C. M. Lampson, London, rejecting sample trade muskets that had been submitted by Lacy.[31]

Parker, Field and Company, London, made a flintlock gun for the trade. One specimen is in the Milwaukee Museum (no. N3588). Metschl states, "This gun was made for the African trade, the natives preferring muskets of this type because of the simple ammunition required." He might have added that similar pieces were distributed in America. The barrel is 35¾ inches long, with an octagonal section at the breach. It has a front sight but none in the rear. English proof marks are stamped near the breech, and the inscription "Parker Field & Co., London, 1875" is on the barrel. The caliber is .58. The stock extends along the full length of the barrel and has brass mountings. The trigger guard is large and clumsy and in all other particulars the piece is similar to the other fusils covered in this account.[32]

Robbins and Martin, Birmingham, is a firm not generally recognized as a manufacturer; it is possible that it was a jobbing house. But on May 16, 1842, the firm wrote to Ramsay Crooks of the American Fur Company, offering to "make" North West guns at 11/6 "here" (Birmingham) or 11/9 "on arrival" in America. The tone of the letter suggests that the firm had previously engaged in the manufacture of trade guns. E. C. Robbins and Company is given as a reference with respect to the integrity of the house and the quality of its product.[33] No gun marked by Robbins and Martin has turned up in my search for material for this book.

George W. Tryon of Philadelphia is well known for his Navy muskets and for the trade rifles he supplied to the U. S. government. In 1846 he and his son also filled orders for North West trade guns requisitioned by the U. S. Indian Trade Office. One Tryon gun is reported by Mr. Serven, who writes, "One of my trade guns has a barrel slightly more than 31″ long, with typical large trigger guard, serpentine escutcheon [dragon ornament], corrugated ferrules, etc., is American-made and bears the famous name Tryon, Philadelphia, on both the lock plate and the barrel. It is a percussion arm." [34] It is quite possible that the specimen Mr. Serven refers to is one of those made in 1846.

Eli Whitney the inventor of the cotton gin, had been a successful contractor for the manufacture of U. S. government muskets ever since 1800, and he was active in this business until 1825, when he was succeeded by his son, another Eli Whitney, who made military rifles well into the 1870's. The factory was in Whitneyville, which later became a part of New Haven, Connecticut. On January 27, 1844, Whitney wrote to Ramsay Crooks of the American Fur Company, "What is called the North West gun I have seen and I can probably manufacture them for $1.50 less than the price you pay, viz 8½ dollars as I understand." Crooks rejected the proposal on January 29.[35] No specimen of the trade gun by Whitney has come to my attention.

A number of years ago, the Teton Hotel in Riverton, Wyoming, exhibited in its lobby a weathered flintlock trade gun which had been found near a small breastwork or fortification erected in the day of the mountain man on the west fork of Sheep Creek, forty-five miles north and west of Riverton in the Owl Creek Mountains. The gun had been presented to the hotel by J. D. Woodruff and Jesse M. Teeters. The barrel of this piece is about thirty inches long and has an octagonal section near the breech. The lock bears the imprint "Wilson 1820." A number of Wilsons have manufactured guns in

London and Birmingham since 1681, but not enough is known about this Wyoming gun to link it with any one of them.

The dragon ornament.—It is practically impossible to trace a definite line of descent for the remarkable cast-bronze ornament used by all makers of trade guns as a side or screw plate (fig. 27, *h*). The eight figures here shown do suggest, however, that in the heraldry of firearms the dragon as a decorative motive was used in combination with mascarons, leaves, and flowers in the early seventeenth century by the master Italian gunsmiths of Brescia, in Gardone, and that through the years the Dutch, German, French, and English gunmakers devised various versions of this ornamentation for their finer products. When those Englishmen who were first concerned with the design of the fusil for the American Indian specified the dragon ornament as a part of the make-up of their distinctive gun, it is unlikely that the scaled creature used as a side plate had any special meaning. It was only after the trade gun had been in use for a time that it became a distinguishing emblem. Mayer has suggested that the mark meant to the Indian that the article was genuine.[36]

Zoömorphs seem to have been popular as ornaments on guns from the very beginning of the seventeenth century. Greener shows a boldly sculptured scaled animal, which he calls a "dolphin," on the forestock of Cardinal Richelieu's ornate matchlock musket.[37] In general appearance, this fishlike figure closely resembles the dragon ornament. Scaled "dolphins" cast in iron and similar in every particular to the animal on Richelieu's gun were mounted as handholds on the large seventeenth-century British mortar used at the Siege of Namur, 1694, and now exhibited (as no. 125) in the Tower of London.[38] The London gunmaker Fisher (1685–1689) used a similar figure as his personal mark which he stamped on his guns; and Jacquinet, Le Hollandois, and Thuraine, mid-seventeenth-century makers of French luxury arms, used side plates which featured the dragon motif.[39]

Going back still further into the story of ornament, one finds that the Romans used the same scaled creature in the decoration created in their mosaic tiles in the first and second centuries. (Exhibit no.

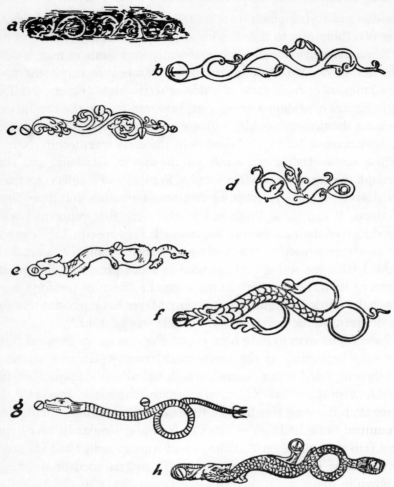

Fig. 27. The dragon ornament characteristic of all nineteenth-century trade muskets. A summary of some of the antecedents of the dragon motif (*h*), in the side plate of the Indian fusil. *a*, rubbing from one of Dr. Joseph Mayer's pistols *ca.* 1650. *b*, screw plate from Cornelis Wynkoop's musket, made in London, 1660–1680. *c*, a German baroque design, 1690–1700. *d*, from the lock plate of a repeating pistol by Michael Lorenzoni, Florence, 1695; in Museum für Völkerkunde, Vienna. *e*, English (Queen Anne) ornament from a trade gun, 1700–1720. *f*, a French ornament, *ca.* 1700, from a musket by Lorenz Pauer; in Stadt Museum, Vienna (no. 929). *g*, ornament from a Lafenmann flintlock gun made in Hesse *ca.* 1740; in Staatlichen Historischen Museum, Dresden (no. 723).

615, Victoria and Albert Museum, London, is an example of this.) It seems, therefore, that the scaled beast was firmly ensconced in the grammar of ornament long before the first trade gun was made. Whether or not the makers of hand firearms in the seventeenth, eighteenth, and nineteenth centuries attached any significance to the dragonlike animals with which they embellished their handiwork is a moot question, but it is interesting to review this phase of their art.

Figure 27, *a,* represents a rubbing from one of Dr. Mayer's Italian pistols of about 1650. Here the dragon is indeed imaginary, but his head (at left) is unmistakable. The screw plate shown in figure 27, *b,* is from Cornelis Wynkoop's musket, a gun made in London in the period 1660–1680. It is a handsome pierced scroll in which the dragon's head and protruded tongue are merely suggested in the first swirl at the left.[40] A German baroque design of about 1690 or 1700 is shown in figure 27, *c.* The dragon's head is at the extreme right.[41] The snaky figure (fig. 27, *d*) is taken from the lock plate of a repeating flintlock pistol made by Michael Lorenzoni, Florence, in 1695. In 1936 I examined the specimen in the Waffensammlung of the Museum für Völkerkunde, Vienna. A closer approach to the trade-gun ornament is shown in figure 27, *e.* It is distinctly English (Queen Anne), 1700–1720.[42] A French ornament of about 1700 is shown in figure 27, *f.* It is on a heavy flintlock musket by Lorenz Pauer, which I examined in the Stadt Museum, Vienna, in 1936.[43] A German ornament (silver on a Lafenmann flintlock gun made in Hesse about 1740 for use at the Court of the Elector of Saxony, Friedrich August II, is shown in figure 27, *g.* In 1936 the gun was in the Staatlichen Historischen Museum, Dresden. The cast-bronze dragon ornament (fig. 27, *h*) on the Barnett trade gun, 1805, is also shown in figure 18. Dr. Mayer points out that after about 1740 the dragon motif disappeared from all guns except the trade muskets. On these guns it persisted in a constant prescribed form through the cap-and-ball period and continued to be the most distinctive feature as long as manufacturers had orders to fill. The most recent trade gun I have found is the J. Hollis & Son specimen of 1886 (fig. 26) described earlier in this chapter. The dragon ornament on this piece differs in no important way from the side plate of the Barnett fusil of 1805 shown in figure 18.

Since the preceding account was written, three important items pertaining to trade guns have come to my attention: Parsons, 1952; Hanson, 1955, and Ewers, 1956. Most significant in the additional material is Mr. Hanson's discovery of the dragon ornament on the Queen Anne light musket which first came to America about 1700 (Hanson, 1955, p. 39 and pl. 1, *b,* p. 57). (See my note 42.)

RIFLES SUPPLIED TO INDIANS

The development of the trade rifle paralleled that of the "Hudson's Bay gun" in large part except that this development was strictly American. Records dating from 1803 show the planned procurement by the U. S. government of several thousands of pieces given to the Indians as a matter of public policy. Correspondence of a somewhat later date from trading companies to manufacturers concerning the specification, prices, and even methods of shipment of the trade rifle is also on record.

Figure 28, *a,* shows the characteristics of the standard early piece. The barrel of the Indian rifle as it came from the factory ranged in length from 36 to 42 inches; it was decidedly shorter than the old Kentucky rifle barrel. The Indian owner would often have the weapon still further shortened (fig. 28, *b*). On the plains, particularly, was this sawing off of the barrel customary, for the mounted rifleman found it much more convenient to carry and use a short weapon. The Plains rifle, discussed in chapter ii and illustrated in figure 11, was a more expensive model of the same type. The affinities of the two are unmistakable. The caliber was about .52.

Although the Indian rifle was plainly finished and sold for a low price, it was not shoddily constructed. On the contrary, it was strong and safe. Specifications were rigidly drawn. Before a rifle was accepted by the government or by the trading companies it was sub-

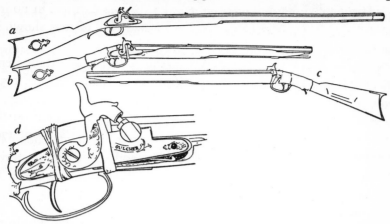

Fig. 28. Rifles supplied to Indians. *a,* typical flintlock rifle of the kind distributed by the U. S. government and by private trading companies to western Indians in the early 1800's. *b* and *c,* an Indian rifle (percussion) after use and abuse at the hands of a savage owner; in the Jefferson National Expansion Memorial, St. Louis. *d,* details of the lock of gun *b.*

jected to a proof charge of 250 grains of the best rifle powder, two wads, and two bullets.[44]

The insistence on quality was implicit in all the dealings of the Indian Trade Office, as the following letter shows:

> The rifles I am instructed to purchase are to answer the following description. They are to be common, plain rifles substantially made. The barrel to be three feet and two inches in length. The workmanship to be such as to pass a strict and rigorous inspection. The caliber such as to fit balls of half an ounce weight. The finish (if the work be good and substantial) will be sufficient if it is like that commonly given to ordinary rifles. The barrels would be preferred round (instead of eight-square) from the tail pipe, or lower thimble, to the muzzle; but of the thickness they would be in the flat part, or thinnest part, of octagonal barrels. The price that will be paid for the rifle complete will be ten dollars, cash.[45]

Tench Coxe, author of the letter just quoted, was the Purveyor of Public Supplies and made the arrangements for the supply of trade rifles from 1803 until 1812. His insistence on rigid inspection standards did much to maintain a consistently high quality in the arms purchased by the government.[46] Sensible of his responsibility as a public servant, Coxe shopped about in various parts of the country for Indian rifles that would be acceptable. Inevitably he was subject to pressure from gunmakers who had had experience with trade rifles.[47] A vociferous group of Pennsylvania rifle makers even exerted influence through other officials. The arms supplied by some of these makers were criticized by certain politicians.

Confident that the inspection was effective, Coxe defended his purchases against reports of poor quality and the criticism of his superiors. Callender Irvine, then Commissary General, assumed the direction of arms purchases after 1811. He urged that "two or three additional U. S. armories be established" to provide the trade rifles needed, but this expansion was prevented by the demands of the War of 1812.[48]

It appears that the Indian rifle of the early nineteenth century played a significant role in clarifying for the U. S. government the problems of arms procurement. The later practice of supplying pattern weapons to guide the contractor grew out of the arguments in 1811 for and against the use of private contractors.[49]

Among the contractors who made rifles for Indians in the years 1803 to 1807 were Peter Gonter, Henry De Huff, Jacob Dickert, and Christopher Gumpf of Lancaster, and John Miles of Philadelphia. In 1803, products from Gonter's shops were shipped directly to government Indian establishments at Chickasaw Bluffs and Tellico, both in Tennessee. Correspondence from Coxe, preliminary to contracts, was sent in 1803 to Solomon Myers, York, Pennsylvania, and to John Buyers, Sunburg, Pennsylvania; but no contracts resulting therefrom are recorded. In his letter to Myers, Coxe was specific in saying that the rifles were needed by the "Indian Factories." He indicated that the prevailing price then was $10.50 for rifles with brass mountings, and $11.00 for those ornamented with "silver thumb-pieces and star," as paid to the gunmakers in Lancaster.

Late in 1807 and early in 1808 there was renewed activity in procuring rifles for Indians. Molan and Finn, Henry Pickel, Henry De Huff, Jacob Dickert, Joseph Henry, Abraham Henry, George Miller,

Christopher Gumpf, John Bender, Peter Gonter, John Guest, and Peter Brong, all in Pennsylvania, are conspicuous in the records of the rifle business conducted by the government during this period. Molan and Finn went into bankruptcy soon after signing their contract, and it is doubtful that they supplied any arms. So many of the rifles by Henry Pickel were defective that Coxe suspended payment for them, and it is questionable that his contract was completed.

Mr. John C. Ewers states that the records of the Indian Trade Office, now preserved in the National Archives, contain an order of March 21, 1808, for 20 Indian rifles to be made by Thomas Crabb of Frederickstown (now Frederick), Maryland.[50] In all probability, this was the Thomas Crabb who in 1799–1801 had manufactured U. S. muskets, Model 1795, under government contract. Mr. Ewers also tells of an order of January 5, 1811, for 30 Indian rifles to be supplied by George Kraps of Hagerstown, Maryland.

One wonders where existing specimens of these early Indian rifles may be. Besides the piece shown in figure 28, *a,* only one possible example has come to my attention. Colonel B. R. Lewis in a personal letter writes: "I have a half-stock (converted to percussion) .525 rifle with c. GUMPF on the barrel and DECKERT on the lock. It is a better quality job than is the usual later Indian trade arm. It may be an 1808 contract rifle meant for Militia use. There is no proof mark." [51]

After the War of 1812, the government seems for a while not to have supplied rifles to Indians. In 1820, however, Thomas L. Mc-Kenney, Superintendent of Indian Trade, obtained from H. Deringer, Philadelphia, 141 rifles, for which he paid $14.75 each.[52] A Deringer contract of July 23, 1819, is a matter of record,[53] and it is likely that production of the rifles McKenney was to supply to Indians was authorized in this document.

The Indian Intercourse Act of 1834 provided the basic authority for the later procurement of the Indian rifles which today are to be found in so many arms collections. Numerous specimens from the factories of Henry E. Leman, Lancaster, Pennsylvania; George W. and Edward K. Tryon, Philadelphia; and Henry Deringer, Philadelphia, are available for study, and the government contracts under which they were manufactured are a matter of record.[54] Another less well known contractor was Jacob Fordney of Lancaster, who had a government contract in 1837 for 250 Indian rifles. He obtained locks for these arms from George Goulcher in New York. Some other rifle makers also used the Goulcher locks, and many rifles commonly attributed to Goulcher actually are mistakenly identified because of the Goulcher name on the locks. There is no record of a Goulcher contract with the U. S. government, but there is reason to believe that James and Joseph Golcher (Goulcher) did make Indian rifles for the fur companies. (See section "Goulcher rifles" near the end of this chapter.)

The known government contracts of 1837 account for 4,250 Indian rifles, a total which seems to be too small considering the demands of the Indians who had been hurriedly moved to the West in the three or four years preceding that date. It is likely that records of additional orders will come to light.

At the time that the U. S. government was procuring Indian rifles from private manufactories, the American Fur Company was doing a rather extensive business along the same lines with John Joseph Henry (until his death in 1836) and with James Henry, the son of John Joseph, at Lancaster, Pennsylvania. The Henrys appear to have been both coöperative and advanced in their thinking. Records show that they designed an improved technique in making the trade rifle, and that their product was praised.[55] The relations between the Henry business and the American Fur Company continued through 1845. The correspondence reveals that meticulous attention was given to the orders placed. A low price, certain details of specification and construction, and good quality of materials and workmanship were exacted from the manufacturer;[56] even the packing and shipping of the rifles had to meet high standards.[57]

Occasionally in the literature of firearms and in the old manuscript records of the traders one comes upon references to "smooth bored rifles." This dissonant terminology, Dillin explains, stems from the practice of some of the old-time gunsmiths in isolated situations of buying barrels bored to caliber from manufacturers who specialized in gun-barrel making.[58] Upon order, the gunsmiths rifled these barrels in accordance with the customers' desires; a small percentage of the smoothbores, however, were passed on by the gunsmiths to customers who were content to fire patch and ball from a barrel which was not rifled. Another explanation is that some owners would have their rifles rebored after the original rifling had through use become so worn that the guns were no longer accurate; these rebored guns then became small-bore shotguns. Ramsay Crooks, in a letter of August 22, 1840, addressed to James Henry, reveals that the Boulton Gun Works was one of the factories that supplied "smooth bore rifles" to the trade. He also makes clear that the western Indians provided no market for such make-believe rifles: "We said in ours of July 29 that the smooth bored rifles would not suit us. The more we reflect upon it the more we are satisfied they will not answer at all for our Indian trade. When the Indians use a rifle it must be a real one, and they will not carry a smooth bore of such weight so long as they can get a North West gun." [59]

Various pieces of evidence are at hand which point to the fact that few rifles were in the hands of far-western Indians before 1820. One bit of testimony comes from the St. Louis fur trader Louis Bissounette, who suffered loss of men and goods at the hands of Indians in the Sauk-Foxes country on May 21, 1820. Bissounette, testifying before John R. Guy, a justice of the peace, in St. Louis on July 6, 1820, said that he "had no doubt the Indians who had so fired on them were the Sac nation; . . . that he has for a great many years followed the Indian trade and is well acquainted with the habits, manners and customs of the Indians." He based his identification on the belt and garter dropped by the attackers, and "by the rifle balls which were fired at them, four of which were found on the field of defeat, as none of the Northern Indians besides the Sacs make use of rifles." [60]

It was not to be long, however, until numerous Indians in the West were armed with rifles. In 1825 came a revival of Jefferson's idea of "Indian removal"; Secretary of War John C. Calhoun, recom-

mended to President Monroe that "permanent" Indian lands be set
aside west of Missouri and Arkansas in order that eastern tribes
might be transplanted from their homes then coveted by white
settlers. Monroe endorsed the plan, and his successors carried it out.
One of the means of placating the displaced Indians was to provide
them with rifles and ammunition.[61] Records show that by 1837 one-
half of the 20,000 immigrant Indian warriors had been presented with
government-owned guns.[62] The practice continued through 1840, by
which time some 60,000 Indians had been moved to the country immediately west of Arkansas. Small numbers of Indian rifles are listed
in the inventories of the Ordnance Department in the opening years
of the 1840's, although the need for such arms as gifts to immigrant
Indians tapered off in 1840. It is interesting to note in the returns
of the Ordnance Office that in 1842 "152 Indian Rifles" were issued
to regular U. S. troops, along with 712 Model 1817 U. S. rifles.[63]

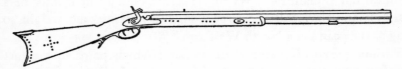

Fig. 29. Cap-and-ball Indian rifle by "J. Henry and Son." A typical
specimen of the trade rifles produced at the Boulton Gun Works by
James Henry and his son Granville. It is one of a lot captured from or
surrendered by the Sioux and Cheyenne soon after the Custer massacre
on the Little Big Horn River, Wyoming Territory, in 1876. It was formerly no. 320 in the collection of the U. S. Cartridge Co. Before Granville
entered the business, James marked his product "J. Henry."

Henry rifles.—The Henry family occupies a prominent place in
the story of American gunmaking. William I (1729–1786), the first
of the line, operated a gun factory in Lancaster in 1751. Even in his
day, firearms for frontiersmen were a principal product. His sons,
Abraham (d. 1811) and John Joseph (1758–1811) also engaged in
gunmaking in Lancaster. A third son, William II (1757–1821), established himself near Nazareth, Pennsylvania, and launched the business of which we read in the American Fur Company Papers. He
trained his sons, John Joseph (1786–1836) and William III (b. 1796),
in the ways of their forebears.[64] These Henrys were relatives of the

previously mentioned Joseph Henry, who had made Indian rifles for the government in 1807–1808 at the Henry factory then situated at 3d and Noble streets, Philadelphia. Dillin states that the Boulton Gun Works was built by William III on Bushkill Creek, Boulton, near Nazareth. It was completed in 1813 and continued to operate under the direction of his nephew James Henry (1809–1894), and his grandnephew Granville (1835–1912), until the 1880's. The factory and the nearby dwellings of the Henrys still stand.[65]

The percussion rifle shown in figure 29 is typical of those manufactured at the Boulton works. It has a full-octagon barrel of .52 caliber and is equipped with a set or hair trigger. The walnut stock is ornamented with brass tacks, perhaps the contribution of an Indian owner. Additional information about the piece, as well as an indication of the confidence felt by the trading companies for the Henry firm, is found in a letter written by Ramsay Crooks in 1837:

> You will have all the orders we receive this year and in the meantime you may go on with the 300 mentioned in my last, viz., 150 rifles American Lancaster pattern @ $9.50; 150 rifles English new pattern, $11.50. Ball 32 to the lb., barrell 40 to 42 inches. It is understood these rifles are to be in all respects fully equal to the best you ever made us of these descriptions, to have a woolen bag or cover, each. The price to include packing and all the charges till delivered in New York and to be paid for in 6 months.[66]

Leman rifles.—The rifles manufactured by H. E. Leman, Lancaster, Pennsylvania, are particularly well represented in collections. His factory was active from 1834 until the 1880's, and beginning in 1837 his contracts with the U. S. government were many and sizable. At all times his business was mainly manufacturing weapons for the Indian trade.[67] In spite of the volume of government business, Leman appears to have been an aggressive salesman. His correspondence with the American Fur Company provides an amusing side light on his persistence in attempting to interest the fur companies in his wares.[68] There is no record in the documents examined that Leman ever sold a rifle to the American Fur Company.

Leman did an extensive business in supplying gunlocks to other manufacturers, and it has been stated that he supplied many flintlock and percussion Indian rifles both to the government and to some of the fur companies.[69] The evidence of his industry is seen in firearms collections all over the United States.

Lieutenant Clark, 2d U. S. Cavalry, took some specimens from the Cheyenne in 1876 which were sent to the Springfield Armory and later sold as relics. One of these is in the Nunnemacher Collection (no. N3601) in the Milwaukee Public Museum. It has an octagonal barrel 34¾ inches long which has both front and rear sights. The caliber is .52. It was altered from the flintlock by enlarging the vent and screwing into this aperture a drumlike cylinder fitted with a nipple. The lock plate is engraved "H. E. Leman, Lancaster, Pa." The barrel is similarly stamped and also bears the word "Warranted." It is equipped with a set trigger.[70]

Of eighteen Indian rifles in the U. S. Cartridge Company's *Catalogue,* eleven (nos. 315–332) are Leman's products. Dillin shows six Indian rifles, "most of them by Leman." [71]

Deringer rifles.—Henry Deringer who made Indian rifles was the son of Henry Deringer, the maker of Kentucky rifles. The elder Deringer, a Pennsylvanian, did business in Richmond, Virginia, from 1800 to 1806, and then returned to Pennsylvania, where he spent the rest of his life making firearms. The younger Henry Deringer was born on October 26, 1786, at Easton, Pennsylvania; he died in Philadelphia in February, 1868. A notable part of his business was done on a contract basis with the U. S. government. Pistols, such as the militia model of 1808; trade muskets recorded in the Invoice Book, 1822–1823, of the Indian Trade Office, Georgetown, D.C.; Army rifles of the period 1820–1830; and Indian rifles made from 1835 until the Civil War were among the items which he manufactured for the government. His mark was H DERINGER PHILADA. Pistols by Deringer bearing dates in the 1870's are not uncommon, yet Henry Deringer died in 1868.

Deringer was especially renowned as the maker of a popular percussion-cap pocket pistol, deeply rifled, short of barrel, and of elegant design and workmanship, whence all similar small pistols of whatever origin were called "derringers." Even after the breech-loader came into use, short-barreled single-shot pistols were called "Deringers," usually misspelled "derringer." The gun used in the assassination of President Lincoln was one of the muzzle-loading Deringer pistols.[72]

Tryon rifles.—George W. Tryon (1791–1878), first worked with Frederick W. Goetz (or Getz), a Philadelphia gunmaker.[73] Subsequently he became the partner of Goetz and finally the owner of the business. In 1811 he established his own business, and in 1814 he combined with John Joseph Henry, temporarily, in filling orders from the U. S. Navy. George W. Tryon and his son Edward K. became partners in 1836. In 1837 they contracted to make 1,000 Indian rifles for the U. S. government at $12.50 each. Edward K. was one of the several contractors who made the Model 1841 military rifle, which was "noteworthy for being the best made and most accurate spherical bullet military rifle in the world, so acknowledged by all Nations." In 1846 Tryon contracted to make 640 muskets at $12.18 each, and in the same year he got orders for North West trade guns. The Tryon product was consistently recognized as of top quality. Dillin states that the firm was still in business in 1937 under the name E. K. Tryon & Co., handling sporting goods and guns.[74]

Goulcher rifles.—Figure 28, *b–d,* shows an Indian rifle with percussion-cap lock from the National Park Service collections, Jefferson National Expansion Memorial, St. Louis. The lock of this bruised and battered specimen is inscribed "Goulcher." As Dillin warns, the lock of a rifle is not always a guide to identifying the maker of the piece.[75] The Goulchers (also spelled "Golcher"), especially Joseph and James of Philadelphia, and George of New York City, specialized in locks, both flintlock and percussion, which were distributed widely among other manufacturers of guns. Musket barrels by Goulcher were obtained by the Committee of Safety in Philadelphia in 1776. A Goulcher is also mentioned as a contractor who made Indian rifles. The relic pictured, however, cannot accurately be attributed to the Goulcher factory in Philadelphia.

John Goulcher of Easton, Pennsylvania, did a great deal to establish the family name among gunmakers in the period between the Revolution and the end of the century. During the Revolution he served as an instructor in the Committee of Safety, and after the War he became celebrated for his Kentucky rifles and the excellent over-and-under revolving-barrel rifles which he produced. He also manufactured a multishot flintlock rifle having a single barrel which took superposed loads fired successively with a traveling lock. His rifle shop still stood in 1920.

Joseph Goulcher had a shop in Philadelphia where he did an extensive business in manufacturing gunlocks. Apparently he was another of the several American gunsmiths who, in the early nineteenth century, were stimulated by the heavy importation of foreign locks, to supply the domestic market. The rifle here pictured is believed to be equipped with one of his locks. Whether or not the entire weapon came from a Goulcher shop is a moot question.

George Goulcher of New York City made many locks, both flint and percussion, which were used on the arms turned out by various makers. It is known, definitely, that James Fordney of Lancaster, Pennsylvania, built into his Indian rifles some of the locks by George Goulcher. A John Golcher also was active in New York City during the percussion period. Percussion locks manufactured by one or another of the Golchers at this time were used on arms produced by G. Morgan, J. H. Lefbett, N. Moll, and Mathias Ringle.

James Goulcher, who died in 1805, was a Philadelphia locksmith during a part of the period in which John of Easton was active. One of his descendants, Manuel Goulcher, was still making shotguns in Philadelphia in 1877. A second James, presumably also a descendant of the James who died in 1805, became a well-known maker of rifles in Philadelphia. He signed his products "James Golcher." He fathered William, who also became a master in the trade. Rifles made by William at this time were marked "James Golcher Manufacturer Philadelphia." James and William moved their business to St. Paul, Minnesota, in the 1850's. While on a buying trip to Chicago in the 1870's, William met the San Franciscan John P. Claybrough, a maker and importer of fine shotguns. In 1878, William, with his sons Henry C.

and William G., moved to San Francisco, where William entered into partnership with Claybrough. William J. and Henry succeeded to this partnership, which lasted until the death of William J. in the 1880's. Golchers have been a fixture in the San Francisco gun trade ever since 1878. Benned Golcher, a son of Henry and last of the line in the gun business, still (1956) presides at the Golcher store, at 508 Market Street.[76]

The tendency of the Indian was to try coercion upon his rifle if it seemed to fail him. With fire and water and brute force he was apt to abuse his weapon, or simply to ruin it through neglect and rough handling. Most of the captured or surrendered Indian rifles now in collections show the damage and crude repair with rawhide evident in the "Goulcher" specimen pictured.

IV

Military Arms of the Fur-Trade Period

The story of the military is closely associated with trapper affairs throughout the period of the western fur trade. Scores of entries in journals of trappers and many official reports attest to the liaison between trappers and soldiers. The wilds were first explored by hunters, and when a territory was established or annexed, it was the military, guided by the trappers, who moved in to consolidate the gain and exercise control. Often the military furnished the only government for a new territory for many years, and it was to the post commanders that the trappers looked for justice and protection, though these were not always forthcoming.

On the whole, the relations between trappers and traders and the Army were good. The military were cognizant of the aid given by the knowledgeable mountain men. Colonel Abert, Corps of Topographical Engineers, wrote concerning the establishment of a chain of posts to protect the road to Oregon:

> It will add much to the efficiency of the commands if the commanding officers . . . were allowed to enrol about 50 of the class of trappers known as "American Trappers" for scouts, guides, and hunters. These will be found to be highly valuable, and even necessary auxiliaries with all exploring expeditions as well from their knowledge of the country and its inhabitants, as from their ability to act as interpreters and the reliance which can be placed on their allegiance.[1]

D. H. Mahan thought it worth while to indoctrinate the students of West Point with this point of view. He remarks, in his *Treatise on*

Field Fortifications, that hunters and trappers "are the best persons to apply to for information . . . in examining the face of the country, and they should be chosen for guides." [2]

The expansion of the military frontier can be divided roughly into three periods. Before the purchase of Louisiana, all the organized military operations were confined to the country east of the Mississippi River. From 1791 to 1803, the small Army, numbering only 2,000 regulars and about 1,000 militia, was occupied in two areas. The Indians of the Old Northwest ravaged the new American settlements in the area that is now the states of Wisconsin, Michigan, Illinois, Indiana, and Ohio. Not until 1795 were these Indians quelled. To the south, along the disputed border between the United States and the Spanish possessions, were the hostile Creeks and Cherokee and the more or less friendly Choctaw and Chickasaw. The Spanish in Florida and Louisiana supplied the Creeks with arms and generally hindered the settlement of boundary questions. Not until 1796 was a treaty negotiated with the Creeks and peace brought to the southern border. The military remained in the area, acting as escorts for survey parties and later as garrison for six forts along the lower Mississippi, which were established in 1804 for the protection of the Louisiana Purchase.

On March 9, 1804, Captain Amos Stoddard with only seven soldiers from Kaskaskia took over the city of St. Louis from the French. This marks the beginning of the period of expansion westward from the Mississippi. Fort Belle Fontaine was built in 1805 and became military headquarters for the region. Lewis and Clark left in 1804 on the first leg of their epoch-making journey to the Pacific. Lieutenant Zebulon M. Pike explored the upper Mississippi in 1805 and in 1806 led another party of soldiers to the Colorado Rockies. The establishment of numerous forts between 1804 and 1821 tightened the grip of the young nation upon its western frontier. The pictures of Fort Osage (end papers) and Fort Winnebago (fig. 31) illustrate the types of construction. Several of these posts were lost to the British during the War of 1812 but were later regained.

Not all military establishments in the northern fur country were

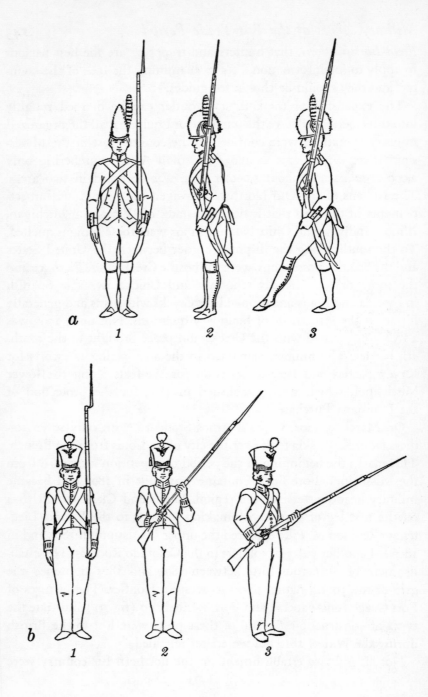

a

1   2   3

b

1   2   3

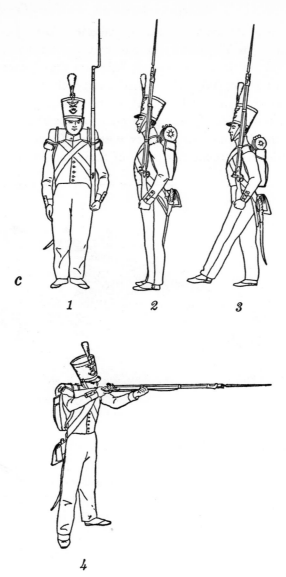

Fig. 30. Soldiers in the West in 1812, the 1830's, and the 1840's. *a*, private of U. S. Infantry, 1812; after pl. 2, "Drill of the Soldier," Smyth, 1812. The flintlock musket shown is the U. S. Model 1795, with bayonet fixed. *b*, private, Militia of the United States, 1830; after pls. 3 and 4, "School of the Soldier," U. S. War Dept., 1830. *c*, U. S. Infantry private of the 1840's; after pl. 5, Scott, 1859, Vol. I. "School of the Soldier" was printed in 1835 and 1842 in editions similar to that of 1859.

bastioned forts protected by enclosing palisades. Fort Winnebago on the important Fox-Wisconsin portage was constructed by the 1st Infantry of the U. S. Army in 1828; Jefferson Davis, then a second lieutenant just out of West Point, had charge of the logging detail and the production of lumber used in the buildings. The Winnebago Indian hostilities of 1827 gave occasion for the establishment of this, the third American military post in Wisconsin. While the post was under construction, a party of these Indians went to Can-

Fig. 31. Fort Winnebago, Portage, Wisconsin, 1828. After an illustration in the 1856 edition of *Wau-bun,* by Mrs. John H. Kinzie.

ada to obtain guns and ammunition with which to make further trouble for the Wisconsin miners and settlers. The Fort Winnebago garrison and its Indian agents, however, successfully restrained the Winnebago Indians during the eighteen years preceding the removal of the tribe to Minnesota and the upper Missouri. In 1832, during the Black Hawk War (with the Sauk and Foxes), the Fort Winnebago warehouses became a central depot for arms, ammunition, and other war supplies.

The years 1821–1842 marked the removal of the largest number of Indians, and the military were closely associated with the process. The weight of responsibility on commanders of small isolated units was great. The Army, in coöperation with the Indian agents, paid to the Indians their annuities; did what it could to suppress liquor trafficking in their villages; regulated and protected legitimate trade, including the overland commerce with Santa Fe; quieted as far as possible the incessant intertribal wars; removed squatters; and whipped down the uprisings that resulted from encroachment by white men upon Indian lands. Not the least of the troubles met by the Army were raids of the "wild" Indians upon the settlements of both the whites and the Indians who had come from farther east and invaded the ancestral domain of the Plains tribes. Along the Indian frontier as defined by an 1834 Act of Congress were no fewer than 100,000 war-loving natives, all people of the plains who were completely at home on the backs of horses. Single tribes could send forth more mounted warriors than there were white soldiers (2,900) stationed on or near the long frontier in the early 1830's.

After the organization of Wisconsin Territory and the admission of Michigan and Arkansas as states, the Army was increased to nearly 8,000 troops on the western frontier. Militia forces were used intermittently. The wars of 1832 and 1836 caused temporary increases. The Seminole War drained off troops to fight in Florida and resulted in the abandonment of several forts. By 1845 the military frontier extended from the northern peninsula of what is now Michigan, across northern Wisconsin to southeastern Minnesota, thence southwesterly across Iowa to the Missouri River in northeastern Nebraska. From Fort Atkinson, just north of the site of present Omaha, Nebraska, the imaginary line extended south through eastern Kansas to Fort Scott, where a city by that name now flourishes, and thence south to Fort Gibson on the Arkansas River in Oklahoma. Here the line trended southwesterly to Fort Washita north of the spot on which Fort Sill, Oklahoma, now stands, and to San Antonio and the Gulf of Mexico at Corpus Christi. At no point, then, did the military have strongholds on the high plains or in the Rockies. With the exception of the Lewis and Clark expedition, Pike's exploring parties, and the later Frémont expeditions none of the Army groups reached the fur fields of the Rockies.

One of the more interesting and the most important of several

Army men who influenced the fur trade was Captain B. L. E. Bonne-ville, a French-born West Pointer who had been an Army officer since 1815. He came to Fort Smith, Arkansas, as a company officer in the 7th Infantry Regiment in 1821. After spending ten years on

Fig. 32. Capt. Benjamin Louis Eulalie de Bonneville. After a portrait in Vinton, 1935, p. 648. Obtained through the coöperation of the Jefferson National Expansion Memorial, St. Louis.

border duty he saw the possibilities of the fur trade in the West. Backed by Alfred Seton of New York, a one-time Astorian, and under instructions from the Secretary of War, Captain Bonneville took leave from the Army and organized a trading expedition which left Fort Osage on May 1, 1832. For three years he engaged in or directed exploration, map making, and trade in the Rocky Mountains, along the Columbia, and across the Great Basin into California. Some of the significance of the Bonneville expedition is implied in the following excerpt from a message sent by the Captain to General McComb from Wind River, July 29, 1833: "The information I have already obtained authorizes me to say this much; that if the government ever intends taking possession of Oregon, the sooner it shall be done, the better." In 1836, after he had been refused reinstatement in the U. S. Army, Bonneville addressed Lewis Cass, Secretary of War: "That I started as a trader and acted as such is something I never attempted to conceal. General Scott, Eustis and even General McComb assisted me to become one, as their letters now in my possession will show. The whole Army knew it. It was deemed more proper for me to go as such." [3]

Some published disparagement notwithstanding, Bonneville's maps of the transmountain region were a credit to him. They were filed in the War Department archives and were not published until 1837, having been preceded, so far as public use is concerned, by the Albert Gallatin map of 1836, which reflected some of the Ashley-Smith findings, and which quite properly has been given high praise. Nevertheless, Bonneville's maps were much better than Gallatin's map in some respects; they provide the first clear and fairly accurate picture of the relationships of the rivers which head in the Yellowstone–Grand Teton summit country, they depict the Humboldt River and its sinks for the first time, and they reveal the true nature of the drainage into San Francisco Bay.[4]

The story of military arms differs from that of the trade and personal weapons in one respect. The traders and fur companies chose arms which were convenient for them to obtain or which were demanded by their customers. The soldiers used the guns which had been issued to them, guns chosen by the chief of ordnance and his advisers. One important aspect of this situation is the attitude of the soldier toward his weapon. Little material has been published in this regard for the period 1804–1843. When it can be discerned, the story of guns in the hands of soldiers is full of dramatic appeal and human interest. Unfortunately, few of the frontier soldiers were given to literary pursuits, and very few of those who did write are specific about identifying the weapons they carried.

In this chapter, material gathered from official records, contemporary news accounts, certain private journals and correspondence, and the guns themselves has been assembled to present as coherent a picture as possible of the models used at given times. The findings have been checked against the standard current books on military arms. Opinions of the users of the arms, results of fire-power tests, and performance reports are discussed.

In the years covered in this book (1804–1843), the Army uniform was changed repeatedly, but the Manual of Arms persisted with no changes of note. The printed guides supplied to infantrymen during the flintlock period always opened with the explanation that the gun carried by the soldier might be known to him as a "fusil" or as a "musket," but to the Army it was a "firelock" and would always be so designated in Army parlance. The four models of the "firelock," Models 1795, 1812, 1816, and 1840, are treated in the pages that follow.

MILITARY MUSKETS

Before the outbreak of the Revolution, the American—or Colonial —troops had been used to the regulation British Army musket, most of the guns being the famous "Brown Bess" already described. It was naturally the "Brown Bess" which served as a pattern for the first American-made muskets procured from local gunsmiths by the committees of safety set up by various colonies when the war broke out in 1775. Peterson points out that many British arms fell into the hands of the Americans with the seizure of colonial arsenals.[5] Many more were captured from British troops, with the result that, at the beginning of the war, most of the weapons were either British made or patterned after British designs. In 1823 there were still on hand in U. S. Ordnance stores 2,729 "British pattern muskets." [6]

During the war, the United States procured some 100,000 French military muskets of various models, some of them made as far back as 1717.[7] Because so many of them were marked "Charleville," it became the custom to refer to all French models as Charleville muskets.

Although the British muskets were in use during the Revolution and several thousand more were purchased in 1794, the British model was not the one finally adopted. When the United States armories were established at Springfield, Massachusetts, in 1794 and at Harpers Ferry in 1796, the French Charleville musket, Model 1763, was adopted as a pattern for making the first American military musket. Production was started in 1795 at Springfield, and the weapon, a close duplication of the 1763 French model, has since become known as the United States musket, Model 1795.

Model 1795.—It would be convenient for collectors if the models had succeeded each other in orderly fashion, but at the end of the century the threat of war with France caused the government officials to bestir themselves to meet the need for military arms. Gun parts were purchased from a variety of sources, and private manufacturers were hired to make them into complete guns. In 1800, the British firm Ketland and Company sold to our government 1,541 musket locks marked "Ketland and Co.—United States." This is but one example of the many importations, most of them not documented. John Guest and the firm William and J. J. Henry, both of Lancaster, Pennsylvania, are among the private makers who are known to have used Ketland locks in manufacturing arms for the U. S. government.[8] At this time, also, the government contracted with twenty-eight private manufacturers to supply 40,200 Charleville-type muskets. Among the contractors was Eli Whitney of New Haven, Connecticut. Whitney had studied a specimen of the 1777 Charleville musket and had recognized in it certain improvements over the model of 1763. To U. S. Ordnance officers, he proposed to incorporate the improvements in the muskets he was making. Approval was given, and the Eli Whitney product after 1801 is characterized by an inclined brass pan having no fence, and by a round-faced cock, or hammer, and a frizzen with a flared head and cutoff toe. Whitney's contract, dated January

14, 1798, called for 10,000 muskets. He did not complete the order until January, 1809, nine years after the date specified in the contract. His improvements were later adopted by the U. S. government as standard specifications for a subsequent model of musket.[9]

By 1801 the Model 1795 was being manufactured at both Springfield and Harpers Ferry armories. Some writers have contended that a distinctly new model was prescribed in 1808. James L. Mitchell, however, has made the following analysis:

> In my opinion the Model 1795 musket was made at both (U.S.) armories until the next model was adopted, that of 1812. It is almost certain that there is no such arm as the Model 1808, which is many times assumed to be a distinct model. Contract arms were authorized in 1808 when Congress appropriated $200,000 annually for arming the militia. While they are different in some respects from the Model 1795, they are practically the same. The main difference was the rounded trigger guard believed by some to have first appeared on the 1808 contract musket, but I have one dated 1806 and have seen another of 1807. The change in trigger-guards, iron-detachable pans, straight projection on the top of the hammer instead of the curl, were merely steps which we today would call streamlining. Virtually all the modifications cut the cost of the finished musket.[10]

Mitchell's observations have been duplicated by other discerning collectors. There is no question that some of the Model 1795 muskets made in the national armories in 1806 and later were inconsistent in their characteristics. Colonel Gluckman has pointed out the reasons for this lack of stability in the Model 1795 and the poor definition of some of the characteristics of the Model 1808:

> Common are the many arms made subsequent to 1808, found with trigger guards and other parts of the Model 1795 type, and in case of Harpers Ferry arms, even with lock plates of the earlier type. The same remarks are applicable even to a greater degree to the contract arms made by the numerous contractors of the 1808 model. Many of these had made state and government arms patterned after the 1795 model, and continued to use serviceable old model parts until the old stock of parts was exhausted; others bought up old type stock parts from subcontractors in order to make deliveries on time. These variations often make positive identification and classification of a musket model confusing and difficult.

When one is confronted with such a specimen, probably his classification should be based on the shape and construction of the lock plate, disregarding other minor difficulties.[11]

Gluckman's analysis of lock characteristics is reprinted in the legend of figure 33. If used with other criteria in his text, the system provides a means of determining the origin and approximate date of almost any bona fide U. S. flintlock musket.

During the summer and fall of 1808, twenty-four private gunmakers contracted to manufacture the so-called "new" model. Eli Whitney wanted to undertake to supply the largest quantity of all, 15,000, but his contract was not signed until 1812. He had not yet completed the order for 10,000 for which he had contracted in 1798. The price which the government in 1798 had agreed to pay Whitney was $13.40 a musket; in 1812, $13.00. Since other contractors were getting only $10.75 a musket in 1812, Commissary General Callender Irvine argued for the cancellation of the Whitney contract, but the Secretary of War did not uphold Irvine's recommendation. It was generally conceded that the Eli Whitney muskets "were probably as fine arms as had been made anywhere," and the price as in 1808 was allowed to stand.

Various alterations of the Model 1795 were undertaken after delivery was made to the government. In 1796–1800 some fifteen thousand muskets had the bayonets soldered permanently to the barrels. Secretary Henry Dearborn in 1806 ordered that this mutilation be discontinued. In 1813 six or eight thousand muskets were shortened by sawing off twelve inches of the barrel, and others by cutting off ten inches. This lack of uniformity detracted from the value of the weapons to the Army. As early as 1809, Tench Coxe, Purveyor of Public Supplies, had recommended that ten thousand of the substandard muskets then on hand be sold. In 1815 the sawed-off muskets were sold to William Cramond of Philadelphia "on account of the shortness of their barrels." Thus it may be inferred that a large number of specimens of the Model 1795 and of the so-called Model 1808 were distributed at an early date to American civilians and to foreign lands.

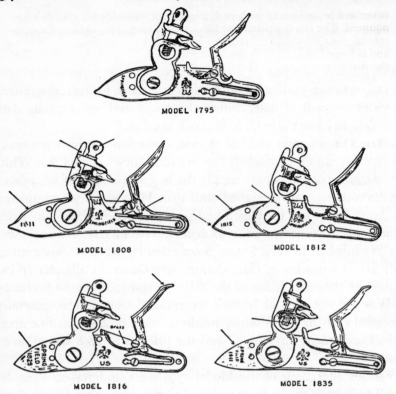

MODEL 1795

MODEL 1808

MODEL 1812

MODEL 1816

MODEL 1835

Fig. 33. Locks of United States muskets, 1795–1840. From *United States Muskets, Rifles and Carbines,* 1948, by Arcadi Gluckman, Col., U. S. Army (ret.); reprinted here by permission of the author and The Stackpole Company, Harrisburg, Pa. (Page numbers refer to Gluckman's text.)

Springfield flintlock musket, Model 1795 (p. 67).—The lock plate is marked between the cock and the frizzen spring with a small spread eagle which faces to the rear. "U. S." in script appears below the eagle. Behind the cock is stamped, "SPRINGFIELD"; (from 1804 the date appears here also). The lock plate is about 6⅜ inches long, by 1¼ inches wide; the flat face is beveled at the edges and slopes to a decided point at the rear. The cock is flat bevel-edged, double-necked, and the comb ends in a curl above the upper jaw. The head of the flint screw is pierced and slotted. The removable iron pan has an outer surface of three bevels tapering into each other at the bottom, and has a fence to the rear. The tail of the frizzen ends in an ornamental iron curl.

Model 1808 (p. 102).—The lock differs from the lock of the Model 1795 in the following respects: It is about ¼ inch longer (6⅝ in. × 1¼ in.). The upper rear portion behind the cock is more rounded, giving more cover and protection to the sear spring; the point at the rear is more pronounced. The comb tip and the battery heel are plain, without the ornamental curls of the Charleville model; the pan is rounded at the bottom and is forged integral with the lock plate. With the exception of the date, the marking is placed in the area in front of the cock.

Model 1812 (p. 128).—The lock differs from the lock of the Model 1808: The lock plate comes to a point at the rear without the prominent tit, and is 1/4 inch shorter and 1/16 inch wider (6 3/8 in. × 1 5/16 in.). The cock face is rounded instead of flat and bevel-edged.

Model 1816 (p. 142).—The lock differs from the lock of the Model 1812: The lock plate is 1/4 inch longer (6 5/8 in. × 1 5/16 in.). The rear surface of the lock plate is rounded; the pan is brass; the top of the frizzen is bent forward toward the muzzle.

Model 1835 [1840] (p. 162).—The lock differs from the lock of the Model 1816: "Had a redesigned, narrower lock bridle and a shorter main spring. These were responsible for the shortening and change of appearance of the musket lock plate,"—which is 3/8 inch shorter and 1/16 inch narrower (6 1/4 in. × 1 1/4 in.). The rear end surface is more rounded and the end is more pointed. There is a fence on the pan. The throat hole in the cock is round instead of heart-shaped.

The Model 1795 went along with the American troops that took over Louisiana, and this and the 1808 type served as the principal weapons with which the United States fought the War of 1812. In its various "issues" the Model 1795 was consistent in being always close to .69 caliber [12] and always having three bands. The length of its stock, however, ranged from 54 1/4 inches to 56 1/2 inches; the barrel, from 42 to 44 3/4 inches. In accordance with differences in these dimensions, the total length ranged from 57 to 59 3/5 inches. The trigger guard also ranged in length from 10 1/4 to 13 inches, and the shape of its ends varied from pointed to round. A bayonet, triangular in cross section, was always a part of the equipment of an infantryman in the regular service. The earlier bayonet blades for the Model 1795 musket were 14.12 inches long; later blades were 16 inches. The lower (or rear) sling swivel was always affixed to a stud just in front of the trigger guard. (See fig. 34, *a*.)

It was regular practice for the Army to supply the soldier with cartridges when they were available. Ordinarily, the ratio of powder to ball in these loads was about one to four; the ball weighed 1/18 pound, and the charge of powder weighed 110 to 154 grains. Flints were issued in the proportion of one flint to twenty rounds.

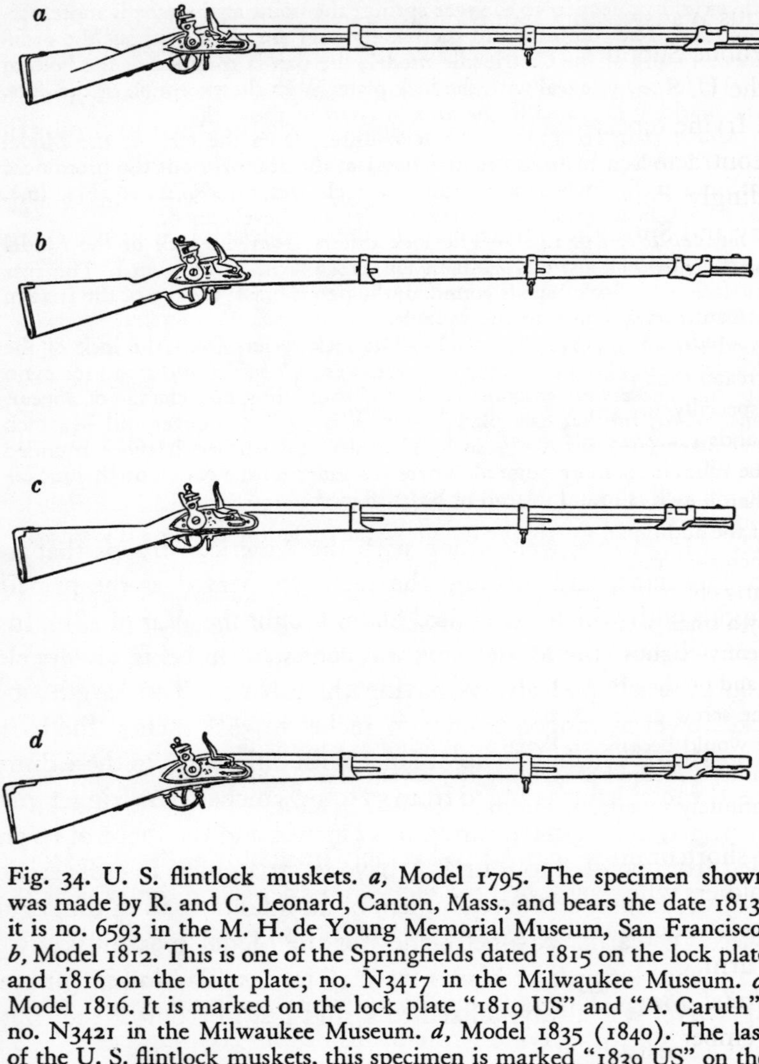

Fig. 34. U. S. flintlock muskets. *a,* Model 1795. The specimen shown was made by R. and C. Leonard, Canton, Mass., and bears the date 1813; it is no. 6593 in the M. H. de Young Memorial Museum, San Francisco. *b,* Model 1812. This is one of the Springfields dated 1815 on the lock plate and 1816 on the butt plate; no. N3417 in the Milwaukee Museum. *c,* Model 1816. It is marked on the lock plate "1819 US" and "A. Caruth"; no. N3421 in the Milwaukee Museum. *d,* Model 1835 (1840). The last of the U. S. flintlock muskets, this specimen is marked "1839 US" on the lock plate and "1840" on the tang. Lemuel Pomeroy, Pittsfield, Mass., made the piece; no. N3432 in the Milwaukee Museum.

The official correspondence indicates that the 1795 Model was not altogether an admirable weapon in the eyes of officials. Continual attack was made upon it by Callender Irvine, Commissary General;

Decius Wadsworth, Colonel of Ordnance; and Tench Coxe, Purveyor of Public Supplies. In 1809, Coxe recommended that 10,000 muskets in the U. S. armories be sold because of their substandard qualities, and Irvine repeatedly took exception to the arms then in production by contractors. He referred to them as faulty in pattern and as "exceedingly defective and exceptionable"; in his eyes the Harpers Ferry and Springfield muskets also were "not as good as they ought to be." Colonel Wadsworth wrote:

> Can it be seriously intended to place that musket on a parallel with a good French musket? If I am not deceived its weight is considerably greater than the average French weight; the barrel is thicker and heavier especially toward the muzzle; the bayonet heavier and clumsier; the bands unnecessarily stout, and this additional weight disposed toward the muzzle so as to carry the center of gravity further from the breech than it exists in the French musket. The consequence is that independent of the additional weight the fatigue of the soldier in handling it is greatly increased and his power over the bayonet materially impaired. I particularly object to the method of fastening the bayonet, which is to be effected by a small screw, perhaps an inch long and weighing only two or three pennyweights. . . . So diminutive is it that by falling out of a soldier's hand on the ground it will be lost. A screw driver must be used to loosen the screw everytime of fixing and unfixing the bayonet. In a short time it would become so loose by wearing as to drop out. I am surprised so faulty a method of securing the bayonet should be resorted to when one infinitely superior is shown in the French musket.[13]

The shortcomings of this musket notwithstanding, the thousand or so soldiers who garrisoned the western border when the War of 1812 broke out depended largely upon the Model of 1795 as their regulation arm.

Model 1812.—The repeated complaints had some effect, for on November 30, 1813, Irvine wrote to his deputy commissaries:

> Experience has shown since the commencement of the war [War of 1812] that an improvement in the quality of our arms is indispensably requisite. To accomplish which I procured a French manufactured musket having all the latest improvements. I consulted practical, ingenious men in whose integrity I could confide, and requested them to point out such alterations from the French musket as they might deem of impor-

tance. I caused a musket to be constructed under the direction of a superior artist, one who had been employed for many years as Master
Armorer at Harpers Ferry [M. T. Wickham]. This musket was forwarded to Washington for examination and approval of the Secretary
of War. I shortly after had the satisfaction to learn that it was approved
of, not only by the Secretary of War, but all the officers of government
resident at Washington, one only excepted, and adopted as the *Standard
Musket* of the United States. . . . It is intended that the locks, bands,
plates and screws of one musket may be fitted to any other musket of
100,000, all the component parts being made precisely on the same
models.[14]

The pattern musket to which Irvine referred was completed in
December, 1812, and the arms which later were copied from it are
referred to as the Model 1812. Some of the contractors who were still
working on their orders of 1808 were requested to incorporate the
changes of 1812 as they completed the arms which were still in work
in their shops. Eli Whitney's product already included most of these
innovations and some other characteristics which the United States
officials later specified as standard. The national armories did not
begin to assemble the parts and produce the finished musket, Model
1812, until 1815.

The U. S. musket, Model 1812, was 57½ inches in total length
(fig. 34, *b*). The barrel was 42 inches long and of .69 caliber; it was
held to the forestock by three bands. The stock (including the forestock) was 54 inches long. The lock plate was 6.37 inches by 1.31
inches; the trigger guard was 11 inches long, with rounded ends. The
rear sling swivel was mounted immediately in front of the trigger
bow. The bayonet had a 15½-inch blade, and it was secured to the
barrel by a device which was presumed to be an improvement over
the earlier method of fastening with a removable screw.

Since Eli Whitney's contract specified that his Model 1812 would
be like "the muskets which the said Whitney hath heretofore manufactured for the State of New York," [15] the Whitney product differed
slightly from the regularly specified pattern in being shorter in barrel
and in total length. The stock had but a slight comb. Details of the
lock—the pan of brass at a slight incline and without fence, the friz-

zen with flared head—were similar to the earlier Whitney muskets, and in these respects were unlike the Model 1812 produced by other contractors and by the public armories.

At the Springfield Armory, a cheek recess was cut in the left side of the butt stock after the fashion of the Charleville musketoon, Model 1777.[16]

In effect, the Model 1812 as manufactured by the government and by private makers provided a somewhat miscellaneous batch of arms which collectively constituted a step toward a new regulation piece. Few, if any, Model 1812 muskets were issued in the West in time to be of service in the War of 1812, but they were distributed very soon thereafter and when available were used wherever regular infantry units and the militia served.

Model 1816.—The next action attempting to increase and improve the armament for infantry came in 1816. This time the Charleville musket, Model 1777, served as the pattern for the lock, a pattern which Eli Whitney had been following for fifteen years. Among the characteristics specified in formal contracts was a stock with straight lines (that is, with little or no comb), another feature which Whitney had adopted, with the approval of the War Department, in 1801. The round-faced cock, inclined brass pan, and frizzen with flared end, typical of the Charleville musket of 1777 and continuously supplied on the Whitney muskets since 1801, were now standard in the specifications written by the government. The new arm was commonly referred to as the Model 1816. It was turned out in both bright and brown finishes. The caliber remained .69, and the barrel was 42 inches long. A heavy screw extended through the stock, holding the barrel tang to the trigger-guard plate. Except for a longer lock plate (6.87 inches), a shorter trigger guard (9.75 inches), and a longer bayonet (16 inches as against 15½ inches), there was no notable difference between the early Model 1816 and many of the Whitney muskets which preceded it.

In 1822 a change was made in the method of attaching the lower (rear) sling swivel; the forward part of the trigger bow was provided with an enlargement which was drilled to receive the sling-swivel rivet. Previously, the sling swivel had been affixed to a stud in front of the trigger bow. Of this change Fuller writes: "This was the outstanding innovation adopted with the model and was the one feature that remained standard for years; it provides reasons why this arm should be designated Model 1822." [17] In the reports and publications of the U. S. Ordnance Department [18] this musket is referred to as the Model 1822, but many recent authorities classify it as a continuation of the Model 1816. It was one of the arms selected by an Ordnance board of 1855 as being worthy of conversion to the percussion system and of being rifled to take the Minié ball. [19]

From 1822 until 1831 the U. S. musket was given a brown finish. Except for the discontinuance of the browning in 1831, [20] no major changes were made in the 1822 type in the twenty-two years that it was produced. Ordnance records reveal that it was manufactured until the end of September, 1844, at government armories. It and its progenitors in the Model 1816 series were in some use everywhere on the western military frontier after 1823; however, it did not supplant entirely the Model 1812 then in the hands of some regular troops and the militia on the border. Lieutenant Colonel Bomford asserted that 36,687 muskets of all descriptions had been shipped to western states and territories in the years 1813–1821. [21]

Model 1840.—In 1831 a U. S. Ordnance board instituted a study of foreign armament with a view to recommending improvements of American weapons. By 1833 a French musket made in 1822 had been selected by this board as the ideal pattern for future U. S. muskets. In the Harpers Ferry Arsenal, pattern muskets were prepared which bore the mark "Model 1835." Not until 1840 [22] was production begun in earnest on this, the last U. S. flintlock musket. [23] In the literature of the U. S. Ordnance Department the arm is referred to as Model 1840, and Fuller [24] points out that in the years between 1835 and 1840 no changes were made in the 1835 specifications; production was based on a new pattern marked "Model 1840." The new arm was manufactured in the Springfield Arsenal and by two contractors, Lemuel Pomeroy of Pittsfield, Massachusetts, and

Daniel Nippes of Mill Creek, Pennsylvania. Production continued at Springfield until 1847 and in the factories of the contractors until 1848.[25] Distribution to troops was limited, and it would appear that the greater part of the output of the Model 1840 was converted to the percussion system before the arms were extensively used in the field. Although there were various inconspicuous mechanical improvements in the new musket, it is unlikely that the soldier made any sharp distinction between the 1822 type and the Model 1840 flintlock. Except that the later model had a longer bayonet with clasp, an increase of three-tenths of a pound in total weight, and a stock with a comb, the two arms looked alike and handled similarly. Mordecai provides full nomenclature for each model and gives comparative dimensions and weights.[26]

The designers of the 1840 model anticipated that the arm would eventually be rifled and made the barrel at the muzzle .03 inches heavier than earlier muskets, in order to facilitate the job of rifling. In 1842 the barrel was rifled and a leaf sight was mounted at its rear end. The resulting rifled musket is known as the Model 1842 flintlock rifle. Even though alteration of the model was in progress at Springfield, the contractors, Lemuel Pomeroy and Daniel Nippes, continued for several years to manufacture the 1840 musket in its original design.

Thus there came to an end the series of models of flintlock muskets made or procured by the U. S. government, a series begun half a century before, in 1798, and numbering in all some 850,000 muskets.

In a review of the history of the U. S. flintlock muskets, probably only technicians, arms historians, and the more technical-minded collectors of old arms will want to find particulars that will enable them to recognize more models than the four which have been identified in the preceding pages. In any large collection of U. S. flintlock muskets the characteristics of the different models are so intergraded that it is impossible to assign an exact date for every individual piece. Ordinarily, however, any flintlock military musket which comes to hand can be ascribed to (1) the Model 1795, which was made during the period 1795–1812; (2) the Model 1812, manufactured from 1813 to 1817; (3) the Model 1816, made from 1817 to 1844; or (4) the Model 1840, produced from 1840 to 1848.[27]

During an eleven-year period in the 1830's and the early 1840's, the War Department issued 93,109 flintlock muskets to the Regular Army and the militia, an average of 8,464 muskets a year. Surprisingly enough, the smallest issue for this period was in 1832, when 264 muskets went to regular troops and 544 went to the militia—this in spite of the increased activity of the Black Hawk War. The "big year" was 1836, when 21,279 muskets were issued to regulars and 10,588 went to the militia.[28] At this time, General Macomb was begging for an increase in the size of the Regular Army,[29] but its actual strength that year was less than 8,000. It may therefore be concluded that most of the 21,279 muskets recorded as issued to the Regular Army and to the Marine Corps were placed in reserve in the several arsenals situated at strategic spots throughout the country and in the more important "permanent" military posts.

In April, 1808, the Congress had enacted a law which authorized the U. S. Ordnance Department to supply arms to the militia of the states and territories. In the trans-Mississippi country, the governors of Arkansas, Iowa, and Missouri [30] found repeated occasions to call out the militia to put down strife between Indians and settlers.

The formula for apportionment of arms to all militia organizations throughout the nation yielded an average annual issue of 5,449 muskets during the decade 1830–1839. At this time, the militia of the Louisiana and Missouri regions, combined, obtained an average annual issue of 262 muskets, a rather inconsequential drain upon the nation's stores.

Performance and safety of muskets.—The process of loading muskets, the accuracy obtainable in shooting them, and the safety measures used to insure the issue of serviceable weapons will be briefly reviewed in the paragraphs that follow.

The manual of arms for the flintlock musket (always termed "firelock" by the Army) did not change in any important way throughout the period.[31] The process of loading the piece entailed placing the hammer at the half cock, opening the pan, removing a cartridge from the cartridge case which the soldier carried at his side, carrying the cartridge (in the right hand) to the mouth, and tearing the paper with the teeth. A priming charge was then poured from the broken cartridge into the open pan and the steel was pulled back, shutting the pan; the butt of the musket was dropped to the ground; the powder was poured from the cartridge into the muzzle and the ball was inserted; the ramrod was drawn and turned end for end and inserted upon the ball and the wadded cartridge paper; these were rammed home with two forceful blows. The ramrod was then withdrawn from the bore, turned with its small end to the first pipe, and forced down to its place under the barrel. The piece was then ready for cocking and firing. Obviously, in loading the long-barreled musket the soldier had to stand erect.[32]

Mahan, a professor at West Point, writing in 1836 stated:

> It is generally admitted that not more than four or five rounds can be fired in two minutes, allowing the men time to aim deliberately; three may be fired in one minute, but at the expense of a good aim. . . . As the point blank of the musket fired with the bayonet off is at about 120 or 130 yards to attain a point at this distance it must be directly aimed at; when it is at a distance short of this the aim must be below it; and when at one over this the aim must be above it.[33]

Mahan's figures indicate that the percentage of hits on a target the size of a company front dropped from 75 per cent at 85 yards over smooth ground to 5 per cent at 510 yards over rough ground. "On ploughed ground," he added, "fire is less effective than on an even, firm surface; in the latter they *ricochet,* and thus attain their mark. Under favorable circumstances about ⅓ of the balls produce their effect in this way."

That the marksmanship of the soldier armed with a flintlock musket, and his personal reliance in his piece, were somewhat desultory is suggested by the foregoing evidence. The idea is given additional weight by further remarks of Professor Mahan: "Beyond 220 yards the effect of the fire is very uncertain. Beyond 450 yards the ball seldom gives a dangerous wound, although the musket fired with an elevation of 4° or 5° will carry from 600 to 700 yards, and with greater elevations over 1000 yards." [34]

Whatever unfavorable impression the inaccuracy of his flintlock musket may have made on the early-day American soldier, contemporary documents would have us believe that he had little reason to worry about the strength and safety of the gun. The contracts of 1798 provided that

> the stocks of the muskets shall be made of well seasoned black walnut timber, when the same can be obtained by the contractor, otherwise of well seasoned tough maple timber; or the United States shall cause to be delivered at [   ], to the party of the Second Part, if the same shall be required—[ONE THOUSAND]—well seasoned black walnut stocks in the rough, as they have been usually received into the public stores, at the rate of twenty-five cents each.[35]

Farmers throughout the eastern states were called upon to supply the seasoned hardwood planks from which contractors sawed the rough stocks. In finished state the stocks had to pass inspection for quality of the wood, "straight grain, well seasoned, and free from sap and worm holes"; for workmanship, "free from splints; that it has not been split and glued up; that the handle [grip] and comb are of the proper size and form; that the stock has the proper fall or crook, and is of the right length," and so on.[36] Sometimes the contractors' inability to obtain seasoned wood caused considerable delay in the manufactories.

The barrels, of course, were safeguarded with particularly rigid specifications. The contracts of 1798 specified that they were

> to be put on the proof rack and fixed and confined so as not to rebound. They are immediately fired twice: the first time with a charge of powder equal in weight to the eighteenth part of a pound avoirdupois, and the second with a charge one fifth less, or the twenty-second part of a pound weight. In both instances a ball of the caliber of the piece is to be put in . . . The powder with which this proof is to be made will be first proved with a five and a half inch mortar, one ounce whereof must propel a twenty-four pound ball eighty yards.[37]

These specifications persisted with little change at least until the Civil War, the only difference in the later proving being the placing of wads in the proving charge: "one on the powder and the other on the ball, and the charge is well rammed with copper rods. The wads occupy when rammed about ¾ inch in the length of the barrel." [38]

To bolster the morale of the musket-shooting soldier or, perhaps, to ease the public conscience, Ordnance offices published the following data on the strength of musket barrels:

> The regulation fixing the duration of small arms in the French Service at 50 years is founded on the durability of the barrel, which is the most important part of those arms. Experience has shown that a musket barrel will bear 25,000 discharges without becoming unserviceable, and even in time of war a musket is not fired more than 500 times a year. The wear caused by firing is therefore small, and the principal cause of the rejection of barrels is the diminution of .09 in the diameter of the breech. With good management and care, that diminution will take place very slowly, and it ought not generally to occur in the space of 50 years. It has been ascertained by direct trials, that the strength of the barrel furnishes every requisite security against the accidents of service and the want of care on the part of the soldier; and that even after being reduced in diameter .09 inch at the breech, it is still perfectly safe against the effect of the charge. In experiments made in 1806, barrels reduced .13 inch at the breech, bore a double and triple charge with one ball, or two cartridges placed one over the other.
>
> Other trials were made in 1829 at the manufactory of Mutzig, on arms sent there for repairs, which had been a greater or less time in the hands of troops. They furnish the following results:
>
> 1st. When a musket barrel is charged with a single cartridge, placed in any part of it, or with 2 or even 3 cartridges inserted regularly without any interval between them, there is no danger of bursting; with 4 cartridges inserted regularly over each other, or with 2 or even 3 cartridges placed over each other with slugged balls (or balls driven in, as in a rifle) there is danger only in case of some defect in fabrication, or some deterioration in the barrel. With more than 4 cartridges inserted regularly one over another, or with 2, 3 and 4 cartridges with intervals between them, it is not safe to fire.
>
> 2nd. No danger of bursting is occasioned by leaving a ball screw in the barrel. There may be danger from a plug of wood driven tight into the muzzle, when the barrel has been loaded with 2 cartridges; or from a cork rammed into the barrel to a certain distance from the charge with another cartridge over it.

Snow, clay and sand, which may be accidentally introduced into the barrel are not dangerous, if they lie close to the charge; but they are so when there is a space between them and the charge; in this case sand is more dangerous than clay and snow.

Balls or pieces of iron inserted over the charge were not attended with danger when placed close to the charge, even when their weight amounted to 1¼ lb.; but there is danger from a piece of iron .5 inch square, weighing ¼ lb., if placed 20 inches or more from the breech.

3d. A barrel with a defect which might have escaped the inspector at the armory, bore the explosion of three cartridges, regularly inserted. After mutilation which may have caused a reduction of metal in some parts, it may still be used without danger.

Finally, the diminutions of exterior diameter which may be produced in ordinary service are never sufficient to be dangerous. In these trials, barrels originally .272 inch thick at the breech, did not burst when loaded with 2 cartridges until the thickness was reduced to .169 inch, and with one cartridge to .091 inch.[39]

This queer testing may seem silly, today, but actually it was based on a sound understanding of the peculiar psychology of troops in combat. A report on the use of muzzle-loaders in battles of the Civil War period clearly shows that the test procedures were justified:

The official report of the examination of the arms collected upon the battlefield of Gettysburg states that of the whole number received (27,575) we found at least 24,000 of these loaded; about one-half of these contained two loads, each; one-fourth from three to ten loads, each, and the balance one load each. In many of these guns from two to six balls have been found with only one charge of powder. In some the balls have been found at the bottom of the bore with the charge of powder on top of the ball. In some as many as six paper regulation caliber-58 cartridges have been found, the cartridges having been put in the guns without being torn or broken. Twenty-three loads were found in one Springfield rifle-musket, each loaded in regular order. Twenty-two balls and sixty-two buckshot with a corresponding quantity of powder all mixed up together were found in one percussion smooth-bore musket.

In many of the smooth-bore guns, Model of 1842, Rebel make, we have found a wad of loose paper between the powder and ball and another wad of the same kind on top of the ball, the ball having been put in the gun naked. About six thousand of the [Confederate] arms were found loaded with Johnson and Dow's cartridges; many of these cartridges were about half way down in the barrels of the guns, and in many cases the ball end of the cartridge had been put into the gun first. These cartridges were found mostly in the Enfield rifle-musket.[40]

The assurance that the barrels of the military muskets were very strong probably was well founded. Contemporary accounts of field experiences by trappers and traders contain numerous references to the explosions of light muskets in the hands of Indians and civilians (see chap. iii), but in the literature of the day there is little mention of similar accidents with military muskets.

MUSKETOONS AND CARBINES

Mounted troops were employed to some extent throughout the early years of military action in America. "Carbines" for the use of troopers are mentioned by the General Court as early as 1675. Cavalry served during the Revolution and on the western frontiers from the 1790's until the 1830's. Volunteer mounted units usually known as rangers were raised at several times in the Louisiana-Missouri section. They were reorganized into the 1st Dragoons of the Regular Army in 1833.[41]

Traditionally, mounted troops carried saber, pistols, and a shoulder weapon much shorter than the regulation musket or rifle. On the frontier, the mounted volunteers were commonly armed with rifles.[42] Since the seventeenth century the arm of the cavalryman in Europe had been the musketoon, or carabine. During the Revolution and for a decade or so thereafter, American forces had obtained a small supply of French flintlock musketoons,[43] and these weapons continued to be used by some artillerymen and rangers throughout the early years of the U. S. Army. They were not available in numbers adequate to permit mass issues to troop units that might use short-barreled muskets; therefore, in 1813 an attempt was made to meet the demand by sawing off ten inches of the barrels of about six thousand regulation muskets, Model 1795. As mentioned earlier, the results were not satisfactory, and within two years the modified muskets were disposed of. From time to time, special short-barreled and light muskets were specified and manufactured by the Ordnance Department; but they were not made in large quantities, and it can be said that there was no large production of U. S. military arms in the carbine class until after 1833, when Hall's carbine was requisitioned by the War Department.

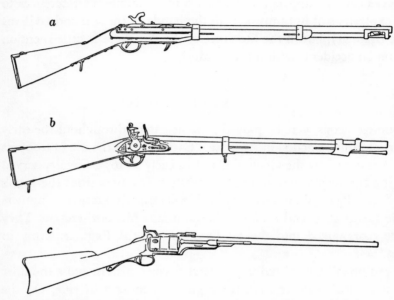

Fig. 35. U. S. carbines and musketoons. *a,* U. S. carbine (Hall's), Model 1833. The first percussion arm adopted by the War Dept., it was manufactured both as a rifled piece and as a smoothbore. (From Mordecai, 1861.) *b,* U. S. musketoon, Model 1839. One of the last of the flintlock muskets. Note the ramrod 25.7 in. long, with the trumpet-shaped end. (From U. S. Ordnance Dept., 1841.) *c,* Colt's revolving carbine, Model 1837. The loading lever appears on the right side of the frame. The 6-chambered cylinder is marked "Ormsby." This Paterson Colt is in the Milwaukee Museum (no. N4149).

Hall carbine, Model 1833.—The Hall carbine, illustrated in figure 35, *a,* had been preceded by the Hall rifle, Model 1819, which was a breech-loading flintlock that had been tested from 1813 to 1816 and first manufactured on a production basis in 1824. That piece and Hall's career are discussed in the section "United States Rifles." The breech-loading arm was an innovation in the fixed military picture, but the Hall mechanism had withstood attacks of the die-hards and was quite firmly established in Army usage by the time (1833) that dragoons became a part of the regular U. S. forces. In order that the mounted regiment might be equipped with a weapon especially suited to its needs, a smoothbore arm of rifle caliber was devised which had a barrel about twenty-six inches long. Another novelty which distinguished the model was its employment of the percussion system; it was the first cap-and-ball gun to be adopted by the War Department.

The contractor, Simeon North, already engaged in manufacturing Hall rifles, made models of the carbine in 1833 at the request of the War Department. R. V. Mason, Major of the newly established Dragoons, subjected the pattern guns to testing. On June 3, 1833, he wrote to Colonel George Bomford of the Ordnance Corps:

> After making a trial of the new gun proposed for the Dragoons, I find that it shoots a ball with more force and accuracy than either the French carbine or Harpers Ferry musket, but its caliber prooves too small for buck shot, carrying only a half-ounce ball. . . . In point of accuracy and close shooting, the French carbine and the Harpers Ferry musket bear no comparison to this new gun. I can, at the distance of 100 yards with this gun, put more balls in a small target in 20 shots than either of the others can in fifty. In firing the new gun I find that the recoil with a full charge is scarcely perceptible; while that of the French carbine and musket is so great that one man can not fire more than a few shots.[44]

Simeon North was awarded a contract for 1,000 carbines at $20.00 each. Because of the immediate demand for the new weapon, North rushed his first order and made deliveries in January and May, 1834.[45] Seven hundred fifty of these arms were at once placed in the hands of the dragoons then organizing at Jefferson Barracks and Fort Gibson. Numerous reports attest to the use of the carbines by dragoons and other military parties.[46] Todd reproduces the painting by Fritz Kredel which shows a mustachioed dragoon astride his horse and equipped with a full field accouterment.[47] The carbine is carried alongside the mounted man's right thigh, its down-pointing muzzle supported in a leather cup at one end of a sling, and its grip held within the loop of the sling strap which passes to the pommel and ends close to the soldier's right hand. Incidentally, after 1837 the Hall carbine was manufactured with a sliding-ring sling attachment similar to the traveling-ring device used on the French flintlock musketoon, Model 1766.

The records of the Ordnance Office indicate that 18,858 Hall carbines were manufactured at Harpers Ferry and in the shops of the contractor Simeon North from 1834 through 1843. During those years, 7,920 of these arms were issued to regular troops, and some 3,000 went to the militia. In the nine-year period (1844–1852) following the period with which this book is concerned, the total production was 28,858.[48]

North made at least one hundred carbines with rifled barrels for the State of Alabama. This model was modified in 1836, and after that year it became known as the "U. S. rifle carbine, Model 1836." [49] North was awarded a contract for 2,500 of these rifled arms.[50] Two thousand more carbines were made at Harpers Ferry in 1837 and 1840, in the flintlock system, which were of musket caliber and smoothbore.[51] These stands had the sliding-ring sling attachment. The change in caliber may have been made in response to the recommendation made by Major R. V. Mason of the Dragoons in 1833: "From the experiments made today, I am clearly of the opinion that by increasing the caliber to carry 24 balls to the pound [.58 cal.] it will be sufficiently large for buckshot and answer every purpose for which it is intended." Finished model pieces in the larger caliber were prepared in the North shops, as indicated by North's letter of December 24, 1838, addressed to Colonel Bomford.[52] A "Hall's carbine, musket caliber" was one of the guns tested in the trials conducted at the Washington Arsenal in 1839, but it was tested with 90 and 100 grains of powder—"charges too great for service." [53] In the early 1840's, the Harpers Ferry Arsenal went back to the smaller bore and adopted a 21-inch barrel. These stands were made with percussion locks.

The early type represented by the specimen shown in figure 35, *a,* was made in both rifle and musket calibers (.54 and .69). The piece shown has a 26½-inch barrel provided with a knife-blade front sight. The ramrod is 24¼ inches long.

The method of loading the Hall was unique. A pull on the lever in front of the trigger guard released a spring catch under the receiver, causing its forward end to spring upward until its opening was above the frame. Into the chamber thus exposed was poured the charge of 75 grains of rifle powder. On top of this, the half-ounce ball was seated by the simple process of inserting it in the bore of the receiver and forcing it down with the thumb. The tilted receiver was then pressed back into its place in alignment with the barrel, where it was held securely in place by the pressure of its shoulders against the chocks in the two side straps, and by the spring catch under the frame. Since the barrel was bored to .52 caliber and the ball was .525, there could be no misplacement of the ball until it was driven forward against the lands of the rifling by the explosion of the powder charge. Loading was completed by placing the percussion cap upon the nipple, which is to be seen under the cocked hammer. The piece was then ready for firing.[54]

As one might expect, so radical an innovation stirred up controversy in the War Department. A board of Ordnance officers reported very favorably on the Hall for use by mounted troops (see section "United States Rifles"), in 1837. But nine years later another board reported adversely on all breech-loading weapons:

> After duly considering the subject the Board has the honor to report that there have been innumerable trials made of arms loading at the breech. The principal advantages of these kinds of arms are a greater and more exact range with less recoil . . . unfortunately, these advantages appear difficult to obtain, combined with sufficient solidity, simplicity, and durability. . . . The general objections: want of solidity of the parts most exposed to the action of the charge, the liability of the movable parts to become unserviceable by their getting fast from rust or dirt deposited at each discharge, and the escape of the gas through the joints or junctions of the different parts. The defects inherent to this method of loading have been such that . . . [it] has not been adopted for arming troops in any country, except partially in this, nor has it been brought into general use, for other purposes.[55]

Lieutenant Colonel H. K. Craig, Chief of the Ordnance Department, pressed this report on the Adjutant General of the Army and added his personal remarks:

> No time of any consequence is saved by loading at the breech; indeed when the pieces become foul the gun loading at the muzzle can be fired with more quickness, and it is infinitely better in all respects. I have never yet seen a gun that loaded at the breech that was not more liable to accidents than the whole barrel, and I am convinced that eventually these "broken back" guns will be pronounced imperfect and discarded altogether. The stocks of Hall's carbine that we now have in use are continually splitting and flying in all directions. The facts and views thus elicited led to the adoption of the present cavalry musketoon, an arm with a whole barrel and a swivel for its ramrod. If it be not a suitable arm for cavalry, I know not where to look for one that will answer.[56]

In keeping with the attitude displayed by Lieutenant Colonel Craig and beginning with 1846, the old-time cavalry-type musketoons were manufactured and issued in ever-increasing numbers in an attempt to meet the demands created by the Mexican War. In the years following that war, the production and use of this type of gun, together with the Colt's arms, far exceeded the production of the Hall carbine. After 1852, the Hall carbine was no longer made, but it did remain in service even after the U. S. rifled carbine, Model 1855 (.58 cal. using the Minié bullet) came into use. In 1857, more than three thousand of the regulation U. S. pistols with carbine butt were placed in the hands of mounted soldiers. Also in that year, the Sharp's carbine made its appearance in the U. S. Cavalry equipment, and the Burnsides and Merrills arms were under experimentation by the Army. The Hall carbine, although issued in small numbers through the 1860's, went into an eclipse.

G. Talcott, Chief of Ordnance, in explaining the decline of the Hall carbine, addressed the Secretary of War as follows:

> Jan. 14, 1845. The United States long since adopted Hall's rifles, after such trials as appeared to satisfy all objections, and that they were overcome is fully shown by the reports and statements made. The First Regiment of Dragoons when first raised was armed with carbines of this model, and they received the most unqualified approbation. How is it

that the opinion of their utility has recently been changed? It is because no attention has been paid to keep the arms in the hands of troops in good condition, nor have the soldiers been properly instructed to use them. Neglecting to keep the joint closed, a blast has been suffered to exist and ruin the stocks. I am practically acquainted with the use of Hall's arms, and assert unqualifiedly that if my honor and life were at stake and depended on the use of firearms I would sooner take one of these carbines than any other weapon. But fashions change and what is good today will be cried down tomorrow. Upon due consideration of the subject the department decided on abandoning the manufacture of breech-loading arms, and have followed in the steps of the great powers of Europe, deciding that a diversity of arms was productive of evil, and adopting those of ordinary construction which are the simplest and easiest managed by the common soldier.[57]

Even as early as 1858, Lieutenant C. M. Wilcox, a U. S. Army observer in Europe, in referring to American breechloaders, completely ignored the Hall arms and their history.[58] Nevertheless, this carbine, the first percussion arm for the U. S. Army, cut a mighty swath in the tradition of military arms in America, and in spite of its shortcomings, the story of its twenty years of use in the Cavalry seems eminently worth the telling.

U. S. musketoon, Model 1839.—In 1839, patterns were made at Harpers Ferry for a .69 caliber musketoon which had a 26-inch barrel and a lock of the type used on the Model 1840 musket. The specimen shown in figure 35, *b,* is 41 inches long and weighs 7 pounds 3 ounces. The lock, barrel, and all mountings were given a bright finish. The front sight is a brass knife blade. On both butt plate and lock is the mark "US." In the reports of the Ordnance Department little light is thrown upon this, the last of the flintlock musketoons, but it is given a place in the 1841 *Ordnance Manual.* The text says of it:

This model is similar to that of the musket of 1840. The parts are the same, omitting the bayonet and the middle band and band spring, and observing that one swivel is on the lower band and the other near the butt of the stock, on a plate fastened by 2 wood screws; the lower band and the swivel plate have studs for attaching the swivels. The regular bayonet model (1840) may be used with it if occasion requires.[59]

Special flintlock muskets.—The Springfield Armory in 1809 and 1810 made 1,202 33½-inch-barrel, .56 caliber muskets. They had underpin fastenings in place of bands, and there was no provision for a bayonet. Nine hundred and fifty of these light muskets were still in the armory in 1830. It is presumed that these guns were made for distribution to Indians, but they were not welcomed by the tribes. On January 24, 1830, George Bomford of the Ordnance Department inquired into the practicability of putting them to use as cadet muskets, and some were so used.[60] A special musket of .69 caliber, with a 33½-inch barrel, held by two bands, was made at Springfield in 1816. One hundred and twenty-six stands were produced; their use is not recorded. In 1818–1821 about fourteen hundred special flintlock muskets of .69 caliber and with a 36-inch barrel were made at Springfield, and some of them were put to use at West Point. Colonel Wordsworth's orders to Lieutenant Colonel R. Lee at Springfield specified that this arm should be exactly in the pattern of the Model 1816 musket except for length of barrel. On September 3, 1821, Bomford wrote to Lee directing him to discontinue making these short muskets. "The number already made is greater than will ever be required by the cadets." [61] This musket is sometimes referred to as the "Artillery musket, 1817." It weighed about ten pounds, a weight which proved to be too great for cadets. A gun of .54 caliber was designed proportionately smaller than the standard musket but was like the Model 1816 in general appearance. The barrel was 36 inches long, and the total weight was 7½ to 8 pounds. Three hundred of these were made at Springfield. The arm is referred to as the "U. S. Cadet musket, Model 1830"; it was the first regulation cadet musket.[62]

In summary: the U. S. special light-weight, short-barrel muskets and musketoons recognized above are: (1) the 1809–1810 shotgun of .56 caliber; (2) the sawed-off 1795 muskets improvised in 1813; (3) the 1816 musket of .69 caliber, with a 33-inch barrel; (4) the 1818–1821 "Artillery musket" with a 36-inch barrel; (5) the Cadet musket, Model 1830; and (6) the U.S. musketoon, Model 1839. A flintlock carbine which is inconspicuous in government records but which turns up occasionally in collections is the W. L. Evans arm reported to have been made for the U. S. Navy. Serven figures a specimen of which he writes, "Lock marked 'W. L. Evans—v. FORGE USN 1831.' The 24½" barrel is held to the stock by two brass bands." [63]

Colt revolving carbine.—The War Department purchased 160 carbines in 1841 like the one shown in figure 35, *c*. The "1842" marked on the frame of this specimen identifies it as one of the last to be made in the Paterson factory. It is a .52 caliber piece with a 23⅞-inch round, rifled barrel. The total length is 43 inches and the weight 10½ pounds. The six-chambered cylinder is revolved by the cocking action.

UNITED STATES RIFLES

The rifle-shooting forefathers of the United States Army established traditions which would of course guarantee the adoption of the rifle among the earliest of American military arms. Frontiersmen armed with the Pennsylvania-Kentucky rifle had distinguished themselves in the Revolution,[64] and in 1792 a battalion of riflemen was organized within the very young U. S. Army. The rifles for this battalion were purchased by the government from some of the well-known Pennsylvania rifle makers. These long-barreled, comparatively small caliber flintlocks and their progenitors "changed the whole course of world history, made possible the settlement of a continent, and ultimately freed our country of foreign domination." [65]

This sweeping assertion of John Dillin does not go unchallenged by the military historian. Harold L. Peterson in his manuscript "American Colonial Arms and Armor" provides a fair and convincing account of the status—or lack of status—of the rifle in the American Army of Revolutionary times. It is a fact that the rifles in use during the Revolution were few in comparison with the number of muskets which records show were used by the great majority of the 300,000 men who fought the British. Battle tactics of the day required that opposing forces meet in mass formations and that engagements take place at close quarters. The prime requisites for small arms under such circumstances were facility in loading and a bayonet for hand-to-hand fighting. The rifle available to the Revolutionary soldier did not meet these requirements. However, a succession of special circumstances developed during the War which enabled American riflemen to harass the enemy and, on a few occasions, to win phenomenal victories by virtue of their Indian-warrior tactics and the long-range accuracy of their arms. The psychological effects of these American successes were felt by both the enemy and the musket-shooting Americans. That the American rifle was superior to all other small arms was the belief of many people in all parts of the world soon after the end of the Revolution. The several demonstrations made by American backwoodsmen during this conflict and in the War of 1812 played a notable part in hurrying the day when armies everywhere would make greater use of rifled arms.

U. S. rifle, Model 1803.—The first regulation U. S. rifle was produced at Harpers Ferry early in 1803. Although reports of the Ordnance Department indicate that the pattern rifle was made in 1804,[66] substantial evidence exists that actual production started earlier. Henry Dearborn of the War Department wrote in 1803:

> I have had such convincing proof of the advantage of short rifles over the long ones (commonly used) in actual service as to have no doubt in my mind of preferring the short rifle, with larger calibers than the long ones usually have and with stiff steel ramrods instead of wooden ones. The great facility which such rifles afford in charging, in addition to their being less liable to become foul by firing, gives a decided advantage to men of equal skill and dexterity over those armed with the common long rifle.[67]

Dearborn specified that the barrel of the proposed new rifle should not exceed 33 inches and that it should carry a ball of one-thirtieth of a pound weight, about .54 caliber.

> The barrels shall be round from the muzzle to within ten inches of the Britch, and not of an unnecessary thickness, especially in the round part. The stock shall not extend further than the tail pipe; from thence to within three inches of the muzzle an iron rib should be substituted for that part of the stock. The mountings should be brass. There should be at least 2000 of these rifles made . . .[68]

It is known also that in 1803 the Lewis and Clark party obtained a few pieces of this model.

The first lot of the Model 1803 was manufactured at Harpers Ferry from 1803 through 1807. The number of stands requisitioned by the War Department in 1804 was 4,000. Colonel Bomford of the Ordnance Department in a report on November 30, 1822, indicates that 4,023 were made during the five years of this first production. When Colonel John Whiting inspected the Harpers Ferry Armory in March, 1810, he found in the stores at that place 188 "long rifles" and 3,113 Harpers Ferry Model 1803. Satterlee accounts for 4,965 produced before 1808.[69]

The load for the arm is described as 90 to 100 grains of fine-grained rifle powder, loaded into a paper cartridge with a half-ounce (.54 cal.) ball. The bullet was wrapped in linen or encased in a thin leather or bladder patch well greased with tallow.[70] With the heavier load the recoil is recorded to have been "tremendous."

Tench Coxe, Purveyor of Public Supplies, took violent exception to many features of the arm. He advocated that the rib under the barrel be done away with and that the half stock be replaced by a full stock. He anticipated that the iron ramrod would damage the rifling and advocated that the rod be tipped with brass. He wanted future rifles to have 38-inch barrels. He found the mechanism of the lock too cramped within the small space available to it; the sear, in his opinion, was

> so sharp at the point that there is danger of it flying especially in severe dry frost. . . . The plate through which the trigger passes is brass, which will too soon wear out where the female screw thread passes and so become loose. . . . The butt-box for the wiper, flint and Rag is made to open by a pin near the bottom of the butt where it is liable to be struck by stones and stumps and opened. . . . The cock is flat, thin and not strong. . . . Cock screw is very weak in the shank. . . . Cuts in the screw heads are not well made to admit a driver.[71]

The objections of Coxe notwithstanding, the Model 1803 continued in production with no change in basic design for another seven or eight years.

The War of 1812 served to enlarge the good reputation of the rifle and brought about a plan to create three new regiments of riflemen. In 1813, four pattern rifles were made which for all practical purposes were the same as the arms made from 1803 through 1807; and in 1814 the Harpers Ferry Arsenal began making a second lot of the rifles of the 1803 design. The Springfield Armory also manufactured parts for this rifle in 1814.[72] Henry Deringer and Robert Johnson contracted in 1814 to make the improved version of this arm, and fifty-one rifles were completed by Deringer,[73] but both Johnson and Deringer later changed over to the Model 1817 rifle in accordance with instructions from the War Department.

Some of the rifles made in 1814 had 36-inch barrels but were otherwise similar to the basic specifications of 1803. As a matter of fact, some of the specimens made in 1807 and earlier also had 36-inch barrels. Actually, there is considerable variation among the examples available for study. The barrel ranges in length from 32 to 36 inches, the octagonal part from 11 to 13 inches, and occasional specimens are equipped with a set trigger. The half stock, iron rib, semipistol-grip trigger guard, flat-faced cock, curved butt plate, and brass furniture seem to be consistent characteristics, as is the caliber, .54. No provision was ever made for attaching a bayonet to this model.

Satterlee gives statistics regarding the production of the Model 1803 through 1818. In existing collections there are specimens which bear the date 1819, and Bomford's report of November 30, 1822, leads to the conclusion that the model continued in production through 1819.[74] In all, 19,726 U. S. rifles, Model 1803, are accounted for in the Ordnance records.[75]

The specimen shown in figure 36, *a,* is typical. The 35-inch barrel is rifled with seven grooves and is of .54 caliber. The letters "US" and the head of an eagle over the letter "P" are stamped on the barrel, which is octagonal at the breech. The bright-finished lock plate is marked, in front of the flat-faced cock, with an eagle and a shield enclosing the letters "US"; behind the cock appear the words "Harpers Ferry 1818." The butt is curved to fit the shoulder and has a large patch box with a brass cover. All mountings are brass. The bright

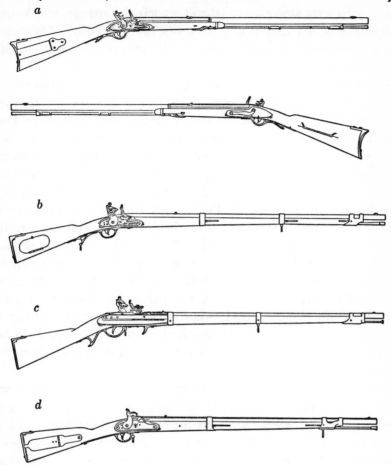

Fig. 36. U. S. rifles. *a,* U. S. rifle, Model 1803 (flintlock), two views; Nunnemacher Collection, Milwaukee Museum (no. N2184). *b,* U. S. rifle, Model 1817, flintlock (the "common rifle"); Nunnemacher Collection, Milwaukee Museum (no. N3439). *c,* U. S. rifle (Hall), Model 1819, flintlock, breechloader; Milwaukee Museum. *d,* U. S. rifle, Model 1841, percussion; Harold's Club, Reno, Nev.

steel ramrod is carried below an iron rib which extends under the barrel from the end of the half stock to within three inches of the muzzle. The trigger guard is extended to form a semipistol grip.

Colonel Gluckman is of the opinion that some of the barrels of these arms were smoothbore when they left the armory, and known specimens which lack rifling may support this idea.[76] Also, some early inventories list "smoth" (*sic*) Model 1803 rifles; that is, smoothbore arms of .54 caliber.

Since the Lewis and Clark party had obtained some of the earliest pieces, it is from their reports of 1804–1806 that we get the first accounts of the behavior of the Model 1803 on the target range. During the winter of 1803–1804, while the party was encamped opposite the mouth of the Missouri River, some of the twenty-six enlisted men with the expedition kept a practicing party on the rifle range firing one round daily, "off-hand," at fifty yards. The journals kept by Meriwether Lewis and William Clark are replete with stories of hunting adventures experienced by the party while en route to the Pacific and on their way back. The rifle gave a good account of itself except when fired into a half-ton of grizzly bear. A good summary of the Lewis and Clark encounters with grizzly bears is contained in Bakeless. After a number of experiences in riddling charging grizzlies with rifle bullets, Lewis observed, "These bear being so hard to die rather intimedates us all; I must confess that I do not like the gentlemen and had reather fight two Indians than one bear." [77]

It is likely that the rifles carried by Zebulon Pike's men (one sergeant, two corporals, and sixteen privates) on their expedition into the far Southwest, 1806–1807, were the Model 1803. At South Park in Colorado, Pike wrote: "Bursted one of our rifles which was a great loss as it made three guns which had bursted and the five which had been broken on the march. One of my men is now armed with my sword and pistols." [78] The Lewis and Clark party also had trouble with broken rifles, but extra parts were carried with which to make repairs.

The party of Major S. H. Long on the trip to the Rockies in 1819 was accompanied by some riflemen. Long in his journal states that the soldiers were armed with the "yauger, or rifle gun." [79] On the Arkansas three of the men "went over the hill" on the night of August

30 and took with them some of the first specimens of the Model 1803 to enter into civilian use.

Regiments of regular Infantry often had "light" companies within their make-up, and it was customary to arm these special companies with rifles. Philip St. George Cooke, then a lieutenant with the 6th Infantry, tells of traveling in 1829 from Jefferson Barracks to the Arkansas with four companies of the 6th as escort for a party of Santa Fe traders. Except for one "light" company armed with the "half-stocked" (Model 1803 rifle), his command carried muskets. In Cooke's view, his riflemen had the respect of the hostile Indians whom they encountered on several occasions. While traveling between Fort Leavenworth and Council Bluffs in 1831, Cooke killed a doe at a distance of a hundred yards with a service rifle. He also "shot a curlew sixty yards off hand with a rifle ball. The bird's bill was more than four inches long and the size of a rye straw." [80]

In addition to the pieces that were taken into the West on the shoulders of marching riflemen, 2,429 rifles were shipped from Pittsburgh to western states and territories in the period 1813–1821. By the time that the Model 1817 was issued, the Model 1803 had been carried through the country which later became the states of South Dakota, Kansas, Nebraska, Colorado, New Mexico, Oklahoma, Arkansas, and Texas, and to a large degree had supplanted the traditional long rifle in the West, so far as the regular Army was concerned.[81] So many rifles of this model were in use, both in the frontier regions and in the settled country east of the Mississippi, that it can be assumed that civilians along the lines of march became interested in it.

In general, this first regulation U. S. rifle, of which nearly 20,000 were manufactured, had a certain influence upon subsequent American weapons. It led the way to the "common rifle," or U. S. Model 1817, and its handiness and pleasing lines inspired private makers to copy some of its features as they manufactured the "plains" or "mountain" type of sporting rifle, the weapon which for a quarter of a century was the first choice of the mountain man.

That the Army did not discard the Model 1803, even in its later years, is evidenced by the fact that 67 stands were issued to regular troops in 1836. At this time there were not less than 15,000 Model 1817 rifles in store.

U. S. rifle, Model 1817.—While the Model 1803 was still being manufactured at the Harpers Ferry Arsenal and in the shops of Henry Deringer, a new model of rifle was designed by the Ordnance Office. Nine pattern rifles were made at Harpers Ferry in 1818, and two more were produced in 1819.

Deringer, on March 17, 1814, had entered into a contract to supply 2,000 Model 1803 rifles, improved by changes prescribed by Marine T. Wickham, Armorer at Harpers Ferry. As has been explained, Deringer had made but 51 stands under this contract when his agreement was modified so as to make it pertain to the Model 1817 rifle.[82] Robert Johnson of Middletown, Connecticut, also had contracted, in November, 1814, to make the improved Model 1803; but before he had manufactured any, his agreement was changed to cover the Model 1817. Both Deringer and Johnson made deliveries (2,340 rifles) in 1822. Records of the Ordnance Department show that some 18,000 stands were ordered from four contractors between 1821 and 1823.[83]

Deringer was instructed to make his deliveries to the U. S. Arsenal in Philadelphia; the other three contractors made deliveries in Middletown. By 1830, 25,539 stands had been supplied, and then came a lapse of seven years. Between 1837 and 1842, due to demands of the Seminole War, an additional 3,079 were manufactured.[84] The total number of Model 1817 rifles accounted for by the production and procurement records of the Ordnance Department was thus 28,618. This figure is rather nicely balanced by the total number recorded as issued to regular troops and to the militia. The annual reports of the Ordnance Department up to and including 1842 show that 7,198 of these rifles (always referred to by Ordnance officers as the "common rifle") were issued to regular troops and 21,275 to the militia —a total of 28,473. The greatest demand for the rifle came during the period 1836–1840. As a matter of fact, this arm was issued to regular troops for the first time in 1836. The militia had used it, however, since 1829. S. N. D. and R. H. North report some interesting correspondence concerning the details of design, manufacture, and proof of this rifle.[85]

This weapon as specified was .54 caliber, like its predecessor. It differed from it, however, in having a round barrel 36 inches long, a full stock held by three bands, a grip slightly larger in diameter than that of the Model 1803, an oval patch box of iron, a sling swivel on a projecting arm behind the bow of the trigger guard, and a brass-tipped ramrod. The butt plate did not curve to fit the shoulder. As in the Model 1803, the pan was brass, but most of the other parts were iron. The cock was round-faced, and the lock was like the 1816 musket lock but smaller. Sling swivels were fastened to the semipistol grip and to the second band. The admonitions of Tench Coxe in 1811, previously quoted, apparently were heeded in part, at least, when this rifle was designed. Figure 36, *b,* shows a Model 1817 rifle bearing the inspection mark *M* (of Justin Murphy?) over the letter *P.* On the lock plate is an eagle and "R. Johnson US Middn. Conn." Behind the cock is the date, "1821."

Model 1819 (Hall breechloader).—John H. Hall of Yarmouth, Maine, in 1811 invented and patented a method of loading flintlock muskets, rifles, and pistols at the breech. For a few years he manufactured his breechloaders for sporting use in a plant which he built in Portland, Maine. It is not surprising that he should have attempted to sell his invention to the United States government; the astonishing aspect of his history is that he *did* sell it. By virtue of his ingenuity and sincerity he overcame the deep-seated opposition of the military to breechloaders and in 1813 arranged for Army tests of his arms. The Ordnance Department was impressed by the possibilities they presented.

In a letter of January 24, 1815, addressed to Colonel Bomford of the U. S. Ordnance Bureau, Hall stated, "I invented the improvement [in method of loading] in 1811, being at that time but little acquainted with rifles, and being perfectly ignorant of any method whatever of loading guns at the breech." [86] The weapons spoke for themselves, however, and in 1816 further government trials were conducted. One hundred Hall rifles were purchased and were issued to a company of riflemen, who were enthusiastic about the performance of the new arm. In association with William Thornton of Washington, D.C., Hall devised a means of obtaining a tighter closure of the breech, and in 1819 the rifle was adopted officially by the U. S. government.

Under the terms of his contract, Hall was employed at the Harpers Ferry Armory as assistant armorer at a salary of $60.00 a month. He supervised the making and installation of the necessary machinery, and by 1823 the plant went to work on the first 1,000 rifles. Hall received a royalty of $1.00 a rifle. On completion of the first 1,000 in 1824 (the cost was $20.59 a rifle), a second work order for 1,000 rifles was issued. This lot was finished in 1827 at a cost of $17.82 a rifle. The U. S. Congress became inquisitive regarding the Hall setup, and a committee conducted an investigation of the expenses involved and the procedure followed.[87] The findings were favorable to the continuance of manufacture of rifles by Hall.

Further tests of the efficiency of the Hall gun were conducted in 1825. One of the rifles was fired 7,186 times, and as a check a U. S. musket was fired 7,061 times. The Hall rifle was demonstrated to be superior in every way, from durability to rapidity of fire and accuracy. In 1825, two companies of "regulars" stationed at Fortress Monroe were armed with the Hall in order that it might be subjected to further trials. After two years of this use, the committee of the staff of the school at Fortress Monroe reported "its perfect conviction of the superiority of this arm over every other kind of small arm now in use." [88] Production continued at Harpers Ferry in 1828, and arrangements were made for a further supply to be obtained from the factory of Simeon North at Middletown, Connecticut. North's contract for 5,000 Hall rifles at $17.50 each was dated December 15, 1828.

Interchangeability of parts was a feature of Hall's work at Harpers Ferry, and "perfect uniformity of the respective component parts" was a requirement written into the North contract. Interchangeability of parts was not new to the North establishment, but it was an innovation in the public armory. A second contract for 4,000 Hall rifles was entered into by North in 1835. Upon completion of this order and until his death in 1852, North manufactured only the Hall carbine, an arm which has already been covered in this chapter. His total production of Hall rifles was 9,000. At Harpers Ferry the Hall rifle continued in production until 1844, by which date 22,870 stands had been manufactured. Hall died in 1841. In addition to his salary and certain expense allowances during his twenty-two years of employment, he or his estate had received $20,220.00 in royalties on his arms.

The rifle shown in figure 36, *c,* is a well-balanced piece 53.12 inches long, with a barrel 32.62 inches long. The chamber is .54 caliber; the .52 caliber sixteen-grooved barrel is slightly funnel-shaped where the chamber fits against it. The piece weighs 10 pounds 4 ounces without bayonet. The stock is black walnut. Stamped on the breech block is "J. H. Hall, H. Ferry U.S. 1832." The breech piece containing the chamber is raised for loading by pulling back the projecting lever in front of the trigger guard. Hall personally wrote the following description:

> The gun consists of a receiver which contains the charge, and to which the lock is attached. The receiver has two shoulders near the muzzle end, by which it is kept to the barrel and is prevented from recoiling when it is discharged; these shoulders bear against the casehardened chocks placed behind the shoulders. But no direct support is given by the butt-piece behind the receiver, nor by the axis-pin on which the receiver turns; on the contrary, the receiver does not even touch the butt-piece; a vacancy is left between that and the end of the receiver to freely permit all the expansion which takes place in the receiver as it grows warm with repeated discharges, viz: all the expansion from the back part of the shoulders to the back end of the receiver. That expansion which takes place forward of the shoulders is provided for in the joint where the receiver meets the barrel. The holes in the receiver through which the axis pin passes are made long for the same purpose, viz: to freely admit of expansion in the afterpart of the receiver. The bore of the barrel increases gradually in size toward the breech beginning about one foot from the muzzle and enlarging very rapidly the last ½ inch next to the re-

ceiver somewhat in the form of a trumpet so as to be rather larger at the butt than the bore of the receiver.[89]

It may be added that Hall's rifling differed from the usual rifling in that there were sixteen grooves. There was one turn in eight feet. The barrel (bore) diameter without the grooves was .51. The "interchangeability of parts" was no mere figure of speech. Instructions to inspectors required them to disassemble the finished Hall arms, "say 10 in every 100 of the first 400 arms; after that about 10 in 400, and interchange the component parts of each of these lots of 10." [90]

There is a noticeable inconsistency in the written comment regarding the Hall arms in the published papers of Army officers of the day. It would appear that some of the officers expressed disapproval without having any great personal knowledge of the weapon.[91] Some of them advocated the use of muskets only and blanketed all rifles—breechloaders and muzzle-loaders alike—in their objections.[92] Others limited their protests to breech-loading mechanisms or to the newfangled percussion cap locks.[93] Professor Mahan of West Point, however, made an intelligent effort to enlighten the future Army officers. Writing in 1836 for cadets at the Military Academy, he observed:

> Rifle fire.—When the distance is under 170 yards and the mark large, the effects of the two arms [musket and rifle] are nearly equal. But for distances of 220 yards and beyond the balance is greatly in favor of the rifle. This superiority of the rifle is more particularly observable in the latest improvements of this arm, by Hall, in loading at the breech.[94]

Of Hall, the man, and his program of work at Harpers Ferry, his contemporaries were complimentary, to say the least. When Colonel Bomford, on January 31, 1827, responded to a resolution of the House of Representatives questioning the expenses of manufacturing and the utility of the Hall rifle, he concluded his report with a bow to its inventor: "It is but an act of justice to Mr. Hall, the inventor, to state that during the whole of this period [1813–1826] he has devoted himself with the greatest zeal and assiduity to the perfecting of this arm and of the means for fabricating it, and that in both he has been eminently successful. To him is due the merit of effecting so great an improvement in firearms." Lieutenant Colonel G. Talcott, who followed Colonel Bomford as Chief of Ordnance, was equally complimentary in his appraisal of Hall and his work. An exhaustive review of the Hall program with a reprinting of reports by investigating boards of Army officers is given by Fuller, who judged Hall and his weapons as follows:

> The Hall arm represents an outstanding achievement in the development of firearms not only because it was the first breech-loader adopted by any government, but that its construction was undertaken under the interchangeable system which at that time was considered as presenting too many obstacles to ever be successfully accomplished. Hall succeeded in developing the system to a point of perfection unsurpassed by even the modern methods of today, and considering the handicaps of working with the crude machines of the time, manually operated or at the best driven by water power, his work is deserving of the greatest credit.[95]

Samuel Colt encountered in the Hall breechloader an obstruction to his own program for selling revolvers to the government. Partly as a result of the pressure exerted by Colt to obtain governmental recognition for his revolving arms, a board of Army officers met on February 20, 1837, in the Washington Arsenal, for the purpose of examining certain guns. In testing for comparative rapidity of fire, the board supplied the Hacketts, Halls, and U. S. standard muskets with cartridges, and the Colts and Cochrans with loose ammunition, in order that the weapons "might be placed on an equity." A second series of tests was conducted in June of the same year, at the Military Academy, West Point, New York, by the same board.

The Hall arm was found to be adapted best to convenient loading when the user was in "constrained position or mounted."

> An arm which is complicated in its mechanism and arrangement deranges and perplexes the soldier. . . . The guns of Hall, and apparently of Hackett, are more easily managed, present less accountability to the soldier and are less liable to get out of order. . . . The experiments with Hall's guns in 1825 gave results satisfactory with regard to character for resisting the effects of long firings. . . . The advantage [when used by Cavalry] is believed to be altogether in favor of arms that load at the breech, and with receivers that contain only one charge; such arms being

conveniently handled and loaded on horseback, are peculiarly adapted to the Cavalry Service; and the ball being larger than the diameter of the barrel it is not changed from its position in the receiver by the movement of the horse. The many-chambered arms, because of difficulty of loading receivers while on horseback, are deemed inapplicable to the service of Cavalry. . . . The board is confirmed in the opinion that the arm of Hall is entitled to all the favorable consideration which has heretofore been bestowed upon it. . . . It is the unanimous opinion of the undersigned that the standard arms now in use—the U. S. Musket and U. S. Rifle, Hall's musket, rifle and carbine with such improvements in construction as they are susceptible to, combine in a higher degree all the requisites of convenience, durability, simplicity, and effect than any that have been suggested for the general armament.[96]

In issuing the Hall rifle, the Army placed a preponderance of stands with the militia. Before 1843, some thirty thousand had been produced; [97] about nine thousand of the arms went to the states, and approximately one-third of that number went to regular troops. The greatest number of these rifles, as well as of the "common rifles," were issued in the period 1836–1840. The Mexican War called out more stands, and to a limited extent the arm was used during the Civil War, both in Confederate hands and in the Union Army. Damaged rifles and surplus parts were left in the ruins of the Harpers Ferry Armory when in April, 1861, Lieutenant Roger Jones and his garrison of Union troops set fire to the plant and retreated before the advance of a Confederate force. The Confederates salvaged the abandoned arms of all descriptions, and from the parts of the Hall rifles they improvised some remarkable cap-lock weapons.[98] Roberts shows one of these relics, which was captured and brought home by William Bailey of the 118th New York Regiment. The original flintlock breech action had been removed by the Southern gunsmiths, and a breech plug with nipple and a percussion hammer had been installed to make of the arm a muzzle-loading cap-and-ball rifle.[99]

Model 1841 (percussion).—Early in 1841, the model for a full-stocked percussion rifle was prepared in the Harpers Ferry Armory, and the Ordnance Board placed its stamp of approval upon it the same year. Official records indicate that both the Harpers Ferry and

Springfield armories tooled up to make this, the first percussion rifle to be adopted by the United States. Colonel Gluckman, however, states that no specimen from Springfield is known to him. Some of the Harpers Ferry locks bear the date 1841, but production records show that finished rifles were not turned out until 1846.

The Tryon family records suggest that Edward K. Tryon and Company, Philadelphia, contracted with the Republic of Texas on April 3, 1840, to supply 1,500 Army rifles of the Model 1841 specifications. I have found no record of their production. However, the Tryon Company did make 5,000 of these rifles for the U. S. government, at $12.875 each, in accordance with a contract of April 22, 1848.

Eli Whitney, Jr., of Whitneyville, Connecticut, obtained a government contract on October 22, 1842, for 7,500 Model 1841 rifles at $13.00 each, to be delivered by January 1, 1847. Thomas Warner, one-time master armorer at the Springfield Armory, directed the tooling-up for Whitney and superintended the production of his rifles. Shipments of the Whitney Model 1841 rifles went to New Orleans in time to supply the regiment of volunteers called the "Mississippi Rifles," organized in 1846. Colonel Jefferson Davis commanded this regiment, which became renowned for its part in the Mexican War. He had insisted that his men be armed with the new weapon rather than with the flintlocks which were being issued at the time. Because of the effectiveness of the regiment and the notoriety attained by it, the Model 1841 has been known ever since as the "Mississippi rifle." [100]

Whitney, on March 27, 1848, contracted to make another 7,500 rifles at $12.875, and on February 6, 1849, he entered into a third contract for 2,500 of the arms at the same price. His fourth contract was signed May 24, 1855, for 100 additional Model 1841 rifles at $11.625 each. Some contemporary writers refer to the Model 1841 as the "Whitney rifle," and "Yäger" is another popular name for it.

John Griffith of Cincinnati contracted on December 6, 1842, to make 5,000 of the rifles. He failed to meet his obligations, however, and his contract was taken over by the Remington Arms Company, Ilion, New York. Remington also obtained another contract for 7,500 additional rifles. On August 11, 1862, he obtained an order for 10,000 "modified" Model 1841 rifles at $17.00 each, and this order was followed by another on December 13, 1863, for 2,500 at the same price.

On February 18, 1845, Robbins, Kendall, and Lawrence of Windsor, Vermont, contracted to make 10,000 stands at $11.90 each. This contract was followed by another for 15,000 at $12.875 on January 5, 1848. In the meantime, Kendall had sold his interest to his partners; the second contract is in the name of Robbins and Lawrence.[101]

In 1855, Colonel H. K. Craig of the Ordnance Bureau recommended to Jefferson Davis, then Secretary of War, that "the bore of this arm [the U. S. rifle, Model 1841] be reamed up [to .58 caliber] and rerifled; that it have a rear sight similar to the rifle-musket of 1855, and that a stud and guide [be provided] for attachment of a sword bayonet." Davis placed his "O.K." on the proposal on July 5, 1855,[102] and the weapon thereafter used the Minié bullet and boasted a bayonet.

The original model is shown in figure 36, *c*. The piece has a 33-inch barrel of .54 caliber, rifled with six grooves having one turn in 6 feet. All mountings are brass. On the 5-inch lock plate forward of the cock is a spread eagle looking rearward and the letters "U.S." To the rear of the cock is "Harpers Ferry 1841." The total length of the arm is 48.8 inches; of the ramrod, 33 inches. The black-walnut stock is 43.5 inches long. The piece weighs 9.68 pounds. With 70 grains of powder and a ball 32 to the pound, an initial velocity of 1,750 feet was obtained. The regulation musket with 110 grains of powder and a ball 17 to the pound gave an initial velocity of 1,500 feet.

Harold's Club, in Reno, has a rifle of this model, complete with leather sling. The M. H. de Young Memorial Museum, San Francisco, exhibits one (no. 53461) dated at Harpers Ferry, 1850. The Milwaukee Museum has one (no. N3467) marked "Remington's Herkimer, N.Y., U.S. 1849," which was made under a contract of 1842.

It is interesting to note that Callender Irvine, Commissary General, in 1813 had a model sword bayonet prepared for use on a new rifle which he attempted to "sell" to General John Armstrong, Secretary of War. Irvine wrote:

The sabre to cut or thrust may be used as such, or as a bayonet fixed, alternately. When as the latter, it will have advantage over the common musket by three inches in length, and is a more certain, and to the enemy, dangerous weapon. It will readily pass through an inch pine plank. It requires great force to pass a fixed [musket] bayonet through the same substance. . . . Knowing how much riflemen acting as flankers are exposed to the charge of cavalry, and believing that mounted riflemen ought to be so equipped as to be able to act as cavalrymen and riflemen, alternately . . . it is my opinion that carbines so equipped [with sabre bayonet] would be the best arms.[108]

The Secretary of War advised Irvine to submit his proposed rifle to the governor of Virginia for his inspection, and he did so on February 24, 1814. However, there is no evidence of the adoption of a saber bayonet by Virginia or by any other state or by the federal government before the "modification" of the U. S. rifle, Model 1841, in 1855.

The Model 1841 did not, of course, get to the West either as a military weapon or as a civilian's arm in the heyday of the beaver trade. There is evidence, however, that it found use in the hands of mountain men and emigrants on the Oregon and California trails during the rush to the "promised lands." Robbins and Lawrence found that some of the product resulting from their 1848 contract could not be "received" by the government. The rejected arms are said to have entered channels of trade, and some of them turned up "on the road to Oregon" and in the gold camps in California. It is a fact also that a law of March 2, 1849, authorized the Ordnance Office to issue U.S. arms to emigrants who were about to travel to New Mexico or California or Oregon. Some of the Model 1841 rifles known to have been used by civilians on the far-western trails may have been drawn from government store in accordance with this law.

Colt rifles and carbines.—We have seen that some traders and trappers of the beaver days used revolving-cylinder arms while the muzzle-loading flintlock was still the vogue. Just as some frontiersmen demonstrated revolvers to the Army, so the military introduced the repeating weapons to more than a few of the mountain men. These introductions took place in Florida and Texas and along the Santa Fe route.

The number of repeaters used by the frontiersmen was not large, but the comparatively few presaged a new era in armament; they occupy a significant place in this outline of the history of firearms in the West. The Colt, of course, was preëminent among them.

By 1837, Samuel Colt's patents were secure (see section "Pistols" in chap. ii) and the "Patent arms" were coming off the production line in Paterson. What Colt needed was buyers for all types of arms: rifles, carbines, and handguns. From the beginning of his promotion program, he knew that government purchases would be essential for any great volume of business. He concentrated on the matter of placing his product before government officials, and in February, 1837, some of his muskets and rifles were included in the assortment of breech-loading and repeating arms to be tested by the Board of Army officers that examined the Hall rifle. The first trials were conducted in the Washington Arsenal and were designed especially to be used in a comparative study of the rapidity of fire. The Colt revolving arms were contrasted with Hackett's breech-loading musket, Hall's breech-loading musket and rifle, Cochran's revolving musket and rifle, Leavitt's rifle, and the standard U. S. flintlock musket. (See note 96.)

The results of the tests were decisive: the penetrating power of the Colt was greater, but the Hall weapon was judged to be best when the user was mounted or "in a constrained position."

> The many-chambered arms on the contrary requiring a variety of append-ages to aid in charging them and the application of considerable manual force in placing the charge, cannot be loaded either in constrained posi-tions or on horseback without inconvenience; and it is believed conse-quently that Hall's rifle and Hackett's gun are the only descriptions of arms loading at the breech that can be considered as suitable for the serv-ice of light troops either on foot or mounted. These remarks might not be applicable to the many-chambered guns could it be supposed that they would at all times be supplied with a number of loaded cylinders, but this is not to be admitted as being practicable at all times and in all situations.

It was pointed out that four loaded seven-shot Colt receivers or cyl-inders for the musket weighed 13 pounds 14 ounces. These, together with the cylinder in the musket provided 35 rounds—"The same rounds carried for the ordinary musket weigh 2 pounds, twelve ounces." [104]

The mechanism of the Colt was thought to be too complicated. The loading of the Paterson Colt entailed the removal of the barrel and the putting of powder and ball into each of the chambers, followed by a ramming of the charges with a special loading tool. The weapon and its accessories as first devised did indeed mean much juggling of hardware in the loading.

In spite of the fact that the Hall percussion carbine had then been in Army use for more than three years, the board observed: "The application of the percussion primer to arms for the use of troops has not yet been made with success. . . . The system if improved may be used by troops in extended order. The liability [of percussion caps] to annoy and maim the contiguous men was fully illustrated by the experiments. . . . The many-chambered guns use the percussion cap." The investigators ruled out the Cochran arms entirely, but they acknowledged, cautiously, that the Colt weapons might be successful "when an operation is of a special kind and brief character and it is desirable to throw a mass of fire upon a particular point for a limited time"; but their final verdict canceled even this faint praise:

> The massive burden of its [Colt's] parts condemn it as wholly unsuited to the general wants and exigencies of the service in the field. . . . It is the unanimous opinion of the undersigned that the standard arms now in use . . . combine in a higher degree all the requirements of convenience, durability, simplicity, and effect than any that have been suggested for the general armament.[105]

The adverse report of this board of Army officers was a blow to Samuel Colt, but he was not downed by the verdict. That same year, he journeyed to Charleston, South Carolina, where state officials were about to invest in arms for the South Carolina Militia. He did not obtain orders for his weapons in quantity, but he sold seventy-five pistols to individuals. Early in 1838, Colt went to Florida, where two thousand "Regulars" and an equal number of volunteers were fighting the Seminole Indians. There he enlisted the interest of Lieutenant Col. William S. Harney of the 2d Dragoons, who recommended to his superior, General T. S. Jesup, that Colt arms be purchased for the use of his "outfit." Fifty revolving eight-shot rifles were sold to the U. S. government by Colt at this time and saw field service in the hands of dragoons.[106]

In 1839 a transaction took place which amounted to a turning point in Samuel Colt's fortunes, but its effects could not be anticipated immediately by any of the principals. Edward Ward Moore, in command of the very new Texas Navy, purchased a consignment of Colt arms while he was outfitting in Baltimore. For four years these weapons, "among the first manufactured by the inventor," served that navy, and after that they were turned over to the Texas Rangers.[107] One of the earliest printed references to the success of Colt's weapons in the hands of mounted Indian fighters appeared in the *Telegraph and Texas Register,* November, 1840: "In the late Indian fight, Captain Andrews used one of Colt's patent rifles which he discharged ten times while a comrade could discharge his rifle only twice. He believes that these rifles in proper hands would prove most useful of all weapons in Indian warfare." A far more momentous incident occurred in 1844, when fifteen rangers under Colonel John Coffee Hays gave battle to eighty mounted Comanche Indians. The Rangers were armed with Colt weapons obtained from the Texas Navy. Forty-two of the eighty Comanches were left dead on the field of battle, the first concrete evidence that the mounted white man possessed an arm that placed him upon at least an equal footing with the wild horsemen of the plains. This battle of the Piedernales received wide publicity and served to clinch in the minds of many Texans the fact that Colt revolving weapons provided a solution to one of their problems.[108] It was at this time that Samuel H. Walker (of Whitneyville-Walker renown) first became identified publicly with the Colt revolver. He was one of the Jack Hays men who killed the Comanche Indians, and his qualifications as a judge of the merits and weaknesses of the Paterson-Colt were hard-earned and genuine.[109]

Before the end of 1839, Sam Colt had taken steps to meet some of the Army's objections to his arms. He devised and patented an attached loading lever, which made it unnecessary to disassemble a weapon for loading, and he worked on a waterproof foil cartridge, which would be consumed when the weapon was fired. In 1840, he succeeded in placing the improved arms before another government board of experimenters; this time it was a U. S. Navy committee, which met in Washington. These officers acknowledged the percussion system to be better than the flintlock, but they decided that the revolving arms were too complex and were liable to get out of order; they advised against their adoption for use by boarders and marines.[110] In response to a Congressional resolution of July 20, 1840, three officers, all of junior grade, at the Dragoon School, Carlisle Barracks, looked into the fitness of the guns and the merits of the new cartridge developed by Colt. Their findings were less damaging than was the Navy report, and it may be presumed that the government purchases of 160 Colt's carbines in 1841 resulted from the Dragoon trials.[111] By this time Colt had expended much money, time, and energy in social lobbying in Washington and in cultivating the good will of state officials and Army and Navy officers in many parts of the country. Economic conditions in the United States were bad, to say the least, and the Patent Arms Manufacturing Company had not had enough business to keep management and stockholders happy. John Ehlers, who had managed the business, criticized Colt for his profligate public relations activities, and Sam, in turn, accused Ehlers of cheating him out of some of his commissions. Colt brought suit, and in 1842 Ehlers threw the company into bankruptcy. The early agreements had been such as to cause the Colt patents to revert to Sam, personally.[112]

It was a closed and practically empty Colt factory upon which Ehlers turned his back in 1842, but he had managed to salvage enough stands of Colt arms to enable him to set up business in New York City. If, as some students of firearms assert, government officials were able to buy Colt arms in New York in 1845, it is likely that the supply came from Ehlers. One Crosby, once of the Colt factory at Paterson, also salvaged guns and parts of guns when the company became defunct, but he is said to have had no more than twenty-five complete pieces, whereas Ehlers' loot ran into the hundreds, according to unconfirmed reports. In any case, these two men provided some source of supply during the years following the closing of the original Colt factory, and the fact that some stands of their Colt arms were made up after the production lines were dismantled may account for the existence, in present-day collections, of those specimens of Paterson Colts which lack serial numbers.

Sam Colt was not idle at this time (1844–1845), but with his propensity for creating needed products he had turned to one of his earlier interests, the manufacturing of waterproof cable for submarine electrical and telegraphic purposes. In this industry he did have the support afforded by government orders. Unknown to him were the dramatic exploits then being staged in Texas by such doughty Rangers as Jack Hays, Samuel H. Walker, Ben McCulloch, Mike Chevaille, Rip Ford, "Big Foot" Wallace, George T. Howard, and I. S. Sutton. In all these fights the Colt arms became closely identified with victories.

In 1846 the long-continued troubles with Mexico flamed into warfare. On April 25 an American patrol was attacked from ambuscade and suffered sixteen casualties. Captain S. B. Thornton of the 2d Dragoons, armed with his own pair of Colt revolvers, shot his way out of this scrape, and the story of his prowess spread far and wide. General Taylor soon learned that more than a few men in the Texas Rangers, who by this time had joined his forces, as well as a goodly number of his more experienced officers, were warmly attached to their Colt guns. They argued for a general acquisition of the remarkable revolvers and revolving rifles or carbines. The moment had arrived for Sam Colt to collect on his investments in mechanics and good will and at the same time to make his critics in the Ordnance Bureau eat crow.

General Taylor sent Captain Sam Walker of the Texas Rangers to Washington to arrange for the purchase of Colt guns, and of course there were no Colt guns. The rest of the story is of great interest, but it extends beyond the chronological limits of this book. Here it suffices to say that Sam Walker and Sam Colt reached agreement, and the Colt firearms industry was reëstablished largely on the basis of the U. S. Army's urgent need for Colt handguns. More will be said about the Walker-Colt interchange in the section on "United States Pistols."

Josiah Gregg testifies regarding some rather nonconsequential use of Paterson-Colt carbines in the Mexican War,[113] but, generally, the record of the use of this arm by the military ends with the Florida episodes of 1838 and the Ordnance Office purchases in 1841. Probably these 160 carbines made for the Dragoons were about the last weapons manufactured in the Paterson factory.[114] No doubt greater use of Colt long arms would have been made by our troops in Mexico had there been a ready supply upon which to draw.

In concluding the review of the history of the Paterson long arms, it is to be noted that a new line of revolving rifles and carbines, generally known as the Model 1855, grew out of the 1836 and 1837 types. These were made in the Hartford factory, established in the early 1850's, and were characterized by improvements initiated by Elisha K. Root, who was employed by Colt to superintend his enterprises. The Model 1855 was purchased by some foreign governments and found use in many parts of the world. True to his old form, Colt saw to it that voluble testimony in regard to the merits of his revolving rifles appeared in print. H. W. A. Cleveland, in his book *Hints to Riflemen,* was loud in his praise and attempted to counteract the devastating criticism that Frank Forester had directed at the 1836 and 1837 models. Hans Busk, a first lieutenant in the Victoria Rifles, published *The Rifle and How to Use It,* which appeared in England in several editions in the 1850's. He gave much space to both the Colt Revolver and the Colt carbine and printed testimony obtained from British and American officers who favored the arms. In England, however, there was not universal acclaim of the revolving long arms. John Scoffern wrote:

> Fire a revolving pistol at night; observe the escape of lateral flame like the halo around the head of a saint. How would you like your arm to be in that burning halo of flame? Colt tells you his carbines need not be held with two hands. I tell you they *cannot* be held with two hands; the coat sleeve would be burned through presently. And see how manufac-

turers of revolver long arms steer clear of big or moderately big bores; a condition which would speedily try out conclusions. They stick to thick barrels and small bores and low charges. I tell you revolving full length arms are a failure.[115]

Between January 1, 1856, and December 30, 1865, the U. S. government purchased 6,693 Colt rifles and carbines.[116] Fuller states, "When used in the Civil War the soldiers in all branches of the Service disliked them exceedingly on account of the flash and loud report so close to the face, and the fearful recoil when several chambers went off at once." [117] Endorsements of the kind given by Cleveland and others did not engender for the Colt rifles and carbines the degree of public favor accorded the Colt handguns; the revolving long arms soon became obsolete.

UNITED STATES PISTOLS

Before 1843, about 110,000 flintlock pistols had been made or procured by the U. S. government. The greater number had been manufactured in the private plants of contractors. War Department records account for the issuance of about three-fourths of these handguns before the War with Mexico. For reasons not entirely clear, federally owned pistols did not go to the states in any numbers until 1829; [118] after that year the great preponderance of the issues went to the militia.

Of the eleven models of flintlock pistols treated in the following pages, five were of musket caliber; the others were of rifle caliber (.54), but none was rifled. Barrels were 8½ to 11 inches long. Total weight ranged from 2¼ to 3¼ pounds. In general, it may be said that these arms were rugged and could withstand rough usage, but they were rather clumsy and were ineffectual except at close range. Even a cursory survey of the military pistols used in France during the last half of the eighteenth century will reveal that most of the characteristics of the American flintlocks were borrowed from those European progenitors.[119] In all countries the pistol was essentially the horseman's weapon, but officers in other branches of the U. S.

Army, as well as the Cavalry, carried it. In the contemporary writings of men who were armed with it are numerous references to the inability of the men to meet a crisis because of the failure of their pistol to fire. Wet weather and high winds rendered the flintlock mechanism quite undependable. Hostile Plains Indians, mounted on their fleet steeds, were contemptuous of the white soldier's handgun and took joy in demonstrating the superiority of their bow and arrow. Frequently they committed their depredations under the very noses of military units, and they had little fear of reprisals, because even the mounted soldiers, armed with flintlock weapons, could not cope with them in a very effective manner, and the infantrymen of that day were completely ineffectual before the wild horsemen.

Two percussion single-shot pistols, Model 1842 and Model 1843, came into use by the military just at the end of the period with which this book is concerned, but they did not bring about a revolution in fighting tactics, as the Colt handgun had done after being adopted by the Army in spite of Ordnance Department judgment. Not until the revolver came into use did the Army have a pistol which could command the respect of the mounted Plains Indian.

As has been told in chapter ii, men of the fur brigades, as well as the Army personnel, contended with the inadequacies of the flintlock pistol. Traders and trappers often carried military flintlock pistols. However, the mountain men seized upon percussion pistols long before the government adopted a regulation percussion handgun. The traders also availed themselves of the new types of repeating pistols; in some quarters they played an active part in demonstrating to the Army that Sam Colt had indeed opened a new era in weapons.

Model 1799.—Pistols had made up a part of the armament of our Revolutionary Army; some of them had been purchased in Europe and some from the small shops of loyal American gunsmiths. The committees of safety had procured some of these arms; the Continental Congress had bought others. A small number of French weapons came as a gift from the Marquis de Lafayette, and a greater number were obtained as a result of our formal alliance with France. Long after the Revolution, the French influence was as decidedly predominant in our flintlock pistol models as it was in our early muskets.

In 1799, the U. S. government adopted its first regulation pistol. The French Army pistol, Model 1777, served as the pattern, and Simeon North of Berlin, Connecticut, initiated his half-century program of martial arms making when on March 9, 1799, he signed a contract to make 500 of these .69 caliber handguns. His product was satisfactory to government officials, and a second contract for 1,500 was awarded to him on February 6, 1800. Both lots were marked, on the underside of the brass frame, NORTH AND CHENEY, BERLIN or S. NORTH AND E. CHENEY, BERLIN. The Elisha Cheney referred to was Simeon North's brother-in-law. S. N. D. and R. H. North disclaim any partnership between Simeon North and E. Cheney,[120] but it would appear from these markings that there must have been some business agreement at the time the Model 1799 pistol was manufactured. However, this family combination is not recorded on any of the several models of U. S. arms which the North factory produced subsequently, nor is there reference to any partnership in the North correspondence preserved in family and government archives.

One of these North Model 1799 pistols is shown in figure 37, *a.* Having a total length of 14½ inches, the piece weighs 3 pounds 4 ounces. It has an 8½-inch smoothbore, round barrel, bored for the musket ball. The frame and mountings are brass; the walnut grip is one piece, without a fore end. On the underside of the frame are the words "North & Cheney Berlin," and on the top of the barrel under the breech are the letters "US," "P," and "V."

Only about a score of the Model 1799 pistols are to be found in present-day collections, and specimens in fine condition stand close to the top of dealers' lists of market values. The weapon which Simeon North sold for $6.00 is now valued at approximately $2,400.00. Yet specimens of the French pistol which served as the pattern can be bought for a comparatively few dollars.

Model 1806.—A great deal of interest attaches to this, the first handgun to be made in a national armory. Some writers designate it as Model 1805, some as Model 1806, and others as Model 1807. The Chief of Ordnance records eight pattern pistols as having been made at

Harpers Ferry in 1806.[121] From these patterns came some four thousand pistols produced in the Harpers Ferry works in 1807 and 1808. Gluckman observes that more than eight locks bearing date of 1806 were manufactured, but they were not built into pistols until 1807.[122] The Montana specimen shown in figure 15, *a,* has an 1806 lock. Serial numbers for the entire output were stamped on the barrels; the Montana specimen is no. 89.

Of all the U. S. flintlock pistols, this half-stocked, 16-inch pistol of .54 caliber is the most trim in line and pleasing in balance. The flat-faced cock is bevel-edged and double-necked. The horizontal iron pan has a fence and is forged into the lock plate. The barrel of the specimen shown in figure 37, *b,* bears a serial number and the letters "US" and "P." On the lock plate in front of the cock is the spread eagle looking rearward, and under the eagle, "U.S." To the rear of the cock are the words "Harpers Ferry 1806." The Model 1806 is as distinct among military pistols as the U. S. rifle, Model 1803, is different from other Army rifles of the time. In general appearance, the Model 1806 is like the ancient *pistolet de carabiner* of the French; [123] but its short stock, rib under the barrel, and better balance seem to reflect the influence of the British officers' pistols of the mid-eighteenth century.[124] It weighs 2 pounds 9 ounces. Although it proved to be rather fragile for military use, it continued to be used by the Army for many years. Some specimens were in store in 1848 when the government converted serviceable flintlocks to percussion. The Nunnemacher Collection contains a converted Model 1806 which appears to be a government conversion.

No subsequent U. S. model had the short forestock with rib; but the Virginia Manufactory at Richmond and a "Bielry and Co.," listed by Carey as in Philadelphia, produced pistols patterned after the Model 1806 for private sale during the War of 1812 and in the period immediately thereafter. They are not marked "US."

As indicated in chapter ii, the Model 1806 was used to some extent in the fur fields of the Far West.

U. S. pistol, Model 1807.—The biggest flintlock pistol of the martial series is of .69 caliber and has an 11-inch barrel. The superin-

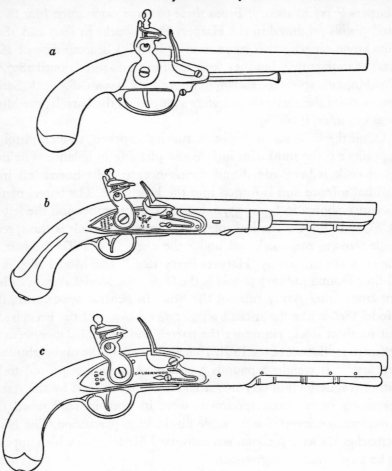

Fig. 37. U. S. pistols, flintlocks, Models 1799, 1806, contract 1807, 1813, 1819, 1836. *a*, U. S. contract pistol, Model 1799; after Serven, 1952, p. 5. *b*, U. S. pistol, Model 1806; Milwaukee Museum (no. N74). *c*, U. S. contract pistol, Model 1807; after Serven, 1952, p. 6, no. 25. *d*, U. S. pistol, Model 1813; Milwaukee Museum (no. N4062). *e*, U. S. pistol, Model 1819; after a photograph by Serven. *f*, U. S. pistol, Model 1836; Milwaukee Museum (no. N4076).

tendent at the Springfield Armory was instructed on October 26, 1807, to start making pistols of this model, but by the next spring Army officials had decided that they wanted no more handguns of

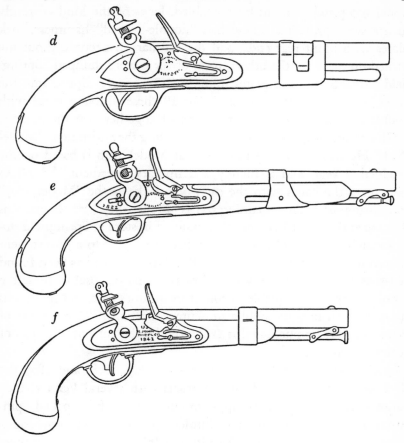

musket caliber, and the work was stopped. The unassembled parts manufactured in 1807 and 1808 remained on hand until 1817, when the Ordnance Office decided to make them into finished weapons. These parts apparently included stocks for the complete order, but the locks were sufficient to supply only about half of the 1,000 pistols that had been ordered. The locks for these 500 pistols had the early-type flat, bevel-edged, gooseneck cock. Upon the resumption of work on the arms, they were stamped "Springfield 1818." The lock plate had a projecting point at its rear end, and the frizzen was provided with a turned-up toe. In order that the remainder of the lot—an additional 500 pistols—might be assembled, locks of the kind currently in use were provided. These had "double-necked" hammers, lock plates with blunt rear ends, and the ordinary frizzens without the turned-up toe. Like the others, most of these were stamped "Springfield 1818." Some lock plates stamped "1815" were slipped into the order, adding further confusion. On all these pistols a band with double strap held the barrel and forestock together near the muzzle.

Gluckman lumps both lots together, calling the entire 1,000 "Model 1818." He states, "Dating this pistol as Model 1818 is based on the production year, and is merely a temporary expedient." [125] Hicks recognizes the batch with the early-type locks as the "Model 1807" and distinguishes the remaining 500 as "Model 1817." [126] He explains that the entire lot of 1,000 pistols remained in store at Springfield until Lieutenant Colonel J. W. Ripley had them sent to a government arsenal in New York in the fall of 1850. No evidence has been found of issues to troops, nor any record of the final disposal of these big pistols. They were available to collectors in times past, and specimens are to be seen in some public museum collections.[127] That some of them still may be purchased is evidenced by the current offerings of dealers in old arms.[128]

U. S. contract pistol, Model 1807.—In 1807, 1808, and 1809 the U. S. government entered into contracts with several Pennsylvania gunmakers for a total of approximately 4,500 full-stocked, pin-fastened, .54 caliber, smoothbore, flintlock pistols of a type now sometimes referred to as "Kentucky pistols." It is said by some writers that the Model 1806 served as the pattern for these, but there is little about the U. S. contract pistol, Model 1807, to suggest this relationship. Rather, in its lines it resembles the usual 10-inch-barrel horse pistol which had been used throughout Europe in the late eighteenth century.[129]

The "Kentucky-type" pistol in figure 37, *c*, was made by William Calderwood under a contract of 1808, which called for 120 pistols.[130] The full-length stock extends nearly to the muzzle of the 10-inch barrel. The total length is 16 inches. It has a flat gooseneck cock and a brass pan attached to the barrel. The ramrod is wood. On the barrel are stamped the letter "P" and an eagle head; on the lock plate in front of the cock is "Calderwood Phila.," and to the rear of the cock, "US 1808."

Most of the appropriations for payment for these pistols were made in accordance with the Act of 1808 for arming the militia,[131] but the Regular Army also received this contract arm. William Calderwood, J. Guest (with A. Henry and P. Brong), J. Henry, J. Shuler, Molan and Finn, Jacob Cooke, A. and J. Ansted, Adam Leitner, and Martin Frye, all of Pennsylvania, delivered their products to the Schuylkill Arsenal. Their pistols were marked "US" behind the hammer. A few years later, T. French of Canton, Massachusetts, also made this model and marked his output "US." Henry Deringer, John Miles, and Dan. Switzer and Co., all of Pennsylvania, and the Virginia Manufactory of Richmond also made the arm, but the "US" does not appear on specimens from their shops. Presumably, they sold directly to the states, and their pistols were used by various citizen military organizations as well as by the militia.[132] The demands made by the War of 1812 absorbed the supply, and some of these pistols were taken into the West during that war, but details of their possible use in the fur fields are lacking.

Contractors were paid $10.00 a pair; the same arms now bring $200.00 to $395.00 a pistol in the collectors' market.

Miscellaneous contract pistols, 1808 and 1811.—On June 30, 1808, Simeon North, Berlin, Connecticut, contracted to make 1,000 Navy pistols of .64 caliber with iron belt hook at $11.75 a pair. The contract was extended on December 4, 1810, adding 500 pairs at $12.00 a pair. The usual designation of this North pistol is "U. S. pistol, Navy Model 1808." The pan, butt cap, and trigger guard are of brass. The smoothbore barrel is 10½ inches long, and the total weight of the piece is 2 pounds 14 ounces. The "S. North" impress is behind the hammer. In front of the hammer is the American eagle and "U States." [133] There is no evidence that this Navy model was used in the West.

In 1811, at the same time that the patterns for the North U. S. pistol, Model 1811, were under study, Tench Coxe, Purveyor of Public

Supplies, seized upon a pair of French Navy pistols, year XIII (1804), which he considered to be superior. The ungainly proportions of the arms brought from him only the remark, "rejection of expense on the score of appearance." Eventually, this French pistol became the pattern for the so-called "Valley Forge pistol" made by O. and E. Evans. Gluckman points to the fact that specimens examined by him bear the date 1814 on the underside of the barrel. They are of .689 caliber, and the barrel is 7.87 inches long. Like its French progenitor, this Evans pistol has an iron ramrod. Details of production and distribution of the Valley Forge pistol have not been found, but specimens are available in several public and private collections. There is no evidence that the arm was used in the West.[134]

U. S. pistol, Model 1811.—On November 18, 1811, Simeon North signed a contract for 1,000 pairs of .69 caliber, smoothbore pistols. This model was very much like the North Navy pistol, Model 1808, except that it had a slightly larger bore, a barrel that was but 8⅝ inches long, and no belt hook. Apparently, the U. S. Army had forgotten its decision of 1808 to use no more pistols of musket caliber. While the arm was still in the pattern stage, Tench Coxe took exception to the weakness of the stock at the muzzle: "there is the want of a firm band to the upper part of the stock to prevent its splitting." The North factory proceeded to make the arm as originally specified, but in the course of producing the model, North changed the style of the arm in accordance with instructions from the Ordnance Office. M. T. Wickham, at that time U. S. Inspector of Arms, devised a double-band fastening for the stock. North turned out a part of his order equipped with this band, and on the pistols with this modification he also shortened the stock, terminating it abruptly at the forward edge of the band. In this respect, some of the Model 1811 pistols resemble the Model 1813.

U. S. pistol, Model 1813.—On the strength of his growing business, Simeon North invested in a new arms factory on a never-failing stream of water at Middletown, Connecticut. He contracted to make 20,000 pistols of .69 caliber for Army use at $7.00 each. The contract, dated April 16, 1813, specified that "the component parts of pistols are to correspond so exactly that any limb or part of one pistol may be fitted to any other pistol of the twenty thousand," the first formal provision for interchangeability of parts. Some of the Model 1813 pistols are marked BERLIN CT, some MIDL^N CON., and others MIDL^{TN} CONN.

The model is shown in figure 37, *d*. The 9-inch barrel has a semi-octagonal section at the breech; it is smoothbore and of .69 caliber. The total length of the gun is 15¼ inches; the weight, 3 pounds 6 ounces. The rear band of the double-strapped ring is fluted, and there are no sights. The stock ends at the ring. The tilted brass pan has no fence. The 1813 contract under which Simeon North made this pistol specified that all parts, except the parts of the lock, should be interchangeable; it was the first of such contracts in the history of the War Department. Only 1,100 of the 20,000 pistols specified in the original contract had been produced when Army authorities decided that the terrific "kick" of this "short-barreled musket" was more than should be tolerated by any user of a handgun. Under orders issued in May, 1816, North made up the rest of this lot in .54 caliber. The barrel of this gun is round throughout its length, and the front strap has a knife-blade sight of brass. Both straps are fluted. The stock extends beyond the end of the barrel band. The gun weighs 3 pounds 3 ounces. In the revision of the contract North was required to make the parts of the 1816 lock interchangeable.[135] Provision was made to pay him $1.00 more for each pistol, and the duration of the contract was extended. Pistols made under the specifications of the revised agreement are generally known as the U. S. pistol, Model 1816. (One is exhibited at Harold's Club, Reno.) Arms of this type were used by various classes of troops during the Black Hawk War and were taken to the West via Florida at the time of the Seminole War. They were also carried by U. S. soldiers in the Mexican War, and there is evidence that some pieces which were rejected by the government and which do not bear the mark "US" were used by civilians.[136] Among specimens now in collections it is not unusual to find the marks of various state militia, in addition to the eagle and the "US." Some specimens with belt hooks suggest that this model was used by the Navy also.

U. S. pistol, Model 1819.—In June, 1819, Simeon North received from the Ordnance Department two pattern pistols of a design quite different from that of former military pistols. The next month he signed a contract to supply 20,000 of the arms at $8.00 each. Records show that he filled the order in 1823, more than a year in advance of the time limit set by the contract.

This .54 caliber smoothbore pistol has a round, 10-inch barrel (fig. 37, *e*). There is a single spring-fastened band which resembles the lower band of the French Army pistol, Model 1765. The stock extends well beyond the band, and the iron ramrod is held to the barrel near the muzzle by a swivel fastening. This is the first model of U. S. pistol to have such an attachment of the ramrod, but the device had been in use on both English and French martial pistols for many years. It obviated the danger of dropping the ramrod while the arm was being loaded, and the United States continued to use it on pistols until muzzle-loaders were no longer used.[137] The piece has an open rear sight and a knife-blade front sight. It weighs 2 pounds 10 ounces. On the barrel are the letters "P" and "US." On the lock plate is the spread eagle, with "S. North" above and "U.S." and "Midltn Conn." below it. Behind the cock is the date, "1822."

An innovation was the safety bolt which held the hammer at half cock. It was operated by a sliding thumb catch behind the hammer. This device proved to be impracticable. It was not included in any succeeding models.

The longer tapered barrel and the design of the forestock gave to the arm a better symmetry and balance. Among flintlock pistols it is distinguished in appearance, but there is nothing in the record to indicate that it gave unusual service. It was in use throughout the western military border wherever mounted troops were sent, and during the Mexican War the stores of this pistol were absorbed by the Volunteers.

U. S. pistol, Model 1826.—In 1826, 1827, and 1828, Simeon North entered into three government contracts for pistols (3,000 guns in all) similar in most respects to the Model 1819 except for the omission of the safety device and the shortening of the barrel to 8⅝ inches. The Navy received a portion of this output, and most of these pieces have the usual belt hook. The Milwaukee Museum has one of them (no. N4065), which is marked "US" but lacks the usual eagle. Some of the pistols destined for use at sea were supplied with tinned barrels to minimize corrosion. These were the last pistols made by North.

W. L. Evans, owner of the Valley Forge, Chester County, Pennsylvania, also made pistols of this model, some of which were marked v. FORGE and others E. BURG, for Evansburg, the home of Evans. The assembling of parts and the finishing of the arms were done at Evansburg. Gluckman writes, "Similar in all respects to the S. North Model 1826 pistol; most parts being interchangeable. Probabilities are that a North 1826 pistol was used as a pattern." [138] John Joseph Henry of the Boulton works near Nazareth, Pennsylvania, made an unrecorded number of pistols of the Model 1826 type which do not appear to be government contract arms. They are marked on the lock plate, between cock and frizzen: J. J. HENRY BOULTON. Presumably they were sold privately and directly to the states.

The Black Hawk War (1831–1832) called out more than four hundred regular infantrymen and some four thousand mounted Illinois militiamen or volunteers. The demand for arms, especially pistols, caused the government to "scrape the bottom of the barrel." There are unexplained gaps in the Ordnance Department's published records of production; for example, the 3,000 U. S. pistols, Model 1826, supplied by Simeon North are not reported as "procured," and there are similar gaps in the record of pistols issued to regular troops and to the militia before 1829. However, beginning with the period of the Black Hawk War, there is a rather good accounting of all handguns obtained for and issued to the U. S. Army. It is obvious that in the early 1830's a notable number of U. S. pistols were taken to the lower Wisconsin River valley and the Rock River country of Illinois and Wisconsin. It is understandable that a large number of these pistols never returned to government stores. The record of the activities of pistol-packing horsemen during the Black Hawk War—a record not altogether favorable to the reputation of some of the volunteers—gave substance to the arguments for a mounted branch of the Regular Army. By dint of writing numerous petitions, the Army and the civilian chiefs of the War Department were able to get authorization for one regiment of dragoons in 1833.[139] The regiment was so successful that it was kept on the western frontier even during the Seminole War. A second regiment of dragoons, one thousand infantry and artillery, and about two thousand volunteers were sent into the Florida campaign in 1836–1837.[140] This caused a heavy drain on the stores of U. S. pistols and accounts for the contracts to replenish them.

U. S. pistol, Model 1836.—On June 27, 1836, Robert Johnson of Middletown, Connecticut, contracted to make 3,000 flintlock pistols of .54 caliber and having an 8½-inch barrel which, like the iron mountings of the arm, was to be polished bright. The pan and front sight were to be of brass. Metschl appraises this model:

> The lock-plate, frizzen and cock were case-hardened in mottled colors; the frizzen spring, trigger, barrel tang and all screws were blued; the other steel parts were left in the bright condition and polished. The black walnut stock was smoothed, finished with linseed oil, rubbed off, and left dull. Pistols of this model were elegantly shaped, conspicuous by their colors and nearly the equals of the old-time dueling pistols in the matter of excellent workmanship.[141]

The piece shown in figure 37, *f*, is a good example. It is 13¹³⁄₁₆ inches in total length and weighs 2 pounds 9 ounces. The brass pan is conspicuous against the mottled lock plate, which bears the inscription "US R Johnson Middn Conn 1842" in front of the round-faced cock.

Johnson received $9.00 each for the 3,000 pistols produced under his 1836 contract. On March 14, 1840, he signed a contract for 15,000 more at $7.50 each. Asa Waters of Milbury, Massachusetts, in 1836 (4,000 pistols) and 1840 (15,000 pistols) entered into contracts similar to the Johnson agreements. These pistols, the last of the flintlocks, were received by the government from both Johnson and Waters in

1837 and through 1844. The Waters arms in 1844 were stamped A. H. WATERS & CO., instead of A. WATERS, which had been the mark on the pistols produced in the first seven years. A remarkable series of the arms, representative of both the Johnson and the Waters factories and of each of the eight years of production, is owned by the Milwaukee Museum.

This type of flintlock pistol was supplied to both regular soldiers and militiamen for many years after the percussion model was adopted. Not only was it figured in the 1841 edition of the *Ordnance Manual,* but it was issued both in unaltered form and converted to percussion all through the years of the Mexican War and for a long time thereafter.

U. S. pistol, Model 1842.—This was the first percussion pistol in the U. S. series. On November 23, 1841, Colonel George Bomford, Chief of Ordnance, instructed Major J. W. Ripley, of the Springfield Armory, with respect to the patterns for a new percussion pistol,

> to be made of the same form and dimensions as the present model, except the strap and side plate which will be made of uniform width, without a swell in the middle. A percussion lock on the same principle as for the other arms [U. S. musket, Model 1842; Cadet musket, Model 1841; and U. S. rifle, Model 1841] is to be adopted to it. The band and side plate, the butt plate, the guard bow and plate, and the sight are to be of brass.[142]

On June 10, 1842, Lieutenant Colonel Talcott of the Ordnance Office specified that twelve pistols were required for pattern purposes.

H. Aston, once an armorer with Simeon North, Middletown, Connecticut, and I. N. Johnson, also of Middletown, contracted in 1845 and 1851 to make 40,000 of these percussion pistols. Specimens exist which were made by A. H. Waters and Company (dated 1844) [143] and by the Palmetto Armory, Columbia, South Carolina (dated 1842),[144] but they lack the "US" on the lock plate.

The pistol shown in figure 38, *a,* is one made by Aston. It is substantially a cap-and-ball version of the U. S. pistol, Model 1836. The total length is 14 inches, and the weight is 2 pounds 12 ounces. Except for a change in the design of the side plate opposite the lock, the new weapon had the same form and dimensions as its predecessor. The side plate, band, butt plate, trigger guard, and knife-blade sight are brass. Soon after the patterns for the Model 1842 were distributed from the Springfield Armory in 1845, many Model 1836

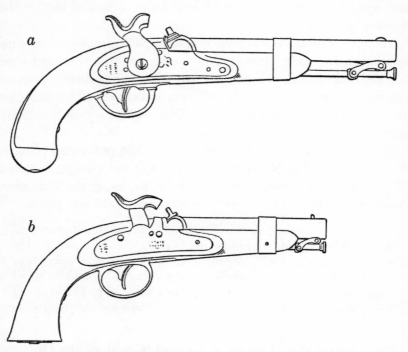

Fig. 38. U. S. pistols, percussion, Models 1842 and 1843. *a,* Model 1842. It is an H. Aston and Co. product from Middletown, Conn., now exhibited at Harold's Club, Reno, Nevada. *b,* Model 1843. This specimen is one of the 2,000 made by N. P. Ames of Chicopee Falls, Mass. It is also in the Harold's Club exhibit.

pistols were converted to percussion by replacing the pan with a brass plug into which a cone with nipple, also brass, was screwed. The M. H. de Young Memorial Museum has a Johnson specimen (no. 6380), dated 1842, which has been so converted.

The Aston specimen shown in figure 38, *a,* is one of 30,000 made under a contract of February 25, 1845. Several other contractors made this model, and some of their arms are dated 1842, presumably because the pattern pistols were so dated. All evidence indicates that patterns did not reach manufacturers before 1845.

Before Aston and Johnson got the Model 1842 into production, another official pistol, the Model 1843, was designed, manufactured, and issued to troops; thus, although the Model 1842 was the first percussion pistol to be formally prescribed by the U. S. government, it was not the first to be "received." However, it is the pistol which was selected to represent the handgun among the illustrations of small arms in the *Ordnance Manual,* editions of 1850 and 1861, and it was the standard-issue pistol until it was superseded by the rifled U. S. pistol-carbine, Model 1855. Lewis quotes a letter from General Talcott, written in 1849, which asserts that the 1st Dragoons preferred this pistol (Model 1842) even after the Colt revolver was available to them.[145]

U. S. pistol, Model 1843 (percussion).—In designing this pistol, someone among the armorers in the U. S. Ordnance organization seems to have turned back to pre-Revolutionary days in reviving a type of lock known to the English as "box-lock." The hammer is attached inside the lock plate. There seems to be no published account of the advantages that may have been claimed for this mechanism.

N. P. Ames of Springfield, Massachusetts, and Henry Deringer of Philadelphia contracted to make a comparatively few (several thousand) of this model in 1843.[146] A number of specimens by Ames are known which are marked "USN" on barrel and lock plate; some are dated 1843, some 1844, and others 1845. No sights are found on the Ames pistols. Deringer turned out some of his order as rifled pistols (seven grooves), the first rifled single-shot handguns in the U. S. series. This model, therefore, not only was the first percussion pistol to be used by U. S. troops, but it was the first rifled pistol to be specified by the government. Deringer's rifled specimens are equipped with front and rear sights; his smoothbore product lacked sights. Some of Ames's pistols and some of Deringer's are marked "USR" on the lock plate, for "U. S. Mounted Rifles." The Deringer specimens are not dated.

The typical specimen in figure 38, *b,* shows the Ames product: a pistol 11.62 inches long, with a 6½-inch smoothbore barrel. It is .54 caliber.

It is interesting to note that the "USR" pistol is a sort of souvenir of the conversion of the 2d Dragoons to riflemen. They were soon restored to cavalry status. During the winter of 1845–1846 they were stationed on the Nueces River in Texas, where in target practice they were able to try out the rifled pistols against the Colt-Paterson revolvers in the hands of the Texas Rangers.[147]

In March, 1846, the Dragoons led the way across the disputed country south of the Nueces. It was one of their patrols which was set upon by the Mexicans opposite Matamoras on April 25, an ambuscade referred to previously as the clash which started the fireworks.[148] Here was the beginning, also, of the widespread interest in Colt's revolvers. Quite fortuitously, the two arms—the U. S. pistol, Model 1843, and the Paterson Colt—so far apart mechanically were brought together in a military way at what proved to be a big moment in military-arms history.

Colt Paterson pistols in the Army.—At this point, it is only necessary to relate the Paterson revolvers to the Walker-Colt revolver commonly referred to by arms historians as "United States repeating pistol, Model 1847."

After Sam Colt had been told several times by boards of Army officers that his revolving arms of the 1836 design were not suitable for military use, he busied himself in making changes from the original model. Two of these holster pistols are those shown in figure 39, *a* and *b*. They should be compared with figure 16 in chapter ii.

The gun pictured in figure 39, *a,* is a Colt Paterson revolver without loading lever. It has a 9-inch octagonal barrel, .36 caliber, rifled with eleven grooves having a slight right twist. The cylinder contains five chambers which are chamfered at the muzzle end. The nipples take the no. 9 percussion cap and have four shoulders which can receive a wrench. The two-piece, flared grip of walnut is typical, although some straight grips also were used on Colt Paterson re-

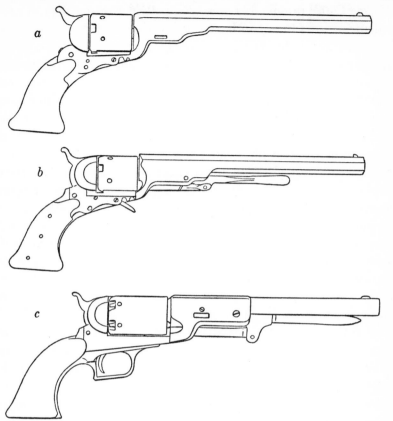

Fig. 39. Colt revolvers used by rangers and the military. *a,* the Colt Paterson without loading lever, now in Wadsworth Atheneum, Hartford, Conn. *b,* a similar model with the loading lever, in the John E. Parsons Collection, New York City; after a figure in Serven, 1946 (p. 20), by permission of Mr. Serven and Mr. Parsons. *c,* the famous "Walker Colt," the U. S. repeating pistol, Model 1847; no. F23 in the exhibit at Harold's Club, Reno.

volvers. The revolving mechanism is an arrangement of slots on the rear end of the cylinder, which receive a pawl extending forward from the base of the hammer. The cylinder stops are round. The rear sight is in the hammer nose; the front sight is a short, low blade. This large-framed, long-barreled holster pistol, usually classed as a "Texas Colt," presumably was produced in 1838 or 1839 to meet the demand for a handgun having greater power than could be obtained from the earlier belt sizes made by Colt.

In figure 39, *b,* is the pistol with a loading lever. The dimensions of this specimen are similar in many ways to those of 39, *a,* described above. Its distinguishing characteristic is the built-in loading lever, a device upon which Colt obtained a patent on August 29, 1839. The barrel lug is cut away to permit clearance for the loosely seated balls which are brought in line with the two-piece plunger with which they can be rammed down upon the powder charge. The recoil shield is cut away to permit the placing of caps upon the nipples. Like all Colts with loading lever, this one has a cylinder with rounded rear shoulder. The loading device overcame some of the criticism formerly directed at the Colt revolver, but even this improved handgun still had the defect that an exploding cap might cause a jam when fragments of the metal were caught between cylinder and recoil shield—a difficulty which, however, was remedied in part by the cutting of a ring slot in the recoil shield in the subsequent model.[149]

The improved loading lever made these 1839–1840 revolvers rather direct progenitors of the Walker Colt. It is a foregone conclusion that both the "belt" size, Model 1836, and the "holster" size, Model 1839, were represented among the Colt revolvers that were carried as personal arms by some Army officers,[150] and as official arms by some Texas Rangers before the Mexican War; but it was the larger holster size which brought forth the greatest praise in the West, and it is this larger .36 caliber gun with 9-inch barrel, rifled with eleven grooves, which has become known as the "Texas Paterson."

Repeatedly it has been said by a number of writers that Captain Sam Walker of the Texas Rangers gave Colt advice with respect to the improvements which are the features of the 1839 patent; but rather conclusive evidence has been presented by Hicks (1940*a*), Serven (1946), and Parsons (1949), indicating that Walker and Colt did not correspond or otherwise get together until General Zachary Taylor, in command on the Mexican border, sent Walker, then with the U. S. Mounted Rifles, on his journey of 1846 to buy Colt guns.

Walker was authorized to represent the Secretary of War, and the first contract for one thousand revolvers, which bears the date January 4, 1847, was entered into between Samuel Colt and Samuel H. Walker. It was signed by Walker, personally, and was approved on January 6 by the Secretary of War.[151]

In collaboration with Walker, Colt devised the rugged .44 caliber, six-shot weapon (fig. 39, *c*) which was to be known as the Walker Colt, a gun which from the beginning anticipated the use of elongated bullets. In accordance with the contract: "The barrels to be nine inches long and rifled, made of the best hammered cast steel; and of a bore suited to fifty round balls to the pound; and with strength sufficient for firing an elongated ball of 32 to the pound." The cylinder, rounded at the rear, has six chambers. The total weight of the gun is 4½ pounds. On the right side of the barrel lug is stamped "US 1847." This revolver, made after Captain Walker had given advice in regard to dimensions and certain mechanical details in 1846, was manufactured in accordance with a contract for one thousand entered into in 1847. The arms are marked "Address Sam'l Colt, New York City, U. S. 1847," but the first lot was made in Eli Whitney's factory at Whitneyville near New Haven during that interval in 1847–1848 when Colt was on his way to Hartford, fame, and fortune.

The contract with the government provided for "a larger number than one thousand if desired by the War Department," and Colt urged Walker to lay the groundwork in Washington for additional orders. On January 30, 1847, Walker wrote to Colt:

> I have lost no opportunity in recommending your arms and have succeeded in attracting public attention to them, but everybody wishes to see them. . . . If you can get the pair complete I will return here with them expressly to exhibit them to the Military Committee who have the matter now under consideration and much depends on their recommendation. Houston and Rusk [Senate Military Committee] will give the highest recommendation to these arms and you may have no fears about their being adopted for general use by all the U. S. Cavalry if you can only get some of them complete. Nine men of ten in this City do not know what Colt's pistol is and although I have explained the difference

between yours and the six barrel popgun that is in such general use a
thousand times they are still ignorant on the subject.[152]

Obviously, Captain Walker was a successful agent. In July, 1847,
William L. Marcy, Secretary of War, ordered that another contract
for one thousand Colt revolvers be entered into. Colt had planned
his own factory, in the meantime, in Hartford, Connecticut. This second government order, dated November 2, 1847, yielded the "first-
model Dragoon" and launched Colt and his Hartford factory upon
a program of arms making which has been continued to this day by
his successors.

Colt died in 1862[153] without witnessing the effect the general use
of metallic cartridges was to have on his business, but he lived to see
the great westward movement of his fellow Americans and the
devastating rupture in national affairs resulting from the dispute
over slavery, both of which caused a great increase in the volume of
sales for his handguns. Enriched through successful business activities, bemedaled as he was by foreign governments and honored at
home,[154] he had every reason to feel that his accomplishments were
of high order. His biographers [155] now are numerous, and the appraisals of his over-all contributions to America's success at arms vary,
but there is unanimity of opinion regarding the significance of the
Paterson pistols in the history of the western frontier during the
critical period of the 1830's and 1840's. Walter Prescott Webb, who
published his "The American Revolver and the West" in 1927 and
his *The Great Plains* in 1931, led the way among accredited historians
of the present generation in acknowledging the role of the Colt in
the West. Of the Rangers, Dragoons, Santa Fe traders, and mountain
men and the Paterson pistols they used De Voto writes, "They had
promptly worked a revolution in warfare comparable to and more
immediately important than that heralded by the American light
artillery at Palo Alto." [156]

V

Powder, Ball, and Accessories

The flintlock firearm and all its appurtenances prevailed through the greater part of the era of the mountain man. It was not until 1816 [1] that the percussion system of detonation was perfected, and even for many years thereafter there was a reluctance among many of the men on the western frontier to abandon the flintlock. This resistance to the change was especially manifest among the Indians, and the example set by the military, both British and American, did not hurry the improvement. The old-style flintlock guns were in some demand through most of the period with which this book is concerned (through 1843) and some manufacturers continued to cater to the die-hards by producing flintlock arms even after metallic cartridges and breechloaders were commonly used.

GUNPOWDER

Gunpowder, of course, was and still is basic in the preparation of the load in any firearm, whatever its period or system. For hundreds of years, gunpowder in the form of fine dust or meal persisted as the proper charge for small arms as well as cannon, but sometime in the sixteenth century it dawned upon some of its users that greater power, as well as added convenience in loading and uniformity of behavior, was obtained with powder that was granulated. Ignition was observed to be accelerated by the ready passage of the flame between the grains of the charge. Powder manufacturers thereupon became more scientific in their experimenting and in the processes of their production of the explosive; yet for a long time there continued to be a wide divergence in the methods used and in the results obtained. Even the proportions of the basic ingredients of gunpowder differed in the various countries in which it was produced. The English government specified that its powder should contain 75 parts of saltpeter, 15 of charcoal, and 10 of sulphur. In France and Belgium it was prescribed that there should be 75 per cent of saltpeter and 12½ per cent each of charcoal and sulphur; in Germany and Austria the proportions were 76 parts of saltpeter, 14 parts of charcoal, and 10 parts of sulphur. In manufacturing gunpowder under conditions of stringent economy, as in production for some trade purposes, the amount of saltpeter was reduced to a minimum.[2]

The reader who desires to learn of the eighteenth-century materials, equipment, and methods of making gunpowder in the manufactories of France is referred to the nineteen large plates and accompanying explanatory text published by Denis Diderot in his forty-five-volume *Encyclopedie*. The significance of the French gunpowder enterprise in the story of gunpowder in the United States will receive some attention in the account of the young chemist from Essone, E. I. du Pont de Nemours. First, however, the basic processes in preparing the ingredients of gunpowder and the crude "home industry" practiced by Americans in meeting their needs for ammunition will be described.

The first step, of course, was the procurement of the ingredients. Saltpeter was and is available in the natural state in many of the limestone caves of Virginia, Georgia, Tennessee, and Kentucky. By a process of leaching the raw material with wood ashes, followed by evaporation, unwanted salts and earthy matter could be separated from the saltpeter. The resulting product was still too crude to be useful in making gunpowder; a series of washings, straining, melting, crystallization, drying, sifting, and packing in barrels or molding in cakes was necessary before the saltpeter was sufficiently purified. Powder mills in the vicinity of the deposits of saltpeter usually refined their own supply, but many others had the refined ingredient shipped to them.

Sulphur occurs in volcanic regions and is refined from its crude state by sublimation—by heating it until it is vaporized. The subsequent cooling and solidifying forms a powder called "flowers of sulphur." In the making of gunpowder, this was melted and run into molds to make "roll brimstone." Usually, the powder manufacturer depended upon importers to supply his sulphur.

To obtain the ingredient carbon, charcoal often was prepared from willow or poplar cut in the spring and stripped of its bark. The wood was charred in pits or "distilled" in an iron vessel. The iron container, closed except for a pipe which permitted the escape of gases, was heated in a furnace until the wood was reduced to charcoal.

The next step was to grind and mix the ingredients in proper proportion, the most important part of the process. In pioneer times this was done by pounding the materials in a mortar made from an oak or other hardwood log. The pestle was bronze or some very hard wood. First, the charcoal was ground, after being moistened by a little water; then measured amounts of saltpeter and sulphur, previously pulverized, were added. Further pounding and mixing by hand served to blend or "incorporate" the ingredients. The pounding or grinding process took several hours, and water in small quantities was added from time to time until a cake was formed. The cake was then taken from the mortar and dried.

Some powder makers, as a part of their grinding process, placed the ingredients (except the saltpeter) in a "rolling barrel" made of leather or rawhide stretched on a frame which had its slats on the inside. Into this was put a load of zinc or copper balls equal in weight to twice the weight of the mixture of charcoal and sulphur. The barrel was rolled for an hour or two, then the saltpeter was added and the barrel was set in motion again. At the end of another two hours the meal was moistened with water and pounded in the mortar to make a cake.

To granulate the cake, one method was to pass it between wooden rollers and sift it; another was to place it upon a sieve made of pierced parchment, where it would be broken up by the action of a five-pound disk of hardwood. In either method the final sifting was done with a series of sieves having apertures of different sizes. A sieve with 14 to 16 meshes to the inch would pass the "Fg," or coarse powder used for cannon loads; 16 to 24 meshes to the inch would pass the "FFg" powder, suitable for musket loads; and 24 to 46 meshes to the inch separated the "FFFg," or rifle powder.

Powder was "glazed" (that is, each grain was given a hard, smooth surface) in order that it might be somewhat resistant to the action of moisture in the air. The granulated powder was placed in a barrel, which could be revolved at the rate of fifteen or twenty times a minute for several hours.

The secret of the explosive force of black powder is found in its property of burning when confined without air. A part of the abundant supply of oxygen in the saltpeter in the powder in the gun barrel is released under the effect of the ignition of the powder in pan or primer, and thus provides the load with its own oxygen for the combustion of the whole charge. This combustion releases a tremendous volume of gas, which is confined behind the ball until the pressure is so great as to drive the missile beyond the confines of the barrel. More than half of the products of combustion of black powder are solids which, together with the powder gases, produce a cloud of white smoke. Some solids also remain in the bore and touchhole, fouling the piece and making it necessary to clean it frequently.[3]

In America the colonists lived by the gun to a far greater extent than their relatives in the mother countries. As might be expected, the problem of survival mothered invention and the perfection of arms. The development of the Kentucky rifle is a fair example. Even in the seventeenth century the Colonial fathers sought to promote progress in the making of gunpowder. In 1666 when Richard Wooddey of Boston and Henry Russell of Ipswich began an experiment in powder making, the General Court gave them special privileges and ordered that they be given all aid and encouragement possible.[4] Yet, in spite of the official encouragement that was generally forthcoming, no great advances in powder making were brought about in America in the Colonial period. Right up to the time of the Revolution the much-needed explosive continued to be made in small quantities only, on a hand-to-mouth basis, very much as American bullets were made in the homes of the hunters. War necessitated great expansion of the powder industry in America, but even after the successful conclusion of the Revolution there was little falling off in the demand for gunpowder. On the contrary, so great was the demand for it that many new powder mills were established in all parts of the country at the beginning of the nineteenth century. The census of 1810 listed more than two hundred mills in sixteen states, with an estimated output of 1,500,000 pounds. Yet demand exceeded the supply, and many of the makers hurried to fill the need, paying small attention to the quality of their product and giving little or no thought to scientific standards to be adhered to if uniform results were to be obtained.

On New Year's Day in the year 1800 there came to the United States a Frenchman who was destined to revolutionize the powder industry in America. This was Éleuthère Irénée du Pont de Nemours, who had once been a chemist in the French government's gunpowder works at Essone. Under the training of the noted head of that enterprise, Lavoisier, the young Du Pont had learned how to refine saltpeter and sulphur; to combine the two with charcoal derived from willow wood; and to press, grain, and polish the product into high-grade "black powder." He also had learned how to operate machinery and how to guard against carelessness in the hazardous business of powder making.

By chance or as a result of someone's deliberate planning, Du Pont went hunting with a Colonel Louis de Toussard, near the town of Wilmington, Delaware. When he bought gunpowder at a country store he became angry at the high price demanded and the inferior quality of the gunpowder foisted upon him. This circumstance stirred him to look into the possibilities of engaging in the manufacturing of gunpowder as a private undertaking. He visited some of the small mills then operating on the eastern seaboard and determined quickly enough that he could compete with them very effectively. Thomas Jefferson, already a friend of the Du Ponts, was approached in the matter. Jefferson, General John Mason, and John Hancock urged that the proposed new industry be started. Du Pont went back to France in 1801 and obtained promises from officials in the French powder department to provide needed machinery and to lend trained workers. Articles of incorporation were drawn up and Du Pont was named director of the new firm, E. I. du Pont de Nemours and Company. Young Du Pont then returned to America and explored for a millsite. He selected a spot on Brandywine Creek near Wilmington, Delaware, and in 1802 the original Du Pont establishment was started. One of the first jobs undertaken in the plant was the refinement of some saltpeter for the U. S. government. By 1804, shipments of gunpowder were made from the Brandywine to New York. In that year, 44,907 pounds of gunpowder were manufactured; and in 1805, coastal schooners and wagon teams were taking the Du Pont product north to Boston, south to Charleston and Savannah, and west to Pittsburgh.[5]

Before the War of 1812, imported gunpowder sold in the United States for 37½ and 40 cents a pound, as shown by the invoices of the U. S. Indian Trade Office and the American Fur Company.[6] During the War of 1812 it was as high as 62 cents a pound.[7] Soon after the war, American-made powder of equal quality was to be had for 20 cents.[8] Beyond doubt the Du Pont mills did much to bring about this change. The invoices of both the American Fur Company and the U. S. Office of Indian Trade indicate that in the 1820's American gunpowder was being purchased quite regularly in two- and three-thousand-pound lots at 20 cents a pound, and that the imported product at 30 to 62½ cents a pound was limited to occasional purchases of one hundred to four hundred pounds.[9]

In 1827 the Du Pont mills employed 140 men and had a capacity of 800,000 pounds of powder annually. E. I. du Pont computed in 1832 that he had produced 13,400,000 pounds during the thirty years he had operated. "The bulk of this had been used for hunting, a use which demanded a powder superior to blasting powder." [10]

The patronage and commendation of the U. S. government were extended to the Du Pont Company through the years, yet some of the government officials, in the early stages of dealing with the company, took nothing for granted. On December 28, 1807, the superintendent of the U. S. Office of Indian Trade admonished Mr. du Pont: "The good quality of the powder used by the Indians is a great object with them. They are good judges of the quality and much dissatisfied if they do not procure that which they like." This warning was accompanied by an order for forty quarter casks of best rifle powder, "to be in casks well coopered and carefully sewed in canvas, marked U.S.N. and numbered 1 to 40." [11] That this order was filled satisfactorily there can be no doubt, for subsequent entries in the records of the Indian Trade Office pertain to numerous additional orders, and other government offices also availed themselves repeatedly of the service provided by Du Pont. On April 24, 1827, the commanding officer at the Frankfort Arsenal published a report which showed that the Du Pont gunpowder had proved superior when checked against such European gunpowders as Pegou, Andrews and Wilkes's three grades—"single seal," "double seal," and "canister"—and unnamed brands from Edinburgh and London. In official tests it was demonstrated that the Du Pont product excelled in strength, quickness in burning, and cleanliness, [12] yet the cost to the user was scarcely more than half the price of the other powders.

A Du Pont advertisement of the flintlock period refers to the Du Pont Eagle Gunpowder: "Fine grain for sporting in canisters, pound papers, and 6¼-pound kegs. Coarser grain expressly for water fowl shooting in canisters, 6¼ and 12½-pound kegs. Gunpowder of superior quality F, IF, and HF glazed and rough in 25, 12½, and 6¼ lb. kegs." [13] In designating grades and characteristics of his gunpowder, Du Pont informed the Superintendent of the U. S. Indian

Trade Office, in 1809, that the following markings would be used: "FG, coarse grain glazed; FFG, finer; FFR, same size grain not glazed, FFFG, very fine grain glazed." [14]

The matter of containers in which to ship the explosive into the wilds where it found greatest use was a problem in itself. One of the earliest comments on this problem in the Far West is found in the records of the Lewis and Clark expedition. On August 6, 1805, near the Three Forks of the Missouri, one of the canoes in the flotilla turned over. Meriwether Lewis wrote in his journal:

> About 20 pounds of powder which we had in a tight keg, or at least one which we thought sufficiently so, got wet and entirely spoiled. This would have been the case with the other had it not have been for the expedient which I had fallen on of securing the powder by means of the lead having the latter formed into canisters which were filled with the necessary proportion of powder to discharge the lead when used [as bullets], and those canisters well secured with corks and wax. [15]

Two thousand pounds of gunpowder shipped from Kentucky to the Tombigbee country in 1810 was carried in kegs (probably 40 of them) which were billed to the U. S. Indian Trade Office at $60.00. [16] In 1821 the American Fur Company allowed 50 cents each for kegs holding fifty pounds of powder. [17] The Du Pont mills finally added a cooperage to the establishment and made their own casks and kegs on their premises. Specially designed freight wagons [18] also were added to the Du Pont equipment, and freight costs were reduced accordingly. Before this expanded freight service was provided by the company, much of the trucking of the dangerous product was done under contract by independent operators. Ramsay Crooks of the American Fur Company wrote to Pratte, Chouteau and Company of Philadelphia and St. Louis, on February 4, 1835: "Messrs. Dupont have advised us that the enormous price of $3.25 is asked by the waggoners for freight to Pittsburgh and they do not think it will be cheaper 'till the canals of Pennsylvania are open. Last year the price was only $2.12½ per 100 lbs. from Brandywine to the Ohio." [19]

Shipments of gunpowder destined for the Mississippi River or St.

Louis and the Far West encountered still greater obstructions after they arrived in Pittsburgh.[20] Ramsay Crooks on January 12, 1835, admonished Joseph Rolette, agent of the American Fur Company at Prairie du Chien at the mouth of the Wisconsin:

> I am disappointed in not receiving your domestic order, particularly for gunpowder which is got to St. Louis with the greatest difficulty. We cannot send it from this port [New York] by New Orleans with any certainty for our ships dislike it and the St. Louis steamboats [at New Orleans] refuse to take it. You cannot even get it carried from Pittsburgh in a steamboat as the fact of its being aboard deters passengers from embarking. There is then no resource left but that of a keel boat which is now almost unknown [on the Ohio], and the only opportunity I can hear of is that which Messrs. Pratte, Chouteau & Co. have annually to prepare to take their own gunpowder. If your order comes in time I have secured freight for it in their boat which is to leave Pittsburgh the first week of March, but if your memo arrives too late for that conveyance I know of no other way of getting your powder to you than by the Lakes on the opening of navigation the latter part of April.[21]

Apparently Rolette's "memo" arrived soon after the foregoing letter was written, for on January 21, 1835 Ramsay Crooks addressed Rolette:

> We have already directed 100 kegs gunpowder of 50 lb. each FF 5% 5%, to be forwarded so as to leave Pittsburgh early in March by Pratte, Choteau & Co. boat,—the remainder shall go by the Lakes as you request, and you will please inform me at what time you want it at Green Bay. I presume you intend your boats that bring your skins over to take this powder back on their return to the Mississippi.[22]

POWDER CONTAINERS

The canisters provided by the powder makers afforded convenient containers which many hunters used for their immediate individual reserve supply of gunpowder, and more than a few of the frontiersmen depended upon the 6¼-pound kegs also made by the powder factories. Others utilized water casks or canteens of wood as storage receptacles. One such powder cask is preserved by the Los Angeles

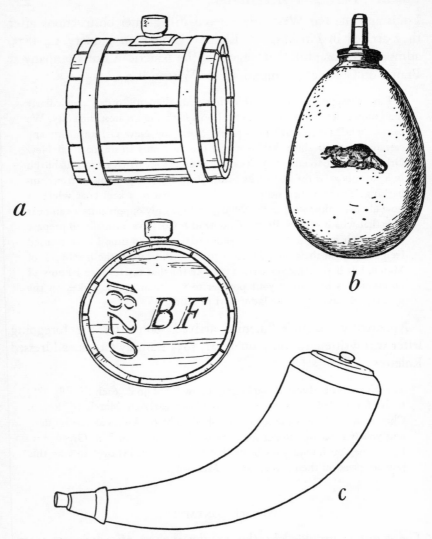

Fig. 40. Powder horns and other powder containers. *a,* canteen of wood used as a container for gunpowder, two views; Otis Collection, Los Angeles Museum (no. A 992/1523). *b,* Hudson's Bay Co. powder flask of lead (the cast figure is a beaver); C. Stanley Jacob Collection, Plainfield, N.J. *c,* a 13-in. powder horn made from the horn of an ox that was driven from Tennessee to Ohio in 1802; Colorado Historical Society Collection (no. H. 147). *d,* powder horn made from the horn of a buffalo; it has a high polish; C. Stanley Jacob Collection. *e,* powder horn made from a buffalo horn, which has been scraped but not polished; C. Stanley Jacob Collection.

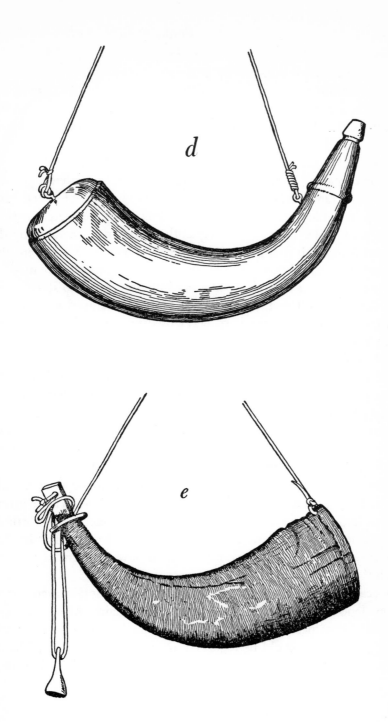

Museum. It is a round cask with ten staves. The ends, which are approximately nine inches in diameter, are of one piece of wood with a slightly concave surface. Two iron hoops, one inch wide, enclose the staves. One of the staves is wider than the others and has a raised circular section which contains the bunghole. A plug of wood, called the bung, closes the opening. This cask is engraved on one of the solid end pieces "BF 1820." (See fig. 40, *a*.)

The container carried on the hunter's person was either a powder flask or a powder horn. Flasks were usually made of metal (fig. 40, *b*), and they were seldom the product of home craftsmanship, whereas powder horns were frequently made and decorated by the hunter himself. It is apparent, however, that powder horns were also stocked by supply houses. The horns of oxen (fig. 40, *c*) were used for these containers most commonly, but buffalo horns also served (fig. 40, *d* and *e*). When the entire horn had been scraped smooth and thin, the large end of the horn was closed permanently with a carefully fitted piece of hardwood, embellished with carved rings and a knob, as the maker saw fit. The small end contained a smooth, tight-fitting but removable plug of wood. The horn was carried slung by a strap beneath the hunter's right arm, if he was right-handed. The strap passed transversely over the left shoulder, and upon the strap where it passed across the hunter's back "his bullet mould, gun screw, wiper, awl, etc." were sometimes affixed [23]—an arrangement which might suffice for the march, but which was decidedly irregular so far as the hunt was concerned. The accessories mentioned were usually carried in a pouch. Col. John Johnston in 1802 at Fort Wayne inventoried large powder horns at $1.00 each; small ones were worth 45 cents apiece. Powder flasks in 1809 were listed at $2.75 each.[24] In 1821 the American Fur Company valued small powder horns at 65 cents each.[25]

Occasionally, the powder containers of the mountain men served as evidence in the identification of human remains. Also, a marked powder container found in the hands of an Indian whose conduct was questionable could be regarded as some evidence that a bloody murder had been committed. The Boston trader N. J. Wyeth at Fort

Union in 1833 wrote: "A Mr. Patten of Fort Union shewed me a powder flask which he traded from the Blackfeet. I immediately knew it to be one of mine and on examination found 'No. 4 H.G.O.M.' graven with a point on it. It was Mores' flask who was killed in Little Jackson Hole last year on his return [trip] home after rendezvous." [26]

Rifle makers of the muzzle-loader days often supplied a charger which would hold just the right amount of powder for an ideal load to be used in a particular rifle sold to a customer. The maker also advised, "Use coarse powder. FG or FFG; it is much better than fine." Roberts, who provides a wealth of information on the practical aspects of muzzle-loader rifle shooting, states:

> The pioneer rule for ascertaining the correct charge of powder for a round ball rifle was: place a ball in the palm of the hand and pour out from the powder horn enough powder to completely cover the ball. Then, from a piece of bone hollowed out, or the tip of a small horn, or from a brass tube with a cork in one end, make a charger which this quantity of powder fills exactly to the top—"stricken measure." This measure is still the best for ascertaining the correct charges for the different gauges of round ball rifles. Another old-time rule for this purpose was: use 3 grains weight of powder for each 7 grains weight of ball, which applied to the above caliber round balls works out very nearly the same charges.[27]

LEADEN MISSILES

Although the smoothbore gun could not be depended upon to hit even a sizable target at a range greater than fifty to a hundred yards, it had the advantage of being easily and quickly loaded, and it had the further virtue of throwing a handful of shot in lieu of a single ball when occasion called for the use of the "scatter-gun." These characteristics and the simple mechanism commended the musket to the Indian and to a goodly number of white hunters of Canadian and Creole origin on the western frontier. It remained the popular weapon of the Indian for many years after the precision accuracy of the Kentucky rifle had been demonstrated and made famous by revolutionists and backwoodsmen in the East.

The rifleman of the days of the muzzle-loaders found it necessary to force his bullet into the rifle barrel. The hunter who carried a musket was able to push his ball into place without great effort. Actually, the musket ball without a patch could be seated upon the powder charge by merely jarring the butt of the gun against the ground or the saddle, for the lead ball was made a size or two smaller than the bore. Even the dirt and powder residue adhering to the inside of the gun barrel did not usually greatly impede the musket ball as it was being loaded. This advantage strongly appealed to the Indian of the Plains and the Rockies, for he hunted buffalo from the back of a horse.

The inaccuracy of the musket at long range was not a disadvantage to this buffalo hunter, for he commonly rode alongside his lumbering quarry and discharged his gun point-blank into the vitals of the beast. This practice, together with the prevailing mode of hand-to-hand combat in intertribal war tended to perpetuate the big bore and the heavy ball of the musket. Range might have been increased by using a smaller bore and ball, and there would have been a corresponding economy in the use of lead; but since it was much more important for the weapon to have great shocking power at short range than for it to throw a ball a long distance (with little or no accuracy), the musket always retained its large caliber.

Captain Levinge, writing at the end of the period of the western fur trade, gave his views regarding the advantages of the shotgun in the wilderness:

> One word as to the best sort of gun for Upper Canada. There is not the facility of carrying about several kinds of guns, and a smooth-bore "double gun" which will throw ball true at 60 yards,—and most guns will—is the best weapon for deer shooting, as most of the shots got in the woods are within that distance. It is, therefore, available for small game. There is a prejudice against firing ball from a smooth-bored gun, as it is supposed to injure it for shot. No sort of damage is done by having the balls cast in a mould one size smaller than the gauge of the barrel; and by placing them in the ends of the fingers of kid gloves, cut off long enough to cover the ball they will fly quite true, and will not injure the

gun in the slightest degree. In 99 cases out of a 100, a ball will fly nearly as true at 60 yards as one fired from the best rifle turned out of Moores or the Lancaster shops. It is to be remembered, however, that only ⅔ of the charge of powder used when shooting with shot is required when the same gun is to be loaded with ball.[28]

Lead was commonly taken into the wilderness in the form of small bars. Musket balls and rifle bullets were molded by the hunters as needed. A piece of one of these bars from the Grignon-Porlier post, Butte des Montes in Wisconsin, is preserved in the collections of the Wisconsin Historical Society at Madison. The account book of the Wisconsin trader Francis X. Des Noyers records the sale of such lead bars at 50 cents each.[29] In 1802, Colonel John Johnston at Fort Wayne invoiced 600 pounds of small bar lead at $50.40, or 8⁴⁄₁₀ cents a pound. In the same year 1,050 pounds of Illinois lead was invoiced at 15 cents a pound. By 1809, Johnston valued his small-bar lead at 10 cents a pound.[30] The American Fur Company in 1821 carried lead on its books at 20 cents a pound. This was in the Illinois country, and the lead was heavy bar lead, sometimes referred to as pig lead. The bars averaged about sixty pounds each.[31]

The smaller sizes of shot of course were not readily made in the field. The traders' inventories reveal that "pigeon shot," "duck shot," "beaver shot," and "buck shot" were commonly supplied to the trade. The American Fur Company in the early 1820's in the Great Lakes region inventoried all sizes of shot, and musket balls as well, at 20 cents a pound; the same value as was placed on bar lead. At Fort Wayne in the opening years of the nineteenth century, the price of shot was 13 to 19 cents a pound.[32]

Among the many interesting objects taken from the ground at Tadoussac, at the mouth of the Saguenay on the St. Lawrence, is a collection of shot and musket balls of the period of the earliest French activity in America. The missiles range in size from no. 4 shot to ¾-inch balls. The smaller sizes predominate.

Containers for shot were commonly made by the hunters or by their Indian women from buckskin, but the traders also provided them. In 1802 at Fort Wayne, "12 shot pouches with double gores" were valued at $15.00. Subsequent entries indicate the price of shot bags to have been $1.25 each.[33]

Bullet molds were of the utmost importance to the Indian and the white hunter alike. A wide variety of molds are to be found in collections throughout the country. Some of these iron and brass matrices are very simple and provide for the casting of but one ball at each operation. Occasionally specimens of molds are to be seen which were made from steatite, or soapstone. Most of these home-made molds consist of two blocks of soapstone so shaped and fitted that they can be held together by pins of wood. With a metal "cherry" the hunter hollowed out depressions in each half of the mold and by means of a canal joined these half holes to a groove in the edge of the block of stone. After the two parts of the mold were adjusted to fit and were pinned together, molten lead was poured into the trench, or groove, from which it then streamed down the canal into the round cavity enclosed by the two blocks. This cavity was of the exact size of the desired ball. Removal of the wooden pins enabled the hunter to open the mold to extricate his musket ball from the half of the mold that held it. A little work with a knife would trim from the ball the edges and "tits" of lead along the line where the two parts of the mold joined, and the resulting projectile was fairly spherical. A soapstone mold made to cast these balls is in the Wisconsin State Historical Society Museum. It came from Mishicot, Manitowoc County, Wisconsin.

Among the more interesting molds are those heavy brass devices in which larger numbers of balls could be made in one operation. A typical example is the one shown in figure 41. It consists of two bars of brass 14½ inches long and 2 inches wide. One end of each bar has been shaped so that it can be fitted into the end of the other bar to make a hinge. The ends of both bars opposite the hinge have been drawn out to make a tang some 4 inches long. Handles of wood 6 inches long enclose the tangs. One bar has a protruding pin which, when the faces are brought together, fits into a depression in the opposite bar. In both bars are twenty-four carefully made round depressions, or cups, about ⅜ inch in diameter, arranged in two parallel series. Each cup constitutes an exact half of a hollow sphere. A depressed channel, U-shape in section and ⅛ inch wide, extends from each cup to the edge of the bar of brass. All parts of this mold are accurately machined, and when the two brass bars are swung on their hinge so as to bring their cupped faces together, the protruding pin or lug of one fits into the opposed well of the other, and the two halves of the mold are thus stabilized in closed position. A continuous median trench extends along the long edges of the closed mold,

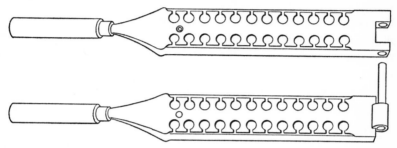

Fig. 41. Brass bullet mold for twenty-four balls. In preparing the mold for use, the pin in the hinge is withdrawn; after the two halves of the mold are fitted together, it is reinserted. The balls produced by this mold are .60 cal., a usual size for the Hudson's Bay fuke, or trade gun. The mold was used in Canada as recently as 1837; Chateau de Ramezay, Montreal (no. 18).

and the small channels leading from the spherical hollows within the mold open into this trench. By holding the mold with one of these trenches upward, the bullet maker could pour hot lead into it and so fill twelve of the spherical openings. When the other edge of the mold was turned upward, the other trench was ready to receive the molten lead and the remaining twelve holes could be filled. It was then only necessary to open the mold by pulling the wood handles apart to remove the twenty-four balls of lead.

A mold similar to the one just described but 9⅞ inches long and 1 inch wide has two rows of round depressions in which forty-six buckshot can be cast. By military standards, buckshot are .31 inch in diameter and weigh about 150 or 155 to a pound. This buckshot mold was used by the trader Louis B. Porlier at the Grignon-Porlier trading post, Butte des Morts, Wisconsin, and it is preserved in the collection of the Wisconsin Historical Society.[34]

GUNFLINTS

Because of the almost universal use of flintlock arms in the fur fields, gunflints were a standard article of trade. Traders did their utmost to obtain satisfactory flints—an ideal not always attained. Edward Umfreville, writing from the Hudson Bay region in the last half of the eighteenth century, bemoaned the inferior gunflints imported into the wilderness by the Hudson's Bay Company: "One-half of the gun flints,—a commodity about which the Indians were most particular since their lives depended upon them,—were found unfit in contrast to the clear and black flints of the Canadians [the North West Company] which never missed fire." [35] Through the hundred years following Umfreville's complaint other traders in many places in America had occasion to register similar protests regarding quality or size of the all-important flints. A fair example of one of the later complaints is found in Benjamin Clapp's letter to George Wilde and Company, London, August 31, 1836: "The gun flints sent last season did not suit, being too large. This article though a small item in amount is very important in the country. They are required of small size for rifles—those sent before were of the size used for muskets, and quite too large." [36]

Some of the best gunflints were made at Brandon quarries not far from London, England. Here in the chalk deposits the official manufactures of flints began in the seventeenth century and continued until 1835 as an enterprise for the British government. The gunflints were shaped by a flaking process called knapping. The finished products were packed in tubs or sacks containing from 5,000 to 20,000 flints. For export the flints were repacked in half casks holding 2,000 to 4,000 flints each and weighing sixty-five to seventy pounds. In the later days of the flintlock period the size of the casks and barrels used by the knappers for shipment to the trade was increased to a capacity of 7,500 to 14,700 flints.

Flints were obtained not only from the quarries at Brandon but also from Icklingham, Suffolk, Norwich, Cavenham, Tuddenham, Mildenhall, and Salisbury. The nodules of flint came from layers of chalk. Pits from which the nodules have been dug ever since the Stone Age are scattered everywhere over the ancient quarry sites. The best flints for use with firearms were quarried in damp weather, and the nodules were dried out at a fire before the knapper undertook to work on them. A good flint knapper "reckoned up" his finished gunflints by the hundred. He tallied each hundred by laying a spare flint to one side. His finished products sold at the quarry at about $1.00 a thousand, or *per mille,* as the flint knappers said, using the French term.

In the judgment of the English, the very best gunflints were the common black ones which abounded at Brandon. Fine-quality flints were also produced in France in Champagne and in Picardy, but the French government banned the exportation of them in the eighteenth century. The English flints were sent to all parts of the world from the ports of Liverpool, Bristol, and Birmingham. During the eighteenth and early nineteenth centuries the Hudson's Bay Company depended upon the firms of Joseph Railton (1785–1791), Burgon (1792), and William Melton (1815) to supply its needs for gunflints.[37]

The *Ordnance Manual* of the U. S. Army said of gunflints:

> The best flints are translucent, with a smooth surface, of a uniform tint of light yellow or brown, and slightly conchoidal fracture. . . . The parts of a flint are: the *edge* or *bevel,* the *back,* the *sides,* the *face* which is slightly convex, and the *bed* or lower face slightly concave. In using the flint the bevel is placed uppermost [in the flint vise]. There are three sizes for military service; musket, rifle, and pistol flints. A good musket flint will last for more than 50 fires. Flints are issued to the troops in the proportion of 1 flint to 20 rounds.
>
> In the inspection of flints first verify their dimensions with a gauge, giving the maximum and minimum dimensions; see that the bevel is

free from spots and irregularities of surface, that the face and bed are nearly parallel, and have not too great a curvature.

Having thus made a science of issuing flints to its soldiers of the flintlock days, the U. S. Army in the *Ordnance Manual* quoted above presented meticulous instructions for boxing flints and concluded:

> After the flints are placed in the boxes, all the interstices are to be filled with dry sand, in order to exclude the air from them as much as possible; and for the same purpose the boxes should be well made of seasoned wood, and with close joints. Each box should be plainly marked on the end with the number and description of flints contained in it, and with the year in which they were manufactured, if this be known; if not known, then with the year in which they were procured. Flints should not be placed in the upper stories of a building, but in the basement or cellar, where the air is damp and cool.[38]

Obviously, the procuring, storing, issuing, and using of the gunflints were not taken lightly by the military. Soldiers were not allowed to snap their locks in play or practice unless the flint was replaced with a wooden dummy called a snapper, and when a flint did become blunted through ordinary use in firing, its soldier owner was required to sharpen its bevel by chipping flakes from the striking edge. This was done by working from the edge backwards.

Colonel P. Hawkers' *Instructions to Young Sportsmen* advises: "The flint should be put in [the flint vise] with the flat side upward. Screw it in between a piece of leather, as lead strains the cock, and cloth is dangerous from being liable to catch fire." [39]

Colonel Hawker's advice notwithstanding, it was regular practice in the U. S. Army to mount flints in the cock by placing them between layers of lead before tightening the flint screw. Sometimes two separate disks of lead were used, one above the flint and the other below. Or one thin disk was folded over the flint so as to enclose it, top, bottom, and rear. These lead "grips" were formally designated "flint caps" in Ordnance terminology. They were used on military muskets, rifles, and pistols throughout much of the flintlock period, but in Ordnance reports they show up most prominently in connection with rifles. The government contracts with the private concerns that made military rifles of the Model 1817 specified that "each box is to contain twenty rifles with flint and flint caps complete . . . and there are to be twenty spare flint caps." This provision is not found in contracts for the Hall breech-loading flintlock rifle, nor does it appear in the musket and pistol contracts. Colonel Lewis states that "the extra flint cap was required in these contracts [for the Model 1817 rifle] because it was regulation to place a flint cap along with an extra flint, a scourer tip for cleaning, and a combination screwdriver and spanner in the patch box" [40]—and only the Model 1817 rifle had a patch box.

Flint caps totaling about 280,000 are listed in the records of "articles manufactured and procured" at the Springfield Armory during the period 1829–1844. The numbers acquired annually range from 70,792 in 1829 to none whatever in 1843. After 1844, the flint cap does not appear in the Springfield records.

In 1945, Cal N. Peters, Curator of History, Los Angeles Museum, unearthed a rather large collection of flint caps on the site of the first Fort Crawford (1816–1829), at Prairie du Chien, Wisconsin. These specimens are all of the kind that requires the use of two separate disks. Mr. Peters writes: "In fitting them in the jaws of the hammer of a Harpers Ferry flintlock musket, M 1816, I found that they would fit snugly, and by gently screwing them tight with a flint in between, would bed the flint." [41] A representative series of the flint caps found by Mr. Peters is now exhibited in the Los Angeles Museum. Arthur Woodward observes: "Judging by their size, they were made to fit military muskets, and I suspect they were made locally. One still has the casting sprue on it, and the letter *C* is on the face of it." [42] (See fig. 42, *d, e, f.*)

In the collection of Colonel Arcadi Gluckman is a rifle with a patch box containing a flint cap:

> a mint STARR rifle, Model 1817, dated 1824. In the patch box is a packet with original brittle, coarse paper wrapping, containing a curved screwdriver, a bullet worm and a gadget of lead, properly called a FLINT CAP, chalky white with a century or more of age; it looks like a corn plaster. It is oval, about $\frac{1}{32}$nd-inch thick except at the slightly thicker

rim. It has an oval hole in the center. When the lead is wrapped around
the rear of a flint the hole permits the flint and its wrapping to fit against
the jaw screw, making a firmer contact. Also in the past, I have had FLINT
CAPS [see fig. 42, *a*] for muskets.[43]

Colonel Lewis writes (March 8, 1954) that he has a U. S. flintlock
rifle in new condition which is accompanied by its original accouterments, including the flint cap. This flint cap, though similar to
Colonel Gluckman's specimen in other respects, is equipped with
lateral tabs to be folded down over the sides of the flint when it is
mounted in the jaws of the cock (see fig. 42, *b* and *c*).

Flint caps are not conspicuous in collections, but gunflints, as
might be expected, turn up by the hundreds on the sites formerly
occupied by the traders and the military and on Indian village sites.
Museums everywhere have these relics. An especially large collection is exhibited in the Fort Joseph Museum, Niles, Michigan. These
specimens came from the old fort site and vicinity and represent
eighteenth-century relics of both the French and British. The Colorado Historical Society, Denver, owns a small (3 in. × 2 in. × 1 in.)
hand-carved wooden box—which had been used by a soldier named
Bacher in the Revolution—in which gunflints were carried in the
pocket. Containers for "spares" must have been in common use
throughout the flintlock period, but few of them seem to have been
preserved. The one here referred to accompanies a British Tower
musket of 1779, which had belonged to the same soldier. The musket
is no. OH96 in the Colorado Historical Museum.

In 1748 at the Hudson's Bay Company post York Factory, sixteen gunflints were exchanged for one beaver.[44] At Miamies, in 1761,
twelve flints could be had by an Indian in exchange for one beaver.[45]
At that time a beaver skin was worth about a dollar, or a trifle more.
The cost of the flints to the traders was not more than one cent each.
Sir William Johnson at Detroit in 1761 gave a thousand gunflints to
his Indian allies. He inventoried these flints at £2:0:0.[46] By 1802 the
U. S. government Indian factory at Fort Wayne, Indiana, had reduced the price of a flint to about two-thirds of a cent,[47] and in 1823
the government price at St. Louis was less than one-third of a cent.[48]

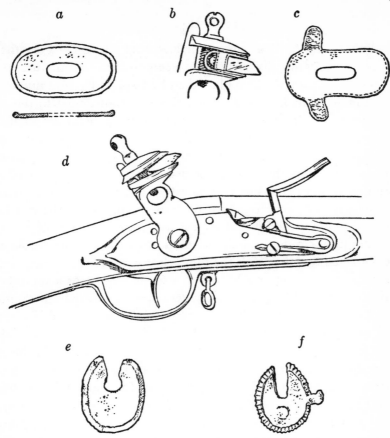

Fig. 42. Flint caps. *a*, oval flint cap with oval perforation; Col. Arcadi Gluckman Collection. *b* and *c*, flint cap with lateral tabs; Col. B. R. Lewis Collection. *d*, U. S. musket lock with flint held between two flint caps; Los Angeles Museum. *e*, flint cap of the type used in *d*, from Ft. Crawford; Los Angeles Museum. *f*, flint cap, from Ft. Crawford, with casting sprue still attached; Los Angeles Museum.

In the Far West, however, the trader's price even to the white man was considerably higher. When, in 1826 at the Great Salt Lake, William H. Ashley sold his business and his remaining merchandise to his friends Smith, Jackson, and Sublette, his bill of sale included gunflints at fifty cents a dozen.[49]

PERCUSSION CAPS

Early in the nineteenth century the Reverend Alexander Forsythe of Belhelvie, Scotland, discovered that a certain chemical mixture could be more easily ignited by a blow than by a spark. By 1814 numerous experimenters in Europe and America had contributed to the production of a fulminating powder suitable for general use in firing the guns of the day. At first the new priming powder was formed into small pellets, and special pill locks were devised to use these primers; but in 1816 came the copper percussion cap. This container of the priming powder could be carried safely and conveniently; it could be quickly and securely adjusted upon the nipple of the cap lock devised to use it; and it had the further great advantage of making a water-tight closure over the nipple so that the powder would not be damaged by rain. With the flintlock it was practically impossible to keep the priming powder dry in a heavy shower or a continuous drizzle of rain. The percussion system was so marked an improvement over the flintlock that one may wonder why percussion guns did not quickly supersede the old-style weapons in the fur fields. The fact remains that they were not noticeably popular in the Far West during the period covered in this book. The United States Army did not adopt a percussion weapon for the Dragoons (the Hall carbine) until 1833, and Infantry units did not obtain percussion arms until still later. A somewhat similar lag marked the change-over among traders and trappers. Indians were even slower to adopt the better weapon. In the meantime, the metallic cartridge and the breech-loader revolutionized the entire firearms industry.

Some percussion guns did get into the West, however, before the period of emigration. They found rather general use among the Santa Fe traders, and occasionally a few were carried up the Platte and into the transmountain region or along the upper Missouri to the increasing number of trading posts in that vast area. Some of the bourgeois adopted them, and more than a few of the personal flint-lock weapons of the leaders in the business—muskets, rifles, and pistols—were converted to the new system. This conversion was often done in the field.

Although the day of the percussion system was brief in the fur fields, cap-lock guns make a notable showing in collections, and percussion caps deserve a place in the story of the fur trader's weapons. The cap itself is made of thin-gauge copper. It is slightly conical with a flaring rim round the open end. Four slits extend halfway from the rim toward the dome of the cap, assuring ready and secure adjustment of the cap upon the nipple of the gun. The powder with which the caps are charged usually consists of fulminate of mercury mixed with half its weight of saltpeter. Half a grain of this percussion powder constitutes the charge, which is compressed into the cap and made waterproof and airtight by a drop of varnish. In military service the caps were distributed in bags of strong linen, 10,000 in a bag. Such a package weighed only 12½ pounds.[50]

The growing fraternity of twentieth-century muzzle-loader enthusiasts, together with a notable number of Indians in Canada who still hunt with cap-lock guns, create a current demand for percussion caps. They are available in six or eight different sizes from the Winchester Repeating Arms Company and the Remington Arms Company in this country, and from Eley Brothers, Ltd., in London, England.

Figure 43 shows the top from a container for Eley Brothers pistol caps which is exhibited by Harold's Club, Reno, Nevada. The cylindrical box is thin-gauge iron with lacquer finish. It is two inches in diameter and about an inch and a half deep and contains 250 caps. The diagram in this figure shows a corrugated copper cap, three-sixteenths of an inch in diameter, seated on the nipple of the U. S. pistol, Model 1842.

CARTRIDGES

Loads for the musket, rifle, and pistol, both for military and civilian use, have been encased in handy cartridges ever since the early seventeenth century. Many American frontiersmen in the period of the western fur trade carried their ammunition in cartridge form. In the literature there are several good reviews and descriptions of the making of sporting and military cartridges.[51]

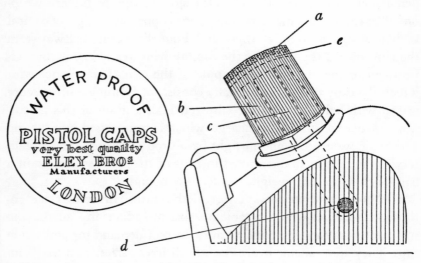

Fig. 43. Percussion caps. The Eley Brothers box top is exhibited in Harold's Club, Reno. The diagram shows the relationship of the fulminate of mercury within the cap to the touchhole leading to the powder charge in a military pistol. *a*, fulminate of mercury. *b*, nipple. *c*, channel through which flash passes to touchhole. *d*, touchhole which conducts flash of fire to powder in the chamber of the pistol. *e*, shellac to protect fulminate from moisture.

Government records show the costs at various times of making musket cartridges in the U. S. Arsenal at Pittsburgh, Pennsylvania, in the years 1813–1819.[52] During that period, 3,445,700 musket cartridges were transported by the United States Army from Pittsburgh to the military establishments in the West. It cost the government about sixty cents for the handwork necessitated in making a hundred cartridges. In 1842 the Ordnance Office gave the cost of musket cartridges, labor, and materials as $11.00 a thousand.[53]

It was regular practice in the Ordnance Department to make up rifle cartridges as well as musket cartridges. In general, the procedure was the same for both types of ammunition. The rifle ball was a half-ounce (.525 cal.) spherical bullet enclosed in a cloth patch or a thin envelope of leather or bladder. The Pittsburgh Arsenal records indicate that in the period 1816–1817 the government could obtain bladders for this purpose for a trifle more than six cents apiece. Each bullet with its tied and trimmed patch was dipped in hot tallow and then fitted, pucker-end foremost, into the open end of a paper cylinder which had within it a charge of one hundred grains of rifle powder. The bullet end of the cartridge was tied shut with a double-hitch of linen thread in such a manner as to place two loops between the ball and the powder and one loop at what had been the open end of the paper cylinder. The powder end of the cartridge had already been closed by an ingenious fold of the paper. (See fig. 44, *a–d*.) In loading the rifle with this type of ammunition, the soldier tore open the paper, poured the powder into the muzzle, rammed the patched ball home, and threw the paper away. U. S. rifle cartridges in the percussion period were bundled in lots of ten. "A package of 12 percussion caps is placed in each bundle of 10 cartridges at the end of the bundle." [54] Cartridges for the Service pistols also were charged with rifle powder—ordinarily fifty grains.

The making of cartridges was not confined solely to the federal arsenals; large bodies of troops carried with them the materials necessary to supply their needs in the field. A rather detailed account of the preparation of musket cartridges is given by Smyth:

> The ammunition wagon [one to a brigade] shall contain 20,000 cartridges; and in order to keep the same complete the conductor shall as deficiencies arise apply to the Brigade Quartermaster for a supply, or otherwise for the necessary materials of cartridges, and to the Brigade Inspector for men to make them up under the direction of the conductor; and for this purpose the Brigade Inspector shall order out a party of the most careful soldiers. [55]

"The necessary materials of cartridges" consisted of paper, thread, powder, and ball. The paper was cut into "trapezoids" 5.25 inches long, 3 inches wide at one end and 4.33 inches wide at the other. A round piece of hardwood 6 inches long and the same diameter

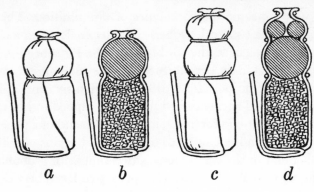

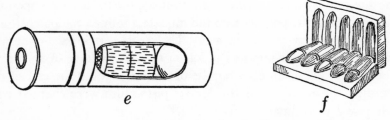

Fig. 44. Cartridges. *a*, paper cartridge for the U. S. musket, .64 cal., 2.37 in. long, 18 balls to the pound. *b*, sectional view, U. S. musket cartridge. *c*, paper cartridge, buck-and-ball, for U. S. musket, .64 cal., load 2.55 in. long. *d*, sectional view of buck-and-ball cartridge. *e*, sectional view of modern 12-gauge shotgun shell loaded with a single ball, .645 in. in diameter; exhibited at Harold's Club, Reno. This charge is to be fired from a cylinder-bore gun and can be expected to give a fair grouping at 60 yds. The muzzle velocity is about 1,300 ft. a second. (Johnson and Haven, 1943, pp. 22, 194.) *f*, Colt's combustible envelope cartridge (see note 59).

as the ball, one end convex and the other end concave, served as the "former." Round this former a strip of the paper was wrapped to make a hollow cylinder, one end of which was "choked" by tying with thread and folding the paper against the end of the partially withdrawn former. A ball was inserted and pushed down into this closed end of the paper cylinder and was held there by "two half hitches of the thread." With a copper powder measure and a small funnel, 110 grains of musket powder (154 grains in the earlier years) was then poured into the cylinder, and the open end was folded down over the powder by making two rectangular folds in the paper. The finished cartridge thus produced was 2.6 inches long. The cartridges were wrapped, ten to a "bundle," in paper which had been sized with a varnish of beeswax, turpentine, and linseed oil. The bundles were then placed in paper-lined packing boxes made of one-inch pine boards, a thousand cartridges to the box. Each box, when packed, weighed about one hundred pounds.[56]

The U. S. Ordnance return of February 15, 1805, lists 12,578 cartouche boxes among military stores "fit for service." No mention is made of cartridges. Thereafter, cartridge boxes and cartridge-box belts are listed in the annual returns. Ball cartridges were fabricated by the millions; the return of 1838, alone, reported 2,344,535 cartridges "purchased or fabricated." Of these, 2,061,446 were "musket ball and buckshot cartridges," principally destined for use against the Seminole Indians, no doubt. At this time the regular troops and militia in Florida numbered about 4,000.[57]

The fur companies that maintained large and more or less permanent posts in the wilderness commonly transported the ingredients for cartridges to these remote establishments and there put the materials together in the form of fixed ammunition. For example, in 1813 at Astoria, Oregon, John Jacob Astor's men had in store a supply of cartridge paper, 1,211 pounds of gunpowder, 2,065 pounds of bar lead, 1,677 pounds of pig lead, 1,338 pounds of buckshot, 414 pounds of musket balls, and 125 pounds of "patent shot." [58] A comparatively small proportion of the powder and lead was put up in cartridges at the central post, but a limited program of cartridge making was a part of the Astorian's industry—cartridges were "Columbia made," in the parlance of the place.

Eventually, the Colt company devised a combustible cartridge for use in its revolving arms (see fig. 44, *f*). This self-consuming cartridge consisted of a load of powder held in a paper or parchment container in one end of which a lead bullet was cemented.[59] The paper or parchment used for these cartridges had been impregnated with niter and thus made highly inflammable. The container, of course, was consumed in the heat of the explosion when the charge was fired. To protect the fragile container until the time came for loading, it was customary to enclose the cartridge in a light linen case. Colt's instructions which accompanied a new revolver offered "Directions for Loading with Colt's Foil Cartridge."

> Strip the white case of the cartridge, by holding the bullet end and tearing it down with the black tape. Place the cartridge in the mouth of a chamber of the cylinder, with the pointed end of the bullet uppermost, one at a time, and turn them under the rammer forcing them down with the lever below the surface of the cylinder so they can not hinder its rotation. To insure certainty of ignition, it is advisable to puncture the end of the cartridge, so that a small portion of gunpowder may escape into the chamber while loading the pistol.

Following Colt's lead, some other private makers produced combustible cartridges, but the use of metallic cartridges soon rendered them obsolete. Representative combustible cartridges are exhibited in the museum of the Wisconsin State Historical Society, Madison.

CARTRIDGE BOXES

Little evidence remains of the cartridge boxes used by civilians in the days of the muzzle-loaders, but examples and descriptions of those used by the Armed Forces are to be found in many collections and in military records. On January 3, 1810, Lieutenant-Colonel John Whiting reported on his inspections of the Springfield and Harpers Ferry armories. He wrote, "The best model of a cartridge box is that established by long use in the Revolution, and will contain 29 rounds in the wood, and 11 in the tin at the bottom, which also has a compartment for spare flints. On the outside is a receptacle for oily cloths, worms, and screwdriver. A large flap secures the whole from rain. [The box] is supported by a shoulder belt." [60]

During the days of percussion arms, the infantryman was equipped with a cartridge box of "black bridle leather," which was 7 inches long, about 6 inches high, and 1½ inches thick. Inside were two tin compartments, each having a "lower division, 3 inches by 3.3 inches, open in front to contain a bundle of 10 cartridges; and two upper divisions, 2.7 inches deep," one of which was large enough to contain 6 cartridges, the other 4—a total capacity of 40 cartridges. The cartridge box was supported on its own 2¼-inch leather belt. Twelve percussion caps were wrapped with each of the two bundles of cartridges in the box; in addition, the soldier had a supply of caps in his black leather sheep-lined cap pouch, which was 3 inches by 3 inches by 1¼ inches. The cone pick also was kept in this pouch, which was carried on the waist belt.

The rifleman of this period carried a cartridge box and cap pouch of the same dimensions as given above, but with five "upper divisions" within the tin lining of the cartridge box instead of four. The rifleman was equipped also with a light leather pouch, approximately 7 inches by 5½ inches, which could expand by virtue of the "gussets" in its side and bottom walls. In it he was expected to carry such accessories as a ball screw, a wiper tip for his ramrod, a supply of cloths for cleaning the bore, and a box of grease. A copper powder flask about 7 inches by 4 inches by 2 inches, with a capacity for 8 ounces of powder, was another item of special equipment for the rifleman. It was fitted with two chargers, one of which would measure out 75 grains, the other 100 grains of powder. The pouch and flask were attached by brass hooks to straps of the "flask and pouch belt." [61]

GUN WORMS

Gun worms (see fig. 45) were a necessary part of the accouterments carried by all users of muzzle-loading arms. They served to meet emergencies in removing charges, and the regulations of the early U. S. Army also required their routine use: "The non-commissioned officers of each company will be provided with gun worms and every day those men who have returned from duty are to bring their arms and have their charges drawn. The First Sergeant to receive the powder and ball and deliver the same to the quarter-master." [62]

Traders included gun worms in their stocks of goods, and the Canadian companies made it a practice to hand out the small "gadgets" as gratuities.[63] Indians did not always use the screwlike objects for the purpose for which they were designed. Governor Simpson of the Hudson's Bay Company, while traveling on the Columbia in 1824, observed: "The dress of the men [Chinook Indians] consists of a woodrat skin robe or blanket fastened over the shoulder by a gun

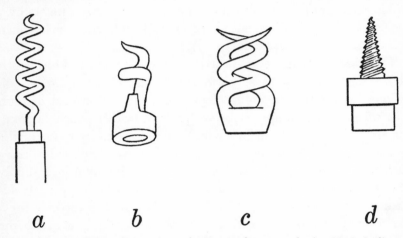

a   *b*   *c*   *d*

Fig. 45. Gun worms. *a*, worm device on the ramrod of a U. S. Indian rifle of 1807. Holding the wiping cloth was probably its principal use. *b*, gun worm of the type distributed to Indians in the Columbia River region in the 1820's, now in the Museum of the Washington State Historical Society. *c* and *d*, gun worms used in U. S. percussion arms; from the U. S. National Museum.

worm, or wooden pin." [64] In 1837, Jim Bridger's trapping party, which included Joe Meek, found it necessary to give battle to a band of Blackfeet Indians near Henry Lake, Idaho. Newell, one of the trappers, attempted to scalp a fallen warrior. The victim proved to be alive. His coiffure was ornamented with "gun screws," and Newell's sleeve was caught in one of them; the resulting spectacle was vividly remembered by Meek through the more than thirty years that elapsed before he related the story to Mrs. Victor, his biographer. The luckless Indian finally was dispatched, and his scalp and gun worms were taken by Newell.[65]

VI

Small Cannon of the Traders and the Military

Cannon not only provided greater firepower for wilderness forays; these larger guns by their mere presence in the armament of a trading party had a great psychological effect upon the hostile wild tribes. The possession of cannon, in the eyes of the Indian, marked the field expedition of the white man as militant and superior. For those Indians who knew nothing about cannon, the traders quite commonly put on a show with the "big guns" in order to impress them, but when occasion demanded, the cannon were unlimbered in bloody combat.

Even before the purchase of Louisiana by the United States, cannon were taken to the upper Missouri country, and after the Lewis and Clark expedition, ordnance was regularly in use in the Far West. Incidentally, Lewis and Clark had with them one swivel gun on the part of their journey that was made in river boats. Roughly, the cannon of both the traders and the military may be classified in three groups: (1) small cannon or "swivels" mounted on keelboats; (2) small wheeled cannon of six-pounder size and larger; and (3) cannon mounted within the fortifications of military establishments and trading posts. In this last group, many of the guns were the same as those in the first or second group, put to this special use, although the Army posts sometimes mounted guns of larger sizes.

SWIVEL GUNS

Mechanically, swivel guns were of two types: those of the usual design of small cannon with the trunnions held upon the forks of a Y-shaped mounting (fig. 46), and those that were hardly more than

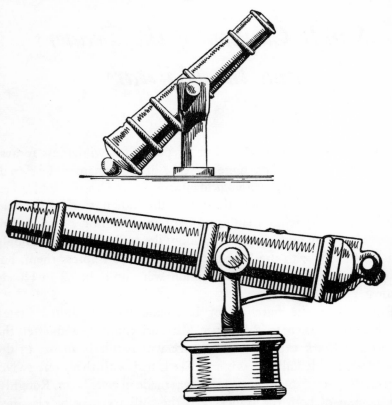

Fig. 46. Swivel guns of the cannon type. Both guns are of British origin. The upper one has a barrel 16 in. long and a bore of slightly more than 1 in.; the lower is 28 in. long, with a bore of 1¾ in.

gigantic muskets with a pin through the forestock, which permitted their being mounted on a Y-shaped support (fig. 48). In the use of both types, the lower projection of the Y-shaped support, or swivel, was placed in a hole bored in the gunwale of a boat, very much as a large oarlock would be used. When an arm of this type was mounted on a parapet of a fort, it was spoken of as a "wall piece." In early terminology, such a rampart gun was often called an "amusette," a term which persisted in America at least until the end of the Revolution.

Figure 46, upper, is a gun of the first type from the British brig *Natalia,* of Revolutionary days, said to have been wrecked in Monterey Bay in 1834. Its total length is 16 inches; the diameter at breech, 3½ inches; the diameter at muzzle, 2¾ inches; the bore, 1¼ inches. The swivel stands 7½ inches high and has a 3-inch base; the trunnion is 4¾ inches long. This gun is exhibited in the old Custom House, Monterey, California.

Figure 46, lower, is a small cannon from a British war vessel which was in the fleet that captured Charleston, South Carolina, in 1780. It is 28 inches in total length; the bore is 1¾ inches. The British crown and the initials "ECL" stand in relief on the top of the barrel just ahead of the touchhole. This specimen was a part of the collection of firearms once owned by the U. S. Cartridge Company. Its present whereabouts is unknown; but the M. H. de Young Museum, San Francisco, has a swivel gun so similar as to suggest that it was cast at the same foundry. The de Young specimen (no. 9003), classed as a carronade, is "believed to have come from H.M.S. *Bounty.*"

The use of these small swivel guns was not limited to naval actions. Among the notable instances of their early use by land forces in America was the renowned fight between the English and French at Fort Necessity in Southwestern Pennsylvania, on July 3, 1754. Nine swivel guns were included in the armament of George Washington's regiment of Virginians. The French and their Indian allies, in their initial attack upon the English position, exposed their flank to the entrenched Virginians, and the first volley fired from the fort included a blast from the swivel guns; as recorded by a participant, "the combined volleys killing many of the Indians." [1] Upon the capitulation of the English at the end of the day of fighting, only the surrender of the swivel guns was demanded by the victorious French; the English troops were permitted to carry their muskets back to

Virginia. In the spring and summer of 1953, the National Park Service conducted archaeological studies at the site of Fort Necessity to determine the size and shape of the one-time stockade and the related trenches. In the course of the excavating, a few relics of the battle were brought to light. Among them were nine iron balls about an inch and a half in diameter, each weighing approximately seven ounces. Presumably these were cannon balls for the swivel guns.[2] Additional smaller iron balls, about seven-eighths of an inch in diameter and weighing about an ounce and a quarter each, were found buried in the earth on the fort site. Their presence there suggests that some of George Washington's swivel guns may have been as small as the "falconet" pictured in figure 46, upper. No guns or parts of guns were found, although contemporary French testimony records that the swivels were broken up as soon as the English marched away from the scene of their defeat.

SMALL CANNON MOUNTED ON BOATS

At the end of the eighteenth century while Spanish interests were still striving to hold the Missouri and Platte rivers, cannon were taken upstream from New Orleans by Spanish traders. On July 18, 1794, the Spanish Missouri Fur Company, was granted the exclusive privilege of trade for ten years, by Baron de Carondelet of New Orleans. Parties of traders were sent by this company up the Missouri River in 1794 and 1796. In 1795 James MacKay, a Scot with Spanish leanings led the party in the field. He "encountered a persistent hostility on the part of the Indians which was attributed to the activities of the English traders who had established themselves upon the Upper Missouri." MacKay said later that through his hands "were distributed the presents [from the Spaniards] of merchandise to secure the friendship of the Indians and to estrange them from the British."[3] A line of Spanish forts along the Platte and westward to the sea was planned to further counteract the British influence. On petition of Jacques Clamorgan, chief director of the Spanish Missouri Fur Company, Carondelet provided "ten swivels for the Company's forts."[4]

Some details about the Spanish ordnance on the Missouri may be gleaned from the documents quoted by Nasatir. The usual swivel guns employed by the subjects of His Catholic Majesty at that time were described as "swivel-guns or little cannons of one pound caliber." [5] Carondelet's ten swivel guns "with their balls, arms and utensils" were shipped from the government's arsenal at Barrancas (now Memphis, Tenn.) to St. Louis, and from there they were to be taken to wilderness forts then being built by the agents of the Missouri Company. One of these establishments was near the mouth of the Platte in a village of the Oto Indians; one at the Omaha village about six miles below the site of present Omadi, Nebraska; one at the Mandan villages, which had been seized from the British and rebuilt; and another at Fort Carondelet, well up on the Osage River among the Indians of that name.[6] The guns were the property of the King of Spain, and the company was held accountable for them.

As the Missouri Company in 1795 extended its trading activities into the upper Missouri country, where British traders already had a following among the natives, some of the Spaniards—especially Carondelet—advocated a patrol of the river, "with one or two galliots of small tonnage, flat-bottomed, and armed with six two-pound cannons, some swivel guns and manned by twenty sailors," to be provided by the government. In the E. G. Voorhis Collection, Missouri Historical Society, St. Louis, is an original drawing of "The galley that Gov. Gayoso de Lemos stays abord of." In 1796 Gayoso followed Carondelet as Governor General of Louisiana. His little gunboat carried one six-pounder and eight swivels. It had a crew of twenty-eight men and presumably was somewhat larger than the armed vessels Carondelet had in mind for patrol duty, but it is representative of the early-day galleys on the Mississippi and Missouri rivers. The positions of the guns and types of mountings shown in this eighteenth-century drawing, a tracing of which is reproduced in figure 47, are indicative of the manner of arming the later government vessels and privately owned keelboats that swarmed on the Ohio, Mississippi, and Missouri rivers during the first few decades after the acquisition of Louisiana.

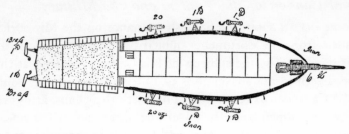

The Galley that Gov.ʳ Gayoso de Lemos stays abord of 28 Men 240 ars One 6/pounder & 8 Swivels   Called

Fig. 47. "The galley that Gov. Gayoso de Lemos stays abord of." This craft is representative of the small Spanish gunboats that patrolled the Mississippi and the lower Missouri rivers in the 1790's. One six-pounder and eight swivels made up its armament. The contemporary drawing is owned by the Missouri Historical Society and is here reproduced with the permission of Mr. Charles van Ravensway, Director.

Beginning in 1798 and continuing through 1813, American ship-builders in shipyards at Pittsburgh, Marietta, Eddyville, and Louis-ville constructed gunboats somewhat like the Spanish galleys. Some of these boats were equipped with cannon as heavy as twenty-four-pounders. All of them carried swivel guns. Stirring accounts of the use of these gunboats in fights with British forces and with Black Hawk's Sauk and Fox warriors at Prairie du Chien and at the mouth of Rock River in 1813 and 1814 are given in Baldwin.[7]

SWIVEL GUNS OF THE MUSKET TYPE

Musket-shaped swivel guns had always been smoothbores until Americans introduced rifled wall pieces during the Revolution for use on the navigable rivers of Virginia. These arms weighed about fifty pounds, and some of them fired a ball weighing four ounces. There is some evidence that they were made in the Fredericks-burg Manufactory, Virginia, in 1776, and several specimens are pre-served which are definitely known to have come from the Rappa-hannock Forge across the river from Fredericksburg. However, there is no evidence that rifled swivel guns were used on the interior rivers in the fur-trade days. Hicks accounts for experimental "wall rifles" made in 1847 at both the Springfield and Harpers Ferry arsenals, but apparently they were never actually used. They fired a three-ounce ball and weighed about thirty pounds. They were percussion arms, "mounted on convenient tripod stands adapted to being carried on a pack horse." The only two specimens known are in the Springfield Armory Museum.

On November 7, 1807, Henry Dearborn of the War Department wrote to James Stubblefield, Harpers Ferry Arsenal, enclosing a sketch for a swivel gun: "The work is to be done very strong, but need not be highly polished. A common musket lock will answer. The barrel should be thicker so as to bear high proof. The swivel should be strong enough to support a very heavy charge without giving in any part. The breech of the stock should be strong and about the usual length of that of a musket. You will have it well proved before you send it on. Let the pivot of the swivel be about four-and-a-half inches long, and when you prove the gun, let the pivot be put into an auger hole in a piece of timber, so as to try its strength, as well as the strength of the gun." On December 23, 1807, Dearborn acknowledged receipt of the "wall piece" and asked that six more be made. "Add a sight near the middle and instead of the pins to secure the stock to the barrel, add another grip or hoop [band]. When completed you will forward them to this office." On August 1, 1808, Dearborn acknowledged receipt of the six swivel guns.[8]

Ordnance Office records include few details of the history of swivel guns used by the Army and Navy, but accounts of the use of such arms on government boats on the Ohio, Mississippi, and the Missouri indicate that more of the guns may have been made than are accounted for by the Ordnance Department.

Figure 48, *a,* shows a swivel gun of the musket type specified by Dearborn in 1808, which appears to have been made in the Pittsburgh Arsenal, the place of origin also of all of the heavier ordnance shipped to the West in the period 1813–1823.[9] The round iron barrel is smoothbore, 33 inches long and of 1.25 caliber; the original flintlock has been converted to percussion. The lock plate is marked "U. S. Pittsburgh."

Contracts between the government and Tryon and J. J. Henry in 1814 to make twenty repeating swivels featuring the system invented by Joseph G. Chambers are on record.[10] Apparently still other contracts for this "lost" military weapon were entered into by the federal government and by several states. Formal approval of the Chambers repeaters by the U. S. Navy is a matter of record, as is a directive from the Secretary of the Navy specifying that fifty repeating swivels be procured. Eight of these guns were mounted on the *Guerrière* at Philadelphia in 1814, and George Harrison, the Navy agent at Philadelphia, was ordered to send fifteen of the repeaters to Commodore Chauncey on the Great Lakes in order that they might be tested in actual service on the small gunboats then active there. Today no specimen is to be found.

In a statement of ordnance made and procured by the U. S. government during the five-year period 1817–1821 is an entry "25 1-pounder iron swivels" and another for 1,120 pounds of swivel shot.[11] These guns are listed under "Cannon," and no doubt they were of the type shown in figure 46. As an indication of the relative scarcity of swivel guns in the armament of the War Department, it may be mentioned that the same report accounts for 306 six-pounders and some 500 cannon and mortars of other sizes in the nation's armament.

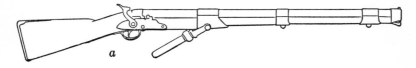

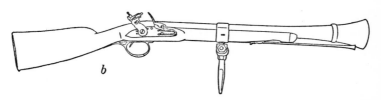

Fig. 48. Swivel guns of shoulder-arms type. *a,* heavy musket-type swivel gun, originally flintlock but converted to percussion. This specimen is said to have been found at the bottom of a bayou near New Orleans; Milwaukee Museum (N7106). *b,* flintlock blunderbuss swivel gun, a type often used on river boats in the late eighteenth and early nineteenth centuries. Barrels were either brass or iron. This specimen was no. 148 in the collection of the U. S. Cartridge Company; its present whereabouts is unknown.

There can be no question regarding the early use of small cannon and swivel guns by the U. S. government in its Indian factory at Fort Osage. Eli B. Clemson, writing to James Wilkinson, November 30, 1808, from the newly established Fort Osage reported, "When the guard was ordered out they [the Osage Indians] showed marks of resistance and in one or two instances they did not leave the boats until a three-pounder was brought to bear on them." [12] Numerous entries in the diary of George C. Sibley, Indian Agent at Fort Osage, reveal that swivel guns were taken to the new post in 1808 on government boats, and that these small cannon were left at the fort.[13]

The introduction of mounted military guns to the western wilds was accompanied by and even preceded by the use of cannon by private traders. Manuel Lisa used swivel guns on his keelboats in the opening years of the century. In 1807, and again in 1811, he took cannon to his post at the mouth of the Yellowstone.[14] When he abandoned this post and built Fort Lisa in 1813 near the site of present Omaha, he again made use of swivel guns. On February 22, 1813, one of Lisa's men, L. Archambeau, was hauling hay with a sleigh across the frozen river near the fort. While in sight of the men in the fort he was shot and killed by Indians. "We . . . placed two swivels on the bank of the river, but unfortunately our balls did not reach across and those [Indians] on this side kept out of reach of our fire. . . . They took Archambeau's scalp and cut him nearly to pieces."[15]

Complete specimens of swivel guns known to have been used in the western fur posts are seldom seen in present-day collections. W. Raymond Wood records the recovery of fragments of one of the small cannon in 1954 in the course of his excavation of Kipp's Columbia Fur Company post at the mouth of White Earth River, Mountrail County, North Dakota. Scattered about the site of the 182?-1829 establishment were cannon fragments. "The number and form of these fragments suggest that the cannon had exploded. It was about 2½ feet long, had a muzzle bore of about 2 inches, and was equipped with a circular pivot for mounting."[16]

Dr. Thomas, with the St. Louis Missouri Fur Company party en route to the Mandan villages in 1809, testified: "On the 28th of June all the boats having arrived [at the Osage River] we set out and on the 8th of July arrived at Ft. Osage which we saluted by a discharge of several guns from our ordnance barges, and was politely answered by an equal number from the fort."[17] Even the firing of salutes sometimes entailed casualties. July 4 had "closed with a ball. We feel it a painful duty to state that an accident happened which threw a damp over the general joy. In firing a cannon the piece by some cause went off whilst a soldier was in the act of ramming down the charge. . . . His recovery is very doubtful."[18]

In the period 1813–1821, the U. S. Army took 108 cannon from Pittsburgh to its establishments in western states and territories. With these weapons went 29,079 cannon balls and shells weighing about 174 tons. Eighty-five hundred rounds of fixed ammunition for cannon, in addition to the shells and cannon balls, were also transported to the western forts.[19]

The first important instance of the use of this ordnance against the Indians was the Arikara fiasco of 1823, which is described in detail by Chittenden and in War Department reports published in 1823.[20] Two six-pounders, one twelve-pounder howitzer, and several small swivel guns were taken by Colonel Henry Leavenworth, with his command of about three hundred white men and eight hundred Sioux Indians, from the old Council Bluffs and from Fort Atkinson and points north to the Arikara stockaded villages near the mouth of the Grand River. The distance traveled from Council Bluffs was about 640 miles, and the cannon and other heavy equipment used in the campaign were transported in keelboats. Lieutenant Morris and Sergeant Perkins had charge of the artillery which bombarded the Arikara village on August 10, 1823, from eight o'clock in the morning until noon. The infantry attack was postponed, while peace parleys were held, until the third day, August 12, and in the meantime the Arikara warriors and their women and children made good their escape from their besieged town. Chittenden, writing eighty years after this fight, judged that

> the bombardment caused very few casualties [other than the death of the Arikara Chief, Grey Eyes, killed by the first shot], for it is evident from the hint dropped by Little Soldier [a subchief who participated in the peace parleys] that the Indians lay on the ground and that most of the shot passed over them. The effect of the shot on the mud huts was inappreciable.[21]

Some of the trappers, contrary to Colonel Leavenworth's orders, set fire to and destroyed the Arikara villages.

Occasional references to continued military use of some of the Army's big guns in the West are found in the contemporary writings of Army officers. Philip St. George Cooke, always to be depended upon for a record of what he saw and did, tells of his experience while serving as escort to a party of traders en route to Santa Fe in 1829, when Arapaho and Comanche surrounded the camp.

> I then marched round towards the front of the camp which was wholly exposed; the 6-pounder as we passed threw a round over our heads, and I saw it strike just in the midst of the body of the enemy, perhaps a mile from the piece; it made a great commotion among them. The piece was then directed against a party of the enemy galloping four or five hundred yards off, along the hill side in front; the grape shot struck like hail among them, but seemed to hit but one.

The Indians withdrew, but on August 11 this band again galloped round the camp in the early morning. "We observed the fire of cannister from a six-pounder near camp upon the Indians who were galloping by beyond musket range; one was shot down." Late in the fall of 1829, Cooke's party returned to Fort Leavenworth. "The piece of artillery which had been pulled out in fine style by six mules came back with a yoke of oxen." [22] Figure 49 depicts a six-pounder of this type.

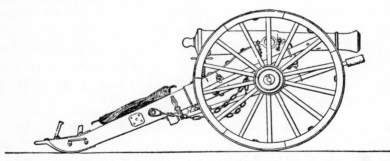

Fig. 49. A 6-pounder field gun. From the Confederate edition of the U. S. *Ordnance Manual* (Mordecai, 1861, pl. 2).

Rodenbough, an officer in the 2d Dragoons, reports on the use of small cannon in extremely unfavorable circumstances—among the cypress swamps and saw palmettos of Florida during the Seminole War: "We had a six-pounder and a howitzer throwing grape, shells and Congreve rockets into the densest part of the hammock—if such there could be where every part was so thick that a man couldn't see three feet beyond him—while the Tennesseans entered on the left flank, the dragoons on the right, and the artillery in the center." [23]

Captain Philip St. George Cooke, about to start westward from the Missouri in 1844 with five companies of the 1st Dragoons, wrote: "You must now take notice of those two brass howitzers on the left of the line—we take them with us. They are 12-pounders and are said to be very effective against Indians. The Indians say they can stand before the bow and arrow, or even the rifle pretty well, but, they 'object to being shot at by a wagon.' " [24] The twelve-pounders here referred to were of the same model as the Frémont cannon shown in figure 53.

The later trading companies made it regular practice to mount small cannon on the bows of their keelboats and on the parapets or in the blockhouses of their forts. Not many of these old guns have been preserved. In the collections of the Missouri Historical Society, St. Louis, is the bronze specimen shown in figure 50, *a*. It has a bore of about two inches and is thirty-six inches long. It was cast by A. Fulton, Pittsburgh, Pennsylvania, about 1839 and was carried on boats of John Jacob Astor's American Fur Company on the upper Missouri as a defense against Indians and as a signal piece for announcing the arrival of the boat at trading posts. Probably it was mounted on a truck carriage similar to the one shown in figure 50, *b,* and to the one on the Fort Nisqually piece illustrated in figure 55.

Before his company became active on the Missouri, Astor had equipped his representatives on the Columbia with swivels and four-pounders convenient for use on river boats and for mounting on wheels.[25] Ross relates that the Astorians separated in the summer of 1813 to make one last call at field stations—"Shewhaps, Spokane, Wallamette, Okanagon and the Snake"—before dissolving Astor's company. En route up the Columbia, the Astorians encountered a large party of Indians—about 2,000 in 174 canoes—near the site of present Walla Walla. The old chief, Tummeatapam, who had consistently befriended the Astorians, urged them to turn back because of the hostile disposition of his people. "We took him, however, to one of our boats and showed him a brass four-pounder, some hand

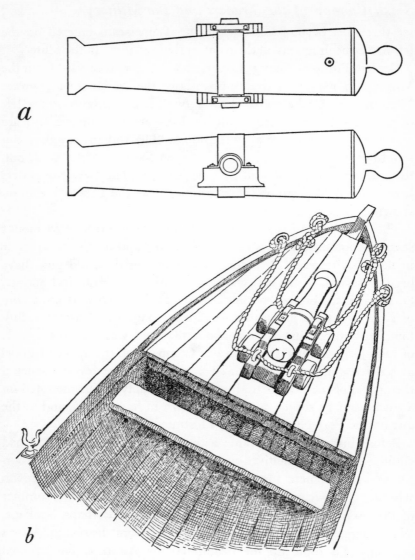

Fig. 50. The American Fur Company's boat cannon. *a,* two views of the 36-in. bronze barrel of an American Fur Co. boat gun used on the Missouri River. The bore is approximately 2 in. The specimen is exhibited by the Missouri Historical Society, St. Louis. *b,* a common method of mounting small cannon on a truck carriage for use on river boats. When good cordage was lacking, the back-country boatmen occasionally substituted local vegetable fibre for hemp. Papaw bark was sometimes used in improvising rope on the Ohio and Mississippi rivers.

grenades, and skyrockets." The white men were allowed to pass upstream without a fight. "We supposed that Tummeatapam's account of our big gun influenced their conduct not a little." [26]

In December, 1813, after the sale of Astoria, Ross and his party descended the Columbia en route to the new Fort George. "At the head of the Cascades, a place always notorious for its bad population, we encamped and were disturbed all night by the whooping and yelling of savages who kept prowling in the woods round us. . . . We fired several shots into the woods from a three-pounder which kept the Indians at a distance."

Soon after this trouble of the Astorians (in January, 1814), the new proprietors—the British North West Company—sent an expedition up the Columbia to take supplies to the interior. It was attacked and robbed at the Cascades. In reprisal, McTavish led a heavily armed party to the troublesome place. "Besides the ordinary arms and accoutrements, two big guns, six swivels, cutlasses, hand grenades and handcuffs," mostly from the Astor properties, were taken along. Circumstances did not permit infliction of punishment upon the Indian culprits, elaborate American armament notwithstanding.[27]

Occasional entries in the early nineteenth-century records of the Hudson's Bay Company indicate that its boats on Athabaska Lake and elsewhere on Canadian waters commonly mounted small cannon. Reference to these pieces as "cohorns" does not necessarily indicate that they were the mortars technically designated as cohorns.[28]

WHEELED CANNON IN THE FUR FIELDS

Because William Ashley's cannon of 1827 was the first wheeled vehicle to cross the mountains by a northern route, the fur traders' "big gun" of the howitzer type has received more publicity than the swivel guns for boats and the pieces that were installed in forts.

The earliest account of a wheeled cannon in the West is in Alexander Henry's journal. When he was on the Panbian River in 1808, he wrote: "Got a carriage made for my cohorn," and said that he loaded this weapon with a pound of powder and thirty bullets. It

was fired with a match.[29] The cannon found practical use in repulsing an attack by the Sioux. Alexander Ross while employed on the
Columbia by the Hudson's Bay Company in 1824 took a large brass
cannon mounted on wheels eastward from Spokane House. His party
set out overland for the country east of the Rockies on a buffalo hunt
and trapping expedition. They followed a trail which took them past
the sites of present Butte and Missoula and into the regions of the
present De Smet and Kootenay. On Hell Gate River their camp was
visited by eight Piegan. "As the Piegans were going off he gave them
a salute of honor from the brass gun, 'just to show them,' he explains, 'that it makes a noise.' " [30] On this same trip in June, 1824, a
party of Piegan captured two members of the Ross expedition while
they were trapping on the Snake River. The captives were forced to
guide the Indians to the main camp of the Hudson's Bay Company
party. When they approached the camp, Ross "instantly pointed the
big gun, lighted the match and sent the women away. The party hove
in sight. Seeing John with them, restrained me from firing." The
members of Ross's party took up positions of defense, but they later
relaxed and permitted the Indians to come into camp and spend the
night there. "In the morning I gave the Piegans presents and told
them to be off and play us no tricks as we would follow them and
punish them. The big gun did it." [31] This British gun had been delivered to the Columbia by ship.

The notable wheeled cannon which made the first wheel tracks
in the transmountain country is represented in figure 51. This drawing represents William H. Ashley's gun headed westward in 1827. In
a letter addressed to the War Department, March, 1829, Ashley
stated:

> In the month of March, 1827, I fitted out a party of sixty men, mounted
> a piece of artillery (a four-pounder) on a carriage which was drawn by
> two mules; the party marched to or near the Grand Salt Lake beyond the
> Rocky Mountains, remained there one month, stopped [places not given]
> on the way back fifteen days, and returned to Lexington in the western
> part of Missouri in September, where the party was met with everything
> for another outfit and did return (using the same horses and mules) to
> the mountains by the last of November in the same year.[32]

Soon after this pioneer venture with a wheeled vehicle in the roadless wilderness, George Nidever's associates on the Arkansas bolstered their armament with a wheeled cannon. The party was about 450 miles from Fort Smith on the north side of the Arkansas River when it was besieged by a band of Pawnee. Nidever wrote, "We had a small cannon with us and having loaded it with 60 bullets we discharged it in the direction of our enemies, and succeeded in silencing their fire." [33]

Fig. 51. William H. Ashley's wheeled cannon, en route, 1827. In sending this 4-pounder and its improvised carriage to the Great Salt Lake, in the summer of 1827, Ashley broke the way for the many wheeled vehicles which later were to follow the South Pass route into the West.

Smith, Jackson, and Sublette apparently were encouraged by their experience with Ashley's cannon in 1827, for on the ill-fated Santa Fe trip of 1831 they took with them a mounted gun. Eighty-five men and twenty-three wagons set out from Independence, Missouri. Ten wagons belonged to Jackson and Sublette, ten to Mills and Chadwick, one to a Mr. Flournoy, and "one was owned jointly by Smith, Jackson, and Sublette, which had a small field piece mounted upon the hind axle. The wagon was so constructed that it could be readily uncoupled and the hind wheels with the piece of artillery mounted thereon drawn out ready for action." [34]

The use of wheeled cannon on the trail in the Rocky Mountain region was initiated by the Canadian Alexander Ross, and his example was followed by his successors within the Hudson's Bay Company. When John Work was traveling with a pack outfit from the Columbia into what is now Montana in the fall of 1831, he had a cannon with him. On October 31, 1831, on Monteur Creek in the Clarks Fork Country, western Montana, the Blackfeet threatened his party in broad daylight. "Our cannon was fired twice to apprise our men who were out of the enemy's approach." Later, on the Beaverhead, the Blackfeet attacked and the cannon was used in repulsing them. On January 30, 1832, in the Salmon River country, Work's party again was attacked by Blackfeet. On this occasion the cannon was also brought into action, but it burst when fired.[35]

The Santa Fe traders continued to include privately owned cannon in their caravans as long as the Southwestern tribes, especially the Comanche, constituted a threat; for on only three occasions—1829, 1834, and 1843—did the U. S. Army send troops as escorts for the wagon trains. Gregg describes two swivel guns, of a heavier type properly classed as cannon, carried by his wagon train in 1839.[36]

FRÉMONT'S CANNON

Few of the cannon that were hauled over western trails in the days before roads were built have been preserved. Of these the number with known histories is small indeed. This Frémont gun therefore commands attention. Mrs. Paden classes it as one of the three most interesting historical relics in the West—"The Sir Francis Drake plaque found in Marin Co., Calif.; the cap to Frémont's telescope, found on an island in the Great Salt Lake, and the Frémont cannon." [37]

Frémont obtained this gun from Colonel S. W. Kearny, who was in command of the Department of the Mississippi Valley, and he took it with him on his second exploring expedition, which started in May, 1843. It went with him to Great Salt Lake, to the Snake and Columbia River valleys, and to the Klamath Lake country, through eastern Nevada, and part way up the eastern ascent of the Sierra Nevada in the neighborhood of what is now Sonora Junction. There he abandoned it on January 29, 1844.[38] A contemporary picture of the

Fig. 52. The Frémont cannon in camp at Pyramid Lake, Nevada, Jan. 13, 1844. From an engraving published in Frémont's official report, 1845. Charles Preuss, cartographer with Frémont, is believed to have made the field drawing upon which the engraving was based.

gun and its carriage is to be seen in the illustration of Frémont's camp on the shore of Pyramid Lake, Nevada (fig. 52).

An account of the adoption of this type of gun and the procurement of the weapons is given by Woodward:

> In 1835 or 1836 the U. S. Government decided to adopt for frontier usage the light 12-pound brass (bronze) mountain howitzer which the French had developed for their mountain troops in Algiers and in the Spanish border country. In December 1836 Major Gen'l. Thos. S. Jesup, then on campaign in the south against the Creek Indians ordered several "light mountain howitzers for service here, the model of which I was informed had been introduced from France by the ordnance department." He received these cannon fully equipped with their carriages but he complained that the latter having wheels only 36″ dia. and axles 38″ long were not the right type carriages for American frontier terrain. The small wheels and narrow base caused the guns to upset too easily. There wasn't enough clearance to allow the piece to pass over rough ground or tree stumps and he requested changes.
>
> Apparently the first of these guns of American origin were cast at the cannon foundry of Cyrus Alger & Company in South Boston, Mass. Alger had been making iron guns for the army and navy with iron mined on the James and Potomac rivers in Virginia. He also made cannon balls for the Government.
>
> Alger probably began casting the brass howitzers of the new French style sometime between Oct. 1836 and Sept. 1837. There were 12 cannon of this type cast between these dates. General Jesup received several of the howitzers before Aug. 15, 1837.[39]

It appears that the cannon almost cost the expedition the services of its leader before it was actually under way. Irving Stone fancifully quotes the presumptive text of a War Department directive regarding Frémont's use of the howitzer:

> Lieutenant John C. Frémont
> US Army Topographical Corps
> St. Louis, Mo.
>
> You are herewith ordered to turn over your expedition to your second in command, and to repair at once to Washington. An explanation is required of why you have taken a twelve-pound howitzer cannon on a peaceful, scientific survey. Another officer of the Topographical Corps will be dispatched to take charge of the expedition.
>
> Colonel J. J. Abert [40]

Instructions of this type were received and read by Mrs. Frémont in St. Louis. Her husband was at that time with his party, some four hundred miles above St. Louis at the small town of Kansas, now Kansas City, near the mouth of the Kansas River. He was completing his preparations for his second exploring expedition, the objective of which was the examination of the region south of the Columbia River lying between the Rocky Mountains and the Pacific Ocean. By special messenger, Mrs. Frémont advised her husband to be on his way; she did not forward the Abert order. On May 29, 1843, the party set out, howitzer and all. "Three men were especially detailed for the management of this piece, under the charge of Louis Zindel, a native of Germany, who had been 19 years a non-commissioned officer of artillery in the Prussian Army." [41]

> We pulled that cannon from Kansas Landing fifteen hundred miles to the Dalles on the Columbia, then another four hundred miles through the snow and icy passes going south from Oregon to the east side of the Sierra. We even got it part way across the Sierra; there we lost it in snow twelve feet deep. We were hard pressed to save our lives and the cannon had to be abandoned. [42]

In his official report, published in 1845, Frémont makes many statements regarding experiences with the howitzer during the trip. In June, 1843, only a week's trip west of the Missouri, a mounted band of Indians pursued at full gallop one member of the party who had been reconnoitering some miles from the column.

> We were thrown into a little confusion by the sudden arrival of Maxwell, who entered the camp at full speed at the head of a war party of Osage Indians, with gay red blankets, and heads shaved to the scalp lock. They had run him a distance of about nine miles, from a creek on which we had encamped the previous day, and to which he had returned in search of a runaway horse. [43]

Alertness of the guards and the martial appearance of the party repelled the Indians quickly. On August 5, when the party was encamped on the North Platte for the purpose of drying buffalo meat,

> the camp was thrown into a sudden tumult, by a charge from about 70 mounted Indians, over the low hills at the upper end of the little bottom.

Fortunately the guard who was between them and our animals, had caught a glimpse of an Indian's head, as he raised himself to look over the hill a moment before he made the charge; and succeeded in turning the band [of Frémont's horses] into our camp as the Indians charged into the bottom with the usual yell. Before they reached us, the grove on the verge of the little bottom was occupied by our people, and the Indians brought to a sudden halt, which they made in time to save themselves from a howitzer shot, which would undoubtedly have been very effective in such a compact body; and further proceedings were interrupted by their signs for peace. They proved to be a war party of Arapahoe and Cheyenne Indians, and informed us that they had charged upon the camp under the belief that we were hostile Indians and had discovered their mistake only at the moment of the attack—an excuse which policy required us to receive as true, though under the full conviction that the display of our little howitzer, and our favorable position in the grove, certainly saved our horses, and probably ourselves, from their marauding intentions.[44]

On December 10, 1843, on the fringes of Tlamath [Klamath] Lake, Oregon, the howitzer was used again:

The character of courage and hostility attributed to the Indians of this quarter induced more than usual precaution [in making camp]; and seeing smokes rising from the middle of the lake (or savannah) and along the opposite shores, I directed the howitzer to be fired. It was the first time our guides [two Indians from the Dalles on the Columbia] had seen it discharged; and the bursting of the shell at a distance, which was something like the second fire of the gun, amazed and bewildered them with delight. It inspired them with triumphant feelings; but on the distant camps the effect was different, for the smokes in the lake and on the shores immediately disappeared.[45]

There are other incidents recorded by Frémont which indicate that the gun was fired occasionally to assist in guiding to camp foraging parties that remained out after dark; but, generally, the emphasis is upon the psychological value of having the piece of artillery in readiness. Throughout the report, up to the date when it became necessary to abandon the gun, Frémont refers to it in a manner to indicate that it was cherished not only by him but also by other members of his party. As may be imagined, it was not always easy to move the howitzer over the rough and untracked wilderness through which the party traveled, and there finally came a time when even grim determination was not sufficient to keep it in tow.

The daily entries in Frémont's published log of the trip, together with the remarkable map based on his astronomical observations and determinations of longitude and latitude and drawn on the scale of 47.35 miles to the inch, make it possible to determine with reasonable accuracy the location of many of the camp sites along the route followed by the expedition. In January, 1844, the party traveled south from the great bend of the Truckee River, crossed the Carson River, and ascended the East Fork of the Walker almost to the site of present Bridgeport, California. Local Indians, though somewhat taken aback at the idea that this cavalcade should attempt climbing to the crest of the Sierra in the dead of winter, nevertheless advised the party of the most promising route which might be traveled at that moment, and some of them provided guidance during various stages of the journey. Frémont makes clear the fact that he turned northwest from the Bridgeport Valley and traveled along an important Indian trail through a gap which is now known as Devils Gate, through which U. S. Highway 395 passes. He notes the hot springs now known as Fales Hot Springs. From that place he dropped down to a point near the West Walker River, where he camped the night of January 28 not far from the site of the present Sonora Junction. Indians in camp in this vicinity told him of a west-bound party of twelve white men who had traveled through there two years before and had made use of the pass known today as Sonora Pass, which, the Indians said, was good in summer but "impassible now." Frémont, in his report, comments that he sensed this party to have been the Bidwell-Bartleson-Chiles party. What he did not write at this juncture was that back on the Missouri frontier at the outset of his expedition he had talked to J. B. Chiles [46] and had learned some details of the experiences of the previous party in crossing the Sierra. One cannot but surmise that Frémont had in mind using Chiles's route when he deliberately proceeded south of the Carson River and on to the Walker—a roundabout route which delayed him about a month in making the climb over the Sierra.

On January 29, the party proceeded northward along the West Walker River. When they found it impossible to travel along the stream course, they climbed the slopes of the canyon wall. "We ascended a very steep hill which proved afterwards the last and fatal obstacle to our little howitzer which was finally abandoned at this place." [47] Later, Frémont reports,

> The other division of the party did not come in tonight, but encamped in the upper meadow, and arrived the next morning. They had not succeeded in getting the howitzer beyond the place mentioned, and where it had been left by Mr. Preuss in obedience to my orders; and, in anticipation of the snow banks and snow fields still ahead forseeing the inevitable detention to which it would subject us, I reluctantly determined to leave it there for the time. It was of the kind invented by the French for the mountain part of their war in Algiers; and the distance it had come with us proved how well it was adapted to its purpose. We left it, to the great sorrow of the whole party, who were grieved to part with a companion which had made the whole distance from St. Louis, and commanded respect for us on some critical occasions, and which might be needed for the same purpose again. [48]

What disposition was made of ammunition and other impedimenta pertaining to the gun is not explained.

A careful checking of Frémont's map and text against the actual terrain of the West Walker region leads to the conclusion that the cannon was taken to the vicinity of what is now Sonora Junction on January 28. When, on January 29, the detachment of the party which had the howitzer in tow reached the steep slopes of the West Walker canyon wall up which Frémont and the main party had climbed, they could drag it no further. They abandoned it in the West Walker Canyon south of Coleville and probably only a few miles north of Sonora Junction.

After the party and its equipage, minus the howitzer, had traversed the canyon to the Coleville locality, Frémont induced an Indian from a village there to guide them to a pass over which they could cross the Sierra. The route used in leaving the West Walker was obviously the same as that followed by the present-day secondary road from Topaz westward to the Carson River at Markleeville.[49] Here on the Carson, at another Indian village, arrangements were made for further guidance, and on February 2 the ascent of the Sierra proper was started. After eighteen days of exhausting struggle, the party, including "the animals and all the materiel of the camp," attained the pass.[50] There Kit Carson left irrefutable evidence of their presence by carving his name on a tree. A part of the tree with the inscription is preserved in Sutter's Fort Historical Museum, Sacramento, California.[51]

For fifteen years there seems to be no record of the Frémont howitzer. Then, in 1859, two miners, it is said, came upon the gun where Frémont left it. During the Civil War it was confiscated by the government as United States property, but afterward it again fell into private hands. For years it was in Virginia City, Nevada; then it was moved to Lake Tahoe, where it was sometimes fired on celebratory occasions. Mrs. Paden says:

> A controversy arose as to its ownership, and an enterprising California congressman succeeded in obtaining an authorization from the War Department to remove it to his home town. Not a bad idea, civically speaking, but it didn't work out.
>
> The howitzer promptly disappeared and remained hidden for many years. It was somewhat of an impasse, for naturally, while the order remained in force no one took an interest in finding it. Meanwhile historians fretted somewhat for fear that through death or other mischance, its hiding place might be forgotten. With these conditions obtaining year after year, my husband finally took it upon himself to write to the War Department asking them to rescind the order and to make such arrangements as would facilitate its return to the general public. In time they wrote back to him releasing the little cannon to whomsoever had it in custody. This communication was forwarded where he thought it would do the most good, and (also in time) the cannon popped up in Carson City.[52]

Dr. and Mrs. Hinkle trace the more recent history of the cannon through devious paths from the West Walker River locality to Carson City, Gold Hill, Virginia City, Glenbrook on Lake Tahoe, Tahoe City, Tahoe Tavern, and finally to the Nevada State Museum in Carson City. The Hinkles conclude that there is "not a shred of evidence to prove that the coveted relic ever belonged to Frémont," and that the U. S. War Department is not in position to release it to anyone. The last assertion regarding present ownership is probably accurate, but the very carefully documented story presented by the

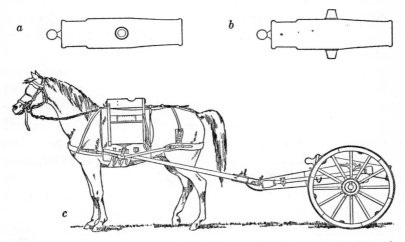

Fig. 53. Frémont's mountain howitzer. The barrel (no. 25-G in Nevada State Museum, Carson City) is shown in *a* and *b*. On the right trunnion is the mark "C. A. & Co."; on the left, "1836." Cyrus Alger and Sons, Boston, made the piece in 1836. The drawing (*c*) of the gun mounted on its carriage pulled by a single horse is from the Confederate edition of the U. S. *Ordnance Manual* (Mordecai, 1861).

Hinkles rather refutes the idea that there is no evidence that the cannon in question is the Frémont cannon.[53] One fact seems certain: the mountain howitzer in the Nevada State Museum is one of twelve twelve-pounders made for and delivered to the U. S. War Department by Cyrus Alger and Company in 1836. The reasonable explanation for its presence on the West Walker River rests in Frémont's own story of his trek to California in 1843–1844.

Figure 53, *a* and *b*, shows the barrel of the Frémont mountain howitzer as viewed from the left side, and from above. The United

States *Ordnance Manual,* 1841, specifies the regulation piece as follows: length of barrel, 32.9 inches; bore diameter, 4.62 inches; length of bore, 28.16 inches; length, rear of base ring to rear of trunnions, 15 inches; diameter of trunnions, 2.7 inches; diameter of muzzle band, 6.9 inches. Weight of bronze barrel, 220 pounds. The Frémont cannon, except for slightly shorter barrel, has dimensions very close to these.

Even at the time of the Civil War, the mountain howitzer had not changed in any important particular to conform to Major General Jesup's recommendations of 1836. The wheels were 38 inches in diameter, which was a slight improvement, but the axletree remained only 38 inches long. The charge was detonated by a fuse inserted into the touchhole at the moment of firing. Shells, spherical case shot (78 musket balls), and canisters (148 balls) were used as projectiles. The shell with its explosive charge (7 ounces of rifle powder) weighed about 9 pounds, and the other two were about 11 pounds each. The charge of powder for driving the projectiles was uniformly 8 ounces, and the range remained 150 to 1,005 yards, according to elevation. Figure 53, *c,* illustrates the gun and its carriage and the manner of harnessing the piece to the single horse that pulled it.[54]

In the western mountains where roads were simple trails, the fur traders ordinarily used two horses hitched tandem to pull guns which weighed less than the twelve-pounder howitzer of the military. (The total weight of the Army gun complete with carriage, ammunition, tools, and portable forge was about three-quarters of a ton. The barrel weighed 220 pounds.) Where rough country was to be traversed, the gun and its carriage could be packed on the back of a horse by using a specially designed pack saddle. There is no evidence that Frémont used a pack saddle in transporting his howitzer on its epic trip to California; however, there were occasions when the barrel was dismounted from its carriage to facilitate travel over particularly difficult stretches of terrain.

Figure 54, *a,* illustrates the method of packing ammunition for the mountain howitzer upon the back of a horse; figure 54, *b,* shows two types of ammunition, "canister" and "shell." Both the canister and the round shell are mounted on sabots of wood. Whichever type was used, the propulsive charge was 8 ounces of gunpowder in bags of woolen cloth tied to cylindrical blocks of wood. When the cartridge and its block were fastened to the sabot of the projectile by means of a collar, the load was referred to as "fixed ammunition." The canister, 4.47 inches in diameter, contained 148 musket balls arranged in four tiers, making a projectile which weighed 11.2 pounds. The round

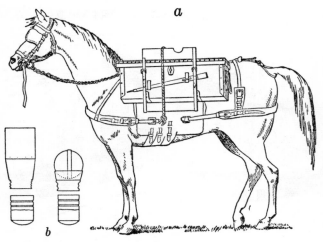

Fig. 54. Ammunition for the mountain howitzer and the method of transporting it. *a,* ammunition chests packed on the back of a horse. The special pack saddle permitted the gunner to place the barrel of the howitzer upon the top of the load. (From Mordecai, 1861, pl. 14.) *b,* canister and shell for the 12-pound mountain howitzer. After Mordecai, 1861.

shell of the same diameter as the canister was charged with 7 ounces of rifle powder, which was exploded by means of a fuse inserted at the moment of firing. The weight of the shell, strapped and loaded, was 9.2 pounds. A third type of projectile was the "spherical case," which resembled the round shell but contained 78 musket balls and a charge of 4½ ounces of rifle powder. The weight of the spherical case was 11 pounds. The ammunition chest ordinarily was packed with two shells, five spherical cases, and one canister; with the fuses, primers, priming tubes, port fire, and slow match also in the chest,

Fig. 55. British ship's gun as it appeared on the parapet at Fort Nisqually about 1833. This 6-pounder (see also fig. 56) was salvaged from a British ship and put to the use here suggested in Ft. Nisqually, the Hudson's Bay Co. post on Puget Sound near the mouth of the Nisqually River. It is now on a parapet in the reconstructed fort, in Point Defiance Park, Tacoma, Wash. (see note 55). The gun now looks southward toward the place where it previously stood.

and the linstock carried on the outside, it made a load weighing 112 pounds. A second chest packed on the opposite side of the pack saddle balanced the animal's burden.

CANNON IN THE WILDERNESS FORTS

No doubt small cannon from river boats and the wheeled guns previously described were at times mounted in the blockhouses and on the parapets of the fur traders' frontier forts. In addition, other guns of greater weight were brought to the trading posts. In such places as the Pacific Coast establishments of the Hudson's Bay Company which were served by seagoing vessels, ship's guns could readily be pressed into service as armament for the forts. A typical cannon and its installation on the stockade of a wilderness fort are shown in figures 55 and 56.[55] At the interior forts, river boats conveyed the cannon to certain posts. Jedediah Smith testifies to the presence of several twelve-pounders at Fort Vancouver in 1828.[56]

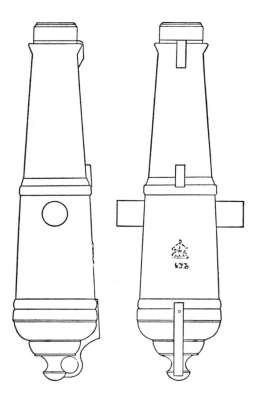

Fig. 56. British ship's gun, Fort Nisqually, about 1833. Details of the ship's gun shown in fig. 55. *Left:* a side view of the barrel. *Right:* the barrel as viewed from the top. The over-all length is 49 in. There is a 4-in. muzzle opening. Near the breech on the top of the barrel is a crown 3½ in. from top to base molded in the metal. Below the crown is the raised inscription "6 PR."

Some of the best records of ordnance at interior forts pertain to Fort Osage, the site of the westernmost post of the government's factory system of Indian trade. In the diary of George C. Sibley, agent at Fort Osage, is this entry for September 23, 1808:

> Capt. Clemson had the ordnance put in firing order round the hill occupied by the guard. This hill commands the bottoms where the camp is. Our camp is now surrounded by Indians who, though friendly, might notwithstanding be tempted by the prospect of getting possession of the factory goods and other stores, to commit some violent outrage.

And on September 24, 1808: "After dinner, Capt. Clemson had the 3-pounder and a swivel fired with shot for the gratification of the Chiefs." [57]

William Clark, in charge of construction at Fort Osage, wrote to Henry Dearborn, September 23, 1808: "As this [Fort Osage] will most probably be an important establishment, I think in addition to the 3-pounder and four swivels which are there, an iron 6-pounder with the necessary quantity of canister and grapeshot may be necessary." [58]

H. M. Brackenridge on April 25, 1811, wrote regarding affairs at Fort Osage: "Great commotions among the Indians. They were excited when some soldiers whipped an Indian for defying a sentry. They rushed forward with their arms, but the soldiers no sooner paraded and made ready a few pieces of cannon, than they thought proper to retreat." [59]

When Lieutenant Loring Palmer assumed responsibility for government ordnance and ordnance stores at Fort Osage on January 9, 1818, he included in his receipted inventory:

> one brass 4-inch howitzer, one iron cannon (6-pounder), three and a half pairs drag ropes, two rammers, two sponges, one gunner's belt, one pricker, two priming wires, two cannon spikes, one hundred and ninety-six (six pound) strap shot, one hundred and two (six pound) case shot, one hundred cannon balls for a six pounder, fifty shells for 4-inch howitzer, two hundred and ninety-three musket balls, four hundred pounds of musket powder, four hundred and seven pounds of rifle powder, sixty-six flannel cartridges (for six pounder), twenty-five and a half pounds slow match, fifteen hundred and one-half pounds of lead, nine pounds of saltpeter, two and a half pounds of sulphur.[60]

All the rather weighty armament and munitions had, of course, been transported to the westernmost government outpost in keelboats.

In the symbolic blockhouse recently (1948) constructed at the Fort Osage site by the Native Sons of Kansas City (Missouri) a beginning has been made in exhibiting ordnance and ordnance stores like those referred to by Lieutenant Palmer. Among the most interesting items are two small bronze cannon of undetermined origin which were acquired in Omaha. These guns are mounted in the same manner as the Fort Nisqually piece shown in figure 55, and presumably they saw service in one of the pioneer forts on the Missouri.[61]

The site of Fort Osage, on which the blockhouse has been built, is on the south bank of the Missouri River, some twenty-five miles east of Kansas City. A restoration drawing of the fort as it was originally constructed in 1808, when it was the westernmost government establishment, is shown in the end papers. At the time of the abandonment of Fort Osage in 1823, all but two of the western forts had at least one cannon, a total of fifty-six guns. The 6-pounder, the most versatile weapon, was represented by twenty-eight pieces. There were eleven 24-pound howitzers, nine 9-pounders, three 12-pounders, three 4-pounders, and two 3-pounders. Fort Atkinson boasted the greatest number—fourteen cannon. Fort Mackinac had ten, and the others had one to five pieces.

After the abolition of the government factory system in 1822, the line of frontier forts was pushed westward until it ran from Corpus Christi, Texas, through Oklahoma and Iowa to Lake Superior. The forts protected the frontier from Sault Sainte Marie in the northernmost point of Michigan to the Gulf of Mexico. They were more than stockades. They were centers of activity for Indian trade and administration of Indian affairs, strong points to control the warlike tendencies of the indigenous and resettled Indians, bases for exploration, and they served to restrain lawless whites, both Americans and foreign neighbors. Equally important, their garrisons maintained communications between the older settlements and the raw frontier, and thus furthered the westward movement. The forts were in general efficacious in keeping the peace; after the War of 1812, there were only three occasions for large-scale shooting: the Arikara campaign of 1823, previously referred to, the Black Hawk War of 1831–1832, and the border scrapes in connection with the fight of Texas for independence in 1835–1836.

State governments and private organizations in Michigan, Wisconsin, Minnesota, Illinois, Nebraska, Kansas, Missouri, New Mexico, Oklahoma, Arkansas, Louisiana, and Texas have done commendable work in salvaging or restoring some of the old federal forts and in preserving a number of the more important fort sites for public use. Within the buildings or on the sites may be traced the story of early military strategy in the then Far West. The guns that have been preserved, of course, constitute highly important parts of these interpretive schemes.

The responsibilities met by the Army in civilizing the West during this early period were highly important, if somewhat lacking in the dramatic, smoking-gun characteristics popularly pictured for military campaigns on a wilderness front. Nevertheless, the U. S. Army in the West "sat on a powder keg," and the official record reflects much credit upon the leadership which kept the mistakes of the Army to a minimum, sustained the western units in a state of preparedness, and held down the warfare to local Indian fights.

In these affairs cannon played a prominent part, as the chapter has shown, and the men who handled them gained a superior ability which blossomed into fame a few years later when Zachary Taylor's guns blasted out a victory at Palo Alto, the first battle of the Mexican War.

Acknowledgments

In the more than twenty years that have elapsed since work on this book was started, many persons have given generously of their knowledge in order that the data here presented should be as accurate and as nearly complete as possible. Libraries, museums, universities, and some other institutions in many parts of the country have made source materials available to me. These sources include not only printed works, manuscripts, and specimens but also personal interviews. This help from archivists, curators, private collectors, and dealers has been extended freely and with a spirit of wholehearted coöperation.

Some brief acknowledgment of my indebtedness is made in the Preface, and throughout the book the usual references are made to documentary sources. The names of the owners of illustrated objects are given, and the present whereabouts of all but a few of the specimens is indicated. For the convenience of readers who wish to review the record of such sources, a "finding list" is appended. Directors, curators, or other responsible officials and private owners have given written permission for the use of their materials pictured in this book. Their coöperation is gratefully acknowledged. Authors, publishers, and other copyright owners have also been generous in permitting the reproduction of some contemporary and copyrighted illustrations. Acknowledgment of these sources is given in the legends under the figures.

The following persons have been of particular help to me in my research and writing.

Albright, Horace M., National Park Service Advisory Board
From the beginning of the research project in Yellowstone National Park in the early 1930's Mr. Albright encouraged my endeavors; his helpful interest sustained the work during the period of writing.

Anderson, James, Historian, Native Sons of Kansas City
Provided basic information for "Fort Osage" end papers. Provided data on ordnance at Fort Osage set forth in chapter vi, read that chapter, and gave me constructive criticism of it.

Dodge, Nat, Santa Fe, N.M.
Made photographs of Spanish small arms, Palace of the Governors, Santa Fe, N.M.

Ewers, John C., Curator, National Museum, Washington, D.C.
Read chapter i and made important suggestions for changes and additions. Provided data on Parker Field and Co. trade gun (chap. iii). Gave permission for reprinting his chart "Intertribal Trade" (fig. 5).

Eustachy, Robert, artist with University of California Press, Berkeley, Calif.
Prepared twenty-five of the illustrations in this book.

Farris, E. M., Editor of *Muzzle Blasts*
In 1944 solicited and obtained the help of many private owners of trade muskets who supplied photographs and data on their fusils.

Gluckman, Col. Arcadi, U. S. Army (ret.)
Read chapter v and gave important criticism. Supplied information on flint caps. Permitted use of his illustration "Locks of U. S. Muskets, Rifles and Carbines" (fig. 33).

Hanson, Charles E., Museum of the American Frontier, Loomis, Neb., and Museum of the Fur Trade, Chadron, Neb.
Provided data on trade guns (chap. iii): C. H. and S. Co.; J. Henry; Ketland; Parker Field and Co.

Hopkins, Dr. Alfred F.
Assembled data on muskets and rifles traded to Indians under the U. S. factory system. Supplied data on Barnett trade gun of 1805 (chap. iii) and information in regard to the significance of the Pigrav-Gabiola fusil (fig. 3).

Houston, Aubrey ("Sam")
Assembled data in regard to saltpeter in Mammoth Cave.

Lewis, Col. B. R., U. S. Ordnance Department
Extended help on parts of chapter iv; supplied information on flint caps.

Mayer, Dr. Joseph R.
Provided data on Billinghurst rifle owned by C. Stuart Martin, Webster,

N.Y. (chap. ii); provided data on dragon ornament (fig. 27); permitted use of his published material on Dutch muskets (chap. ii) and gave valuable suggestions, especially on chapters ii and iii.

Peters, Cal, formerly Historian, Los Angeles Museum
Supplied information on flint caps.

Peterson, Harold L., Arms historian, Washington, D.C.
Read the entire manuscript and reviewed and criticized many illustrations; lent research notes on arms of the colonial period, eastern America; permitted reference use of his MS on early guns in America, "American Colonial Arms and Armor"; assembled data on government contracts under which Alger made howitzers; gave extensive advice on many parts of the book.

Russell, Don, The Westerners, Chicago
Read and criticized chapter iv.

Sauer, Carl O., Professor of Geography, University of California, Berkeley
Gave advice concerning preparation of material and assisted in solving practical problems of expense.

Serven, James E., Serven Gun Room, Santa Ana, Calif.
Permitted use of his *Firearms and Accessories* (1952) as a reference and provided data on the Tryon trade musket. Permitted use of illustration of Paterson Colt shown in fig. 39. Lent photographs of certain rare pistols and permitted study of his arms collection, Santa Ana.

Smith, Dr. Carlyle S., University of Kansas, Lawrence
Provided data on P. Bond trade gun and Lacy and Co. lock from trade gun (chap. iii). Supplied information in regard to various aspects of trade-gun history and lent numerous photographs and notes pertaining to fragments of guns recovered at Indian sites of the Missouri River system.

Stackpole, Gen. E. J., The Stackpole Co., Harrisburg, Pa.
Granted permission to use Colonel Gluckman's key to U. S. musket models from *U. S. Muskets, Rifles and Carbines, 1948* (our fig. 33) and N. H. Roberts' picture of a Billinghurst rifle from *The Muzzle-loading Cap-Lock Rifle,* 1952 (our fig. 13).

Woodward, Arthur, Arms historian and formerly Curator of History and Archeology, Los Angeles Museum
Supplied information on flint caps and gunflints (chap. v). Assembled information on Cyrus Alger & Co., makers of howitzers for the U. S. government (chap. vi), and through a long period gave me guidance and encouragement in this study.

Of the libraries, museums, government offices, and a variety of other institutions in many parts of the United States and Canada which have been of assistance to me in my research and writing those mentioned below have been especially coöperative.

The American Association of Museums, Smithsonian Institution, Washington, D.C.

In connection with the work of the association's Committee on Educational Work in National Parks, I visited many museums in the eastern United States and thus had access to a number of large collections of historic firearms. A tour through parts of Europe in 1936, made possible by a fellowship granted by the Oberlander Trust through the association, enabled me to visit a number of gun collections which contain important early American arms. The American Association of Museums in promoting the museum program of the National Park Service has fostered my research in fur-trade history, including the studies of guns that form the basis of this book.

John Simon Guggenheim Memorial Foundation, New York City

All-important financial assistance in the form of a Guggenheim Fellowship was awarded me by this foundation in 1953–1954, the period in which I did most of the final writing.

Missouri Historical Society, St. Louis, Mo.

This society has rich collections of manuscripts pertaining to the fur trade, on which I have drawn heavily, and many objects that were significant in the life of mountain men, some of which I have used to illustrate this book. In 1948 the society published in its *Bulletin* my "Picture Books of Fur Trade History," reprints of which I circulated among gun collectors when soliciting their coöperation in connection with this study of firearms. Many other helpful acts of officials of the society also facilitated the completion of this work.

New York Historical Society, New York City

Assistance given by the archivists of this society is noteworthy because of the unique nature of the manuscripts which make up the American Fur Company Papers preserved in its archives.

U. S. National Park Service.

Five Directors and many other associates in the National Park Service gave encouragement and valuable assistance throughout the period in which I gathered material for this book. Library materials owned by the National Park Service at offices which at various times have been my headquarters (Yosemite Valley; Berkeley, Calif.; Richmond, Va.; Washington, D.C.) have facilitated my research. Guns and fragments of guns at Morristown National Historical Park, N.J.; Fort McHenry National Monument, Md.; Chickamauga and Chattanooga National Military Park, Miss.; Jefferson National Expansion Memorial, Mo.; Fort Laramie National Monument, Wyo.; Fort Vancouver National Monument, Wash.; Kings Mountain National Military Park, S.C.; Whitman National Monument, Wash.; and Yellowstone National Park, Wyo., have contributed to the firearms materials investigated. A number of workers within the Inter-Agency Archeology Salvage Program, conducted by the National Park Service (Dr. John M. Corbett, Staff Archeologist), have provided data on the guns which recently have been brought to light in the course of the excavation of Indian sites scheduled to be inundated as a result of dams built in the Missouri Basin, in the Columbia River Basin, in the basins of the Arkansas, White, and Red rivers, and in many other localities. National Park Service personnel in many field areas and in central offices (Washington, D.C.; Richmond, Va.; Omaha, Neb.; Santa Fe, N.M.; San Francisco, Calif.) have extended important assistance only a part of which is acknowledged elsewhere. I am also indebted to Miss Louise Murray, Miss Juanita Kesheimer, and Miss Betty Koubelle, particularly, who contributed of their own time in typing various drafts of certain chapters and provided other secretarial help.

U. S. Office of Indian Affairs, Washington, D.C.

Some years ago, when the old files pertaining to the U. S. factory system of Indian trade were in the possession of this bureau, I was given access to this material, which is rich in manuscripts pertaining to the trade gun and the Indian rifle. These files are now in the National Archives, Washington, D.C. (See Hopkins, 1942.)

University of California Library, Berkeley, Calif.

This library and its allied institution, the Bancroft Library, have served as a "home port" during the later years of the gun project. Of particular usefulness were the large collections of Congressional documents owned by the University Library, collections which include the printed reports of the U. S. War Department. Important help was extended by the Interlibrary Loan Department in securing firearms literature, and by the Department of Miscellaneous Services in photostatic copying.

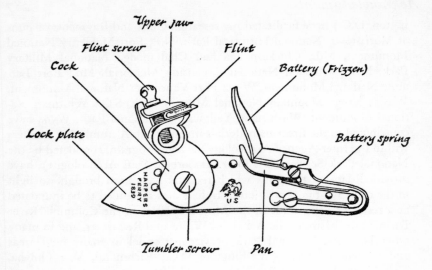

Upper jaw

Flint screw

Cock

Flint

Battery (Frizzen)

Lock plate

HARPERS FERRY 1839

US

Battery spring

Tumbler screw

Pan

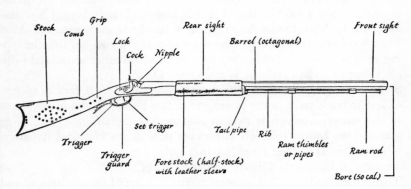

Stock

Comb

Grip

Lock

Cock

Nipple

Rear sight

Barrel (octagonal)

Front sight

Trigger

Trigger guard

Set trigger

Fore stock (half-stock) with leather sleeve

Tail pipe

Rib

Ram thimbles or pipes

Ram rod

Bore (50 cal.)

Fig. 57. Nomenclature of parts of a flintlock and parts of a percussion rifle. *a,* exterior lock parts, U. S. musketoon, Model 1839, according to usage of U. S. Ordnance Dept. in 1839 (courtesy of Col. B. R. Lewis).

UPPER JAW
Margin
Notch
Screw hole

FLINT SCREW
Stem
Screw thread
Shoulder
Neck
Head
Slit
Hole

BATTERY SPRING
Blade
Upper and lower
    branches
Elbow
Eye
Pivot
Chamfer

COCK
Body
Comb
Lower jaw
Throat
Breast
Back
Shoulder
Throat hole
Tumbler hole

FLINT AND FLINT CAP

PAN
Magazine
Face
Margin
Fence
Lining
Groove
Bridge

LOCK PLATE
Screw holes for:
    Side screws
    Battery screw
    Battery spring screw
    Pan screw
    Main spring screw
    Bridle screw
    Sear screw
    Sear spring screw

TUMBLER SCREW

BATTERY (FRIZZEN)
Face
Seat
Back
Top of seat
Seat flute
Eye
Heel
Toe
Hole for battery screw

(Interior mechanism includes main spring, bridle, tumbler, sear, and sear spring.)

b, cap-and-ball Indian rifle (percussion) by J. Henry and Son, Boulton Works, nr. Belfast, Pa., with decorative brass tacks added by Indian owner.

Finding List

COLLECTIONS IN WHICH ILLUSTRATED GUNS AND
APPURTENANCES ARE PRESERVED

California State Parks. Old Custom House, Monterey. *Swivel gun from British ship, fig. 46.*

Kit Carson Museum, Trinidad, Colo. *H. E. Lehman trade musket, fig. 24.*

Chateau de Ramezay, Montreal. *Brass bullet mould, fig. 41.*

Chicago Historical Society. *Pigrav-Gabiola fusil, fig. 3.*

Colorado Historical Society, Denver. *Oxhorn powder horn, fig. 40.*

Colt Museum, Hartford, Conn. *Colt rifle, fig. 12.*

M. H. de Young Memorial Museum, San Francisco. *U. S. musket, Model 1795, fig. 34.*

Will H. Everson Collection, Bozeman, Mont. *U. S. pistol, Model 1806, fig. 15.*

Fort Nisqually, Wash. *British ship's gun exhibited in restored fort, figs. 55 and 56.*

Julius Gans Collection, Santa Fe, N. M. *Sargent Bros. trade musket, fig. 25.*

Col. Arcadi Gluckman Collection, Carmel, Calif. *Oval flint cap of lead, fig. 42.*

E. A. Hawks, Concord, Mass. *H. E. Lehman trade musket, fig. 24.*

C. Stanley Jacob Collection, Plainfield, N.J. *Hudson's Bay Co. powder flask of lead, fig. 40; Buffalo-horn powder horns, fig. 40.*

Benton Kidwell, South Charleston, Ohio. *Whateley trade musket, fig. 25* (now owned by the Museum Association of the American Frontier).

Morgan Livingston Collection, Carlsbad, N.M. *U. S. pistol, Model 1826, fig. 15.*

Los Angeles Museum. *Hawken rifle, fig. 11; canteen of wood (powder flask), fig. 40; flint caps, fig. 42.*

Milwaukee Public Museum. *Astorian's musket, 1811, fig. 10; Billinghurst revolving rifle, fig. 13; Allen and Thurber pepperbox revolver, fig. 16; U. S. musket, Model 1812, fig. 34; U. S. musket, Model 1816, fig. 34; U. S. musket, Model 1835, fig. 34; U. S. Colt revolving carbine, Model 1837, fig. 35, c; U. S. rifle, Model 1803, fig. 36, a; U. S. rifle, Model 1817, fig. 36, b; U. S. rifle (Hall), Model 1819, fig. 36, c; U. S. pistol, Model 1806, fig. 37, b; U. S. pistol, Model 1813, fig. 37, d; U. S. pistol, Model 1836, fig. 37, f; swivel gun of musket type, fig. 48.*

Missouri Historical Society, St. Louis. *Hawken brothers' rifling machine, fig. 17; pocket pistol, flintlock, fig. 14; American Fur Co. boat cannon, fig. 50.*

Montana Historical Society, Helena. *Jim Bridger's Hawken rifle, fig. 11; N. Chance and Son trade musket, fig. 23.*

Museum Association of the American Frontier, Loomis, Neb. *Whateley trade musket, fig. 25.*

Museum of Natural History, University of Kansas. *P. Bond trade musket, fig. 22.*

Museum of New Mexico, Santa Fe. *Spanish escopeta, fig. 4.*

Nebraska State Historical Society, Lincoln. *Belgian trade gun, fig. 23.*

Nevada State Museum, Carson City. *Frémont's mountain howitzer, fig. 53.*

North Carolina Hall of History, Raleigh. *Cannon-barrel pistol, fig. 14; Ketland flintlock pistol, fig. 14.*

Oregon Historical Society, Portland, Ore. *Joe Meek's rifle, fig. 11.*

John E. Parson's Collection, New York City. *Paterson Colt, fig. 39.*

Harold Smith Collection, Harold's Club, Reno. *Paterson Colt revolvers, fig. 16; U. S. rifle, Model 1841, fig. 36; U. S. pistol, Model 1842, fig. 38; U. S. pistol, Model 1843, fig. 38; Walker Colt, fig. 39; percussion cap and container, fig. 43; modern shotgun shell, single ball, Union Metallic Cartridge display, fig. 44.*

Irving Tier, Cheshire, Conn. *Barnett trade musket, Model 1805, fig. 18.*

U. S. National Museum, Washington, D.C. *Gun worms, fig. 45; Dutch musket, seventeenth century, fig. 10* (U. S. Cartridge Co. Collection formerly in National Museum); *Henry cap-and-ball Indian rifle, fig. 29* (U. S. Cartridge Co. Collection formerly in National Museum); *Indian rifle, flintlock, fig. 28* (U. S. Cartridge Co. Collection formerly in National Museum).

U. S. National Park Service. Collections in Jefferson National Expansion Memorial, St. Louis. *Barnett trade musket, 1868, fig. 19; Barnett trade musket, 1833, figs. 20 and 21; Indian rifle, percussion, lock by Goulcher, fig. 28; portrait of B. L. E. Bonneville, fig. 32; drawing of Fort Winnebago, after an illustration in* Wau-bun, *by Mrs. John H. Kinzie, fig. 31; ball cartridge for musket, and buck-and-ball cartridge, fig. 44.*

Victoria and Albert Museum, London. *Short fusil, 1650, fig. 2.*

Wadsworth Atheneum, Hartford, Conn. *"Texas" Colt (Paterson), fig. 39, b.*

Washington State Historical Society, Tacoma. *Gun worm, fig. 45.*

Robert H. Wilcox, Lake Hortonia, Vt. *H. Hollis and Son trade musket, 1886, fig. 26.*

Wisconsin Historical Society, Madison. *De Langlade's flintlock pistol, fig. 14; combustible envelope cartridges (Colt), fig. 44, f.*

William J. Young Collection (see Mayer, 1943). *Seventeenth-century musket, fig. 10, b.*

Notes

1. Biggar, 1922–1936, II, 100–103; quoted by permission of The Champlain Society, Toronto, Canada. The picture of Champlain firing his famous shot faces p. 101.
2. *Ibid.,* pp. 97–100; quoted by permission of The Champlain Society.
3. "Though the new firearms, dismally primitive improvisations, were lamentably capricious in their operation, *a man could fire one after comparatively little training; a competent longbowman was of necessity the product of a lifetime of practice and conditioning.* Perhaps the chemical wonder of early firearms contributed to their success. In those bleak, superstitious days it was agreed by everybody that gunners were in close alliance with the Devil." (Italics mine.) Shields, 1954, p. 2, quoted by permission of Coward-McCann, Inc.
4. Wallhausen, 1615; quoted by Metschl, 1928, pp. 51–52.
5. Greener, 1881, p. 54; Curtis, 1927, pp. 107–133; Hammond and Rey, 1940, *passim;* Powell, 1952, pp. 48, 61, 63, 84, 123, 126–129.
6. Metschl, 1928, p. 53; Peterson, n.d.(*a*), pp. 1–58. For Lemoyne's narrative see Lorant, 1946. Theodore de Bry obtained the Lemoyne paintings, made copper engravings from them, and published them in England in 1591; 43 of these engravings, with Lemoyne's legends, are reprinted in the Lorant book. A score or so of matchlocks appear in the pictures, and details of mechanism are shown. Barrels swell at the breech to give strength "where the powder doth lye," modest scrollwork is engraved at the breech and in the midsection, and the muzzle is enclosed within a ring resembling the end of a "cannon-barrel" pistol. The forestock extends nearly to the muzzle; no ramrod is shown,

and no bands or pins for holding the barrel to the stock are in evidence. The serpentine, or cock, and the flashpan are shown clearly. The trigger is a curved rod ending in a hook for the convenience of the trigger finger. Lieutenants accompanying the arquebusiers carry either halberds or pikes and swords. In only one engraving is a pistol in evidence. In action, the lieutenants wore light armor and steel helmets and carried shields. Like the French on the St. Lawrence, the Laudonnière party in Florida adopted certain tribes as allies and took their guns into action against the enemies of their friends. The artist Lemoyne, armed with an arquebus, accompanied a war party of "Outina" (Utina) Indians in warfare against their neighbors, the "Potanou" (Potano). (See Lorant, p. 65.) Details of the type of matchlock carried by Lemoyne and contemporary instructions for firing these guns with the butt against the breast are given in Jackson, 1923, pp. 2, 4–5. A specimen lock for this type of gun is preserved in the Dexter Collection (no. 827 FB), Burbank, Calif. See also Dexter, 1955, p. 7.

7. Peterson, n.d.(*a*), pp. 50–53.
8. Quoted by Metschl, 1928, p. 54.
9. Schön, 1858, and Montecuculi, 1722; quoted by Metschl, 1928, p. 53. Peter Martensson Lindestrom, a Swedish officer who was present when, in 1655, Dutch forces removed the Swedes from Fort Casimir near the site of present Wilmington, Del., testifies that the Swedish commander, Skute, abandoned the fort at the head of a small contingent of Swedish soldiers, "with loaded guns, burning fuses, pipes and beating drums." That the Dutch military also used matchlocks at this time is revealed by Lindestrom's account of Stuyvesant's dinner party for the vanquished. Behind each Swede seated at table stood "two [Dutch] musketeers with their guns and burning fuses." Ward, 1930, pp. 193–194.
10. O'Callaghan, 1853–1887, I, 182, 388, 389, 392; IV, 57, 126, 236; IX, 408, 409.
11. *Ibid.*, IX, 408–409.
12. Gov. Fletcher to Committee of Trade, 1693, O'Callaghan, IV, 57. The term "firelock" was synonymous with "snaphance" and "flintlock" in the late seventeenth century (see Sawyer, 1910, p. 13; Gluckman, 1948, p. 35). The "fusee," or fusil, was a light flint gun which during the later decades of the seventeenth century was the characteristic arm of Army officers (Peterson, n.d.*a*, p. 43). Diderot, writing in the mid-eighteenth century, stated that the fusil was invented by Frenchmen in 1630 to replace the *mousquet*. The first troops to carry the fusil equipped with bayonet were the Regiment Royal Artillerie, 1671. In 1699–1700 the fusil had replaced the *mousquet* for artillery and cavalry use, and three years later Louis XIV ordered the reduction of pikemen and the adoption of the bayonet by the infantry. Diderot

observed, "the fusil with bayonet is very redoubtable." Diderot, XV, 563–565.

13. Lords of Trade to Gov. Fletcher, 1696, O'Callaghan, IV, 256.

14. O'Callaghan, IV, 126, 236.

15. Gov. Thomas Dongan's report, Feb. 22, 1687; quoted by Mayer, 1943a, p. 55.

16. Peterson, 1947a, pp. 203–205; Sawyer, 1910, p. 13.

17. Schmidt, 1877, p. 33; Lahontan, 1905, p. 377. As early as 1689, Lahontan, who had for several years traveled among the Indians of the Great Lakes region, in the Illinois country, and along the upper reaches of the Mississippi, reported that the short and light fusee was the favorite of the red man. In his list of recommended items for the French trade in Canada he emphasized the importance of this type of gun. That the longer barrels (50–60 inches) had been abandoned by the English traders is evidenced by the invoices of the Hudson's Bay Co. during the century following Lahontan's published comment. Trade muskets seldom exceeded 4 ft. in total length, with barrels 33 in. long. In 1748, English guns having 27-in. and 33-in. as well as 21-in. barrels were distributed from Hudson's Bay Co. posts in the north country. At York Factory, muskets of all three lengths were sold for 14 beavers each. At Moose River and Albany (James Bay), the price was 10 beavers for the gun with 21-in. barrel, 11 beavers for the intermediate length, and 12 for the 4-ft. gun (33-in. barrel). (Woodward, 1948b, pp. 3–4.) The tradition of short barrels for trade muskets persisted throughout the years that such guns were made. The specimens considered in chap. iii are representative of the period 1805 to date; none has a barrel longer than 36 in., and most of the specimens are still shorter.

18. C. W. Brown, 1918, p. 73.

19. It is said that a few Iroquois had and used the flintlock rifle as early as 1750, "but it remained for a fragment of manuscript in the St. Louis Mercantile Library, part of the Journal of Auguste Chouteau, to establish the fact that in 1736, the Chickasaw were not only armed with rifles, but were generally good shots." Dillin, 1924, pp. 89–92.

20. The principal groups: Abnaki, Algonkin, Chippewa, Eskimo (Labrador), Foxes, Huron, Kickapoo, Malecite, Menominee, Miami, Micmac, Montagnais-Naskapi, neutral Iroquois, Ottawa, Penobscot, Pennacook, Potawatomi, Sauk, Susquehanna, Tionontat, and Winnebago. Swanton, 1952, *passim*.

21. At this time the principal tribes of the upper Mississippi–Missouri–James Bay sector were the Assiniboin, Arapaho, Cheyenne–Sutaio, Cree, Dakota, Hidatsa, Illinois, Iowa, Mandan, Missouri, Osage, and Pawnee. The Cree, long-time customers of the French, and the Assiniboin divided their business between the French and the English after the

Hudson's Bay Co. posts on James Bay were established in the 1670's. The Illinois, firm friends of the French, were temporarily broken up by the Iroquois after 1682. Swanton, 1952, *passim*.

22. The Hudson's Bay Co. Committee, meeting March 4, 1671, instructed "That Mr. Bailey . . . treate with such persons as he thinks fitt . . . for supplying 200 fowleing pieces . . . first bringing patterns of the guns to be bought unto the next committee." The Frenchmen Radisson and Des Groseilliers were to advise the committee with respect to the fitness of the arms. Hudson's Bay Co. Minute Book (in Canadian Archives), Oct. 24, 1671, p. 30; quoted in Innis, 1930, p. 127.

23. Wilson, 1951, pp. 50–55. The fighting ended in 1697, but no conclusive victory was attained. Of the British forts seized by the French, only York Factory remained in French hands by terms of the Treaty of Ryswick.

24. Turner, 1891, p. 32.

25. Lahontan, 1905, pp. 93, 373–377, 576. Lahontan in the 1680's referred to the French trade gun as a "firelock," a term which may have meant either snaphance or flintlock; but since the French military had used the flintlock for some years, it may be presumed that most of the French trade guns of that period also were flintlocks. The French during a hundred years of gunmaking apparently did not improve the quality of their fusees for Indians. Mackay of the Spanish firm known as the Upper Missouri Company—"The Company of Explorers of the Upper Missouri"—wrote from the Maha (Omaha) village on the Platte, in October, 1795, to Gov. Carondelet: "This village contains seven hundred warriors and I have promised them two hundred muskets for next year. . . . They care only for the English guns and not the French ones, which burst in their hands." Nasatir, 1952, I, 358.

26. In the Gulf Plain, southern lowlands, and the southwestern plains the noteworthy tribes or groups with which the French came in contact included the Acolapissa, Alabama, Bayogoula, Biloxi, Chakchiuma, Chatot, Chawasha, Chitimacha, Choctaw, Comanche, Houma, Kiowa and Kiowa Apache, Koroa, Mobile, Natchez, Natchitoches, Quapaw, Taensa, Tawasa, Tohome, Tunica, Wichita, and Yazoo. Swanton, 1952, *passim*.

27. These gunmakers were identified by Dr. Alfred F. Hopkins and Dr. Thomas T. Hoopes.

28. Diderot (1751–1777, under "Fabrique des armes, fusil de munition" in Tome III of *Planches*) provides seven plates of drawings and descriptive material pertaining to eighteenth-century French guns and the machinery employed in the manufacture of flintlocks used during the French and Indian War. Contemporary pictures of French trade guns in the hands of Indians are to be seen in Lahontan (1905, p. 430)—a late seventeenth-century piece—and in Carver (1779, p. 228)—an Ot-

tigaumies (Fox) warrior and his gun of the 1760's, ostensibly a French
musket.

29. Jacobs, 1948, pp. 245-256.
30. Secoy, 1953, p. 73.
31. More than 100,000 muskets were absorbed by English regulars, militiamen, and Indian allies during the French and Indian War. These
ranged from antiquated matchlocks to the "Brown Bess" musket and
the shorter flintlock fusee preferred by the Indian. Many matchlock
guns were fitted with flintlocks to make them more like the other
arms. The original Brown Bess musket was adopted during Queen
Anne's reign (1702-1714) and continued to be manufactured with
but little change until the day of George II (1727-1759), when the
lock was improved, and the ramrod of wood was replaced by one of
steel. Through the French and Indian War, the barrel was 46 in.
long and the bore was 11-gauge. For a synopsis of Brown Bess history see chap. ii and accompanying notes.
32. Most of the barrels for French muskets of the eighteenth century were
forged in Paris, and the best locks were manufactured there. These
vital parts were supplied to gun factories in Paris, Sedan, Charleville,
Abbeville, Forez, Franche-Compté, and lesser industrial centers. Musket stocks were made of walnut, ash, and maple; ramrods were made
of oak, walnut, or whalebone. Small shops in the environs of Paris
and in Normandy manufactured them and shipped them in bundles
of 100 to the gun factories. Diderot describes the tools and other equipment used by French gunmakers and includes woodcuts depicting in-
teriors of gun factories. He states that the gunmakers, who were called
Les Arquebusiers, made up one of the larger guilds or societies of
eighteenth-century Paris. (Diderot, III, 435-436.) Strangely, relics
of the French armament are few. Dr. Kenneth E. Kidd of the Royal
Ontario Museum, Toronto, one of the most active students of French
sites, writes: "We have in this museum no authenticated French gun
of any sort of the period previous to 1759, when the French lost
Canada. The nearest thing we have to it are certain parts found in
the course of the excavation of the so-called Ste Marie I, near Midland,
Ontario, a sort of Mission headquarters founded by the Jesuits in
1639 and occupied until 1649. There, in 1939-40, I found fragments
of barrels, and various small parts of the mechanisms. Most of these
are illustrated in my report published in 1949. There would be no
doubt in my mind that these are genuine relics of the decade 1639-
1649, since the site has been well authenticated and there was no
evidence of disturbance where most of these were found. I know
of no other authenticated examples in Canada." Kidd, 1955.
33. Hicks, 1940a, I, 9. There is some evidence that French trade guns also
were shipped to America in the post-Revolution days. Lt. Gov. Gilbert
Antoine de St. Maxent of Louisiana was given the responsibility of

handling postwar affairs concerning Spanish and Indians in the Floridas; along with it he obtained a personal monopoly in the Indian trade. Authority was granted him to import guns and other trade merchandise from France. I have seen no inventories or other documents pertaining to the St. Maxent business, but Mackay of the Spanish Missouri Fur Company provided a hint that there were some French guns in circulation (see note 25). Nasatir, 1952, p. 358.

34. Plantagenet's "Description of the Province of New Albian," in Force, 1836–1846, Vol. II, No. 7, p. 19.

35. "Guns, cannon, powder and clothing for the Continental Army came from the Dutch Island, St. Eustatius, in the West Indies. There on Nov. 16, 1776, Governor de Graff ordered the first foreign salute to the American flag. . . . Rodney, the British Admiral thought it was more important to go and take St. Eustatius, as a source of American supplies than to go to the aid of Lord Cornwallis at Yorktown." Griffis, 1921, pp. 1–11.

36. Ward, 1930, p. 194.

37. Swanton, 1952, p. 94. According to Bolton and Marshall (1930, p. 23): "[Spain found] the Lesser Antilles, the Bahamas, and Florida . . . inhabited by hostile cannibals, who were regarded as fair prize for enslavement. As early as 1494 Columbus suggested that permission be given to sell Caribs. In 1498 he took a cargo of 600 of them to Spain. Soon it became an accepted legal principle that cannibals and rebellious Indians could be enslaved. The idea was encouraged by the lack of Spanish laborers, and by the disappearance of the native population of Española. Slave-hunting was soon extended to the coasts of Florida, Pánuco and other parts of the mainland. The practice was continued, as the frontier advanced, to the eighteenth century when, for example, Apache of Texas and Pawnees of Kansas were often sold to work on plantations in Louisiana or Cuba." Quoted by permission of The Macmillan Company.

38. Conspicuous among the southeastern Indians during the early years were the Apalachee, Apalachicola, Atakapa, Calusa, Chatot, Cusabo, Guale, Karankowan, Potano, Saturiwa, Tacatacuru, Timucua, Yamasee, Yuchi, and Yustaga. Swanton, 1952, *passim*.

39. Ewers (1954b, p. 436) attributes to Ferdinand and Isabella, in 1501, the first Spanish law prohibiting the sale of guns to Indians.

40. Swanton, 1922, pp. 58–59.

41. When William Hilton, commander of an English ship, visited the San Felipe (San Marcos) region in 1663, he took aboard two Edisto (Cusabo) Indians who spoke some Spanish. "They know the use of guns and are as little startled at the firing of a Piece of Ordnance as he that hath been used to them many years." *Ibid.*, p. 62.

42. "Their [the Spaniards'] treatment of the aborigines was hardly short of

diabolical. Well has it been said: 'The Spaniards had sown desolation, havoc, and misery in and around their track. They had depopulated some of the best peopled of the islands and renewed them with victims deported from others. They had inflicted upon thousands of the natives all forms and agonies of cruelty, driving them to suicide as a way of release. They had come to be viewed by their victims as fiends. The hell which they denounced was shorn of its terror by the assurance that the tormentors were not to be there. The true soldiers of the cross, among the Missionaries, protested in vain against these cruelties.' " (Andrews, 1894, I, 21–22.) Dr. Andrews' appraisal of Spain's Indian policy is extreme; yet there are elements of truth in it which, for the United States, make it acceptably descriptive. In moderating such estimates, Bolton and Marshall (1930, p. vi) state that some authors customarily forget "that Florida, New Mexico and Texas were to Spain only northern outposts and they omit the wonderful story of Spanish achievement further south." Some of the achievement in Mexico is very thoroughly analyzed by Powell (1952, pp. 57–148).

43. Curtis, 1926, pp. 327–328; quoted by permission of the Historical Society of New Mexico, publishers of *New Mexico Historical Review*.

44. In the Southwest and in the Mississippi–Missouri River country (Louisiana Territory), which Spain acquired by cession from France in 1762, were approximately 260,000 Indians. Noteworthy tribes in this vast land of particular concern to the Spaniards were the Adai, Apache (Lipan, Jicarilla, and Apache, proper), Arikara, Caddo, Cahuilla, Castanoan, Chemehuevi, Chumash, Coahuiltecan, Cocopa, Comanche, Diegueno, Fernandeno, Halchidhoma, Halyikwamai, Hasinai, Hidatsa, Hopi, Iowa, Jemez, Juaneno, Jumano (see Shuman), Kansa, Kawaiisu, Keresan, Kohuano, Koso, Luiseno, Maricopa, Mohave, Navajo, Omaha, Oto, Paiute, Papago, Pawnee, Pecos, Pima, Pira, Ponca, Quapaw, Salinan, Serrano, Shuman, Tewa, Tiwa, Tonkawan, Ute, Walapai, Wappo, Yavapai, Yokuts, Yuma, and Zuni. Swanton, 1952, *passim*.

45. The international effects of this early trade in guns conducted by the French with the Pawnee is treated by Thomas (1935) and is further analyzed by Secoy (1953, pp. 80–81).

46. In 1720, Don Pedro de Villasur with 42 soldiers and a party of Indian allies was sent northward from Santa Fe to learn firsthand about French activities in the Plains country. On Aug. 13, 1720, near the site of present North Platte, Nebraska, the expedition was surprised in camp by a Pawnee war party. "The devastating effect of the volleys from the Pawnee guns prevented the Spaniards from rallying successfully." Forty-four members of the Spanish party fell, including Villasur. A. B. Thomas, 1924; 1935, pp. 37, 171, and 174; Secoy, 1953, p. 81.

In 1758, the Comanche, with help from Frenchmen, attacked a newly established mission for the Apache on the San Saba River near the site of present Menard, Texas. Capt. Diego Ortiz Parillo with 300 men from San Antonio attempted to retaliate by attacking some Comanche and Jumano (Shuman) in a village on the Red River west of Lake Texoma. The Indians, equipped with French guns and having been coached by the French, easily repulsed the Spanish troops. As a result of the defeat and in the face of growing French prestige, the Spaniards made no further attempt to wipe out the French influence on the Louisiana-Texas frontier. Dunn, 1914; Bolton, 1914, Introd.

47. Ghent, 1936, p. 40.

48. Ewers, 1954b, pp. 429–446.

49. Secoy, 1953, p. 74; Perrin du Lac, in Nasatir, 1952, II, 706. Ewers (1954b, pp. 438–439) cites other contemporary sources.

50. During the Revolution, several firms of Montreal traders combined under the name North West Company to engage in the fur trade throughout much of Canada and the area now the northern states of the American Union. Montreal was the headquarters, and there were four principal outposts: Detroit, Mackinaw, Sault Sainte Marie, and Grand Portage. At its height of development, the company employed 2,000 clerks, voyageurs, laborers, interpreters, and so forth. A transportation line branched off from the main Grand Portage–Assiniboine route to serve the Missouri River tribes, a route which had been used by Frenchmen for half a century before the North West Company was formed. Davidson, 1918; W. E. Stevens, 1926; Wallace, 1934.

51. Nasatir, I, 84–87. This company was commonly called the Spanish Missouri Fur Company.

52. Todd was one of the English merchants from Michilimackinac, who after the Revolution removed his business to Louisiana under permit from Gov. François Carondelet, dated Dec. 21, 1795. On Jan. 8, 1796, Carondelet wrote to the Duque de Alcudia, Secretary of State: "Since Don Andres Todd is one of the principal share holders in our Missouri company; and since the greater part of the merchandise and goods used on its three expeditions were supplied by his house, which will receive in payment part of the skins on its returns, it follows that he will assist its undertakings in every possible way. It also ensues that he will [use his] influence to [get them to] cease their hostility and attacks against the traders in our company, those nations of the upper Mississippi and north of the Missouri, who hold him in great respect and have traded with his house for years." Nasatir, II, 393–394, 407–410.

53. *Ibid.,* pp. 389–390.

54. *Ibid.,* p. 425.

55. Brannon, 1935, pp. 84–85.

56. Gilmore, 1900, p. 198.

57. Bassett, 1911, *passim*.

58. A letter from Gov. Thomas Dudley to the Countess of Lincoln, March, 1631, states: "Diverse Merchants of Bristow, and some other places have yearly for theis [*sic*] 8 years or thereabouts sent shipps hether [to Massachusetts] at the fishing times for Beaver where their factors, dishonestly for their gaines, have furnished the Indians with guns, swords, powder and shott." Force, Vol. II, No. 4, p. 7.

59. Personal letter, Oct. 3, 1955, Clifford P. Wilson of Hudson's Bay Co., Winnipeg, to Carl P. Russell: "We gave up selling muzzle-loading guns several years ago. They were last sold in the Province of Quebec."

60. From "An Abstract of the Laws of New England, 1641," reprinted in Force, Vol. III, No. 9, p. 10.

61. O'Callaghan, I, 182.

62. The more important tribes that were identified with the northern English colonies: Conoy, Delaware, Iroquois, Mahican, Mohegan, Montauk, Nanticoke, Narraganset, Pequot, Saponi, Susquehanna, Wampanoag, and Wappinger. In the mountains and on the lands taken by the southern colonies were the Catawba, Cheraw, Cherokee, Chickasaw, Chowanoc, Cusabo, Eno, Hattera, Machapunga, Muskogee (Creeks), Nottaway, Pamlico, Powhatan, Santee, Shakori, Shawnee, Tuscarora, and Wateree. The Cherokee, Muskogee, Shawnee, and Tuscarora, especially, have left a record of shifting allegiance. Swanton, 1952, *passim*.

63. Anna Lewis, 1924, pp. 343–344, 347; quoted by Secoy, 1953, p. 80.

64. When, in 1752, Georgia changed from a proprietary colony to Royal control, the Creeks, the Chickasaw, and the Cherokee (in part) performed one of their several "flip-flops"; they dropped their English alliance in favor of the French on the lower Mississippi. This did not, however, prevent the three groups from fighting among themselves. Swanton, 1952, p. 222.

65. Harrington, 1954*a*, pp. 25–27.

66. The Hudson's Bay Co. still flies its flag over some 200 trading posts and stores in Canada. Chartered in 1670, the company is the grand patriarch in all fur-trade history and one of the oldest commercial corporations in existence. Its record permeates the story of the Old Northwest and the Columbia. Its impact upon United States history is manifest. For a comprehensive account see Mackay, 1949; for an excellent synopsis see Hudson's Bay Co., 1955.

67. Davidson, 1918.

68. In the country west of Hudson Bay, English activities extended to the Arctic and Pacific oceans and south and southwest to the Missouri, the Great Basin, and California. The English made contact with the following notable tribes in addition to those once served by the French (see note 21) in this sizable section of the continent: Achumawi-Atsugewi, Alsea, Atsina, Bannock, Calapooya, Cathlapotl, Cathlamet, Cayuse,

Chastacosta, Chehalis, Chilluckittequaw, Chimakum, Chinook, Chipe-
wyan, Clackamas, Clallam, Clatskanie (see Chastacosta), Clatsop,
Chowwewalla Columbia, Colville, Cowlitz, Cree, Crow, Duwamish,
Etchaottine, Hanis, Hoh, Kalispel, Karok, Kato, Kowchottine, Klamath,
Klickitat, Konomihu, Kutcha-Kutchin, Kutenai, Kwakiutl, Lassik,
Lillooet, Lummi, Maidu, Makah, Mattole, Methow, Miwok, Modoc,
Multnomah, Mahane, Nez Perce, Nisqually, Nootka, Ntlakyapamuk,
Okanagon, Palouse, Pomo, Puyallup, Queets, Quinault, Sahewamish,
Salish (Flathead), Samish, Sampoil, Sarsi, Sekani, Shasta, Shuswap,
Skagit, Skilloot, Skin (Tapanash), Siksika (Blackfeet), Siletz, Snoho-
mish, Songish, Spokan, Squaxon, Stalo, Suquamish, Takelma, Tenio,
Tillamook, Tolowa, Tsattine, Tsimshian, Umatilla, Umpqua, Walla-
walla, Wanapam, Wasco, Watlala, Wailaki, Wenatchee, Wintun,
Wishram, Wiyot, Yakima, Yani-Yahi, Yuki, and Yurok. Swanton,
1952, *passim.*

69. Nute, 1931, p. 7.
70. Sparks, 1840, IV, 303–323; quoted in Turner, 1891, p. 44.
71. The larger tribes which aligned themselves with the British upon the
    opening of hostilities or soon thereafter: Cherokee, Chickasaw, Choc-
    taw, Creek, Delaware, Foxes, Iroquois, Kickapoo, Miami, Ottawa,
    Shawnee, and Wyandot. A few additional small tribes or detached
    bands from large tribes brought the number of Indians who sided with
    the English to approximately 120,000.
72. Ogg, 1904, p. 45; Swanton, 1946, p. 112; Gilmore, 1899, pp. 158–173.
    Some of these British munitions were seized by the Americans when
    Chief Dragging Canoe's village at Chickamauga was captured in April,
    1779.
73. Ewers, 1939, p. 34.
74. In 1778, Clark sent a row galley up the Ohio and thence up the Wabash,
    while he proceeded overland from Kaskaskia to Vincennes. His land
    force was a detachment of frontiersmen armed with "Kentucky" rifles.
    At Vincennes, well-aimed rifles sent bullets through embrasures in the
    walls of the fortifications and wounded some of the British defenders,
    "which caused them to surrender themselves and garrison, to the great
    mortification of our Boats crew who had not the opportunity of making
    use of their cannon." (A participant quoted by Baldwin, 1941, p. 17.)
    Afterward Vincennes was recaptured by the British. In February, 1779,
    Clark with 172 riflemen made his phenomenal winter attack on Vin-
    cennes. Again the sharp-shooting Americans, shot through embrasures
    and gun slits, picked off the defenders during a three-hour siege, and
    forced surrender of the fort. The long rifle was used in Clark's attack
    on the Miami Indians at Old Chillicothe (Xenia, Ohio), and at Piqua
    (near the site of present Springfield, Ohio) in 1780.
75. Billington, 1952, pp. 174–195.
76. Attempts to inculcate true military discipline had little effect upon the

Indian of the period. He did synchronize his movements with the immediate battle plans of his white comrades, but this was no innovation to tribes practicing the traditional woodland military technique. Secoy, 1953, pp. 67–69.

77. The transfer of upper Louisiana from Spanish ownership to France in 1800–1803, and to the United States by purchase from France in 1803 had little or no effect upon the English trade on the upper Missouri. Lewis and Clark in 1804 observed the evidences of past trading activities and reported on the business being conducted currently by the English companies. Lewis and Clark, 1904–1905, Vol. I, Pt. 2, pp. 189, 206, 215, 232, 238, and 267.

78. Ewers, 1939, p. 67.

79. Turner, 1906; 1921, p. 168; Pratt, 1925; Billington, 1952, pp. 268–289.

80. Capt. Bulger, in command of British troops at the mouth of the Wisconsin River, evacuated his Ft. McKay (Prairie du Chien) on May 24, 1815. As a parting gift to his local Indian retainers, he turned over his surplus of powder and ball. Also, in the spring of 1815, Col. Robert McDouall, British commander at Ft. Mackinac, sent Capt. Anderson of the British Indian Department to the Mississippi tribes with £3,600-worth of guns, ammunition, and general merchandise, "the last rewards in our power for their constancy, fidelity and courage." Beers, 1935, p. 27.

81. *Ibid.*, pp. 37–38.

82. Wesley, 1931–1932, pp. 509–510; Hopkins, 1942.

83. Fort Osage (1808–1825), on the Missouri, was the westernmost U. S. military outpost until Ft. Atkinson was built at Council Bluffs, 1819–1820; and the farthest west of the government trading posts maintained under the factory system was at this fort. President Thomas Jefferson wrote on Aug. 20, 1808: "The Kansa, . . . the Maha and the Ponca adhere to the Spanish interest against us, but if we . . . open commerce for them they will come to us. . . . The factories proposed on the Missouri . . . will have more effect than armies. . . . We must prohibit the British from appearing westward of the Mississippi." Fort Osage represented the first extension of national sovereignty beyond the Mississippi. The restoration of the old fort as a memorial to the westward expansion of the United States, a project of the Native Sons of Kansas City, is contributing significantly to the interpretation of guns of the frontier.

84. In January, 1813, word reached the Astorians at the mouth of the Columbia that the United States and Great Britain were at war. A delegation from the North West Company arrived at Astoria on Oct. 7, 1813, and in the absence of William Price Hunt, who was in charge of Astor's Pacific Fur Company, Duncan McDougal, a subordinate, sold out, "lock, stock, and barrel," to the visiting Canadians. Hunt returned to find Astoria in rival hands, and the British flag flying where the Stars

and Stripes had been. Many of Astor's employees, including some of the partners, remained in Oregon as employees of the new operators. U. S. Cong., 1823*b*, pp. 23, 33–34.

85. The introduction of American-made trade muskets did not do away with the importation of cheap guns for Indians. Congressional documents indicate that immediately after the discontinuance of the factory system, muskets were imported from the British East Indies, Cuba, England, France, the Hanse towns of Germany, Gibraltar, Holland, Mexico, Prussia, the Sandwich Islands, and Spain. Holland, Spain, and England shipped the most muskets—5,000 to 7,000 a year, each. Annually the total number of imported muskets exceeded 18,000. U. S. Cong., 1825*b*, p. 138; 1827*a*, pp. 26–27.

86. Vinton, 1935, I, 157.

87. Russell, 1945, pp. 95–104.

CHAPTER II   PERSONAL WEAPONS OF THE TRADERS AND TRAPPERS (*pages 62–102*)

1. Mayer, 1943*a*.

2. *Ibid.*, p. 43.

3. An interesting story of one personal weapon of a New Netherlander is told in Mayer, 1942. This gun, which in general appearance resembles figure 10, *b*, has a 59-inch barrel, of .75 cal., marked by the London Gunmakers' Proof House. Dr. Mayer considers it to have been made between 1660 and 1680.

4. The elders emphasized the importance of the heavy breech: "He that lovyth the safetie of his own person and delights in the goodness and bewtie of a peece, let him always make choice of one that is double breeched, and if it be possible a myllan peece, for they be of tough and perfecte temper, light, square and big of breech and very strong where the powder doth lie, and where the violent force of the fire doth consist, and notwithstanding, trimme at the end." *Military Treatise* of 1619; quoted by Pollard, 1926, p. 50.

5. U. S. Cartridge Co., n.d., pp. 86–97.

6. Mayer, 1943*a*, p. 34.

7. Sawyer, 1920, p. 390.

8. Metschl, 1928, p. 827.

9. U. S. Cong., 1823*b*, pp. 23, 33–34.

10. Dillin, 1924, pl. 11, fig. 1. The English military weapon of the eighteenth century was the flintlock musket which its soldier-users dubbed "Brown Bess." For many years the story that the gun was named for Queen Elizabeth was popularly believed, but since the "Brown Bess" was not made until Queen Anne's reign (1702–1714) and Queen Elizabeth

died in 1603, there is no basis for the legend. Probably the russet or brown finish given to the gun to make it more nearly rustproof gave rise to the name.

Harold L. Peterson, who has examined several hundred "Brown Besses," writes: "The 'Brown Bess' was adopted by Queen Anne on the advice of John Churchill, Duke of Marlborough . . . It set the pattern for the next hundred years, with but minor variations. The first model had a 46 inch barrel. About 1760 a 42 inch barrel was adopted. Sometime during the American Revolution a 39 inch barrel became standard. Then came the reinforced cock and the combless butt around 1800 . . . In addition to the Infantry muskets there were fusils for officers, artillery, and light Infantry after 1758. Also there were carbines of various lengths, the first of which were often made by cutting down infantry muskets. This accounts for many of the carbines (more correctly musketoons) found without brass fore-end caps." Peterson, 1949.

Lisa may have regarded his "Brown Bess" as a prize, but tests show that a representative specimen of this gun of the period of the American Revolution gave "only 40 per cent of hits on a target covering approximately 12 square feet, at a distance of only 300 feet. A modern military rifle fired at the same range at a target only one-twelfth the area should make 100 per cent. But whereas the modern rifle drills a small hole in a man so suddenly and cleanly that sometimes in the excitement of a battle he barely feels it, the great round ball of the old musket smashed his bones, tore his flesh, let out his blood, and shocked him 'hors de combat.'" Sawyer, 1910, p. 103.

11. The word "Tower" engraved or stamped on the lock of a "Brown Bess" means that the finished gun was checked by government officials at the Tower of London and accepted by them as a satisfactory arm. Beginning with the reign of George I, guns from Birmingham as well as those from London were sent there to be viewed, approved, and marked. These "Brown Bess" muskets are commonly known as "Tower" muskets. Others approved at Dublin Castle were marked with the name of that government arsenal. Pollard, 1926, p. 91; Peterson, 1949, p. 2.

12. In the National Museum, Washington, D.C., in the collection formerly belonging to the U. S. Cartridge Co., there was a George II "Brown Bess," .75 cal., on the lock of which was "Jordan 1743," the crown, the letters "GR," and the broad arrow. Cut in the stock were the initials "CH" and "WD." The gun had been owned by Cornelius Havens, Pomfret, Conn., a member of the 3d Regiment, Connecticut line, during the Revolution. In the U. S. Cartridge Co. *Catalogue* this musket is pictured (fig. 162) and described (p. 35) but is not identified as a "Brown Bess." Satterlee (1939, p. 250), however, quotes J. M. George, who states that it is a George II Brown Bess. I do not know

where this specimen is now; the U. S. Cartridge Co.'s collection was broken up and sold.

13. According to Schmidt (1877), the George III musket was introduced in 1762. J. N. George (in Satterlee, 1939) identifies nos. 157, 158, and 160 in the U. S. Cartridge Co. *Catalogue* as Brown Bess muskets of the George III type. All have the broad arrow on the lock and were carried by Connecticut soldiers of the Revolution. Many of the weapons had been issued to the militia, to the Colonies, and to privateersmen before the Revolution.

14. Satterlee, 1939, pp. 249–250, quoting J. N. George.

15. Leonard, 1904, p. 220.

16. Kurz, 1937, pp. 194–195.

17. Revoil, 1865, I, 274; Parkman, 1920 ed., p. 289.

18. The Rindisbacher painting is reproduced in *The Beaver*, June, 1950, p. 14.

19. Riling, 1951, p. 61. Meyrick's lecture was published in the British Journal *Archaeologia*, II (1829), 59–105.

20. Schmidt, 1877, pl. 8, fig. 46.

21. Nasatir, 1952, I, 374.

22. Lewis and Clark, 1904–1905, Vol. II, Pt. II, p. 189.

23. U. S. Cong., 1823*b*.

24. Brackenridge, 1816, p. 31.

25. *American Rifleman*, April, 1953, p. 28.

26. U. S. Cong., 1822*c*.

27. Metschl, 1928, pp. 96–97.

28. The reader should not conclude that this rifle accompanied Clark on the expedition of 1804–1806. A Kentucky rifle presumably carried by Astorians came to light in 1938 when part of the cargo of a boat believed to be from the William Price Hunt expedition was found at the bottom of the Snake River near Murtaugh, Idaho. The boat had capsized in 1811. The recovered relics are preserved in the State History Museum, Boise, Idaho; the rifle is no. 1886.

29. Tiling, 1913, pp. 59–60.

30. Sawyer, 1920, pp. 51–52; C. Thomas, 1930, pp. 102–103. Some students of firearms history have challenged the propriety of the term "Plains rifle" because there was no contemporary use of the name (Peterson, 1949, p. 3; Barsotti, 1953, p. 155). See also Bingham, 1934, for home-guard use of the Plains-type rifle.

31. Henry Hawkins, a gunmaker of Lancaster, Pa., Harpers Ferry Arsenal, Va., and Hagerstown, Md., removed to St. Louis about 1808. His sons changed the ancestral name to Hawken, in which form it became famous throughout the West. Jacob Hawken was born in Hagerstown, Md., in 1786. He died in St. Louis in May, 1849. Samuel T. Hawken was born in Hagerstown in 1792 and engaged in business in St. Louis

from 1822 to 1860. Metschl, 1928, p. 822. See also *Saturday Evening Post,* Feb. 21, 1920; *American Rifleman,* April 15, 1924, and April, 1951; and Roberts, 1944 (port.), pp. 484–487.

32. The Kit Carson Hawken rifle is owned by Montezuma Lodge No. 109, A.F. & A.M., Taos, N.M. It is illustrated in Sabin (1914, p. 332) and in Dillin (1924, pl. 102, figs. 1 and 2). In appearance it is strikingly similar to the Jim Bridger piece described here and shown in fig. 11. A picture of Kit Carson with his rifle is the frontispiece in Burdett, 1865. Barsotti (1953, p. 155) pictures a Hawken rifle, .50 cal., which was purchased in St. Louis in 1833; it is now exhibited in the Colorado State Museum, Denver.

33. Denig's rifle was sketched by Kurz (1937, pl. 19) on Sept. 14, 1851, at Ft. Union. Except for the sharp drop of the stock, perhaps a liberty taken by the artist, it is a fair duplicate of the Bridger specimen shown in fig. 11. The earlier Hawken rifles were the Kentucky type.

"Paul Anderson's expedition was the first I [Samuel Hawken] fitted out. He and Chambers went to Santa Fe and gave such good reports about my guns that every man going west wanted one. William Ashley's men were the next lot to go out, but they started for the Rocky Mountains and were driven back by the Creek [Arikara] Indians. The boys . . . ran out of provisions and had to kill a mule. Ashley told me he was riding on a white horse looking for game one day and sighted a buffalo. He had no idea of hitting the game, but at the crack of the rifle, over went the buffalo. He could hardly believe the shot was effective at so great a distance, and rode up to take another shot at short range, but found the buffalo dead, shot through. Ashley came back to St. Louis the same year. No, I cannot remember the date [it was 1823]. Ashley's rifle was one I made for his special use. The barrel was three feet six inches long and carried an ounce ball. Ashley was offered $150.00 out west, but he would not take it." From a MS by Samuel Hawken which Otis A. Hawken gave to J. P. H. Gemmer in 1933; a copy of the manuscript is in the Jefferson National Expansion Memorial, St. Louis.

34. Gregg, 1905, XX, 105.
35. Quoted in Sabin, 1914, p. 222.
36. Sawyer, 1920, pl. 5, p. 48. See also Colt's Patent Fire Arms Co., 1937, pp. 9–13; Rohan, 1935, pp. 1–177, 199–208; Satterlee, 1939, pp. 23–24; Gluckman, 1948, pp. 259–260; Serven, 1952, p. 28, fig. C-1.
37. The illustration is based on Serven, 1952, p. 46, fig. 820; and Fuller, 1933, p. 58. For a contemporary "instruction sheet" for the Colt rifle of 1838, see Parsons, 1949*b.*
38. Gregg, 1905, XX, 215–216.
39. The illustration is based on Van Rensselaer, 1947, p. 46. That author also describes an 8-shot specimen, of .36 cal., with a fore end of wood 10

in. long. Another specimen is a 7-shot, .44 cal. rifle with an octagonal barrel 20½ in. long. Satterlee (1939, p. 22) lists a Cochran 8-shot rifle of .44 cal.; and Sawyer (1920, p. 61, pl. 8) pictures one of the arms. Chapel (1947, p. 54, pl. 9, fig. 4) illustrates a Cochran 7-shot turret pistol made by C. B. Allen. It is .40 cal., with a 5-in. round barrel. Its total length is 10 in. Satterlee and Van Rensselaer also list Cochran pistols made by Berry, by H. and C. Daniels, and by C. B. Allen. None of the pistols has a trigger guard; in its place is an underhammer. The grips of the pistols and the heel plates of the rifles are of German silver.

40. A report of Sept. 19, 1837, on official tests of the Cochran, Colt, Hackett, and Hall arms (U. S. Cong., 1837*b*, pp. 334 ff.). A condensed report of these same tests appears in U. S. Cong., 1837*c*.

41. "A Revolving Rifle," Rochester *Daily Democrat,* Aug. 22, 1843, and Aug. 10, 1852.

42. Roberts, 1944, p. 335. The news notes from the Rochester *Democrat* were also reprinted by Roberts, pp. 333–334. Permission to use the material was granted by The Stackpole Company, Harrisburg, Pa., owners of the 1952 ed. of Roberts.

43. Roberts (1944, pp. 333–334) reproduces a photograph of this over-under Billinghurst specimen. A vague reference to a "six-gun" desired by the noted factor Kenneth McKenzie, at Fort Union of the American Fur Co. in the early 1830's, is given in a letter from Ramsay Crooks, Nov. 16, 1832, to Pierre Chouteau, Jr. (quoted in Chittenden, 1935, p. 341): "For Mr. McKenzie's coat of mail I have sent to England, for nothing of the sort could be found here. His *fusil a six coups* is ordered from Rochester; and the medals for his outfit are in the hands of the die-maker." The date of this order belies the idea that the desired six-shooter could have been one of the percussion repeaters elsewhere referred to in this chapter. Since the order went to Rochester, it is likely that it was a Billinghurst repeating arm. If the unusual gun reached Fort Union or any other locality on the Missouri, some record of its use there should turn up eventually.

44. George, 1938, pp. 19, 32, 45, 65, 68, 85, and 94. Pollard (1926, pp. 93 and 95) reminds us that the standardization of the English military pistol had a parallel in the standardization of the French regulation musket.

45. The screw-barrel type of pistol was one of the earliest English pistols. Even in its beginning (seventeenth-century) form it was accurate and powerful. In the percussion model, which began to be produced early in the nineteenth century, it continued on the market, even after the metallic cartridge made breechloaders commonplace. Not until the 1870's did the screw-barrel pistol go entirely out of use; it was displaced at that time by the cheap pin-fire and rim-fire weapons which were made throughout Europe and in the United States. In its various forms it had been a popular type of handgun for more than 200 years.

George (1938, pp. 16–17, 37, 51, 53, 97–99, 135, and 138) traces this history in a very interesting way.

46. A similar pistol of unknown history is no. N4014 in the Milwaukee Museum. Metschl, 1928, p. 456, no. 26.

47. Amer. Fur Co., 1831–1849, LB 1: 154. Letter no. 216 is an order from Ramsay Crooks, Feb. 10, 1835, to Bernard Pratte, Philadelphia: "Be so good as to buy and bring with you 1 pair 4½ inch octagon, iron, rifle-barrel pistols, steel mounted, 45 balls to the pound, short butt, with ball mould and ball screw, percussion locks—made by Deringer, Philada."

48. George, 1938, p. 133, pl. XVIII. John E. Parsons (1952) has written a carefully documented, well-illustrated book on all "Derringer" pistols, including the variety of arms by other makers who appropriated the name as well as the design of Henry Deringer's pocket pistol.

49. De Langlade commanded a French force in defense of Fort Duquesne in the French and Indian War. On one occasion he made a surprise attack on the advancing Braddock (when George Washington was present) and won a victory over the British. After the defeat of the French in 1760, De Langlade was named Indian Agent for the British at Green Bay. Upon the outbreak of the Revolution he was made a captain in the British Army. For account of his life see T. T. Brown, 1932. Kellogg, 1935, also reviews the circumstances of his leadership. The De Langlade pistols shown in fig. 14 were stolen from the Wisconsin Historical Society in 1946 (letter from John W. Jenkins, Oct. 31, 1946).

50. About the time of the American Revolution, officers in the British Army abandoned the heavy holster guns and adopted lighter pistols similar in bore to the earlier weapons but of finer finish and with shorter barrels. The silver-mounted De Langlade pistols are fairly typical, with ornamentation characteristic of good-quality English pistols made from 1750 to 1780. After 1780 the English makers dropped the more elaborate decorations in favor of a plainer style. George, 1938, p. 66.

51. Russell, 1921, p. 22.

52. U. S. Cong., 1827a, pp. 26–27.

53. Sawyer, 1910, pl. 17, p. 170.

54. Parker, 1838, p. 79.

55. Metschl, 1928, p. 485. The gun is now in the Lawrence Collection on the A. M. K. Ranch near the north end of Jackson Lake, Wyo.

56. Ghent, 1936, pp. 250–251. Jedediah's brother, Austin Smith, obtained Jedediah's rifle and pistols from Mexican traders (see Austin's letters of Sept. 24, 1831, in Morgan, 1953, pp. 362–364). Permission to quote from Ghent, 1936, has been given by Longmans, Green & Co., Inc., present holders of the copyright.

57. Sabin, 1914, pp. 627–628.

58. Dawson's, 1926.

59. Pollard, 1926, p. 117; George, 1938, pp. 84–85.

60. "Another form of weapon which fell into disuse in the second quarter of the nineteenth century was the duelling pistol, a type which had been made in vast numbers during the last years of the flintlock era, and to a lesser extent during the transition period, 1820–1830, but which is seldom found among later percussion arms, although pistols of duelling type continued to be made as target weapons for some years after the practice of duelling had been abandoned in England." George, 1938, pp. 127–128.

61. In 1818, Elisha Haydon Collier, an American living in London, patented in England, France, and the United States a flintlock revolver which features a cylinder mounted on a horizontal axis similar to the conventional revolvers of today. The 5-shot cylinder is revolved by hand. A spring presses the cylinder against a sleeve at the end of the barrel, making a joint that is nearly gas-tight. The caliber is .34, and specimens from a factory in England are known to have 9-in., 6-in., and 4-in. barrels. Collier reëstablished his residence in the United States in 1850, but there is no evidence that he manufactured the revolver here or that he even took advantage of the percussion system in perfecting his weapon. Chapel (1947, p. 27, pl. 3, fig. 3) illustrates the gun. See also Pollard, 1926, p. 80, for a good illustration, and George, 1938, pp. 154–165, for illustrations and a satisfying account of the weapon. George states: ". . . it would appear that the inventor was chiefly interested in the application of the revolving principle to sporting guns, and that his revolving pistol was more or less a by-product of his activities as a maker of repeating shot-guns and rifles, and was itself made in relatively small number."

   Pollard, George, and Chapel all seem to suspect that "subsequent finds [of the Collier guns] may show that it was made in the United States also." See the *Gun Collector,* No. 20, pp. 129–131, for a good article on the Collier arms, and also B. R. Lewis, 1953.

62. Ethan Allen of Grafton, Mass., played a leading role in producing the earlier American-made pepperboxes. His arms were placed on the market soon enough to enable some mountain men to buy them. See U. S. Cartridge Co., n.d., p. 119.

63. See Mumey, 1931, illustration on p. 79.

64. George, 1938, p. 171. An exhaustive general treatment of pepperbox arms is available in Winant, 1952. See also the *Gun Collector,* April, 1948, pp. 139–174.

65. Sawyer, 1920, pp. 65–68, and "Pepperbox Shoulder Pieces," in Winant, 1952.

66. Colt's, 1937. This manual contains 28 pages of pictures and text pertaining to Colt history. Several students of firearms history, working independently or in collaboration with the Colt Company, have pub-

lished treatises which have helped to eliminate much of the questionable legend, misinformation, and confusion which have marked the Colt saga in the past. Chapel, Edwards, Gluckman, Hicks, B. R. Lewis, Parsons, Rohan, Satterlee, Serven, and others have contributed to the correction of errors and to the organization and publication of authentic data on the early Colt arms. My condensed interpretation draws upon all these sources. In particular I have relied on Rohan, 1935, pp. 1-177 and 199-208, for the outline, and on Serven, 1946, for the mechanical details. Specimens examined are in Harold's Club, Reno, and the Nunnemacher Collection, Milwaukee Museum.

67. Satterlee, 1939, pp. 23-34; Serven, 1946, p. 28; Pollard, 1926, p. 132; and Fuller, 1946, pl. xviii, illustrate a Paterson Colt with a trigger guard and heavy frame similar to the gun which in 1847 was manufactured at Whitneyville, and which became famous as the "Walker" Colt. Whether or not Capt. Walker of the Texas Rangers had anything to do with the 1839 model or with any experimental models made at the Paterson factory in 1840 and 1841 is not definitely known. The editors of Colt's *Manual* admit that the question is debatable. It seems certain, however, that heavy Colt revolvers with a trigger guard of the "Walker type" were not regularly made at the Paterson factory and that Colt and Walker did not confer regarding changes in design and caliber before production of the 1839 model. Had they done so, Walker would undoubtedly have asked for a revolver bigger than .36 cal. Serven (1946) does not recognize a caliber larger than .36 among the Paterson models, but he does point to the "big Texas Paterson" as the progenitor of the Whitneyville-Walker model. See chap. iv.

68. Gregg, 1905, XX, 105.

69. Sabin, 1914, pp. 199-200. As for the "butcher knife" with which the "white man shoot . . . six times," both the 1836 and 1839 Colts had but five chambers in the cylinder.

70. Chapel, 1947, p. 55; Satterlee, 1939, p. 186. B. R. Lewis (1947) publishes a letter which Colt wrote to President Polk in 1848: "Within a day or two an arm has been presented to the War Department by a Mr. Leavitt which is an infringement on my patent rights and which if ordered by the Department will be doing me a great injustice. . . ."

Rohan (1935, pp. 175-176) states that the Massachusetts Arms Co., Chicopee Falls, Mass., was manufacturing this revolver in 1849. "One Leavett had produced a revolver which was a . . . clear infringement of Colt's patents. This, however, did not worry Sam's enemies. They assumed, without going to the trouble of finding out, that Sam's patent rights would expire by 1853 and by the time a suit for infringement could be tried and a decision rendered there would no longer be any grounds for the infringement suit. As they were to discover later, Sam had obtained an extension of his patent, on the ground that he had been deprived of its benefit and use, and was sitting back watching for some such attempt by his ill-wishers." When the Massachusetts Arms Co. began to produce the Leavitt revolver, Colt brought suit against that company, and the court upheld his claim. The company stopped manufacturing revolvers. The quotation from Rowan is used by permission of the publishers, Harper & Brothers.

71. Sawyer (1920, pl. 7, pp. 59–60) describes a "Wesson and Leavitt" revolver which has an especially long barrel, a special butt, and a detachable stock. In effect the weapon is a repeating carbine which Sawyer classifies as a "buggy rifle." He attributes it to the period "about 1840."

72. De Voto, 1943, pp. 219–221, 509; Webb, 1927 and 1931.

73. The list given below is from Kauffman, 1952. The dates are based on the appearance of the names in St. Louis business directories and do not necessarily represent the limits of the period of each man's activity.

James Lakenan, 200 N. Main St.	1821
Jacob Hawken, 214 N. Main St.	1821
Samuel Hawken, 21 Laurel St.	1836
Jacob and Samuel Hawken	1836–1847
Samuel Hawken, 33 Washington St.	1850
J. Roper, 51 2d St.	1836–1841
Huber and Hoffman, 49 Locust St.	1836–1837
Huber alone	1838–1839
E. T. Jackson, 19 Oak St.	1838–1839
J. Labrau, 120 1st St.	1838–1839
H. M. Brown, 26½ Olive St.	1838–1841
Frederick Hellinghaus, 92 Elams St.	1840–1842
John Hingle, Walnut bet. 3d and 4th	1840–1841
H. G. Huslace, Franklin bet. 8th and 9th	1840–1841
J. F. Diettrich	1840——
Charles and Ignatius Altinger, 73 2d St.	1842
Thomas Bateman, 12th north of Myrtle	1842
Marten Breitenbaugh, St. Georges St.	1842
H. M. Brison, Oak bet. 2d and 3d	1842
Tristma Campbell, 31 Laurel St.	1842
Joseph Curtain, St. Georges St.	1842
Frederick Dohrmann, 53 First St.	1842
John B. LeBeau, 1st and Poplar	1842

The St. Louis census for 1840 records the population as 16,469.

74. Pattie, 1905.

75. Garth, 1949, pp. 309–310; quoted by permission of the *Pacific Northwest Quarterly,* Seattle. The Washington State Historical Society, Tacoma, has on exhibition a set of pioneer gunsmithing tools that were brought across the Plains by Victor Wallace in the 1840's. Wallace was in business in Cowlitz County.

76. M. S. Sullivan, 1936, p. 45; Morgan, 1953, p. 254.

77. Young, 1899, p. 238.
78. U. S. Cong., 1825*a*, pp. 8 and 10 and sheet 32.
79. Ewers, 1954*b*, p. 444.
80. Kendall (1941, pp. 1–34) gives an informative and thorough account of all the steps in the production of the muzzle-loading rifle. Another excellent description is given by Roberts (1944, pp. 437–457). The significance of various procedures in rifle making is reviewed by Cline (1942, pp. 1–162).

CHAPTER III   TRADE MUSKETS AND RIFLES SUPPLIED TO THE INDIANS
(pages 103–141)

1. Dillin, 1924, p. 89.
2. Clifford P. Wilson to Julian C. Spotts, 1943, in National Park Service files, Jefferson National Expansion Memorial, St. Louis.
3. Letter Books of the Indian Trade Office, George Town, D.C.; quoted in Hopkins, 1942.
4. *Ibid.,* May 12, 1809.
5. Hopkins, 1942.
6. Ramsay Crooks of the American Fur Company wrote to his field man, Joseph Rolette, at Prairie du Chien, Wis., April 18, 1835: "Sorry the German guns turned out so badly. Those of this year are all English." (Amer. Fur Co., 1831–1849, LB 1: 334.) This unfavorable report notwithstanding, Crooks subsequently (June 1, 1836) wrote to Geisse and Krockhauss, Philadelphia, and asked for North West guns— "either German or English." Amer. Fur Co. Papers, LB 3: 248, no. 1663.

   See also U. S. Cong., 1827*a*, pp. 26–27. This report of the Secretary of the Treasury for the year ending Sept. 30, 1826, gives the country of origin and the prices paid for guns imported that year: Netherlands, 7,615 pieces at $3.00 each; Germany, 1,489 pieces at $4.00 each; Cuba, 10 pieces at $4.00 each; Spain, 5,411 pieces at $4.20 each; Mexico, 1,576 pieces at $4.50 each; England, 436 pieces at $5.60 each.

   These prices seem ridiculously low, but a letter of Dec. 9, 1819, from Decius Wadsworth, Colonel of Ordnance, to John C. Calhoun, Secretary of War, offers a partial explanation of the price differential between the foreign-made muskets and those produced at the Harpers Ferry Arsenal for $14.25. In it Wadsworth attributes the higher cost in the United States to the wages of $1.40 a day paid to armorers in this country, in comparison with the 40 cents a day earned by the workmen in England and on the Continent, and states that if equivalent wages had been paid to American armorers the weapons could have been produced for $3.90 apiece. Fuller, 1930, pp. 139–140.

7. Woodward, 1948*b*, p. 4.

8. "Charcoal iron is the best quality used for inferior guns; it is made from the clippings of sheet-iron, melted in a charcoal furnace and recast, then forged into a bar and rolled into rods in imitation of stub-twist. The iron when in contact with the charcoal absorbs a certain amount of carbon and becomes hardened, but as the metal from which it is made is originally of a weak description it still remains of inferior quality. Its cost is very low being about 4*d*. per lb., and as it may be made to look well by a method of browning it is much employed by inferior makers, the saving on a pair of barrels in material alone being tenpence to a shilling as compared with stub-twist, besides the reduced cost of forging which adds two more shillings to the saving effected; and this proportion is kept up throughout the subsequent processes." (Stonehenge, 1859, p. 218.) Stonehenge then gives some particulars of the making of cheap "threepenny skelp," "twopenny skelp," and "sham damn skelp," adding: "All of these three kinds of iron are made from scrap of qualities varying in proportion, the scrap used for sham damn being of the worst possible kind. The process of manufacture is smilar to that alluded to under charcoal iron." (*Ibid.*, pp. 219–220.) One method of forging was to shape the iron into bands and, while the bands were hot, twist them into tight spirals approximately of the diameter of the completed gun barrel. These spirals, mounted on a mandril, were welded end to end to provide a length comparable to the length of the developing gun barrel. The twisted tube was further heated and placed upon an anvil in which there was a groove of the same shape as the external surface of the gun barrel. Here the tube was hammered with light hammers until the spiral was consolidated and the barrel was completely forged. This method of twisting a scelp round a mandril was devised in 1806. To make a "plain" barrel, two long bands of iron were each bent longitudinally over a mandril and then were heated to welding heat and welded together on the grooved anvil. Whether the barrel was twisted or plain, it had to be bored, ground, breeched, cut to proper length, proved, polished, and browned. The more important European places where gun barrels were made in the nineteenth century were London and Birmingham, England; Liége, Belgium; Saint-Étienne, France; Brescia, Italy; and Suhl, Prussia. Greener, 1881, pp. 217–254; Stonehenge, 1859, pp. 212–227.

9. Stonehenge, 1859, pp. 218–219.

10. Greener, 1881, pp. 220–221.

11. In April, 1807, the U. S. Armory at Springfield, Mass., started work on an "Indian musket" to be presented by the government to friendly Indians. This gun was a flintlock with 33¾-in. barrel held to the forestock by pins rather than bands. It bears no resemblance to the military musket of its day, nor is it very much like a typical trade gun. Hicks (1940, I, 26–27) states that 1,209 of these arms (pictured in his

pl. 9) were made in the period 1807–1810, and that all but a very few
of them remained in store throughout the time of the Indian factory
system (discontinued in 1822). From the insistence of the Indian Trade
Office, in 1809, upon having "the real North West gun," it would seem
that the government-made Indian gun did not meet the requirements.
It is reported that some of the Indian muskets from Springfield went
to West Point for cadet use in 1813 or 1814, and again in 1830. However, U. S. Cong., 1822*b* (pp. 1–62), records the transfer of forty of the
guns to the Superintendent of Indian trade in 1820. The price paid,
$12.81 each, was considerably more than was paid for a "real North
West gun" at that time. In 1848, 690 of the Springfield Indian muskets
were still at the armory, and Ordnance officials recommended that
they be sold at auction. No record of the actual sale has come to my
attention. A specimen marked with the Eagle and "U. S.—BRIDGEWATER
—1818" is evidence that some additional guns of this pattern may have
been procured through contract with private manufacturers. (Serven,
1952, p. 37.) Gluckman and Satterlee (1953, p. 165) show that Rufus
Perkins of North Bridgewater, Mass., James Perkins of Bridgewater,
and Adam Kinsley of Bridgewater were producing muskets under
government contract just before 1818. It seems incongruous that the
government should add to its supply of unwanted arms, but the
"Bridgewater" Indian musket is not otherwise explainable.

12. In the course of this survey the Barnett trade guns (flintlock) listed below have come to my attention.

1805. Irving Tier, Cheshire, Conn. (Specimen shown in fig. 18.)

1822. J. D. Kimmel, Jenny Lake, Wyo.

1826. Museum Association of the American Frontier, Loomis, Neb.

1833. Montana Historical Society, Helena, Mont.

1833. Dr. Joseph R. Mayer, Rochester, N.Y.

1833. Jefferson National Expansion Memorial, St. Louis, Mo. (Fig. 20.)

1841. Museum Association of the American Frontier, Loomis, Neb.

1848. Ned Frost, Cody, Wyo.

1852. Hudson's Bay Co. Museum, Winnipeg, Canada.

1858. State Historical Society, Bismarck, N.D. (Lock plate.)

1863. L. C. Winant, East Orange, N.J.

1863. Hudson's Bay Co. Museum, Winnipeg, Canada.

1868. Jefferson National Expansion Memorial, St. Louis, Mo. (Fig. 19.)

1869. Clinton A. Russell, Tacoma, Wash.

1871. Hudson's Bay Co. Museum, Winnipeg, Canada.

1876. Hudson's Bay Co. Museum, Winnipeg, Canada.

N.d. Museum of the Plains Indian, Belton, Mont.

Barnett fusils equipped with the percussion system, of the years indicated, are in the following collections:

1847. (Converted.) Hudson's Bay Co. Museum, Winnipeg, Canada.

1883. Arizona Museum, Tucson, Ariz.

1883. Hudson's Bay Co. Museum, Winnipeg, Canada.

1883. D. A. Reynolds, Pittsburgh, Pa.

13. Pollard, 1926, p. 286.

14. Metschl, 1928, p. 519.

15. The description is based on data, photographs, and sketches supplied by Dr. Carlyle S. Smith, Dec. 15, 1953.

16. Amer. Fur Co., 1831–1849, Letter Books, item no. 10237, Feb. 6, 1841.

17. Gluckman and Satterlee, 1953, pp. 123–124.

18. Amer. Fur Co., 1831–1849, Letter Books, item no. 13935, Oct. 19, 1843.

19. Hawks, 1940, pp. 1–2.

20. Amer. Fur Co., 1831–1849, LB 7: 177–178, no. 4216.

21. Woodward, 1946, pp. 22–24. For a history of the "broad arrow" on British guns, see Forbes, 1929, Vol. II.

22. After the Battle of Tippecanoe, a bloody fight with the Shawnee near the site of present Lafayette, Ind., on Nov. 7, 1811, Gov. William Henry Harrison, commander of the American forces, wrote to John M. Stuart of Frankfort, Ky.: "Within the last three months the whole of the Indians on this frontier have been completely armed and equipped out of the King's stores at Malden. . . . The Indians had moreover an ample supply of British glazed powder. Some of their guns had been sent to them so short a time before the action [Battle of Tippecanoe], that they were not divested of the list covering in which they are imported." Ewers, 1939, p. 67.

23. Greener, 1881, p. 219.

24. Dexter, 1940.

25. U. S. Indian Trade Office, Invoice Book, 1822–1823, p. 10; quoted in Hopkins, 1942.

26. Sawyer, 1920, p. 135; Gluckman and Satterlee, 1953, pp. 48–49.

27. Dillin, 1924. See also Gluckman and Satterlee, p. 94; and Irving, 1849, p. 66.

28. Larocque, 1910, p. 19.

29. Sawyer, 1910, p. 221.

30. Pollard, 1926, p. 220.

31. Amer. Fur Co., 1831–1849, LB 7: 177–178, no. 4216.

32. John Ewers, Curator of the National Museum, Washington, in a letter of March 8, 1948, reports that the Hudson's Bay Co. Museum, Winnipeg, has one of these flintlock muskets by Parker, Field & Co., and he mentions another bearing the date 1855, in the possession of Mr. S. E. Johns, Kalispell, Mont. In 1949 Mr. Ewers obtained a specimen dated 1868 for the U. S. National Museum. Mr. Charles E. Hanson, Jr., Loomis, Neb., has supplied good photographs of his Parker, Field & Co. trade gun, which like the Milwaukee specimen is dated 1875. The dragon ornament and all other details are typical of the "Hudson's Bay Co. fuke." On both lock and barrel appears the seated fox superposed upon the initials "EB." Mr. Hanson states that the Museum Asso-

ciation of the American Frontier owns specimens dated 1863, 1871, and 1875. Pollard, 1926, p. 292, lists "Parker, Field and Sons" as London gunmakers for the period 1850–1886.

33. Amer. Fur Co., 1831–1849, Letter Books, item no. 12633, May 16, 1842.

34. Personal letter from James E. Serven, Santa Ana, Calif., to the Jefferson National Expansion Memorial, St. Louis, July 23, 1944. See also Gluckman and Satterlee, 1953, p. 217. Biographical data on five generations of gunmaking Tryons is given in Tryon, 1911.

35. Amer. Fur Co., 1831–1849, Letter Books, item no. 14067, Jan. 27, 1844, and no. 14069, Jan. 29, 1844.

36. This hypothesis was advanced by Dr. Joseph R. Mayer of Rochester, N.Y. Subsequent references to Mayer, 1943*b*, as a source pertain to his letter of Sept. 30, 1943, addressed to me, in which he has outlined the picture very much as it is presented here.

37. Greener, 1881, p. 55, fig. 44.

38. Ffoulkes, 1937, p. 27.

39. Pollard, 1926, p. 220. Grancsay, 1950, engravings 3 and 6.

40. Mayer, 1942, p. 2.

41. Mayer, 1943*b*.

42. *Ibid*. J. N. George, 1938 (p. 48 and pl. 6, fig. 8), describes and figures the dragon side plate shown in fig. 27, *e*. It is on "a brass-barreled pistol made by W. Brazier of London shortly after the year 1700. Both lock plate and mounts are of brass, the latter including a handsome 'dragon' sideplate *of a type which is also found upon some of the Service muskets of Queen Anne*." (Italics mine.) Here, probably, is the Englishman's inspiration for the use of the dragon on his nineteenth-century trade muskets. Trade guns that were made in English shops much earlier than 1805, the date that appears on the oldest "fusee" brought to light in this study, may yet be discovered.

43. *Katalogue des Waffensmuseums-Wien*, Vienna, 1886, p. 94.

44. Sawyer, 1920, p. 55.

45. Tench Coxe to Jacob Dickert and Henry De Huff of Lancaster, Pa., Nov. 16, 1807, Letter Books of the Indian Trade Office; quoted in Hicks, 1940*a*, II, 93.

46. Coxe wrote to Peter Gonter, Lancaster, Pa., in 1803: "Do not lay out for the U.S. any rifle which a customer would decline were he to see it, and were a real judge. If he would leave it and go to another rifle maker, it ought not to be sent in for inspection by the U.S." In the same year, Coxe instructed Peter Getz, a government arms inspector: "You will carefully inspect the rifling and the outside [of the barrel], condition of the lock, the butt boxes, the stocks, and—in short—all the parts; and you will pass none but what are in good merchantable condition. . . . I mention (in confidence between you and me) that some of another small lot was rejected here, for piercing [worm holes] in the stocks, faults in the springs of the butt boxes, want of rifling, rust-

eaten locks, or locks with weak springs. . . . Let everything be done with attention to the public interest and candour towards the manufacturers." *Ibid.*

47. On Dec. 16, 1803, Coxe wrote to Dickert and De Huff of Lancaster: "I am obliged by duty to divide the public business among our fellow citizens in other parts of the United States. We all pay taxes, and manufacturers in every state have a right to a chance if they can work cheap and well." (Hicks, 1940*a*, II, 92.) Nevertheless, the record shows that Pennsylvania rifle makers did get the greater part of the government's orders for Indian rifles.

48. The total number of rifles in the several known contracts was less than 3,000, but a great deal of controversy developed with respect to their quality after representative lots of the arms had been delivered the U. S. Arsenal at Schuylkill, N.Y. William Eustis, Secretary of War, presumably influenced by political advisors, Callender Irvine particularly, wrote to Tench Coxe on Jan. 7, 1811: "It is stated that the rifles and pistols at the U. S. Arsenal on the Schuylkill are an evident imposition on the public and that it would have been far better to have thrown the whole amount of the purchase money in the river than to have procured with it arms only calculated to appear on paper" (Hicks, 1940*a*, II, 101). Identifiable in the documents pertaining to the so-called inferior rifles are the products of Joseph Henry, Henry De Huff, Henry Guest, Peter Brong, and Henry Pickel.

On Jan. 9, 1811, Coxe replied to Eustis: "Many pistols and rifles were rejected, but so far as they are wrong Mr. Thomas Palmer of Philadelphia, Mr. Daniel Pettibone of Boston and Mr. Shough, in a small part must have passed on them. . . . As these arms went into the arsenal at different times from March 2, 1808 to the spring of 1810 and were in most instances inspected there, it is singular and to be considered that Mr. Irvine, the local officer called there hourly by his duty and who is supposed to have his residence there, should never once have taken the trouble to look at them and yet now pronounce in this extreme language. . . . I do not consider the representations to you as correct. . . . I am of the opinion that the inspectors have not done their duty, . . . yet, I am sure the pistols and rifles do not deserve the character Mr. Irvine gives to them. . . . The War Department will find it a fact, also, that no pattern rifles were ever furnished." (Hicks, 1940*a*, II.) In later correspondence Coxe commented further: "I know of no standard of instruction for 'eleven dollar rifles,' and conceive that the true question is whether they [the contractors' arms] are worth the money. I believe the rifles to be just like those supplied these 8 or 9 years, without a single complaint; they are such as the country constantly buys, and such as are meant by the Government. They are the only rifles procureable for the orders." (*Ibid.*) Yet, under the pressure exerted by his superiors, Coxe, on Oct. 21, 1811, wrote to eight of the contractors, requesting them to come to his office for settlement of their business with the government. This conference seems to have terminated his contacts with the private arms makers. Callender Irvine, as Commissary General, carried on the subsequent correspondence with the contractors. His comments and his advice to the Secretary of War were such as to discourage for the time further procurement by the government of privately made arms.

49. Hicks, 1940a, II, 32–127, gives a complete account of the controversy.
50. Ewers, 1954a.
51. Personal communication, B. R. Lewis to C. P. Russell, March 30, 1954. One of the very few contemporary references to the Indians' use of these early trade rifles is found in the official report by Gen. E. P. Gaines regarding the first Seminole war. Gaines stated that repeatedly his sentries were wounded and killed by Seminole riflemen at ranges of several hundred yards. Bosworth, 1846, p. 21.
52. U. S. Cong., 1822b.
53. Gluckman and Satterlee, 1953, pp. 48–49.
54. *Ibid.,* pp. 49, 67, 123, 217.
55. On Jan. 3, 1835, Ramsay Crooks, President of the American Fur Co., addressed J. Joseph Henry: "I have carefully examined your new sample rifle and highly approve it. It is the most substantially good and really serviceable gun I ever saw and the price is not unreasonable. I would be inclined to try them in lieu of the English pattern, but our orders are this year so small that it will be safer perhaps to stick to the old clumsy article; though . . . it may be well to put one of the new pattern in each box of the English." Crooks then added to this letter his order for:

	35			
"20 rifles	P C & Co	English	$10.50 each.
	A		
	T		
"20 rifles	AMF	English	10.50 each.
	W		
"30 rifles	"	Lancaster	9.80 each.

"To be packed in boxes of 10, each." Amer. Fur Co., 1831–1849, LB 1:81, no. 129.

Three weeks later, Crooks ordered 30 additional rifles of the English pattern and again requested that each box of ten rifles include one rifle of the new pattern (*ibid.,* p. 129, no. 177). On March 25, 1835, Crooks paid to J. J. Henry $996.44 for eight boxes of rifles. He asked for a quotation on 300 of the Lancaster pattern and added, "would be pleased to give your rifles the preference if I can." (*Ibid.,* p. 273, no. 333.) Crooks, on April 1, 1835, asked J. J. Henry to name the date of delivery of the 300 rifles and instructed: "We wish no lock longer than five inches for this parcel, and the stocks are to be curled maple stained *tolerably* dark. We can get rifles equal in quality to yours for considerably less than $9.50, six months, and I hope your next will put the price lower." (*Ibid.*, p. 292, no. 352.) Apparently Henry asked Crooks to assist him in locating 5-in. locks. On June 2, 1835, Crooks wrote to J. J. Henry telling of his search for these locks. He had found that Wolfe, Bishop and Co. had "a parcel five to five and a half inches, but they will not break the assortment. The quality might answer but if you take them you will have to keep the larger sizes for some purpose other than ours." *Ibid.*, p. 437, no. 543.

56. On July 15, 1835, John B. Whitten of the American Fur Co. wrote to the Henrys complaining about the quality of the 300 rifles referred to above. He judged the locks to be inferior, "the draw-loops of many of the locks are not polished." Amer. Fur Co., 1831–1849, LB 2:54, no. 668.

Benjamin Clapp of the American Fur Co., on Oct. 22, 1835, wrote to Pratte, Chouteau & Co., a former unit of the American Fur Co., informing them that "$9.00 rifles are up to $9.75, $8.50 rifles are up to $9.50. This difference is owing to a strike and difficulty with the workmen at the manufacturers." *Ibid.*, p. 170, no. 947.

On March 14, 1836, Crooks ordered from J. J. Henry "50 rifles new English pattern, scroll guard, 3 ft., 6 inch barrels, the sort that cost $11¼. Five rifles American pattern, 3 ft., 6 inch barrels, the sort that cost $9½." (*Ibid.*, p. 460, no. 1375.) Crooks again placed an order with J. Joseph Henry on May 4, 1836, insisting that the rifle stocks be "curl'd maple." "Will take fifty from you if you can make so many,—or less if you have not so many stocks of curled wood." (Amer. Fur Co., 1831–1849, LB 3:158, no. 1556.) Crooks wrote to James Henry on Dec. 15, 1837: "We have opened one box of each sort and find the scroll guard as good as ever, but the *outside* of the barrels of the Lancaster pattern have so many flaws as will injure their sale for the Indians cannot be pursuaded that such external imperfection does not extend to the interior of the rifle. We therefore beg you will see that those you send us are free as possible from this objection." *Ibid.*, LB 6, no. 3674, p. 253.

57. Crooks wrote to James Henry, March 16, 1839, reporting that a shipment of rifles had arrived in damp condition. "There is no doubt but the newness of the wood of which the boxes are made is the cause of all the injury." *Ibid.*, LB 9, no. 5803, p. 204.

58. Dillin, 1924, pp. 39, 96.

59. Amer. Fur Co., 1831–1849, LB 13:461, no. 9255.

60. U. S. Cong., 1826*b*, pp. 80–81.

61. U. S. Cong., 1835*b*, p. 52.

62. Beers, 1935, p. 97.

63. U. S. Cong., 1842*b*, p. 224.

64. Gluckman and Satterlee, 1953, pp. 93–95.

65. Dillin, 1924, pp. 17, 18, 47. Interesting views of the establishment are in Dillin, pls. 27, 28, and 62.
66. Amer. Fur Co., 1831–1839, LB 5:130, no. 2794.
67. Gluckman and Satterlee, pp. 123–124.
68. The American Fur Co. Papers clearly reveal Leman's effort to obtain orders for Indian rifles from Ramsay Crooks. On Oct. 24, 1837, Crooks invited Leman to submit two sample rifles for inspection. He specified: "1 rifle single trigger, raised pan, lock chequered and engraved, to cost $11.00, and 1 do, long tang breech." (LB 6:44, no. 3367.) To this request Leman complied, and on Dec. 9, 1837, Crooks wrote: "We prefer the one with the darkest coloured stock and should like it still better if it had the long tang butt plate. The other is a good rifle, too, but the flaws on the outside of the barrel is an objection with the Indians. . . . The lock should be always 5 inches. . . . We care but little for the 'raised pan.' " (*Ibid.*, p. 235, no. 3649.) Apparently these samples were equipped with set triggers, for Leman wrote on Dec. 11, 1837: "Single trigger rifles I have none on hand. They are seldom ordered by our customers; for this reason, and my being so much engaged with Indian rifles for the War Department I would be able to make but one or two dozen in a month."

Yet Leman continued to bid for orders from the American Fur Co. On Nov. 13, 1838, he offered to Crooks Indian rifles "with my own manufactured locks" for $10.50. Rifles made up with imported locks he offered at $10.00, and he would not charge for gun covers and packing boxes. On April 19, 1839, Leman addressed Mr. Whetten of the American Fur Co., offering to make 50 rifles at any terms named by the company. "This proposition I make to induce if possible the American Fur Company to return to the place where they have for so many years purchased rifles." Crooks replied to Leman: "All those rifles furnished from Lancaster to our friends in the West were ordered by themselves *direct* without our ever being made acquainted with either the kind or the quantity. We therefore do not feel at liberty to interfere in the matter. If they should become dissatisfied it is possible they may send us their orders in the future, in which event we shall try to have justice done them, and will cheerfully communicate with you on the subject before we conclude any arrangements for supplying their wants." Amer. Fur Co., 1831–1849, LB 9:402, no. 6066.

Leman, not to be stilled, wrote to Crooks, Dec. 28, 1840, telling of 150 rifles made for the Indian Department in 1838 which had not been picked up by that bureau. "From the Indian Department I was receiving $14 for this article and I offer to sell these to you for $10 on six months credit. A better buy in rifles you cannot possibly get." Amer. Fur Co., 1831–1849, item no. 10002.
69. Dillin, 1924, p. 125; Gluckman and Satterlee, p. 123.

70. Illustrated in Metschl, 1928, pl. 58, fig. 5.
71. Dillin, 1924, pl. 101.
72. Metschl, pp. 119, 481; Hopkins, p. 10; Parsons, 1952, *passim;* Sawyer, 1920, p. 390; Gluckman and Satterlee, pp. 48–49. The assassin's weapon is owned by the U. S. National Park Service, Washington, D.C.
73. Gluckman and Satterlee, 1953, pp. 217–218.
74. Dillin, 1924, p. 132; Sawyer, 1920, p. 141; Tryon, 1911, *passim.* Dillin reproduces (pl. 6, facing p. 109) an interesting advertising poster of "Edw.ᵈ K. Tryon's Gun Store," Philadelphia, of the period 1845–1850.
75. Dillin, 1924, pp. 97–98.
76. *Ibid.,* pp. 89–92, 97–98, 105; Metschl, pp. 498–499; Sawyer, 1910, pp. 207–208; Pollard, p. 32; Gluckman and Satterlee, pp. 77–78. A fine and beautifully ornamented Plains-type Golcher rifle in perfect condition is owned by Benned Golcher. It was made by his grandfather, William, during the early period of his career in Philadelphia. I am indebted to Benned Golcher for information about the later years of Golcher history.

CHAPTER IV   MILITARY ARMS OF THE FUR-TRADE PERIOD (*pages 142–218*)

1. J. J. Abert to Secretary of War, Sept. 15, 1841; in U. S. Cong., 1842*a,* p. 47.
2. Mahan, 1846, p. 132.
3. Vinton, 1935, pp. 432, 434.
4. Washington Irving met Bonneville at the country estate of John Jacob Astor and subsequently (1837) produced from Bonneville's western journal one of the finer literary works of the fur-trade period, *The Adventures of Captain Bonneville.* Some of the Bonneville maps were included in Irving's book. An appraisal of them is given in Gilbert, 1933, pp. 201–202.
5. Peterson, n.d.(*b*), "Colonial Arms and Armor."
6. U. S. Cong., 1823*a.*
7. Gluckman, 1948, pp. 60–61.
8. Hicks, 1942*a,* II, 16–17, 100.
9. Satterlee, 1939, p. 169; Fuller, 1946, pp. 76, 95, pls. I and II; Gluckman, 1948, pp. 55–81.
10. Mitchell, 1947, pp. 122–123.
11. Gluckman, 1948, p. 103.
12. The caliber, .69, suggests that balls for the piece would be 16 to the

pound; actually, the balls were more nearly .65 caliber, or 18 to the pound, and thus allowed clearance in loading. Decius Wadsworth, writing in 1813, declared, "the bullets made use of in service weigh one-eighteenth of a pound, because the cartridge paper which envelopes the bullet will not permit the use of bullets of full caliber." For details of loading see U. S. War Dept., 1830, pp. 18–20; Scott, 1859, pp. 64–65.

13. Letter to Secretary of War, March 12, 1813; quoted by Fuller, 1930, p. 17.

14. Letter from Callender Irvine, Nov. 13, 1813; quoted by Hicks, 1940*a*, I, 43–44. That the stores of "inferior" muskets were used up in the War of 1812 is indicated by testimony from Col. George Bomford of the Ordnance Bureau: "Muskets belonging to the United States at the commencement of the late war [War of 1812] have been estimated at upwards of 200,000 stands, and that the number of muskets manufactured during the War was about 60,000. At the close of the year 1814, scarcely 20,000 stands remained in the arsenals, and great efforts were made to procure an additional supply. Had the war continued another year, the deficiency of arms would have occasioned the most embarrassing consequences. At least 240,000 were expended during the late war; a quantity nearly approaching the number now on hand [in all stores 268,890], as stated formerly. Thus it is seen that nearly 8 years of peace have been required to make good losses occasioned by a war of less than three years duration." Bomford, Jan. 8, 1823, in answer to a Senate resolution, Dec. 23, 1822, questioning the Secretary of War regarding "the number of arms required to supply the militia annually in the west." U. S. Cong., 1823*e*.

15. Fuller, 1946, pp. 94–97.

16. Hicks, 1940*a*, I, 39–44; Metschl, 1928, pl. 21, figs. 9 and 10, pp. 110–111; Sawyer, 1910, pp. 113–118; Gluckman, 1948, p. 126.

17. Fuller, 1946, p. 181.

18. U. S. Ordnance Dept., 1856; Mordecai, 1861, p. 159.

19. In 1855, Col. H. K. Craig of the Ordnance Department recommended that certain arms in use or in store be altered in a variety of ways. Most of these muskets were the Model 1835, but the 1822 musket was also included. "The bore is to be grooved [3 grooves]. Rear sight similar to the new musket, and a front sight of iron attached to the upper strap of the upper band . . . The head of the ram rod is reamed out to fit the pointed end of the [Minié] ball. The lock is altered to the Maynard principle. . . . To adapt the cone seat to this modified lock a portion of the breech of the barrel is cut off and a new breech piece with cone seat attached is screwed on in its place." (U. S. Ordnance Dept., 1856, p. 90.) Thus the 1822 musket became a "rifled-musket"; as such it was used during the Civil War by both Union and Confederate soldiers. Mordecai (1861, p. 159) gives more detailed instructions for the alteration to the percussion system; his

method did not involve cutting off any part of the breech. See Gluckman, 1948, p. 189, for U. S. government-authorized methods of conversion to percussion system; also Fuller, 1933, pp. 82–83.

20. Hicks, 1940a, I, 49–57; Fuller, 1946, pp. 181, 185; Fuller, 1930, pp. 47–48.
21. U. S. Cong., 1823a, Part I, p. 11.
22. U. S. Cong., 1840c, p. 55.
23. Hicks, 1940a, I, 62–67, pl. 35.
24. Fuller, 1946, pp. 191–192.
25. Satterlee, 1939, pp. 174, 220; Hicks, 1940a, I, 62–67, pl. 30.
26. Principal dimensions and weights of U. S. flintlock muskets (from Mordecai, 1861, p. 163):

DIMENSIONS		MODEL 1822 (1816)	MODEL 1840
		Inches	*Inches*
Barrel	Diameter of bore	0.69	0.69
	Diameter at muzzle	0.82	0.85
	Diameter at breech between flats	1.25	1.25
	Length, without breech screw	42	42
Bayonet, length of blade		16	18
Ramrod, length		41.96	41.70
Arm complete	Length without bayonet	57.64	57.80
	Length with bayonet fixed	73.64	75.80
WEIGHTS		*Pounds*	*Pounds*
Barrel, without breech screw		4	4.19
Lock, with side screws		1.23	1.22
Bayonet		0.73	0.64
Arm complete	Without bayonet	9.34	9.78
	With bayonet	10.10	10.42

27. For extensive analyses of the problems encountered in attempting to identify musket "models," see Fuller, 1930; Gluckman, 1948; Hicks, 1940a; Satterlee, 1939. These authors differ in their conclusions, but they offer explanations for them. Colonel Gluckman's key to lock characteristics (see fig. 33) resolves the question in as satisfactory a manner as can be expected.
28. The Annual Reports of the Secretary of War provide very satisfying accounts of the distribution of troops by the general in command of the Army and of the fabrication, procurement, and issuance of arms by the officer in charge of ordnance. The sources used in preparing this chapter are to be found in: U. S. Cong., 1823c; 1823d; 1823h; 1824d; 1825c; 1826d; 1827c; 1828; 1829a; 1830; 1831b; 1832b; 1833; 1834; 1835b; 1836e; 1837a; 1838b; 1839; 1840c; 1841; 1842b; 1843.
29. U. S. Cong., 1837a, pp. 204–214. Some of the troops were fighting the

Seminoles in Florida; others were occupied in protecting the south-western boundary, where trouble with Mexico was brewing. The record of troop assignments shows that in 1836 three companies of the 1st Dragoons and six companies of the 7th Infantry were in the disputed post, Nacogdoches, and that seven companies of Arkansas Mounted Volunteers were brought into service. U. S. Cong., 1836*e*, p. 46.

30. The *Missouri Gazette*, April 3, 1809, printed general orders issued by Gov. Meriwether Lewis authorizing the recruitment of two companies of volunteers, 70 strong, including officers. "These companies [were] to be designated *The Louisiana Spies*." They were to receive the same pay and allowances as regular troops and were to be supplied with ammunition. In an order issued on April 6 the governor directed that muskets and bayonets be furnished to these same units of the Spies at public expense.

31. See Smyth, 1812; Scott, 1821; U. S. War Dept., 1825; U. S. War Dept., 1830; Scott, 1859.

32. W. Stevens, 1797, gives an early manual exercise of loading.

33. Mahan, 1846, pp. xv–xviii. Mahan includes a chart indicating the expectation of hits upon enemy troops deployed and facing into musket fire:

	Distance to target (in yds.)					
	85	170	225	340	425	510
No. of balls (out of 100) that hit the mark:						
On even ground	75	50	27	20	14	7
On rough or plowed ground	67	38	16	6	3	5
	Penetration into pine boards (in in.)					
	3.3	2.2	1.2	0.7	0.4	0.1

34. *Ibid.*, p. 19.
35. Mordecai, 1861, p. 174.
36. *Ibid.*
37. U. S. War Dept. specifications for contractors, 1798; quoted by Hicks, 1940*a*, II, 16.
38. Mordecai, 1861, p. 169.
39. *Ibid.*, p. 197. The author cites (incompletely) *Aide-memoire*, 1819, by Gassend; *Aide-memoire d'art militaire*, 1834, by Lebas; and *Aide-memoire des officiers du genie*, 1840, by Laisné, as his sources of information about the experiments conducted in France.
40. U. S. Navy Dept., *Report of the Bureau of Ordnance*, November, 1864, p. 39; quoted in *Gun and Cartridge Record*, March, 1953, p. 4.
41. Dykes (1952) cites numerous sources which cover the growth and transition of the rangers and dragoons.

42. M. Lewis, 1809: "They will furnish themselves with the usual arms and accoutrements of Riflemen" (April 3). "Such of the Dragoons as have not swords and pistols will arm themselves as Mounted Riflemen" (April 26)—this in the day when the civilian's rifle was still the long-barreled "Kentucky" type.

43. Sawyer (1910, pp. 113–118) describes French musketoons obtained by the Continental Congress during the Revolution as follows: Musketoon (Cavalry) Model 1763; Musketoon (Cavalry) Model 1766 (no sling swivels; a sliding ring on a rod, left side of arm); Artillery musket, Model 1777, 36½" barrel; Marine musket, Model 1777, 36" barrel; Musketoon (Cavalry) Model 1777, 33½" barrel (no sling swivels; rod and traveling ring as in M. 1766; cheek recess in butt, left side).

    Gluckman (1948, p. 61) records that 1,100 carbines (musketoons) were included in a shipment of French arms received in 1777. Cinfontaine (1789, pl. 23) pictures the French musketoon (Cavalry), Model 1766, in two styles: full stock with sling swivels, and half stock with rod and sliding ring. Metschl (1928, p. 107, and pl. 20, fig. 6) presents a Charleville flintlock musketoon, Model 1798 (Milwaukee Museum, no. N3402), 24¼-in. barrel, which was purchased for use in the U. S. Army. This arm has the two finger arches in the iron plate behind the trigger guard, the inspiration for the fingerholds built into the pattern for the U. S. musket, "Model 1835" (Model 1840).

44. Quoted in Hicks, 1940a, II, 111.

45. North and North, 1913, pp. 167–193. Some of the Hall carbines were equipped with a sliding bayonet ("ramrod bayonet"), and a variety of improvements were devised during the seventeen years (1833–1850) that Simeon North busied himself with this arm. The North-Hall story as published in the North and North book is reprinted in Fuller, 1933 (pp. 43–51), and four styles of Hall carbines are illustrated (pl. 1) and described (pp. 40–41, 51–52).

46. Pelzer (1943) lists the writings of twenty or more Army men who participated in Dragoon activities from 1833 to 1847. Frémont (1845, p. 114) tells of stopping a large charging grizzly bear with six shots from the carbines.

47. Todd, 1941, pl. 13.

48. For statistics on production of the Hall arms see the Annual Reports of the Secretary of War cited in note 28. See also abstracts from the Annual Reports of the Ordnance Office, 1844 through 1852, in Fuller, 1930, pp. 154–164.

49. Hicks, 1940a, II, p. 69.

50. Gluckman, 1948, p. 366.

51. Fuller, 1933, p. 40; Gluckman, 1948, p. 362.

52. Hicks, 1940a, II, 114.

53. Mordecai, 1861, p. 373.

54. For all mechanical parts and the use and care of the Hall carbine, see Mordecai, 1861, pp. 162–163, 188.
55. Quoted in Fuller, 1933, p. 4.
56. Quoted in Fuller, *op. cit.* The *Ordnance Manual* took cognizance of the weaknesses decried by Craig: "The shoulders of the receiver must always bear firmly against both chocks; *the piece should never be fired without the chocks being in place,* as in that case the opening between the receiver and the barrel becomes much too great, a part of the charge is perhaps lost, the effect of the remainder much lessened and the stock almost inevitably destroyed by the blast and by the undue strain which it suffers from the recoil of the receiver." Mordecai, 1861, p. 188.
57. Quoted in Fuller, 1933, pp. 65–66. This book (pp. 17–52) provides the most comprehensive reference to Hall arms now available.
58. Wilcox, 1859, pp. 216–218.
59. Fuller, 1930, pp. 57–58; U. S. Ordnance Dept., *Ordnance Manual,* 1841, pl. 11.
60. Fuller, 1930, p. 71 and pl. xvii, A.
61. Hicks, 1940a, I, 57–58.
62. *Ibid.,* pp. 60–61, pl. 28; Fuller, 1930, pp. 73–74, pl. xviii.
63. Serven, 1952, p. 41; see also Gluckman and Satterlee, 1953, p. 61.
64. The backwoodsmen "were employed as sharp shooters, and ere long the British pickets found that it was unsafe to expose their heads even at a distance of 400 yards. The same writer [not identified] . . . says: 'So frequent became the return of officers, pickets and artillerymen shot at long range, that Edmund Burke exclaimed in Parliament, "Your officers are swept off by the rifles if they show their noses." ' In the British camp, the riflemen 'clad in their Indian hunting shirts,' were called 'shirt-tail men with their cursed twisted guns, the most fatal widow and orphan makers in the world.' With this [Revolutionary] rifle-corps, which adopted Indian methods, began the modern system of warfare, fighting in open order as skirmishers, taking advantage of every available cover, and picking off the officers or particular men. The first pitched battle in which rifles were exclusively used by one of the armies was at King's Mountain, where the British, under Ferguson, the inventor of the breech-loader . . . with which some of them [the British] were armed, met the Tennessee backwoods riflemen." Hinkle, 1908, pp. 7–8. See also Russell, 1940; Young, 1939.

Hinkle's interpretation of the importance of the rifle in the outcome of the Revolutionary War is obviously biased. Other sources might be quoted which reveal that Washington, Wayne, and some other American generals did not look upon the rifle as the all-important arm for winning a war. Nevertheless, the American rifleman did lead the way toward a major change in tactics. Among the works of British writers of the muzzle-loading period who took cognizance of the success of American rifles and the importance of rifles in military armament are the following: Ezekial Baker, *Remarks on Rifle Guns,* London, 1800 (11 eds. to 1835). Capt. Henry Beaufoy, *Considerations on the Nature and Use of Rifled Barrel Guns with Reference to Their Forming the Basis of a Permanent System of National Defense,* London, 1808, 231 pp. Col. George Hanger, *To All Sportsmen,* London, 1814, 226 pp. Capt. John Kincaid, *Adventures in the Rifle Brigade, 1809 to 1815,* London, 1830 (3 eds. to 1847). William Surtees, *Twenty-five Years in the Rifle Brigade,* Edinburgh, 1833. Lt. Col. Baron de Berenger, *Helps and Hints with Instructions in Rifle and Pistol Shooting,* London, 1835, 286 pp. Lt. Col. Jebb, *Practical Treatise, Defense,* London, 1836 (4 eds. to 1853); *Practical Treatise, Attack,* London, 1837 (3 eds. to 1853); *Practical Treatise, Siege,* London, 1849, 132 pp. John Boucher, *The Volunteer Rifleman and the Rifle,* London, 1853 (3 eds. to 1860). Capt. Thomas J. Thackeray, *Practice of Rifle Firing,* London, 1853, 44 pp.; also *The Soldier's Manual of Rifle Firing,* 1858, 84 pp. Capt. Jervis-White Jervis, *The Rifle-Musket,* London, 1854 (2d ed., 1859), 81 pp. J. LeConteur, *The Rifle; Its Effect on the War,* London, 1855, 132 pp. Hans Busk, *The Rifleman's Manual,* London, 1858 (8 eds. to 1861). Llewellyn Jewitt, *Rifles and Volunteer Rifle Corps,* London, 1860, 97 pp. Col. Ernest C. Wilford, *Three Lectures upon the Rifle,* London, 1860, 83 pp.

More recent works in which Englishmen have summarized the history of the rifle in warfare, recognizing the influence of the American rifle upon the early nineteenth-century armament of European countries are: Col. E. M. Lloyd, *Review of the History of Infantry,* 1908, 303 pp. (Burgoyne's appraisal, p. 185). Maj. G. Tylden, "Notes on Musket and Rifle, 1739–1859," Society for Army Historical Research, *Journal,* Vol. XVII (1928), No. 66, pp. 112–114. Col. Lord Cottesloe (T. F. Freemantle), *The Englishman and the Rifle,* London, 1945, 270 pp. Maj. Gen. J. F. C. Fuller (ret. British general), *Armament and History,* New York, Scribner's, 1945, 207 pp. Ommundsen and Robinson (1915, p. 19) are very direct in their statement: "It was the use of the sporting rifle in the hands of American backwoodsmen [during the Revolution] that decided the British War Office to investigate its [the rifle's] claim as a military weapon. . . . In 1800, then, we have a committee to find the best rifle with which to arm the newly-formed Rifle Regiment, the 95th Foot."

65. Dillin, 1924, in his "Dedication." Hicks (1940*a*, I, 9) lists gunmakers who supplied rifles to the U. S. government in 1792 and 1793: Adam Augstadt, Jacob Dickert, Peter Gonter, John Groff, Abraham Morrow, John Nicholson, and Jacob Welshams. Contracts with private makers continued until about 1810. In 1809, John Gust of Lancaster was among the contractors.

66. U. S. Cong., 1823*a*, p. 7.
67. Dearborn to Joseph Perkins, Harpers Ferry, May 25, 1803; quoted in Hicks, 1940*a*, I, 25–26.
68. *Ibid.*, p. 26.
69. Satterlee, 1939, p. 172.
70. Gluckman, 1948, pp. 195–196; Metschl, 1928, pp. 118–119.
71. Coxe to William Eustis, Secretary of War, Nov. 11, 1811; quoted in Hicks, 1940*a*, II, pp. 47–48.
72. Hicks, *op. cit.*
73. Callender Irvine, Commissary General, Nov. 22, 1814, reported to Messrs. Houp and Richards, the sureties for the contractor, H. Deringer, that only 51 rifles out of a total of 980 due to be delivered in accordance with his agreement had been received by the United States. He threatened to bring legal action in imposing the penalty of the bond. On Nov. 30, 1814, Irvine wrote to Deringer, ". . . by your failure to execute your engagements with this office, a considerable proportion of the Regular Rifle Regiments on the Northern frontier, the most exposed situation of our country and where these rifles can be used with most effect, have been without rifles. By your ceasing to work for the United States . . . you assisted thereby in withholding as many Rifles from the men stationed on our frontier, where they are used every day in annoying our enemy and in protecting our frontier settlers, so that you have not 'done the best' unless it be for yourself in receiving the same or a higher price for Rifles, inferior to those which would have been received by the United States on your contract." Hicks, 1940*a*, II, 117.
74. U. S. Cong., 1823*a*, p. 7.
75. Satterlee, 1939, p. 172. See also Lt. Col. George Bomford's report of Feb. 12, 1818, reprinted in Fuller, 1930, p. 137, and Bomford's report, U. S. Cong., 1823*a*, p. 7. Also Gluckman, 1948, Appendix III, p. iii.
76. Serven, 1952, p. 38, no. 642.
77. Bakeless, 1947, pp. 201–211.
78. Hart and Hulbert, 1932, p. 137.
79. James, 1905, XV, 192, 227, XVII, 98.
80. Cooke, 1857, pp. 52, 98, 99.
81. Stored in federal armories, arsenals, forts, and other permanent posts in 1822 there were 20,923 serviceable rifles of various kinds (U. S. Cong., 1823*a*, pp. 24–25), and in the stores of the state militias there were 80,193 government-procured rifles, all in serviceable order (U. S. Cong., 1822*d*). It is not inferred, therefore, that the long rifle, which had served so well in the hands of militiamen and members of regular rifle companies before and during the War of 1812, was suddenly withdrawn from military use everywhere as soon as the Model 1803 was issued; there is evidence that the Model 1803 did to a large degree supplant the long rifle in the cantonments and regular Army posts

along the western border. Some of the old and damaged arms from the West found their way to the U. S. Arsenal at Pittsburgh. By 1819, the accounts of Maj. A. R. Wooley of that establishment included many entries which pertained to the repair of "long rifles." Some of this work seems to have been virtually the manufacture of major rifle parts and the complete rebuilding of many stands. Some of the entries:

"June 30, 1819. To Isaac Shunk—For stocking 25 long rifles $51.50; finishing 1 long do. $1.25; finishing 2 long rifles with rods and bullet moulds $3.92; breeching 3 rifle barrels .57¢; looping 3 rifle barrels .60¢; sawing off rifle stocks $1.06 . . . . . . Total $58.61.

"June 30, 1819. To J. Indermaur—Bending and filing 220 rifle pipes $4.40; looping 22 rifle barrels $3.52; for finishing 39 long rifles $46.80; looping 43 rifle barrels $6.88; for filing, dressing and countersinking 42 rifle plates $1.68; filing 36 rifle guards $2.88; bending and filing 116 rod pins $4.06; finishing 16 long rifles $19.20; looping 54 rifle barrels $8.64.

"June 30, 1819. To John Swigley—For finishing 28 long rifles $33.60.

"June 30, 1819. To P. W. Rentgen—For grooving 37 rifle barrels $48.10.

"June 30, 1819. To Alba Fiske—For 162 long rifle barrels $637.00."

Other entries pertain to similar work done on long rifles by Constant White, Silas Pryor, and Henry Boyes in the summer of 1819. Evidently several hundred rifles were repaired. In the fall of 1819, the same gunsmiths were paid for work on a smaller number of "short rifles," probably damaged Model 1803 pieces. Another entry is of particular interest:

"May 3, 1819. To Charles Artz—for 1 rifle of a new construction to break off sideways and load at the breech, and possessing advantages over the rifle patented by Hall . . . $30.00."

In 1823, the U. S. Army had 1,716 "rifles damaged but repairable"; 533 of these were in the Pittsburgh Arsenal, 103 were at Belle Fontaine on the Missouri near its confluence with the Mississippi. U. S. Cong., 1823a, pp. 35, 183, 184, 185, and 188.

After the introduction of the Model 1803, there is no record of issuance of long rifles to regular troops until 1840, when 187 of the old long-barreled arms were issued to the Regular Army. Equally surprising is the fact that 152 Indian rifles were taken from stores and issued to regular troops. U. S. Cong., 1840c; U. S. Cong., 1842b.

82. Apparently Deringer was permitted to use some of the 33-inch barrels with octagonal breech section which he had prepared in connection with his order for the Model 1803 rifle. A number of his Model 1817 rifles now in collections are equipped with such barrels.

83. The contracts, or renewals of contracts, were awarded as follows: April 6,

1821, Henry Deringer, 2,000 Model 1817 rifles at $15.50; Aug. 28, 1823, Henry Deringer, 3,000 Model 1817 rifles at $14.50 (600 each year); Dec. 9, 1823, Nathan Starr, 4,000 Model 1817 rifles at $14.50 (800 each year); Dec. 10, 1823, R. and J. D. Johnson, 3,000 Model 1817 rifles at $14.50 (600 each year); Dec. 10, 1823, Simeon North, 6,000 Model 1817 rifles at $14.50 (1,200 each year).

In August, 1823, Col. Bomford of the Ordnance Bureau issued regulations governing the inspection of the contractors' product:

"*Rifle*. Proof of barrels;—first charge ½₈ lb. of powder and 2 lead bullets each weighing ⅓₂ part of a pound; two paper wads each ½" long after being well rammed,—one to be on top of powder and the other on top of the bullets. Second charge to be ⅓₂ part of a pound of powder with one bullet and two wads. The proving charge to be loaded and fired as in proving musket barrels. The marks of reception will be as follows: the letters U S to be placed on the top of the barrel, and one inch distant from the breech; the initial letters of the inspector's name with the letter P under them, to be placed to the left of the letters U S; which marks will be made by the inspector." From Bomford's report, Dec. 31, 1823, submitted in accordance with a resolution of the House of Representatives Dec. 18, 1823. U. S. Cong., 1824*a*, p. 8.

Detailed instructions concerning the inspection of all small arms are contained in Mordecai, 1861, pp. 164–180.

84. On March 17, 1840, N. Starr and Son, Middletown, Conn., "obtained an additional contract for 6000 flintlock rifles @ $14.50, each, duration five years, at 1200 per year" (Gluckman and Satterlee, 1953, p. 207). The records of the Ordnance Department refer to one delivery of 2,560 stands made by N. Starr and Son in 1841 under this contract; 1,800 in 1845; and 350 in 1846.

85. North and North, 1913, pp. 142–157.

86. Norton, 1880, p. 11.

87. A report by Messrs. Carrington, Sage, and Bell is reprinted in Fuller, 1946, pp. 135–150.

88. Norton, 1880, pp. 11–13.

89. *Ibid.*

90. Mordecai, 1861, p. 177.

91. Gen. William Henry Ashley, of the fur traders' rendezvous fame, in March, 1829, wrote to the Commander-in-Chief of the Army of the United States:

"Gen. A. Macomb

"Dear Sir: You request . . . my opinion, as it regards a military force best calculated for the protection of our western frontier, the fur trade, and our trade and intercourse direct from Missouri and Arkansas to the Mexican provinces, etc.

"This force ought, in my opinion, to consist of about five hundred riflemen, who should be enlisted expressley for that service, anticipating at the time of enlistment the privations peculiar to it, or of suitable selections of men now in the Army. These troops ought to subsist themselves, which they could do with convenience, so soon as the officers become acquainted with the country in which they would have to operate. In addition to the rifle, one-half of the command should be armed with sabres. Four pieces of artillery would be found convenient and useful. The patent rifle [Hall's] which I examined in your office appears, in one particular, to be well calculated for this service, inasmuch as it can be conveniently and quickly charged on horseback; but I have been, heretofore, prejudiced against this description of guns, believing that they were subject, by use, to get out of order, and could not be repaired without much difficulty. Putting, therefore, these guns out of the question of the utility of which I know but little, I would recommend a rifle, the barrel of which should not exceed three feet in length, carrying a ball weighing about three-fourths of an ounce, and having metal sufficient to support a ball of that size. I have used the percussion locks but little, but believe them admirably well constructed for general use, but more particularly for the prairies, where severe winds and rains prevail at certain seasons of the year. Great convenience would be experienced from having every gun of the same dimension, every spring, screw, etc., of the locks, of the same size and form. This being the case every material of one would fit and might be used in any other. The gun stick, or thimble rod, ought to be of large size, and of wood; iron sometimes batters the muzzle, and makes the gun shoot wild. The only difference should be in the breech [stock]; some should in this particular be longer than others, to suit the arms of those who use them. In their weight, and in every other particular except the breech [stock], they ought to be the same. In that case when a man became accustomed to the use of one, he could, with the same convenience, use any one of them." U. S. Cong., 1831*a;* also in Hulbert, 1933, pp. 136–149.

Ashley had owned and used a heavy flintlock Hawken rifle (see chap. ii). His advice about interchangeable parts and a percussion lock was followed four years later, when the government adopted the Hall carbine for Cavalry use. His "prejudice" regarding the breech-loading system apparently did not take into consideration the fact that the U. S. government had been making the Hall breech-loading rifle for ten years prior to his writing.

92. A half century after the U. S. Ordnance Bureau adopted its first regulation rifle, some military tacticians were still decrying the use of rifled arms. J. Roemer, a one-time cavalry officer in the Dutch Army, brought his adverse opinions to America and expressed himself widely in

the Civil War years, when he published his history of cavalry. He gave much space to the imperfections of rifled barrels, sights, powder, and bullets, and to the physics involved in the bullet's flight. "Considering the many causes of inaccuracy of fire, some of which can not be controlled by the most expert marksmen, and the difficulties of teaching principles of accurate firing and proper management of the rifle, we can not expect that this weapon in the hands of the masses will ever be more formidable than the old smooth-bore musket. Indeed, among the uninstructed,—and their number will always be great in any army,—it will be less so. At that supreme moment of life or death when passion takes the place of judgment, we can hardly expect the soldier to go through a series of calculations that require coolness and self-possession. . . . If, therefore, the new rifle prove a formidable weapon in the hands of the few its advantages do not outweigh its disadvantages for the common soldier." (Roemer, 1863, pp. 122–130.) Even William Clark advised against the use of the rifle by the Army in the West. Clark, 1947, pp. 31–32.

93. Lt. C. M. Wilcox summed up the objections of the military to breechloaders: "The objections to, or defects of breech-loading arms are that they are complicated in their mechanism, are liable to get out of order from fouling, or escape of gas at the joints, or want of strength; and as the facility of loading gives great rapidity of fire, it is asserted that in battle, under the influence of excitement the soldier would load and fire without reflection, or without orders of his officers, and when the decisive moment should arrive, he would have exhausted his ammunition. The facility of fire which is the greatest advantage of the system is thus made to appear to be its greatest inconvenience. The future will determine whether or not the breech-loading arm is to be more generally introduced into service or abandoned." (Wilcox, 1859, p. 216.) F. W. Hinkle, writing in an era which gave him greater perspective than Lt. Wilcox could have had, observed: "Two inventions shortly to be made were necessary to make a rifle loading at the breech a success. Its great fault was that using as it did a paper or linen cartridge which was consumed in the discharge, the breech action became clogged and fouled with burnt paper, powder dirt and smut, so that after a few shots it became almost or quite impossible to close the breech. Then, too, the gases escaped through the chinks of the mechanism lessening the range of the bullet and sometimes burning the soldier's face and hands. At times also the breech block would blow out and nearly fracture the holder's skull. Numbers of breech-loading rifles were invented by the Americans during the years . . . 1812 to 1860 . . . but [were] rejected because of the escape of gas at the breech. . . . In 1836, however, a Frenchman patented a heavy paper cartridge with metal base which contained the cap.

From this [gas-tight] cartridge dates the success of the breech-loader
... The other great invention of these years was the [elongated
bullet] Minie ball." Hinkle, 1908, pp. 10 and 12.

94. Mahan, 1846, pp. xviii–xix. (First ed. was 1836.)

95. Fuller, 1930, pp. 18–52. The remains of the Hall Rifle Works are preserved within the boundaries of Harpers Ferry National Monument,
where the National Park Service accords Hall and his history a place
in the interpretation program. Palmer, 1956.

96. The detailed results of the tests (see U. S. Cong., 1837b) in the two
series were as follows:

Kind of Weapon	Times Fired in 1 Minute
Hackett's musket (loads at breech)	5
Hall's musket (loads at breech)	5
Colt's musket (chambered)	3.1
Cochran's musket (chambered)	3
U. S. standard musket	3
Colt's rifle	4
Hall's rifle	3.4
Cochran's rifle	3.2
Leavitt's rifle	1.2

"Colts and Cochrans require 2 minutes to 2 minutes, 10 seconds to
load one receiver."

Musket	Charge of Powder (grains)	Distance from Target (feet)	Penetration in White Oak (inches)
U. S.	134	10	2.3
Hall's	110	10	2.175
Colt's	134	10	2.64
Colt's	110	10	2.75
Colt's	100	10	3.
Cochran's	80	10	1.65

A note added: "The Cochran's chambers will not hold more than 80
grains." The members of the board were: Bvt. Brig. Gen. J. R. Fen-
wick, Bvt. Brig. Gen. N. Towson, Col. G. Croghan, Bvt. Lt. Col.
Worth (Ordnance), Maj. R. S. Baker (replaced Lt. Col. Talcott,
Ordnance), Lt. Col. Wainwright (Marines), and Capt. B. Highes
(Ordnance). 1st Lt. J. N. Macomb recorded the proceedings.

97. In a report to the Senate Committee on Military Affairs, May 2, 1842,
Lt. Col. G. Talcott of the Ordnance Department reported that 23,500
Hall rifles had been made at Harpers Ferry and procured from the
contractor, Simeon North (reprinted in Fuller, 1933, pp. 35–36).
However, the annual reports of Talcott's predecessor, Col. George
Bomford, together with his own reports, enumerate 29,533 Hall

rifles made and procured from 1824 through 1841. See sources cited in note 28.

98. "Perhaps some of the most unusual surviving Confederacy arms are the muzzle-loading rifles assembled in part from components of the Hall breechloading weapons taken from the Harpers Ferry Armory. The breech is of cast brass very roughly finished by hand filing. The stocks of the weapons are completely hand fashioned. They show little similarity one to the other in finer details. These arms are thought to have been made by J. B. Barrett at Wytheville, Virginia, and are sometimes referred to as 'Wytheville Halls.' The records indicate that the Barrett shop was turning out and sending to General Floyd's command in western Virginia as many as ten arms per day. These muzzle loading Halls exist, but positive proof that they were made at Wytheville is lacking." Weller, 1953, p. 9.

99. Roberts, 1944, plate facing p. 175.

100. Todd, 1941, pl. 11. Fritz Kredel's color plate depicts the type of soldier with whom the arm was associated.

101. The record of contracts is summarized in Gluckman and Satterlee, 1953, pp. 81, 136, 162, 176, and 178.

102. U. S. Ordnance Dept., 1856, p. 90; Hicks, 1940a, I, 70, 71, and pl. 38.

103. Hicks, 1940a, II, 43–44, 47.

104. U. S. Cong., 1837b, pp. 1–27.

105. U. S. Cong., 1837b; 1837c.

106. On March 9, 1838, Col. D. E. Twiggs appointed a board of officers consisting of three captains, all of Fort Jupiter, East Florida, to examine weapons brought to Florida by Colt. The board met, conducted their trials, and submitted their report the same day. They recommended the adoption of revolving rifles by one or more units of their regiment, the 2d Dragoons. (See Fuller, 1933, p. 53.) For details of the field use of the 50 rifles supplied by Colt to the 2d Dragoons at this time, see Rodenbough, 1875, pp. 36–38, 45, 504; Brackett, 1865, p. 42; Serven, 1946, p. 13; and B. R. Lewis, 1947, p. 32.

107. The Texas Rangers were organized in 1835. Beers, 1935, p. 157; Serven, 1946, p. 13.

108. Webb, 1931, pp. 170–179; Parsons, 1949a, pp. 81–82.

109. Parsons, 1949a, p. 10. This is Walker's personal account written in 1846.

110. U. S. Cong., 1840a.

111. "There were two schools of thought in the Ordnance Bureau. One, headed by moss-backed brass hats opposed all change and insisted that the smooth-bore musket and the single-shot horsepistol were the last words in military equipment. . . . The other supported by officers mostly in the junior grades, believed that improvements in arms were imperatively needed and were ready to encourage and help anyone trying to make them." Rohan, 1935, p. 89.

112. Colt's patent of 1836 normally would have expired in 1850. When Sam,

as a result of the belated government order for his arms in 1846, obtained a "new lease on life," he took advantage of the law which provided that "an inventor who had lost the benefit of his invention during the continuance of the first term might have an extension." Colt turned back to the government his original patent, and in 1849 he was granted an extension of seven years.

113. Fulton, 1944, pp. 155–156. Serven (1946, p. 12) mentions Texas inventories of 1846 in which Colt carbines appear.

114. Fuller, 1933, p. 58. However, the Milwaukee Museum carbine (N4149) shown in our figure 35, *c,* is dated 1842 on its frame.

115. Scoffern, 1860, pp. 1–95.

116. Norton, 1880, p. 207.

117. Fuller, 1933, p. 54. Fuller (pp. 54–57) reprints an article, obviously of British origin, which tells of the wide use of the Colt weapons in Europe. The unidentified author states: "Garibaldi [Italian general] has been ably sustained by a corps commanded by Colonel Peard, and armed with Colts revolving rifles."

118. The returns for the nation-wide militia organization indicate that the New York State Militia had 2,152 U. S. pistols in 1825, and that at that time these were the only federally owned pistols in the entire militia organization of the country (U. S. Cong., Amer. State Pap., Military Affairs, III, 238). That the report is erroneous is evidenced by the many U. S. pistols antedating 1825, now in private and public collections, which bear the impresses of various state militia organizations as well as the mark "US."

119. For a display of the French pistols, see Metschl, p. 442, pl. 70.

120. North and North, 1913, *passim.*

121. Lt. Col. G. Bomford, in his *Report on Expenses of the Ordnance Department, 1817–1822,* U. S. Cong., 1823a, table D, p. 7.

122. Gluckman, 1939, p. 40.

123. Cinfontaine, 1789, pl. 22, fig. 1.

124. George, 1938, p. 65; Metschl, p. 470, pl. 74, fig. 3; p. 474, pl. 75, fig. 3. It is interesting to note the similarity between the Model 1806 and the English flintlock dueling pistols with half stock which were not produced until ten years later. See George, 1938, pp. 84–85 and pl. XIII, fig. 3, for a specimen made by W. Moore, London, about 1820. These English dueling pistols are rifled, and their caliber is .40, but in general they are "cast in the mould" of the U. S. Model 1806. They were not copied after the United States pistols, however, but the designers of both the dueling pistols and the U. S. Model 1806 were influenced by the same European weapons.

125. Gluckman, 1939, pp. 52–55.

126. Hicks, 1940a, I, 27–29, pls. 10 and 24. Gluckman agrees to this designation (personal letter, 1954).

127. Metschl, p. 483, pl. 76, fig. 13. "The cock is of the gooseneck variety,

which reversion seems strange, as the cock which was reënforced under the jaw had long been used for regulation arms. . . . Some collectors claim that the locks for these Model 1818 Springfield pistols were purchased ready-made in Europe in 1815 due to a shortage of pistol locks in the United States."

128. Serven, 1952, p. 6, figs. 37 and 38.

129. George, 1938, p. 65 and p. 67. "Towards the end of the 18th Century a change was made in the form of the [British] service horse pistol, the long 24-bore [.58 caliber] pistol being replaced by a shorter weapon with a 9-inch barrel. . . ." The Milwaukee Public Museum possesses an extensive series of these pistols of English, French, and German origin. Metschl, pls. 67, 68, and 69.

130. Hicks, 1940a, I, 30.

131. Under the provisions of the Act of 1808, the federal government could appropriate $200,000 annually for arming and equipping the whole body of the militia of the United States, the arms to "be transmitted to the several states composing this Union and to the Territories thereof . . . in proportion to the number of effective militia in each State and Territory, and by each State and Territory to be distributed . . . under such rules and regulations as shall be by law prescribed by the legislature of each State and Territory."

132. The story of the U. S. contract pistol, Model 1807, is complicated and not yet founded upon definitive material. Hicks (1940a, pp. 29–30, pl. 11) recognizes the arm as one of our martial pistols. Gluckman (1939, pp. 101–146) gives much information about the individual contractors; he refers to the pistol as "the 1808 type" and classes it as a secondary martial pistol. Chapel (1947, pp. 18–19) writes: "There is strong argument in favor of classing this as a U. S. martial flintlock pistol." Both Hicks and Gluckman point out that many of the contractors had been making pistols which were "on the borderline between dueling [or Kentucky] and martial types" and that they and some of their contemporaries made and sold this "1808 type" without regard to U. S. contracts. The pistols stamped "US" in accordance with formal government contracts should doubtless be recognized as true martial pistols; and because of the chronology in awarding contracts, there is justification for calling them the "U. S. contract pistol, Model 1807."

133. North and North, 1913, plate facing p. 42, pp. 57–75; Gluckman, 1939, pp. 42–44; Chapel, 1947, p. 19, pl. 1, fig. 4. Gluckman and Satterlee (1953, p. 142) recognize a John Miles pistol "made in resemblance of the North Navy pistols of 1808."

134. Chapel, 1947, p. 19; Serven, 1952, p. 11, fig. 130; Gluckman, 1939, p. 115; Metschl, 1928, p. 482, pl. 76, fig. 9.

135. See Serven, 1952, p. 5; Gluckman, 1939, pp. 49–50; and Hicks, 1940a, I, 44–46, 57.

136. Hicks (1940a, I, 46) prints a letter of Nov. 27, 1814, from a U. S. arms inspector, which tells of North's delivery of pistols to private parties in Boston. North, when told of this report, explained "that he did not have outside contracts but merely sold pistols that had failed to pass inspection. . . . We see from this that a number of North pistols were in use outside of the military service."

137. The photograph from which fig. 37, *e*, was drawn was supplied by Mr. Serven. See also Serven, 1952, p. 5.

138. Gluckman, 1939, p. 59; Serven, 1952, p. 6.

139. Maj. Gen. E. P. Gaines to Congressman Joseph Duncan, March 27, 1828, Amer. State Papers, Military Affairs, Vol. III, Doc. 385. John H. Eaton, Secretary of War, to Pres. Jackson, U. S. Cong., 1829a, p. 30. Gen. Alex. Macomb to House of Representatives, Jan. 4, 1830, Amer. State Papers, Military Affairs, IV, 219. Thos. S. Jesup, Q. M. Gen., to House of Representatives, April 5, 1830, Amer. State Papers, Military Affairs, IV, 371. Lewis Cass, Secretary of War, and Wm. Clark, Supt. Indian Affairs, to the Senate, Nov. 20, 1831, U. S. Cong., 1832a, pp. 10–86. Lewis Cass, Annual Report, Secretary of War, 1831, U. S. Cong., 1831b, p. 158. Summaries of the transactions in justifying mounted troops are given in Beers, 1935, pp. 88–89, 101–103, 110; Shirk, 1950, pp. 2–6; and Upton, 1904, pp. 160–161. Firsthand accounts of dragoon service in the field are given in Pelzer, 1943.

140. B. F. Butler, Secretary of War, to the President of the U. S., U. S. Cong., 1836e, p. 107.

141. Metschl, 1928, pp. 485–486.

142. Quoted in Hicks, 1940a, I, 70–71, and pl. 40.

143. Gluckman, 1939, p. 146, pl. 16, fig. 5.

144. Chapel, 1947, pp. 42–44, pl. 7.

145. B. R. Lewis, 1947, p. 25.

146. Metschl (1928, p. 497) states: "It is estimated that each of these contractors [Ames and Deringer] produced only 2000 pistols of this model."

147. Beers, 1935, pp. 164–169.

148. Zachary Taylor to Adjt. Gen., April 26, 1846, "Hostilities have started." U. S. Cong., 1848, p. 140.

149. See Serven, 1952, p. 28, fig. *c-1*, for another type of improvement of the loading lever. Harold's Club, Reno, exhibits a Colt Paterson (similar to the one shown in fig. 39, *b*) which has the extended lever of the loading device held to the barrel by the Navy-type latch, improvements which were made after the gun illustrated was completed.

150. When Lt. James Henry Carleton, 1st Dragoons, stopped in the Pawnee Village on the Platte in August, 1844, he wrote: "One of the officers showed them [the Pawnees] a spy glass and let several of them look through it at some horses that were feeding on the bottoms on the opposite side of the river. . . . The glass is a fine one and seemed to

bring the animals to within a few yards of where they stood. He then took one of Colt's revolving pistols, and having explained to them how many times it could be fired without reloading—just to hoax them— he made some signs as if he could bring Indians, who would be at a great distance, close to him with the spyglass and then shoot them down by scores with the pistol. This put their pipes out completely. That gun that brought horses from a mile off to within 30 yards was the 'biggest medicine' they had seen yet." Pelzer, 1943, p. 81.

151. Hicks, 1940*a*, I, 76–78.
152. Quoted in Parsons, 1949*a*, p. 41.
153. Sawyer (1911, p. 33) states that "Colt left an estate of $5,000,000.00, all acquired during the fourteen years just preceding his death," at age 47.
154. George (1938, pp. 176–177) describes Colt's success in London; Parsons (1949*b*, pp. 189–201) gives his American awards.
155. Various aspects of the history of Colt arms, the chronology of patents, and the mechanics of Colt's inventions are set forth in Fuller, 1933 and 1946; George, 1938; Gluckman, 1939; Hicks, 1940*a;* B. R. Lewis, 1947; and Horn, n.d. For personal biographical data and appraisals of the historical significance of the Colt story, see Colt's, 1937; Edwards, 1953; Parsons, 1949*a;* Rohan, 1935; Sawyer, 1911; Serven, 1946, 1954; and Webb, 1927 and 1931.
156. DeVoto, 1943, p. 219. Quoted by permission of the copyright holder, Houghton Mifflin Co.

CHAPTER V   POWDER, BALL, AND ACCESSORIES *(pages 219–250)*

1. Sawyer, 1920, p. 41; Chapel, 1939, pp. 57–64.
2. Wardell, 1888, p. 20.
3. *American Rifleman,* October, 1949, pp. 26–30; Hatcher, 1947, pp. 300–306; Hatcher, 1949, pp. 32–34, 36; Mordecai, 1861, pp. 209–216.
4. Peterson, 1947*a*, p. 207.
5. Du Pont de Nemours, 1912, pp. 1–62, 95, 137; Dutton, 1942, pp. 1–75. Peter Bauduy, once a partner in the Du Pont enterprise, helped to select the millsite. He had a son who married Victorine du Pont. After the son's death, Bauduy sold his interests in the powder business to Éleuthère du Pont. By 1816, Bauduy was operating his own powder mill near Wilmington. Later, John Peter Garesche, a son-in-law of Bauduy, owned and operated the plant and by 1832 had developed it to the point of producing 250,000 pounds of gunpowder a year. Bauduy Garesche went from this plant to South Carolina during the Civil War and there made gunpowder for the Confederacy. Conner, 1949.
6. Griswold, 1927, pp. 431, 422; Hopkins, 1942, p. 37.
7. Hopkins, 1942, p. 43.
8. Amer. Fur Co., 1821–1822. The price did not drop overnight, however.

Maj. W. R. Wooley, Pittsburgh Arsenal, on Dec. 31, 1816, paid to James Johnson, Big Crossings, Scott County, Ky., 43¢ a pound for 10,000 pounds of gunpowder delivered to Newport, Ky. On July 30, 1817, Johnson received 40¢ a pound for one lot of 10,000 pounds, and 35¢ a pound for another shipment of 20,000 pounds. (See U. S. Cong., 1823*a*, pp. 67 and 90.) The Johnson powder mill at Big Crossings (also called Great Crossings) during the War of 1812 obtained its supply of saltpeter from Kentucky caves, especially the Mammoth Cave, now a national park; the ruins of the works, hand-hewn wooden pipe lines, and bleaching vats made of tulip poplar and oak are still in place within the cave a short distance from the Historic Entrance. (Bridwell, 1952, pp. 14–15, 63; Houston, 1954.) Some idea of the volume of gunpowder shipments made to western military posts is gained from the reports of the Ordnance Department for 1813–1821; 165,333 pounds went to the West from Pittsburgh during those years. "All the powder, except a small quantity forwarded at the Commencement of the War [of 1812] and all the lead was procured in Kentucky and Missouri." U. S. Cong., 1823*a*, p. 11.

9. Amer. Fur Co., 1821–1822, *passim;* U. S. Indian Trade Office, 1833, *passim.*
10. Dutton, 1942.
11. Quoted in Hopkins, 1942, p. 15.
12. Dillin, 1924, pp. 63–65.
13. Du Pont de Nemours, 1912, p. 137.
14. Hopkins, 1942, p. 33. Hatcher (1947, pp. 305) explains that the power of exploding gunpowder increases as the size of the grain decreases, within certain limits. He gives the Du Pont system of designating gunpowder textures (the numerals indicate the number of meshes in each inch of screen):

Size [of Grain] [The more "F's" the finer the grain]	*Must Pass*	*Must Be Retained On*
Grade A-1 [Army saluting]	6	10
Fg	14	16
FFg [old-fashioned sporting powder]	16	24
FFFg [large-caliber pistol cartridges]	24	46
FFFFg [cap-and-ball pistols]	46	60

For an enlightening discussion of black powder contrasted with modern smokeless powder, see Hatcher, 1949, pp. 32–36.

When the U. S. Ordnance Department conducted trials in connection with experiments with the Minié ball, it was found that "musket powder (coarse-grained) answered much better than the Service rifle powder even for the round balls. The latter not only failed to give as great accuracy as the former, but it frequently clogged the vent so effectually as to require a drift to be passed through it. . . . Musket powder is recommended for all small arms. Du Pont's canister powder of very fine grain was tried in the pistol but not with the same success as with the musket powder; the force of the ball was increased, but its accuracy was much diminished." U. S. Ordnance Dept., 1856.

15. Lewis and Clark, 1904–1905, II, Pt. 2, p. 315. The distribution of gunpowder in canisters seems to have been regular practice even in the very early years of the American fur trade west of the Mississippi. Advertisements in the *Louisiana Gazette,* Jan. 25, 1810, testify to this.

16. Hopkins, 1942, p. 37.

17. Amer. Fur Co., 1821–1822.

18. Du Pont (1912, pp. 95 and 96) pictures early powder wagons of the Conestoga type. The wagons were drawn by six mules or horses; the driver rode the left wheel horse. During the War of 1812 Du Pont delivered powder from the Brandywine to Commodore Perry on Lake Erie in this type of freight wagon.

19. Amer. Fur Co., 1831–1849, LB 1:147–148, no. 203.

20. Attempts had been made to provide a local supply of gunpowder on the Missouri, with some success, but the amount produced was far from sufficient to meet western demands. H. R. Schoolcraft (1819, p. 47) recorded that William Henry Ashley developed a saltpeter plant at Ashley's Cave, 80 mi. southwest of Potosi, Mo., in 1810–1820. It may have been the product of this plant which caused the death of three teamsters employed by Ashley to freight gunpowder from St. Louis to St. Charles:

"In 1824 Ashley started out on another trip to trade for furs. Bill Sublette and his brother were among the number. They started a keel boat up the Missouri to bring down a load of pelts. There were no steamboats on the Missouri in those days and they had to pull the keelboats up by hand with ropes. The boat had started off up the river, and Ashley intended to have his ammunition wagon meet the boat at St. Charles. La Barge, I don't know his first name, but he was a brother of Joe La Barge, a jolly German they called 'Happy-Go-Lucky,' and another man whose name I have forgotten, were put in charge of this wagon loaded with guns, pistols and 300 pounds of powder. They drove out Washington Avenue, about where the University now stands. There was a little schoolhouse at the corner in those early days. La Barge was smoking a pipe and just as the wagon was going by it, he knocked the fire out of his pipe. It fell on the kegs. Every keg in the wagon exploded and blew the men sky high. La Barge went up a hundred feet and came down dead; so did the other man, but Happy-Go-Lucky came down, rolled over a few times and then died. The wagon was torn to splinters, but the horses ran away unhurt. One of the strange things about the explosion was the fact that an old dog was trotting along side the wagon and didn't get hurt a bit, excepting that a little of his hair was singed off. That was a pretty hard lick for Ashley, but I fitted him out again on credit, and I was the first man to be paid when he came back with the keelboat loaded with pelts." From Samuel Hawken's "Memoirs," given to J. P. H. Gemmer in 1933 by Otis A. Hawken. A copy of the MS is in the possession of the Missouri Historical Society.

The saltpeter from Ashley's plant was hauled to a gunpowder factory in Potosi, which Schoolcraft describes as the only powder plant in that part of the country. In the eighteen-month period, Dec. 31, 1816, to June, 1818, it produced 60,000 pounds of gunpowder valued at $30,000.

21. Amer. Fur Co., 1831–1849, LB 1:101, no. 145.
22. *Ibid.,* p. 116, no. 166.
23. Sage, 1855, p. 18. Charges entered in the accounts at the U. S. Arsenal near Pittsburgh, Pa., in April, May, and June, 1819, indicate that several hundred "rifle horns" were prepared by government employees at a rate of pay which would bring the cost of workmanship on these powder horns to approximately 50 cents a horn. U. S. Cong., 1823*a.*

Lt. Cooke in 1829, on the Arkansas River with a battalion of the 1st Infantry awaiting the return of a party of Santa Fe traders, recorded that he and his men whiled away the time by reading, fishing, and hunting. "The only alternative seemed the manufacture of buffalo powder-horns. Hundreds were made in the camp and some very beautiful; the horn is quite black and receives a fine polish, and being exceedingly thick, admits of much carving; [soldiers] with the laborious and patient care of Chinese carved and inlaid some with bone." Cooke, 1857, p. 61.

24. Griswold, 1927, pp. 425, 426, 537.
25. Amer. Fur Co., 1821–1822.
26. Young, 1899, p. 213.
27. Roberts, 1944, p. 165. The charges would average in weight about as follows: 150 balls per pound, 31 cal.—25 grains weight of powder; 100 balls, 36 cal.—40 grs.; 56 balls, 44 cal.—60 grs.; 18 balls, 60 cal.— 85 grs. Permission to quote from Roberts, 1944, has been given by The Stackpole Company.
28. Levinge, 1846, p. 236.
29. C. E. Brown, 1918, pp. 78–79; Revoil, 1865, p. 283.
30. Griswold, 1927, pp. 413, 458, 537. Lead mines along the Mississippi became highly important in the very earliest western commerce and industry. The Missouri lead region, about 60 mi. southwest of St. Louis, was reported to be a region about 100 mi. long and 40 wide. From the towns of Potosi and St. Francis the pig lead was hauled to the Mississippi, at Herculaneum and Ste Genevieve, where shot towers converted part of the lead to shot of various sizes. Shot and pig lead were then floated down the river to New Orleans. See Schoolcraft,

1819; Schaefer, 1932; Dick, 1941; and Beers, 1935, pp. 73 and 79, for additional information.

31. Amer. Fur Co., 1821–1822.
32. Griswold, 1927, pp. 417, 536. In 1809, J. Macklot built a shot factory at Herculaneum about 30 mi. from St. Louis. "He has commenced casting shot equal to the best English patent. . . . In a few weeks the factory will have a capacity of 10,000 pounds per day. . . . Further excavations are being made so as to attain a drop [in the tower] of 130 feet and so be able to make the largest size shot." Editorial in *Missouri Gazette,* Nov. 16, 1809.

An interesting history of the widely known Baltimore shot tower and an account of its products are given in the *Gun and Cartridge Record,* January, 1954, p. 10.
33. Griswold, 1927, pp. 428, 537.
34. C. E. Brown, 1918, pp. 70–71. In 1776, Alexander Nelson of Philadelphia contracted with the Colony of Virginia to supply 600 muskets of the British type. With the arms he was to provide certain accessories: "to every forty guns one pair bullet molds, to mould 16 bullets [¾-inch bore]." Abstract from the 1776 contract, in Gluckman and Satterlee, 1953, pp. 151–152.
35. Innis, 1930, p. 161, quoting Umfreville.
36. Amer. Fur Co., 1831–1849, LB 3:473, no. 1933.
37. Woodward, 1947, pp. 1–3.
38. Mordecai, 1861, pp. 242–243. One can see from the following tabulation that the Ordnance Department expected precise inspection:

Dimensions	Musket flints		Rifle flints		Pistol flints	
	Min.	Max.	Min.	Max.	Min.	Max.
Whole length	1.2″	1.50″	.97″	1.2″	.93″	1.10″
Width	1.08	1.13	.79	.88	.83	.92
Thickness at the back ...	.26	.33	.20	.29	.21	.27
Length of the bevel	.39	.55	.41	.71	.30	.42

39. Dillin, 1924, p. 118.
40. B. R. Lewis, personal communication, March 8, 1954.
41. C. N. Peters, personal communication, Dec. 1, 1953.
42. Arthur Woodward, personal communication, Jan. 24, 1953.
43. Arcadi Gluckman, personal communication. The same paraphernalia, contained within the patch box of a Starr rifle, is illustrated in Hicks, 1940*a*, pp. 124–125.
44. Woodward, 1948*b*, p. 5.
45. J. Sullivan, 1921, p. 535.
46. *Ibid.,* p. 503.
47. Griswold, 1927, p. 413.
48. U. S. Indian Trade Office, April 28, 1823.

49. Chittenden, 1935, pp. 4–5. At Astoria, Oregon, in 1813, the North West Company appraised the value of 3,410 flints belonging to Astor at 3½ cents a flint, which Astor stated was but one-fifth of the real value.

50. Mordecai, 1861, pp. 278–281. John Metschl (1928, pp. 779–783) gives an excellent account of the Rev. Mr. Forsyth's work with the percussion system. Roberts (1944, pp. 190–191) tells of the part played by Joshua Shaw. A comprehensive account is given by Paul B. Jenkins in "The Story of the Primer" (1934).

51. Roberts, 1944, pp. 153–155. See also Peterson, 1953, pp. 197–208.

52. U. S. Cong., 1823a.

53. U. S. Cong., 1842a, p. 54.

54. Mordecai, 1861, p. 248.

55. Smyth, 1812, p. 189.

56. Mordecai, 1861, pp. 245–249.

57. U. S. Cong., 1838b, p. 431. This is General Macomb's report, Dec. 3, 1838.

58. U. S. Cong., 1823b, p. 60.

59. The cartridge was regularly supplied in calibers .31, .36, .44, .52, .58, and .69; "any other size furnished to order." The Wisconsin Historical Society exhibits three wooden containers of the type shown in fig. 44, *f*, each holding "6 combustible envelope cartridges for Col. Colt's new model revolving holster pistol, $^{44}/_{100}$ caliber. Hartford, Conn." Colt advertisements of the day (the late 1840's) claimed that foil cartridges "are more convenient and surer fire than loose powder and ball, and a revolver can remain loaded much longer without injury, when charged with these cartridges."

60. Hicks, 1940a, II, 129.

61. Mordecai, 1861, pp. 201–203; Fuller, 1930, p. 104.

62. Smyth, 1812, p. 189.

63. Innis, 1930, p. 325.

64. Merk, 1931, p. 97.

65. Victor, 1870, p. 230.

CHAPTER VI SMALL CANNON OF THE TRADERS AND THE MILITARY
(*pages 251–282*)

1. Tilberg, 1954, pp. 15–16.

2. Harrington, 1954b, pp. 25–27.

3. Nasatir, 1952, pp. 87–108.

4. Clamorgan to Gov.-Gen. Carondelet, July 8, 1795, cited in Houck, II, 177. A translation is given in *American State Papers,* Public Lands, VIII, 234. See also U. S. Cong., 1852, and Nasatir, 1922, pp. 40–42.

5. Nasatir, 1952, p. 339.

6. *Ibid.,* pp. 102, 320, 360, 444, and 462.

7. Baldwin, 1941, pp. 106, 163, 169, and 224–226.
8. Hicks, 1940*a*, I, 27, 75.
9. U. S. Cong., 1823*a*, pp. 24–27. A flintlock swivel gun of musket type known to have been used at Fort Nisqually is preserved in the museum of the Washington State Historical Society, Tacoma (no. 2584).
10. Gluckman and Satterlee, 1953, p. 217. See also Peterson, 1947.
11. U. S. Cong., 1823*a*, p. 274.
12. Original letter in the National Archives; photostatic copy in the library of the Native Sons of Kansas City.
13. Sibley, 1808.
14. Brackenridge, 1844, p. 117.
15. Drum, 1920, p. 125.
16. Wood, 1954, and Smith, 1955. The cannon fragments found at Kipp's Post when fitted together form a barrel similar in form and proportions to the St. Louis specimen shown in fig. 50. James Kipp dealt with the Mandans at the Big Knife a year or two prior to the establishment of Kipp's Post at the mouth of the White Earth River. At this time the disgruntled Arikara virtually laid siege to the Mandan and Gros Ventre villages. Kipp set up cannon in defense of his friendly hosts, and presumably these guns were given to the villages when he moved north to the White Earth. The cannon were still in Indian ownership and in use when Chardon resided in the nearby Fort Clark. (Abel, 1932, pp. 47, 72–73).
17. *Louisiana Gazette,* Nov. 30, 1809, p. 2.
18. *Ibid.,* July 5, 1810.
19. U. S. Ordnance Department reports indicate the following distribution of ordnance (56 guns) in midwestern and western forts at the beginning of 1823:
    Ft. Claiborne, Ala. Two 3-pounder brass cannon with 169 case shot; two 4-pounder brass cannon with 921 cannon balls; one 24-pound howitzer with 192 shells.
    Ft. Smith, Ark. Two 6-pounder iron cannon with 188 balls and 91 case shot.
    Council Bluffs (Ft. Atkinson), Neb. Nine 6-pounders with 2,221 cannon balls, 247 strapped shot, and 1,730 case shot; one 4-pounder; five 24-pound howitzers with 107 case shot.
    Ft. Armstrong, Rock Island, Ill. One 12-pounder with 80 balls and 102 case shot; three 6-pounders with 200 balls and 36 case shot.
    Ft. Edwards, Ill. Three 6-pounders with 100 balls, 48 case shot, and 50 grapeshot.
    Ft. Crawford, Prairie du Chien, Wis. Two 12-pounders with 359 balls, 530 strapped shot, and 332 case shot; two 6-pounders with 754 balls, 317 strapped shot, and 170 case shot.
    Ft. St. Anthony (later Ft. Snelling), Minn. Three 6-pounders; two 24-pound howitzers with 200 case shot and 125 shells.

Sault Ste Marie (Ft. Brady), Mich. Two 6-pounders with 300 balls and 300 case shot; one 24-pound howitzer with 125 shells.

Ft. Mackinac, Mich. Nine 9-pounders with 84 balls; one 24-pound howitzer.

Ft. Howard, Wis. One 12-pounder with 769 balls and 458 case shot.

Ft. Dearborn, Ill. Two 6-pounders with 380 balls.

Ft. Shelby (Detroit), Mich. Two 6-pounders.

"All the cannon, artillery carriages and cannon balls, except a small quantity forwarded at the Commencement of the War [of 1812] were manufactured at Pittsburgh." U. S. Cong., 1823*a*, pp. 24–27.

Lewis Cass, in his 1831 *Report of the Secretary of War,* observed: "The United States have no armories for the fabrication of cannon. The practice for some years has been to make contracts with the owners of the four foundries at Richmond, Georgetown, Pittsburgh, and West Point to the amount of the annual appropriation allowing about an equal proportion to each and paying such price as the Ordnance Department on the best information, judge reasonable. . . . It appears to me that a public armory for the fabrication of cannon is required by obvious considerations." U. S. Cong., 1831*b*, p. 25.

20. Vinton, 1935, pp. 584–601; U. S. Cong., 1823*g*, pp. 55–108. The English astronomer David Thompson, in the service of the North West Company, visited the Mandan villages in 1797–1798. These towns were very much like the Arikara villages, with their stockades and their mud-walled houses. Thompson quoted a Mandan: "In these straight Streets [of the white man's towns] we see no advantage the inhabitants have over their enemies. The whole of their bodies are exposed, and the houses can be set on fire; which our homes cannot be, for the earth cannot burn; our houses being round shelter us except when we fire down on them, and we are high above them; the enemies have never been able to hurt us when we are in our Villages; and it is only when we are absent on large hunting parties that we have suffered; and which we shall not do again. The Sieux Indians have several times on a dark stormy night set fire to the stockade, but this had no effect on the houses." (Tyrrell, 1916, p. 229; quoted by permission of The Champlain Society, Toronto, Canada). Moats, ramparts, stockades, and even bastions were features of the primitive forts. Defenders equipped with muskets could very well withstand attack from musket-shooting enemies, but cannonading was something that Thompson's informants had not experienced.

21. Vinton, 1935, p. 595. This is Chittenden's estimate of the noneffective cannonading; he was influenced by the acrimonious reports handed down by Pilcher. Col. Leavenworth, after he inspected the abandoned villages, observed that the Indian structures were "completely riddled. We found thirty-one new graves, and we found that several old ones had been opened, and the surface set thick with prickly pears to

conceal the new dirt. We know that 10 men, who were killed by the Sioux in the skirmish on the 9th were buried in five graves; and . . . that more than one was buried in several of the other graves. From the best evidence that we could collect, it is supposed that more than 50 of their people were killed, and a great number wounded." Report of Col. Henry Leavenworth, quoted in Morgan, 1953, p. 76.

22. Cooke, 1857, pp. 35, 52, 57, and 92. Mahan, in 1836, observed that ball and shell had a greater effect on morale than grape, and that shell was particularly effective against cavalry. He advocated late fire and a low aim to produce ricochets, which he declared to be of "considerable moral effect . . . There are so many circumstances that affect the aim of artillery that nothing but the most careful attention to the effects produced by the first few rounds will enable the officer to manage his guns with advantage. The point blank range of 6-pounder field guns is about 600 yards and that of 12-pounders about 700 yards." He then added performance data:

"*Balls* out of 100 which attain a target 6 feet high and 95 feet long:

	at 550 yards	870 yards	1,300 yards
12-pounder	57	38	19
6-pounder	49	32	12

"Number of balls out of 41 in *canister* which hit target 6 feet high 50 feet long:

	220 yards	440 yards	600 yards
12-pounder canister	9	9	4.5
8-pounder canister	8.3	7.4	4

"*Grape.* The usual diameter of grape is about one-third that of the ball. To produce a good effect at a distance grape ought not to be less than one inch in diameter . . . Such grape has sufficient velocity at 880 yards with 12-pounders and 760 yards with 8-pounders to disable men. When the distance is within 500 yards the fire of grape is superior to that of ball against troops.

"*Shell.* The shell of the howitzer imbeds itself in earth and wood, and, bursting produces a considerable crater. The fragments of the shell are often thrown to distances of over 600 yards, and they do great damage to objects near. The wounds from them are very dangerous." Mahan, 1846, pp. xx–xxiv. (Mahan's first edition appeared in 1836.)

23. Rodenbough, 1875, p. 30.
24. Pelzer, 1943, pp. 7, 19, and 92.
25. In the inventory of Astor's property which was turned over to the British North West Company at Astoria in 1813 are the following items of ordnance:

2 brass swivels on carriages @ 15.00 .... $ 30.00
5 brass swivels without carriages @ 13.62½ 68.12½

1 ladle and worm for swivels	1.00
4 iron 4-pounders @ 50.00	200.00
2 brass 4-pounders, short, @ 35.00	70.00
5 rammers and sponges for 4-pounders @ 1.00	5.00
10 cannister shot @ 80¢	8.00
3 grape shot @ 41¢	1.23

From U. S. Cong., 1823*b*, pp. 33–34.

Astor claimed that he received only a small fraction of the true value of his properties. A comparison of the foregoing list with the prices of ordnance in U. S. government estimates of 1842, wherein "cohorns" are valued at $100 apiece and bronze 3½-inch howitzers at $1,009, shows that he had some basis for his claim. U. S. Cong., 1842*a*, p. 54.

26. Quaife, 1923, pp. 267–269.
27. *Ibid.*, pp. 283–284, p. 287.
28. Innis, 1930, p. 294.
29. Coues, 1897, pp. 428, 432.
30. Laut, 1908, II, 249.
31. *Ibid.*, pp. 259–260.
32. Hulbert (1933, p. 146) cites original publication by U. S. Cong., 1831*a*. Sullivan (1936, p. 223) states that the original letter, addressed to Gen. Lewis Cass, Secretary of War, is in the Manuscripts Department, Wisconsin State Historical Society, and explains that Ashley did not accompany this 1827 expedition. Hulbert (1933, pp. 146–149) quotes the Ashley letter. Chittenden (Vinton, 1935, p. 275) refers to the significance of this first wheeled vehicle in the West but places the date as 1826, an error which Vinton (*ibid.*, p. 282) corrects. Since Ashley did finance and direct the 1827 business of supply for his successors, Smith, Jackson, and Sublette, his statement that he sent a wheeled cannon into the wilds in 1827 is entirely plausible. In so doing he marked the route which in another decade was to become a wagon road through the South Pass.
33. Ellison, 1932, p. 13.
34. Warner, 1909, p. 177. Morgan (1953, pp. 326–329) describes the unique field piece as a 6-pounder.
35. Lewis and Phillips, 1923, pp. 96, 107, 127.
36. Gregg, 1905, XX, 105.
37. Paden, 1943, p. 437; quoted by permission of The Macmillan Company.
38. The Sacramento *Bee,* Sept. 20, 1941, magazine section (p. 3), prints an account of the history of the piece; and a comprehensive treatment is given by Hinkle and Hinkle, 1949. See also Frémont, 1845, p. 217.
39. Arthur Woodward, personal communication.
40. Irving Stone, *Immortal Wife* (p. 104), copyright 1944 by Irving Stone, reprinted by permission of Doubleday & Company, Inc. See also Frémont, 1887, pp. 167–168.

41. Frémont, 1845, p. 106.
42. Stone, *op. cit.*, p. 104.
43. Frémont, 1845, pp. 106–107.
44. *Ibid.*, p. 126.
45. *Ibid.*, p. 204.
46. *Ibid.*, p. 106.
47. *Ibid.*, p. 225.
48. *Ibid.*, pp. 225–226.
49. *Ibid.*, p. 227.
50. *Ibid.*, p. 235.
51. Hannah, 1951, p. 57.
52. Paden, 1943, p. 437; quoted by permission of The Macmillan Company.
53. Hinkle and Hinkle, 1949, *passim*. Harold L. Peterson, in searching "Statement of Contracts, Ordnance Department, Book 26," found that Cyrus Alger and Co. delivered to the U. S. government 12 twelve-pounder mountain howitzers on June 11, 1836; 12 more on May 16, 1837; 3 on Dec. 8, 1837; 4 on March 13, 1838; and 5 on April 28, 1838. These records are now in the War Records Division, National Archives, Washington, D.C. (Personal letter from Peterson, May 28, 1954.) The *Ordnance Manual* (Mordecai, 1861, p. 19, and in the earlier eds.) specifies the markings which contractors placed upon the mountain howitzers made for the War Department. The Nevada State Museum specimen is marked in every particular in accordance with these specifications.
54. The *Ordnance Manual* (Mordecai, 1861, pp. 131–148) gives a very detailed treatment of the use and care of the mountain howitzer. The drawings in figs. 53 and 54 are taken from pl. 14 of the *Manual,* which also shows the special Army pack saddle for carrying ammunition.
55. Fort Nisqually, founded on Puget Sound near the mouth of the Nisqually River in 1833, was the halfway house between Ft. Vancouver on the Columbia and Ft. Langley. To make way for commercial use of the site, the old buildings were taken down; they were moved several miles to Point Defiance Park in Tacoma, Wash., and there on a prominence were reërected in their original relationships within a stockade like that of the fort of pioneer days.
56. Morgan, 1953, pp. 288, 347.
57. Sibley, 1808. I have these records through the kindness of James Anderson, Historian, Native Sons of Kansas City.
58. The Clark letter is in the National Archives; a photostatic copy is owned by the Native Sons of Kansas City.
59. Brackenridge, 1844, p. 118.
60. The original documents are in the National Archives; copies are owned by the Native Sons of Kansas City.
61. Anderson, 1948–1949.

Glossary of Gun Terms

Arquebus. See *Harquebus.*

Bandolier. A strap or belt worn by the soldier as a carrier for separate loads or charges.

Bands. Strips of metal looped about the barrel and forestock of a gun, thus holding these parts together. (Band-fastened as contrasted with pin-fastened.)

Battery. See *Frizzen.*

Bluing. The coloring of the metal of any gun by a controlled process of induced rusting.

Blunderbuss. A smoothbore gun with a bell muzzle.

Browning. See *Bluing.*

Butt. The part of a gunstock which is placed against the shoulder in firing.

Butt plate. A metal cover which protects the butt.

Caliber, calibre. The diameter of the bore of a gun. Rifle calibers are expressed in decimals of an inch. See *Gauge.*

Canister. A case containing slugs, bullets, or scrap iron designed to break open when fired from a cannon.

Cap. See *Percussion cap.*

Carbine, Carabine. Originally a shortened form of shoulder arm, either smoothbore or rifled, especially for use in the saddle. More recently the term has been applied to short rifled arms.

Cartridge. Container for a charge of explosive. It may or may not include the ball.

Chamber. The part of the bore which receives the charge for firing.

Cheekpiece. The part of the stock of a gun shaped to support the cheek in order to facilitate aiming.

Cock. The hammer, or movable part of the firing mechanism.

Cohorn, Coehorn mortar. A small, short, stubby cannon invented by the Dutch engineer Baron van Mermo Coehoorn and used by him against the French in 1673. The type continued in use through the U. S. Civil War.

Comb. The top (when in position for firing) of the stock of a gun.

Cylinder. The magazine of a gun of the revolver type.

Firelock. The early U. S. military term for a flintlock musket. In the seventeenth century, English colonists referred to either the snaphance or the true flintlock as "firelocks."

Fixed ammunition. The projectile (shot, shell, case, or canister) and its sabot tied into a powder bag and ready for loading into a cannon.

Flashpan. See *Pan.*

Flint. A hard quartz (silica) which fractures to make sharp edges and which strikes a spark from steel.

Flint gun. See *Flintlock* and *Snaphance.*

Flintlock. A gun equipped with a device for firing the charge by means of sparks struck by flint upon steel. The steel, or frizzen, is a continuous part of the pan cover.

Forearm. Any part of the stock of a gun extending forward of the trigger guard under the barrel (as contrasted with the forestock; see below).

Forestock. The elongated part of the stock which extends beneath the barrel of a full-stocked gun.

Frizzen. The steel of a flintlock against which the flint strikes to make sparks. Dictionaries spell the word "frizzle" and "frizel."

Fuke. From "fusil." A common designation by Englishmen in Canada of the light musket traded to Indians. The word "fuke" was associated with the Hudson's Bay Co. trade guns especially.

Fuse, fuze. A tube or cord filled or saturated with combustible substances and used for setting off explosives, especially the charge of a shell or other projectile fired from a muzzle-loading cannon.

Fusee, fuzee. An English corruption of *fusil,* which see. (To the French a *fusee* is a rocket.)

Fusil. Originally a French term for a light flintlock arm made to replace the heavy military musket (*ca.* 1630). In America the word became synonymous with the flintlock "trade musket" and was eventually applied to cheap muskets with the percussion system also. (*Fusil à piston.*)

Fusil-court. A short, light smoothbore gun. (Fr.)

Fuzee. See *Fusee.*

Gauge. The diameter of the bore of a gun expressed in terms of the number of balls of a corresponding size required to make a pound.

Grape shot. Similar to canister, but with larger iron balls bound in grape-like clusters; bagged in cloth but without a metal case.

Grip. That part of the stock of a gun grasped by the trigger hand in firing.

Gunlock. The mechanism by which the charge of a gun is fired.

Hair trigger. A device for adjusting the firing mechanism of a gun so that it may be fired by the light touch of the finger on the trigger.

Half cock. The position of the cock of a gun when raised part way and held by a catch from which it cannot be moved by pulling the trigger.

Hammer. That part of the mechanism of a gun which falls upon the frizzen or cap to fire the piece. See *Cock.*

Harquebus. An early name (in the period of the matchlock and wheel lock) for the military arm which could be fired from the shoulder, or with butt against breast, without a rest.

Howitzer. A short cannon intermediate between the long-barrel type and the mortar.

Lands. The parts of the original surface of the bore of a rifled arm left between the grooves of the rifling.

Linstock. A forked stick used by the cannoneer in applying the burning slow match to the priming powder in the touchhole of a muzzle-loading cannon.

Lock. See *Gunlock.*

Lock plate. That part of the right side of the lock, the outer surface of which is flush with the stock and the inner surface of which supports the mechanism of the igniting device.

Mandrel. An iron or steel rod around which a strip of iron or steel is wrapped and welded into a gun barrel having a bore the same as the diameter of the rod.

Mask butt. An embossed butt plate of metal (usually silver) for a pistol. The raised design often resembles a masquerade mask.

Match. See *Slow match.*

Matchlock. An early gun, the firing of which was effected by the use of a burning slow match.

Musket (musquet, mousquet, Fr.). Originally the heavy military arm fired from a rest (as contrasted with the lighter arquebus). Later, any smoothbore gun, other than the pistol or blunderbuss.

Musketoon (mousqueton, Fr.). A military musket with short barrel and a forestock extending underneath the full length of the barrel, as contrasted with the half-stock carbine.

Nipple. The short metal tube over the touchhole of a percussion gun. Upon it the cap containing the priming compound is placed for firing.

Pan. The receptacle which holds the priming powder on a matchlock, wheel-lock, snaphance, or flintlock gun.

Pan cover. The device which retains and protects from the weather the priming powder in the pan.

Patch. A wrapper of paper, cloth, or leather for the ball of a muzzle-loading gun.

Patch box. A built-in receptacle with a spring-hinged cover in the stock of a muzzle-loading rifle.

Percussion cap. A small metal cup, often crimped, within which the priming compound is sealed. The cap is designed to fit snugly upon the nipple, where, upon being struck by the hammer, it explodes and sends a flash of fire through the touchhole to the powder charge, thus firing it.

Percussion lock. A gunlock equipped to use percussion caps.

Pins. Pieces of iron to be inserted in openings in the forestock of a gun and further passed through holes in metal studs extending from the barrel, thus "pin-fastening" the stock to the barrel.

Portfire. A type of military fireworks. A kind of slow-burning fuse made up of a composition of 13 parts of niter, 4.5 parts of sulphur, and 2.5 parts of mealed gunpowder contained in a paper case.

Primer. Percussion caps for small arms; also applies to the device for firing some types of artillery.

Priming. The gunpowder (in a flintlock) or the fulminate (in a percussion gun) which ignites the charge.

Ram pipes. The ferrules or guides mounted under the forestock or barrel to carry the ramrod.

Ramrod. A rod of wood or metal for pushing down into the barrel of a muzzle-loading gun the powder charge, the shot or bullet, and the wadding.

Rifle. A firearm in the bore of which spiral grooves have been cut for the purpose of imparting a spinning motion to the bullet as it is propelled from the barrel.

Scelp. A band of iron commonly forged from melted scrap iron of inferior quality. Cheap gun barrels were made by wrapping the scelps round a mandrel to make spirals which were then hammered and forged to make a tube.

Sear, scear. A part of the lock mechanism operating between the trigger and the cock.

Serpentine. The S-shaped cock of a matchlock which held the burning match and conducted the fire to the priming charge. The priming powder, also, and the matchlock gun itself were sometimes referred to as "serpentine."

Set trigger. A second trigger on a gun, the adjustment of which can effect firing by a very light pressure on the firing trigger.

Shell. An explosive projectile or bomb fired from a cannon.

Shot. (*a*) Pellets of lead fired from a fowling piece. (*b*) "Solid shot," a cast-iron cannon ball. "Bar shot" and "chain shot" were variations of the round, solid shot.

Slow match. A cord of combustible material (saltpeter, lead acetate, and lye) which when lighted was used for igniting the priming charge of a matchlock gun. Also, before 1800, the slow match was universally attached to a linstock for use in igniting the priming charge of cannon.

Smoothbore. A gun, the bore of which is not grooved (not rifled).

Snaphance, snaphaunce. An early flint gun with battery (frizzen) separate from the pan cover. The pan cover is opened or closed manually by sliding it horizontally.

Spanner wrench. A flat wrench, often specially designed to be used in operating a specific part of the mechanism of a gunlock. Example: the spanner used in winding the spring of a wheel lock.

Spherical case shot. A hollow cannon ball containing a charge of powder and balls and a fuse for igniting the enclosed bursting charge after the case was propelled from the barrel.

Swivel. Hinged loops of metal mounted on the underside of a gunstock (or on the trigger guard) and on the forestock through which the leather gun sling may be fastened.

Swivel gun. A small cannon or heavy musket mounted on a parapet, wall, or gunwale by means of a movable device similar to an oarlock.

Swivel ramrod. A ramrod attached to a muzzle-loading pistol or carbine by means of a hinged link of steel or iron in such manner as to permit all the movements required in loading the arm.

Touchhole. The opening (vent) near the rear end of the barrel of a muzzle-loading gun, through which the flash of fire from the priming powder passes to the powder charge within the barrel.

Trunnion. One of two pivots that project from opposite sides of a cannon barrel to provide the bearing upon which the barrel is mounted on its carriage.

Wheel lock. An early form of gun which was invented after the matchlock came into use. Ignition of the priming powder was effected by sparks struck by pyrites held against a steel wheel made to revolve by a spring when the trigger was pulled.

Worm. A screw or hooked metal rod which could be affixed to the end of a ramrod of a muzzle-loading gun for the purpose of withdrawing a charge from the barrel.

Bibliography

(Books marked with an asterisk have been particularly helpful to me in this work.)

ABEL, ANNIE HELOISE (ed.)
  1932. Chardon's Journal at Fort Clark, 1834–1839. Pierre: Department of History, S.D. xlvi, 458 pp.

ADAMS, JAMES TRUSLOW (ed.)
  *1940. Dictionary of American History. New York: Scribner's. 6 vols. For ready reference in determining geographic relationships of historic places, identifying persons related to the history of specific happenings, and tracing the general succession of events this is invaluable, particularly when used in conjunction with the "Historical Map of the United States," National Geographic Magazine, June, 1953.

AMERICAN FUR COMPANY
  1821–1822. American Fur Company Invoice Book, Michilimackinac. MS in Chicago Historical Society Library. 267 pp. of longhand entries.
  1831–1849. Correspondence and other manuscript documents pertaining to the business of the American Fur Company. American Fur Company Papers in MS Collections, New York Historical Society, New York City.

In the notes to this book, the letters LB indicate that the document referred to is contained in one of the company's letter books.

ANDERSON, JAMES
  1948, 1949, 1956. Personal communications to C. P. Russell, July 28, 1948; Jan. 17, 1949; March 20, 1956. Attachments include studies by George

ANDERSON, JAMES (*Continued*)
>Fuller Green upon which the restoration drawing of Fort Osage (end papers) is based.

ANONYMOUS
>1949. "Modern Gunpowder," *American Rifleman,* Vol. XCVII, Oct., pp. 26–30.

ANDREWS, E. BENJAMIN
>1894. *History of the United States.* New York: Scribner. 2 vols.

BAKELESS, JOHN
>1947. *Lewis and Clark: Partners in Discovery.* New York: Morrow. xii, 495 pp.

BALDWIN, LELAND D.
>1941. *The Keelboat Age on Western Waters.* University of Pittsburgh Press. xiv, 268 pp., illus.

BARSOTTI, JOHN
>1953. "Mountain Men and Mountain Rifles," *The Gun Digest for 1954.* Chicago: Wilcox and Follett. Pp. 153–156.

BASSETT, JOHN S.
>1911. *Life of Andrew Jackson.* New York: Macmillan. 2 vols.

BEERS, HENRY PUTNEY
>*1935. *Western Military Frontier, 1815–1846.* Philadelphia: Upper Darby. vi, 227 pp.

An exceedingly useful outline of the history of the Army in the early West and a guide to War Department reports and other contemporary documents. In scope and thoroughness it has no equal.

BIGGAR, H. P. (ed.)
>1922–1936. *The Works of Samuel de Champlain.* Toronto: Champlain Society. 6 vols.

BILLINGTON, RAY ALLEN
>*1952. *Westward Expansion: A History of the American Frontier.* New York: Macmillan. xiii, 873 pp.

This great work will assist the reader to gain a sense of perspective and to realize the continuity of the frontier gun story.

BINGHAM, ROBERT W.
>1934. *Early Buffalo Gun Smiths.* Buffalo, N.Y.: Buffalo Historical Society. 18 pp.

BOLTON, HERBERT E.
>1914. *Athanase de Mézières and the Louisiana-Texas Frontier, 1768–1780.* Cleveland: A. H. Clark. 2 vols.
>1915. *Texas in the Middle Eighteenth Century.* University of California Publications in History, Vol. III. x, 501 pp.

BOLTON, H. E., and T. M. MARSHALL
  1930. *The Colonization of North America, 1492–1783.* New York: Macmillan. xvi, 609 pp.
BOSWORTH, N.
  1846. A Treatise on the Rifle, Musket, Pistol and Fowling Piece. New York: J. S. Redfield. Facsimile ed. by Standard Publications, Inc., Huntington, W.Va.
BRACKENRIDGE, H. M.
  1816. *Journal of a Voyage up the Missouri River in 1811.* Pittsburgh.
  1904. Reprint of the foregoing, in R. G. Thwaites (ed.), *Early Western Travels,* Vol. VI, pp. 9–164.
BRACKETT, ALBERT G.
  1865. *History of the United States Cavalry.* New York: Harper. xii, 337 pp.
BRANNON, PETER A.
  1935. *The Southern Indian Trade.* Montgomery, Ala.: Paragon Press. 87 pp.
BRIDWELL, MARGARET M.
  1952. *Story of Mammoth Cave National Park.* Mammoth Cave, Ky.: Bridwell, 64 pp.
BROOKS, VAN WYCK
  1944. *The World of Washington Irving.* New York: Dutton. 495 pp.
BROWN, CHARLES E.
  1918. "Indian Trade Implements and Ornaments," *Wisconsin Archeologist,* XVII (Sept.), 61–97.
BROWN, THEODORE T.
  1932. "Sieur Charles de Langlade," *Wisconsin Archeologist,* XI (July), 143–147.
BURDETT, CHARLES
  1865. *Life of Kit Carson.* Philadelphia: J. E. Potter. 382 pp.
BUSK, HANS
  1858. *The Rifle: And How to Use It.* 2d ed. London. 181 pp.
  1861. *The Rifle and How to Use It.* 8th ed. London: G. Routledge. 255 pp.
CAMP, CHARLES L. (ed.)
  1928. *James Clyman, American Frontierman, 1792–1881.* San Francisco: California Historical Society. 247 pp.
CAREY, A. MERWYN
  1953. *American Firearms Makers.* New York: Crowell. 144 pp.
CARVER, JONATHAN
  1779. *Travel through the Interior Parts of North America in the Years 1766, 1767, and 1768.* 2d ed. London. 543 pp., illus.
CHAMPLAIN, SAMUEL DE
  See Biggar, 1922–1936.
CHAPEL, CHARLES EDWARD
  1939. *Gun Collecting.* New York: Coward-McCann. x, 232 pp.
  1947. *Gun Collector's Handbook of Values.* New York: Coward-McCann. xv, 412 pp., illus.

CHAPMAN, JOHN RATCLIFFE
1848. *Instructions to Young Marksmen.* New York and Philadelphia. Facsimile ed., Goffstown, N.Y., 1941. 160 pp., illus.

CHARDON, FRANCIS A.
See Abel, 1932.

CHITTENDEN, HIRAM MARTIN
1902. *The American Fur Trade of the Far West.* New York: Harper. 3 vols. For 1935 ed. see Vinton.

CINFONTAINE, COLONEL
1789. "Dessins Relatifs aux Travaux d'artillerie executes dans les manufactures, 1773–1789." 125 pp. of MS notes and plates of water-color illustrations and line and wash drawings of French military small arms. Originals in the custody of Dr. Thomas T. Hoopes, City Art Museum of St. Louis.

CLARK, WILLIAM
1808. Letter to Henry Dearborn, Sept. 23. MS, photostatic copy, archives of the Native Sons of Kansas City, Mo.
1947. "Report on the Fur Trade, 1830," *Oregon Historical Quarterly,* XLVIII (March), 31–32.

CLELAND, ROBERT GLASS
1950. *This Reckless Breed of Men.* New York: Knopf. xv, 361 pp.

CLEMSON, ELI B.
1808. Letter, Nov. 30, to James Wilkinson. MS, photostatic copy in archives of Native Sons of Kansas City, Mo.

CLEVELAND, H. W. A.
1864. *Hints to Riflemen.* New York: D. Appleton. 260 pp.

CLINE, WALTER M.
1942. *The Muzzle-loading Rifle Then and Now.* Huntington, W.Va.: Standard. 162 pp.

COCHRAN, J. WEBSTER
1866. *Cochran's Patent Breech-loading Arms.* New York: E. O. Jenkins. 14 pp.

COLT'S PATENT FIRE ARMS MANUFACTURING CO.
1937. *100th Anniversary Fire Arms Manual.* Hartford: Colt Company. 28 pp.

CONNER, WILLIAM H.
1949. "Eden Park Once Busy Powder Yard," Wilmington (Delaware) *Star,* Jan. 6.

COOKE, PHILIP ST. GEORGE
1857. *Scenes and Adventures in the Army.* Philadelphia: Lindsay and Blackiston. xii, 432 pp.

COUES, ELLIOTT (ed.)
1897. *New Light on the Early History of the Greater Northwest: The Manuscript Journals of Alexander Henry . . . and of David Thompson, 1799–1814.* 3 vols. New York: Harper. Vol. 1, xxviii, 446 pp.

CURTIS, F. S., JR.
1926. "The Influence of Weapons on New Mexico History," *New Mexico Historical Review*, I (July), 324–334.
1927. "Spanish Arms and Armor in the Southwest," *New Mexico Historical Review*, II (April), 107–133.

DAVIDSON, GORDON C.
1918. *The North West Company*. University of California Publications in History, Vol. VII. 349 pp.

DAWSON'S BOOK STORE
1926. *Dawson's Book Catalog No. 45*. Los Angeles. April.

DE VOTO, BERNARD
1943. *The Year of Decision, 1846*. Boston: Little, Brown. xv, 538 pp.
1947. *Across the Wide Missouri*. Boston: Houghton Mifflin. Pp. xxvii, 483.

DEXTER, F. THEODORE
1940. [Advertisement, Deringer trade gun for sale], *The Dexter Antique Arms Trade Journal* (Topeka). Vol. II, No. 1.
1955. Sales List. Weapon Arts Museum, Burbank, Calif. 14 pp., mimeo., 10 photo pls.

DICK, EVERETT
1941. *Vanguards of the Frontier*. New York: Appleton-Century. xvi, 574 pp.

DIDEROT, DENIS
1778–1781. *Encyclopédie au Dictionaire Raisonné des Sciences*. Paris, Briasson, Neufchâtel, and Amsterdam. 45 vols. (Ed. of 1751–1772, 28, vols.; ed. of 1751–1777, 30 vols.)

DILLIN, JOHN G. W.
1924. *The Kentucky Rifle*. Washington, D.C.: National Rifle Association. viii, 133 pp., 126 pls. (Later eds. 1944, 1946.)

DRUM, STELLA M. (ed.)
1920. *John C. Luttig's Journal of a Fur-trading Expedition on the Upper Missouri, 1812–1813*. St. Louis: Missouri Historical Society. 192 pp.

DUNN, WILLIAM E.
1914. "The Apache Mission on the San Saba River," *Southwestern Historical Quarterly*, XVII (April), 379–414.

DU PONT, B. G.
1920. *E. I. Du Pont de Nemours and Company, a History, 1802–1902*. Boston and New York: Houghton-Mifflin. 196 pp.

DU PONT DE NEMOURS POWDER COMPANY
1912. *The History of the E. I. du Pont de Nemours Co.* New York: Business America. 224 pp.

DUTTON, WILLIAM S.
1942. *Du Pont; One Hundred and Forty Years*. New York: Scribner. x, 396 pp.

DYKES, J. C.
1952. "Ranger Reading," *The Brand Book* (Denver: The Westerners), Vol. VIII, No. 8 (Aug.). 9 unnumb. pp.

EDWARDS, WILLIAM B.

1953. *The Story of Colt's Revolver.* Harrisburg: Stackpole. 470 pp., Appendix 82 unnumb. pp., illus.

ELLISON, WILLIAM H. (ed.)

1932. *Adventures of George Nidever.* Lancaster: Lancaster Press. 25 pp. Reprinted from *New Spain and the Anglo-American West: Historical Contributions Presented to Herbert Eugene Bolton,* 2 vols. Also a 1937 ed., Berkeley: University of California Press. xi, 128 pp.

EWERS, JOHN C.

1938. *Role of the Indian in National Expansion,* Part I. Washington, D.C.: National Park Service. 26 mimeo. pp.

1939. *The Role of the Indian in National Expansion,* Part II. Washington, D.C.: National Park Service. iii, 190 mimeo. pp.

1954*a*. Personal letter to Carl P. Russell. March 16. 2 typed pp.

1954*b*. "The Indian Trade of the Upper Missouri before Lewis and Clark," Missouri Historical Society, *Bulletin,* X (July), 429–446.

1956. "The North West Trade Gun," *Alberta Historical Review,* Vol. IV, No. 2. Reprint pp. 1–7.

FFOULKES, CHARLES

1937. *The Gun-Founders of England . . . from the XIV to the XIX Centuries.* Cambridge: The University Press. xii, 133 pp., illus.

FORBES, MAJOR-GENERAL A.

1929. *History of Army Ordnance Service.* London: Medici Society. 3 vols.

FORCE, PETER (comp.)

1836–1846. *Tracts and Other Papers Relating Principally to the Origin, Settlement, and Progress of the Colonies in North America . . . to 1776.*

FORESTER, FRANK (pseud.)

See Herbert, Henry William.

FRÉMONT, CAPTAIN JOHN C.

1845. *Report of the Exploring Expedition to the Rocky Mountains in the Year 1842 and to Oregon and Northern California in the Years 1843–1844.* Washington: Gales and Seton. 693 pp., illus., maps.

1887. *Memoirs of My Life.* Chicago and New York: Belford, Clarke and Co. xix, 655 pp.

FULLER, CLAUD E.

1930. *Springfield Muzzle-loading Shoulder Arms.* New York: Francis Bannerman Sons. 176 pp., illus.

1933. *The Breech-loader in the Service.* Topeka: Arms Reference Club of America. 381 pp., illus.

1946. *The Whitney Firearms.* Huntington, W.Va.: Standard Publications, Inc. xvi, 335 pp., illus.

FULTON, MAURICE GARLAND (ed.)

1941–1944. *Diary & Letters of Josiah Gregg.* Norman: University of Oklahoma Press. 2 vols. Vol. I (1941), Southwestern Enterprises, xvii, 1840–1847; xvii, 413 pp. Vol. II (1944), Excursions in Mexico and California, 1847–1850; xvii, 396 pp.

GARTH, THOMAS R.

1949. "A Report on the Second Season's Excavations at Waiilatpu," *Pacific Northwest Quarterly,* XL (Oct.), 295–315.

GEMMER, J. P. H.

1940. "The Hawken-Gemmer Story," *The Gun Trader* (New London, Ohio), Vol. II, No. 5 (June). 3 pp.

GEORGE, J. N.

1938. *English Pistols and Revolvers.* Onslow County, N.C.: Small-Arms Technical Publishing Company. 256 pp.

GHENT, W. J.

1936. *The Early Far West, A Narrative Outline, 1540–1850.* New York: Tudor. xiv, 412 pp.

GILBERT, E. W.

1933. *The Exploration of Western America.* London: Cambridge University Press. xiii, 233 pp.

GILMORE, JAMES R.

1899. *The Rear-Guard of the Revolution.* New York: Appleton. xv, 317 pp.

1900. *The Advance-Guard of Western Civilization.* New York: Appleton. xiii, 343 pp.

GLUCKMAN, ARCADI

1939. *U. S. Martial Pistols and Revolvers.* Buffalo: Otto Ulbrich, 249 pp., 29 pls.; Appendix, pp. i–xxxvii. Another edition was issued in 1944.

*1948. *U. S. Muskets, Rifles and Carbines.* Buffalo: Otto Ulbrich. 446 pp., Appendix, 20 pls. (The Stackpole Co. now owns the copyright.)

This "flagship of military gun books" provides the best keys to identification of all military models; it is replete with notes on the history of the arms, their manufacturers, and their users and is profusely illustrated.

GLUCKMAN, COLONEL ARCADI, and L. D. SATTERLEE

1940. *See* Satterlee and Gluckman.

1953. *American Gun Makers.* Harrisburg: Stackpole. 243 pp.

GRANCSAY, STEPHEN V.

1950. *Master French Gunsmiths' Designs.* New York: Greenberg. 21 pp., 16 engravings.

GREEN, GEORGE FULLER

See Anderson, 1948, 1949, 1956.

GREENER, W. W.

1881. *The Gun and Its Development.* London: Cassell, Petter, Galpin and Co. 674 pp., illus.

GREGG, JOSIAH
  1905. *Gregg's Commerce of the Prairies; or, The Journal of a Santa Fe Trader, 1831–1839.* (Reprint of New York, 1845, ed.) *In* R. G. Thwaites (ed.), *Early Western Travels,* Vol. XIX, pp. 155–349; Vol. XX, 356 pp.
  1941–1944. *Diary & Letters of Josiah Gregg. See* Fulton.
GRIFFIS, WILLIAM E.
  1921. *The Dutch of the Netherlands in the Making of America.* New York: Holland Society of New York. 13 pp.
GRISWOLD, BERT J. (ed.)
  1927. *Fort Wayne, Gateway of the West, 1802–1813.* Indianapolis: Indiana Library and Historical Department. xi, 690 pp.
GROSE, FRANCIS
  1786. *A Treatise on Ancient Armour and Weapons.* London.
Gun and Cartridge Record
  1952–1954. Vol. I, No. 1 (April, 1952) to Vol. III, No. 3 (June, 1954). Pub. at Chagrin Falls, Ohio.
  1953. [Nervous tension of troops in battle and its effect upon the soldier and his muzzle-loader.] Vol. I, No. 12 (March), p. 4. See also Weller, 1953.
Gun Collector
  Published at Madison, Wis., at irregular intervals. Each issue bears a number.
HAMMOND, GEORGE P. (ed.), and AGAPITO REY (trans.)
  1940. *Narratives of the Coronado Expeditions, 1540–1542.* Albuquerque: University of New Mexico Press. xii, 413 pp.
HANNA, PHIL TOWNSEND
  1951. *Dictionary of California Land Names.* Los Angeles: Automobile Club of Southern California. xxii, 392 pp.
HANSON, CHARLES E., JR.
  1955. *The Northwest Gun.* Nebraska State Historical Society Publications in Anthropology, No. 2. Lincoln: Nebraska State Historical Society. xii, 85 pp.
HARRINGTON, J. C.
  1954a. "Fort Necessity—Scene of George Washington's First Battle," Society of Architectural Historians, *Journal,* Vol. XIII, No. 2, pp. 25–27.
  1954b. Personal letter to Carl P. Russell, Dec. 21, 1954. MS.
HART, S. H., and A. B. HULBERT (eds.)
  1932. *Zebulon Pike's Arkansas Journal.* Denver Public Library. lxii, 200 pp.
HATCHER, JULIAN S.
  1947. *Hatcher's Notebook.* Harrisburg, Pa.: Military Service Publishing Co. 488 pp.
  1949. "This Stuff, Gunpowder," *American Rifleman.* Vol. XCVII, No. 8 (Aug.), pp. 32–34.

HAVEN, CHARLES T., and FRANK A. BELDEN
  1940. *A History of the Colt Revolver and the Other Arms Made by Colt's Patent Firearms Manufacturing Company from 1836 to 1940.* New York: Morrow. xxiii, 711 pp.
HAWKEN, SAMUEL
  N.d. "Testimony re Hawken's Rifles." MS in Jefferson National Expansion Memorial, St. Louis, Mo.
HAWKER, P.
  1838. *Instructions to Young Sportsmen.* London (8th ed.). 549 pp., illus.
HAWKS, EDWARD A.
  1940. "The Indian Buffalo Gun," *The Gun Report* (Akron, Ohio), Vol. I, No. 5, pp. 1–2.
HENRY, ALEXANDER
  1897. *See* Coues, Elliott.
HERBERT, HENRY WILLIAM
  1849. *Field Sports.* New York: Stringer and Townsend. 2 vols.
HICKS, MAJOR JAMES E.
  1938. *Notes on French Ordnance.* Mt. Vernon, N.Y.: Hicks, photoprinted. 287 pp.
  *1940a. *Notes on United States Ordnance.* Mount Vernon, N.Y.: Hicks. 2 vols.

This work identifies military small arms, 1776 to 1940, and it includes many government reports and War Department correspondence not in other printed sources. Illustrated with 80 plates of pen-and-ink drawings by André Jandot.

  1940b. *Nathan Starr: US Arms and Sword Maker.* Mount Vernon, N.Y.: Hicks. 166 pp., illus.
HINKLE, FREDERICK W.
  1908. *Army Rifles.* Cincinnati: Ohio Commandery of the Loyal Legion. 20 pp.
HINKLE, GEORGE, and BLISS HINKLE
  1949. *Sierra Nevada Lakes.* New York: Bobbs-Merrill. 383 pp.
HODGE, FREDERICK WEBB (ed.)
  1907–1910. *Handbook of American Indians North of Mexico.* Washington. Bureau of American Ethnology, Bulletin 30. 2 vols.
HOPKINS, ALFRED F.
  1942. Report on Indian Trade Objects Purchased by the US Government through its several Superintendents of Indian Trade at Philadelphia and Georgetown, D.C., 1801–1822. Washington: National Park Service. Typed MS, 56 pp.
HORN, R. F. (ed.)
  N.d. *Colt 1836 to 1857.* Reprint of "A Day at the Armory of Colt" (1857). Grosse Point Woods, Mich.: O. Heinrich and H. Lewis. 29 pp.
HOUCK, LOUIS (ed.)
  1909. *The Spanish Regime in Missouri.* Chicago: Donnelly. 2 vols.

HOUSTON, AUBREY ("SAM")

1954. Letter to Carl P. Russell, Jan. 28. MS. (Summary history of mining saltpeter in Mammoth Cave.) 3 typed pp.

HUDSON'S BAY COMPANY

1955. *A Brief History of the Hudson's Bay Company*. Winnipeg: Hudson's Bay Co. 44 pp.

HULBERT, ARCHER BUTLER

1933. *Where Rolls the Oregon*. Denver: Colorado College and Denver Public Library. xv, 244 pp.

INNIS, HAROLD A.

1930. *The Fur Trade in Canada*. New Haven: Yale University Press. 444 pp., illus., map.

IRVING, WASHINGTON

1849. *The Adventures of Captain Bonneville*. New York. xii, 428 pp. (First ed. 1837.)

JACKSON, HERBERT J.

1923. *European Hand Firearms of the 16th, 17th, and 18th Centuries*. London: Chiswick Press. (Pagination by chapters; profusely illustrated.)

JACOBS, WILBUR R.

1948. "Presents to Indians along the French Frontiers in the Old Northwest, 1748–1763," *Indiana Magazine of History*, XLIV (Sept.), 245–256.

JAMES, EDWIN (comp.)

1905. *Account of an Expedition from Pittsburgh to the Rocky Mountains . . . 1819, 1820 . . . under the Command of Maj. S. H. Long of the U. S. Top. Engineers*. (Reprint of London, 1823, ed.) *In* R. G. Thwaites (ed.), *Early Western Travels*, Vols. XIV–XVII.

JENKINS, JOHN W.

1946. Letter to Carl P. Russell, Oct. 31. MS.

JENKINS, PAUL B.

1934. "The Story of the Primer." *Arms Review*, Vol. I, No. 1. 11 pp.

JOHNSON, MELVIN M., JR., and C. T. HAVEN

1943. *Ammunition; History, Development, and Use*. New York: Morrow. xii, 361 pp.

KAUFFMAN, HENRY J.

1952. *Early American Gunsmiths, 1650–1850*. Harrisburg: Stackpole. xx, 94 pp.

KELLOGG, LOUISE

1935. *The French Regime in Wisconsin*. Madison: Wisconsin State Historical Society. xvii, 361 pp.

KENDALL, DR. ARTHUR I.

1941. *Rifle Making in the Great Smoky Mountains*. Washington. National Park Service Popular Study Series, *History*, No. 13. 34 pp.

Bibliography 367

KIDD, KENNETH E.
1955. Personal letter and attachments pertaining to French arms. MS, 5 typed pp.

KINZIE, MRS. JOHN H. [JULIETTE A.]
1856. *Wau-bun, the Early Day in the North-West.* New York: Derby and Jackson. xii, 498 pp.

KIRKE, EDMUND (pseud.)
See Gilmore, James R.

KURZ, RUDOLPH FRIEDERICH
1937. *Journal of Rudolph Friederich Kurz; an Account of His Experiences among Fur Traders and American Indians on the Mississippi and the Upper Missouri River During the Years 1846 to 1852.* Trans. by Myrtis Jarrell; ed. by J. N. B. Hewitt. Washington. Bureau of American Ethnology, Bulletin 115. ix, 382 pp.; 48 pls.

LAHONTAN, BARON DE
1905. *New Voyages to North-America.* Ed. by Reuben Gold Thwaites. Chicago: McClurg. 2 vols. (Reprint of the English ed. of 1703.)

LAROCQUE, FRANÇOIS ANTOINE
1910. *Journal of Larocque from the Assiniboine to the Yellowstone, 1805.* Ottawa. Publications of the Canadian Archives, No. 3. 82 pp.

LAUT, AGNES C.
1908. *The Conquest of the Great Northwest.* New York: Outing Publishing Co. 2 vols.

LEMOYNE, JACQUES
1875. *Narrative.* Translated from Latin of De Bry, with heliotypes of engravings taken from Lemoyne's original drawings. B. F. Perkins trans. Boston: Osgood. 15 pp., 44 pls., map, facsim. *See also* Lorant, 1946.

LEONARD, ZENAS
1904. *Leonard's Narrative; Adventures of Zenas Leonard, Fur Trader and Trapper, 1831–1836.* Ed. by W. F. Wagner. Cleveland: Burrows Bros. 317 pp., map, illus. Reprinted from the orig. ed. of 1839.

LEVINGE, CAPT. R. G. A.
1846. *Echoes from the Backwoods; or, Sketches of Transatlantic Life.* London: H. Colburn. 2 vols. Vol. II, pp. 1–258.

LEWIS, ANNA
1924. "La Harpe's First Expedition in Oklahoma," *Chronicles of Oklahoma,* II (Dec.), 331–349.

LEWIS, MAJOR B. R.
1947. "Sam Colt's Repeating Pistol," Parts 1 and 2, *American Rifleman,* Vol. XC, No. 5 (May), pp. 31–33; No. 6 (June), pp. 23–25, 32.
1953. "Capt. Wheeler's Revolving Guns," *American Rifleman,* Vol. CI, No. 4 (April), pp. 38–40.
1954. Personal letter to Carl P. Russell, March 8. MS.

LEWIS, MERIWETHER

1809. "Orders to Missouri Militia, the Louisiana Spies," *Missouri Gazette* (St. Louis), April 3, 12, and 24.

LEWIS, MERIWETHER, and WILLIAM CLARK

1904–1905. *Original Journals of the Lewis and Clark Expedition, 1804–1806.* Ed. by Reuben Gold Thwaites. New York: Dodd Mead. xiii, 273 pp. 8 vols. in 15 books.

LEWIS, WILLIAM S., and PAUL C. PHILLIPS (eds.)

1923. *The Journal of John Work.* Cleveland: A. H. Clark. 209 pp.

LONG, S. H.

See James, 1905.

LORANT, STEFAN

1946. *The New World: The First Pictures of America.* New York: Duell, Sloan and Pearce. 292 pp.

Louisiana Gazette, St. Louis, Mo.

Succeeded *Missouri Gazette* on Nov. 30, 1809 (Vol. II, No. 71). In July, 1812, title was changed back to *Missouri Gazette.*

McBARRON, H. CHARLES

1949. "U. S. Mounted Ranger Battalion, 1832–1833," *Military Collector and Historian* (Washington), Vol. I, No. 4, pp. 5–6, pl. 16.

MACKAY, DOUGLAS

1949. *The Honourable Company.* Toronto: McClelland and Stewart. 396 pp., illus.

McKENNEY, THOMAS L., and JAMES HALL

1933. *The Indian Tribes of North America.* Edinburgh: John Grant. 3 vols. Previous editions: 1836, 1837, 1838, 1842, 1844, 1848–1850, 1854, 1855, 1856, 1858, 1865, 1868, 1870, and 1872–1874.

MAHAN, D. H. (Professor of Engineering, U. S. Military Academy)

1846. *A Treatise on Field Fortifications.* New York: Wiley and Putnam. 168 pp., 12 pls. (1st ed. was 1836.)

MANUCY, ALBERT

1949. *Artillery through the Ages.* Washington. National Park Service Interpretive Series, *History,* Vol. 3. 92 pp.

MAYER, DR. J. R.

1942. "Cornelis Wynkoop's Musket," *Museum Service* (bulletin of Rochester Museum of Arts and Sciences), April.

1943a. "Flintlocks of the Iroquois, 1620–1687," Rochester Museum of Arts and Sciences, *Research Records,* No. 6, pp. 1–59.

1943b. Letter addressed to Carl P. Russell, Sept. 30. MS.

MERK, FREDERICK

1931. *Fur Trade and Empire.* Cambridge, Mass.: Harvard University Press. xxvi, 370 pp., map.

METSCHL, JOHN

1928. "The Rudolph J. Nunnemacher Collection of Projectile Arms," Parts I and II, Public Museum of the City of Milwaukee, *Bulletin,* Vol. IX. 1017 pp., 20 text figs., 113 pls.

Military Collector & Historian. Washington, D.C.
1949–

Missouri Gazette
1808–1822. Title changed to *Louisiana Gazette,* Dec., 1809, then back to first title, July, 1812. Continued through March 6, 1822, when it was succeeded by *Missouri Republican* (1822–1919).

MITCHELL, JAMES L.
1947. "United States Musket Model 1795," *Antiques,* LI (Feb.), 122–123.

MONTECUCULI, GENERALISSIME
1772. *Memoirs.* (Trans. from Italian into French.)

MORDECAI, MAJ. A. (comp.)
1861. The Ordnance Manual for the Use of Officers of the United States Army. 2d (Confederate) ed. Charleston, S.C. xx, 475 pp., 19 pl.

The Confederate revision of the 1841 and 1850 editions. The text harks back to the 1830's; flintlock mechanisms and the earlier procedures, as well as the percussion armament, are given thorough treatment. My copy, an "association" relic of the Civil War, is inscribed on the fly leaf: "To Lt. A. H. Russell by E. F. Dodge. Captured this day at Richmond, Va. Apr. 4th, 1865."

MORGAN, DALE
1953. *Jedediah Smith.* New York: Bobbs-Merrill. 458 pp.

MUMEY, NOLIE
1931. *The Life of Jim Baker, 1818–1898.* Denver: World Press. xiii, 234 pp.

NASATIR, ABRAHAM P.
1922. "The Chouteaus and the Indian Trade of the West, 1764–1852." M.A. thesis, typed MS, University of California Library. iv, 280 pp.

NASATIR, ABRAHAM P. (ed.)
1952. *Before Lewis and Clark: Documents, 1785–1804.* St. Louis Historical Documents Foundation. 2 vols.

National Geographic Magazine
1953. "Historical Map of the United States," Vol. CIII, June.

NORTH, S. N. D., and RALPH H. NORTH
1913. *Simeon North First Official Pistol Maker of the United States.* Concord, N.H.: North. xii, 207 pp.

NORTON, CHARLES B.
1880. *American Inventions and Improvements in Breech-loading Small Arms.* Springfield, Mass. 407 pp.

NUTE, GRACE LEE
1931. *The Voyageur.* New York and London: D. Appleton. viii, 289 pp.
1945. *Calendar of the American Fur Company's Papers.* Washington. American Historical Association, *Report for the Year 1944,* Vol. II, 1831–1840; Vol. III, 1841–1849.

O'CALLAGHAN, EDMUND B.
1853–1887. *Documents Relative to the Colonial History of the State of New York.* New York. 15 vols.

OGG, F. A.
1904. *The Opening of the Mississippi.* New York: Macmillan. xi, 670 pp.

OMMUNDSEN, H., and E. H. ROBINSON
1915. *Rifles and Ammunition.* New York and London: Funk and Wagnalls.

PADEN, IRENE D.
1943. *The Wake of the Prairie Schooner.* New York: Macmillan. xix, 514 pp.

PALMER, GEORGE A.
1956. Personal letter, Feb. 15, with photographs and descriptive matter pertaining to Hall Rifle Works.

PALMER, LT. LORING
1818. Receipt for ordnance and ordnance stores, Fort Osage, Jan. 9. MS, photostatic copy in archives of Native Sons of Kansas City, Mo.

PARKER, SAMUEL
1838. *Journal of an Exploring Tour Beyond the Rocky Mountains.* Ithaca, N.Y. xii, 371 pp.

PARKMAN, FRANCIS
1920. *The Oregon Trail: Sketches of Prairie and Rocky Mountain Life.* New York: Macmillan. 362 pp.

PARSONS, JOHN E.
1942. *Catalog of a Loan Exhibition of Percussion Colt Revolvers 1836–1873.* New York: Metropolitan Museum of Art. x, 41 pp., 40 pls.
1949a. *Sam'l Colt's Own Record of Transactions with Capt. Walker and Eli Whitney, Jr. in 1847.* Hartford: Connecticut Historical Society. 157 pp.
1949b. "Samuel Colt's Medals from American Institute," New York Historical Society, *Quarterly,* XXXIII (July), 189–201.
1952a. *Henry Deringer's Pocket Pistol.* New York: William Morrow. 242 pp., illus.
1952b. "Gunmakers for the American Fur Company," New York Historical Society, *Quarterly,* XXXVI (April), 181–193.

PATTIE, JAMES OHIO
1905. *Pattie's Personal Narrative. In* R. G. Thwaites (ed.), *Early Western Travels,* Vol. XVIII. (Reprint of Cincinnati, 1831, ed.) 379 pp., illus.

PELZER, LOUIS (ed.)
1943. *The Prairie Logbooks; Dragoon Companies to the Pawnee Villages in 1844, and to the Rocky Mountains in 1845, by Lieutenant James Henry Carleton.* Chicago: Caxton Club. xviii, 295 pp.

PETERS, CAL. N.
1953. Personal letter to Carl P. Russell, Dec. 1. 1 typed page, 2 photographs of flint caps.

PETERSON, HAROLD L.
1947a. "The Military Equipment of the Plymouth and Bay Colonies, 1620–1690," *The New England Quarterly,* XX (June), 197–208.

1947b. "The Lost U.S. Repeating Flintlock," *The Gun Collectors Letter,* No. 14 (July 22), pp. 1–5.

1949. Memorandum to Herbert Kahler, National Park Service, Washington, D.C., Dec. 19. 4 typed pp.

1953. "Early Paper Cartridges," *American Rifleman,* Vol. CI, No. 2 (Feb.), pp. 33, 67.

N.d.(*a*). "American Colonial Arms and Armor." [Eighteenth-century arms.] 85 typed pp.

N.d.(*b*). "Sixteenth and Seventeenth-Century Arms." 53 typed pp.

POLLARD, MAJOR H. B. C.
1926. *A History of Firearms.* London: Geoffrey Bles. 320 pp., illus.

POWELL, PHILIP WAYNE
1952. *Soldiers, Indians, and Silver: The Northward Advance of New Spain, 1550–1600.* Berkeley and Los Angeles: University of California Press. 317 pp.

PRATT, JULIUS W.
1925. *Expansionists of 1812.* New York: Macmillan. 309 pp.

QUAIFE, MILO M. (ed.)
1923. *Alexander Ross's Adventures of the First Settlers on the Oregon or Columbia River.* Chicago: Lakeside Press. 388 pp. Ross's book was first published in London in 1849.

REVOIL, BENEDICT H.
1865. *Shooting and Fishing in North America.* London: Tinsley Bros. 2 vols. Vol. I, 291 pp.

RILING, RAY
1951. *Guns and Shooting, a Selected Chronological Bibliography.* New York: Greenberg. xviii, 434 pp.

ROBERTS, NED H.
1944. *The Muzzle-loading Cap-Lock Rifle.* Manchester, N.H.: Clarke Press. xvi, 528 pp. A 1952 ed. was published by Stackpole and Heck, Harrisburg, Pa., now The Stackpole Company, Harrisburg, Pa.

RODENBOUGH, T. F.
1875. *From Everglade to Cañon with the Second Dragoons . . . 1836–1875.* New York. 561 pp.

ROEMER, J.
1863. *Cavalry; Its History, Management, and Uses in War.* New York: Van Nostrand. 515 pp.

ROHAN, JACK
1935. *Yankee Arms Maker; the Incredible Career of Samuel Colt.* New York: Harper. xii, 301 pp., illus.

ROSS, ALEXANDER
1849. See Quaife, 1923.

RUSSELL, CARL P.
1940. "The American Rifle at the Battle of Kings Mountain," *The Regional*

RUSSELL, CARL P. (*Continued*)
>   *Review*, Vol. V, No. 1 (July), pp. 15–21. Reprinted in National Park
>   Service Popular Studies, *History*, No. 12 (1941), pp. 8–18.
>   1944. "The Trade Musket," *Muzzle Blasts*, June, pp. 4–5, 11.
>   1945. "Trapper Trails to the Sisk-ke-dee," *Annals of Wyoming*, XVII
>   (July), 89–105.

RUSSELL, DON
>   1954. Personal letter to Carl P. Russell, March 20, about United States
>   military history. 7 typed pp.

RUSSELL, OSBORNE
>   1921. *Journal of a Trapper; or, Nine Years in the Rocky Mountains, 1834–
>   1843*. Boise, Idaho: Syms-York. 149 pp.

SABIN, EDWIN L.
>   1914. *Kit Carson Days, 1809–1868*. Chicago: McClurg. 2 vols. 669 pp.
>   (numbered consecutively).

Sacramento *Bee*
>   1941. "The Fremont Cannon," Sacramento *Bee*, Sept. 20, magazine section,
>   p. 3.

SAGE, RUFUS B.
>   1855. *Wild Scenes in Kansas and Nebraska, the Rocky Mountains, Oregon,
>   California, New Mexico, Texas, and the Grand Prairies*. Philadelphia.
>   303 pp.

SATTERLEE, L. D.
>   1939. *A Catalog of Firearms for the Collector*. Detroit: Privately printed.
>   334 pp., illus.

SATTERLEE, L. D., and ARCADI GLUCKMAN
>   1940. *American Gun Makers*. Buffalo: Ulbrich. 186 pp.
>   1953. *See* Gluckman and Satterlee.

SAWYER, CHARLES WINTHROP
>   1910. *Firearms in American History, 1600 to 1800*. Boston: Publ. by author.
>   237 pp., illus.
>   1911. *Firearms in American History: The Revolver 1800–1911*. Boston.
>   216 pp.
>   1920. *Our Rifles*. Boston: Cornhill. 409 pp., illus. Editions of 1941 and
>   1946 were published by Williams Book Store, Boston.

SCHAEFER, JOSEPH
>   1932. *Wisconsin Lead Region*. Madison. Wisconsin State Historical Society,
>   *Domesday Book* III. vi, 341 pp., 3 maps.

SCHMIDT, RODOLPHE
>   1877. *Les Armes a feu portatives*. Paris. 195 pp., 58 color pls. (French ed.
>   of *Handfeuer Waffen*, 1875.)

SCHOEN, CAPTAIN J.
>   1855. *Rifled Infantry Arms . . . Adopted in the Various European Armies*.
>   Trans. from the German by J. Gorgas. Dresden.

1858. *Geschichte der Handfeuerwaffen . . . von ihrem Entstehen bis auf die Neuzeit*. Dresden.

SCHOOLCRAFT, H. R.
1819. *A View of the Lead Mines of Missouri*. New York: Charles Wiley. 299 pp.

SCOFFERN, JOHN
1860. *The Royal Rifle Match on Wimbledon Common*. London. 96 pp.

SCOTT, MAJOR-GENERAL WINFIELD (comp.)
1821. *General Regulations for the Army; or Military Institutes*. Philadelphia: M. Carey and Sons. Pt. I, pp. 13–355, fold. tables.
1859. *Infantry Tactics in Three Volumes*. Vol. I, School of the Soldier and School of the Company. New York: Harper. 202 pp. (Earlier eds. carry many details back to 1834. The 3-volume work appeared first in 23d. Cong., 2d sess., H. Doc. 121, 1835.)

SECOY, FRANK RAYMOND
1953. *Changing Military Patterns of the Great Plains*. Locust Valley, N.Y. Monographs of the American Ethnological Society, XXI. viii, 112 pp.

SERVEN, JAMES E.
1946. *Paterson Pistols*. Dallas, Texas: Carl Metzger. 32 pp., illus.
1952. *Firearms and Accessories Featuring the Charles D. Cook Collection*. Santa Ana, Calif.: Foundation Press. 55 pp., illus.
1954. *Colt Firearms 1836–1954*. Santa Ana: Serven Gun Room. ix, 385 pp., illus.

SHARPE, PHILIP B.
1938. *The Rifle in America*. New York: William Morrow. 641 pp.

SHIELDS, J. W., JR.
1954. *From Flintlock to M 1*. New York: Coward-McCann. 220 pp.

SHIRK, GEORGE H.
1950. "Peace on the Plains," *Chronicles of Oklahoma*, XXVIII (Spring), 2–41.

SIBLEY, GEORGE C.
1808. Diary of George C. Sibley, Indian Agent, Fort Osage. MS in Sibley Collection, Lindenwood College for Women, St. Charles, Mo. (Dr. Kate L. Gregg, Curator).

SMITH, CARLYLE S.
1955. Sketches and personal letter to C. P. Russell, March 1, regarding cannon at Kipp's Post. MS.

SMYTH, COLONEL ALEXANDER
1812. *Regulations for the Field Exercise, Manoeuvers and Conduct of the Infantry of the United States*. Philadelphia: Fry and Kemmerer. xv, 225 pp., 34 pls.

SPARKS, JARED (ed.)
1840. *The Works of Benjamin Franklin*. Boston: Hilliard, Gray. 10 vols.

STADT MUSEUM, VIENNA
1886. *Katalog des Waffen Museums*. Vienna.

STEEN, CHARLIE R.

    1953. "Two Early Historic Sites on the Southern Plains," *Texas Archeological Society Bulletin,* XXIV (Oct.), 177–188.

STEVENS, WAYNE E.

    1926. *The Northwest Fur Trade, 1763–1800.* Urbana. University of Illinois Studies in the Social Sciences, XIV, No. 3 (Sept.). 204 pp.

STEVENS, WILLIAM

    1797. *A System for the Discipline of the Artillery of the US Army.* New York. 206 pp., 22 pls.

STONE, IRVING

    1944. *Immortal Wife, the Biographical Novel of Jessie Benton Fremont.* Garden City, N.Y.: Doubleday. 456 pp.

STONEHENGE (pseudonym of John Henry Walsh)

    1859. *The Shot-gun and Sporting Rifle.* London: Routledge, Warne, and Routledge. xvi, 448 pp.

SULLIVAN, JAMES (ed.)

    1921. *The Papers of Sir William Johnson.* Albany: University of New York. Vol. III. xiv, 997 pp.

SULLIVAN, MAURICE S.

    1936. *Jedediah Smith, Trader and Trailbreaker.* New York: Press of the Pioneers. xiii, 233 pp.

SWANTON, JOHN R.

    1922. *Early History of the Creek Indians and Their Neighbors.* Washington. Bureau of American Ethnology, Bulletin 73. 492 pp.

    1946. *The Indians of the Southeastern United States.* Washington. Bureau of American Ethnology, Bulletin 137. 943 pp.

    *1952. *The Indian Tribes of North America.* Washington. Bureau of American Ethnology, Bulletin 145, vi, 726 pp., 5 maps.

The master plan for showing the distribution of tribes. It is a dependable guide for the usage of tribal names, estimation of populations, and establishment of dates in the history of intertribal relationships and contacts between the Indian and the white man.

THOMAS, A. B.

    1924. "The Massacre of the Villasur Expedition at the Forks of the Platte River, August 12, 1720," *Nebraska History Magazine,* VII (July–Sept.), 67–81.

THOMAS, A. B. (ed.)

    1935. *After Coronado.* Norman, Okla.: University of Oklahoma Press. xii, 307 pp.

    1941. *Teodore de Croix and the Northern Frontier of New Spain, 1776–1783.* Norman: University of Oklahoma Press. xiii, 273 pp.

THOMAS, CHAUNCEY

    1930. "Frontier Firearms," *The Colorado Magazine,* VII (May), 102–109.

THOMPSON, DAVID
　1916. *See* Tyrrell, 1916.
THWAITES, REUBEN GOLD (ed.)
　1904–1907. *Early Western Travels, 1748–1846: A Series of Annotated Reprints of Travels in the Middle and Far West.* Cleveland: A. H. Clark. 32 vols. *See also* Brackenridge, Gregg, James, Pattie.
　1904–1905. See Lewis, Meriwether, and William Clark.
　1905. See Lahontan, Baron de.
TILBERG, FREDERICK
　1954. *Fort Necessity Battlefield Site.* Washington. National Park Service Historical Handbook Series, No. 19, 44 pp.
TILING, MORITZ
　1913. *The German Element in Texas, 1820–1850.* Houston, Texas: M. Tiling. viii, 225 pp.
TODD, FREDERICK P.
　1941. *Soldiers of the American Army, 1775–1941.* New York: H. Bittner. 24 pls. (drawings by Fritz Kredel).
TRYON, CHARLES Z.
　1911. The History of a Business. Philadelphia: Edward K. Tryon.
TURNER, FREDERICK J.
　1891. *The Character and Influence of the Indian Trade in Wisconsin.* Baltimore. Johns Hopkins University Studies in Historical and Political Science, 9th ser., XI–XII. 75 pp.
　1906. *Rise of the New West, 1819–29.* New York: Harper. xvii, 366 pp.
　1921. *The Frontier in American History.* New York: Henry Holt. 375 pp.
TYRRELL, J. B. (ed.)
　1916. *David Thompson's Narrative of His Explorations in Western America, 1784–1812.* Toronto. The Champlain Society Publications, Vol. XII. xcviii, 582 pp.
UPTON, EMORY (Maj.-Gen. U.S.A.)
　1904. *The Military Policy of the United States.* Washington, D.C.: Government Printing Office. xxiii, 495 pp.
U. S. CARTRIDGE COMPANY
　N.d. *Illustrated Catalogue of U. S. Cartridge Company's Collection of Firearms at Lowell, Mass.* Boston: Conant. 140 pp., illus. (An edition of 1902 had 104 pp.)
U. S. CONGRESS
　1789–1838. *American State Papers, Military Affairs.* 1st Congress through 25th Congress. Washington: Gales and Seton. 7 vols. (A reprinting of what was considered to be the most important government documents in the field of military affairs for the period indicated. Papers are numbered consecutively through the seven volumes, but these numbers bear no relation to the original documents and are not to be confused with the numbering of the originals.)

U. S. CONGRESS (*Continued*)

1789–1838. *American State Papers, Public Lands.* Vol. VIII.

1818. Documents in Relation to the Seminole War. Dec. 3. 15th Cong. 2d sess., H. Doc. 14. 165 pp.

1822*a*. A Report of the Sec. of State with Documents Relating to a Misunderstanding between Andrew Jackson, Act. Gov. of the Floridas and Elijius Fromentin, Judge of a Court Therein. Jan. 29. 17th Cong., 1st sess. H. Doc. 42. 326 pp.

1822*b*. Committee on Indian Affairs. Documents Relative to Indian Trade. Feb. 11, 1822. 17th Cong., 1st sess., S. Doc. 60. 62 pp.

1822*c*. Committee on Naval Affairs. Reports of Committees, Vol. 1. Report . . . on Naval Stores. Statement of the Condition of Navy Ordnance and Ordnance Stores. March 4. 17th Cong., 1st sess., H. Rept. 55. 32 pp.

1822*d*. Report of the Secretary of War. *In* Message from the President of the U.S. March 9, 1822. 17th Cong., 2d sess., H. Doc. 91.

1823*a*. Report of the Secretary of War . . . Expenses of the Ordnance Department for the Years 1817 . . . 1822. *In* Message of the President of the U.S. Jan. 6. 17th Cong., 2d sess., H. Doc. 111, Pts. 1 and 2. (See Pt. 1, pp. 11, 65, 178, 183.)

1823*b*. Documents Relating to an Establishment at the Mouth of the Columbia River. *In* Message from the President of the U.S. Communicating the Letter of Mr. Prevost and Other Documents. Jan. 27. 17th Cong., 2d sess., H. Doc. 45, pp. 1–65.

1823*c*. Letter from the Secretary of War . . . Expenditures at the National Armories and of the Arms Made and Repaired Therein . . . 1822. Feb. 15, 1823. 17th Cong., 2d sess., H. Doc. 69. 3 pp. and fold. table.

1823*d*. Message from the President of the U.S. . . . Expenditures of the Ordnance Department [1817–1821]. Feb. 17. 17th Cong., 2d sess., H. Doc. 73, 16 pp. and 13 fold. tables.

1823*e*. Letter of Col. Bomford . . . to the Secretary of War, Relative to the Number of Arms Required to Supply the Militia of the West. Feb. 24. 17th Cong., 2d sess., H. Doc. 83. 6 pp.

1823*f*. Treaty of Ghent and the Treaty with Spain in 1819. March 1. 17th Cong., 2d sess., H. Doc. 91. 15 pp.

1823*g*. Correspondence Relative to Hostilities of the Arikaree Indians. *In* Message from the President of the U.S. Dec. 2. 18th Cong., 1st sess., H. Doc. 2, pp. 55–108.

1823*h*. Report of the Secretary of War, 1823. Dec. 2. 18th Cong., 1st sess., S. Doc. 1, pp. 8–109, 17 fold. tables.

1824*a*. Contracts for Cannon . . . Muskets, etc., 1820–1823. Jan. 6, 1824. 18th Cong., 1st sess., H. Doc. 23. 43 pp.

1824*b*. Moneys Appropriated for the Military Establishment, 1823. Jan. 23, 1824. 18th Cong., 1st sess., H. Doc. 45, pp. 1–80 and 3 fold. tables.

1824*c*. Message from the President of the U.S. . . . Transmitting a Report on the Expenditures of the Ordnance Dept. . . . Feb. 12. 18th Cong., 1st sess., H. Doc. 73. 179 pp.

1824*d*. Report of the Secretary of War, 1824. Dec. 7. 18th Cong., 2d sess., S. Doc. 1, pp. 57–108.

1825*a*. Indian Agents' Disbursements for 1824. 18th Cong., 2d sess., S. Doc. 109, pp. 8 and 10, and sheet 32.

1825*b*. Letter of the Secretary of the Treasury . . . on the Commerce and Navigation of the United States . . . for the Year Ending 30th Sept., 1824. Feb. 17, 1825. 18th Cong., 2d sess., H. Doc. 90. 304 pp.

1825*c*. Report of the Secretary of War, 1825. Dec. 6. 19th Cong., 1st sess., S. Doc. 2, pp. 8–92.

1826*a*. Letter from the Secretary of War Transmitting a Report . . . Trade with the Indian Tribes. March 1. 19th Cong., 1st sess., H. Doc. 112. 115 pp.

1826*b*. Memorial of the State of Missouri and Documents in Relation to Indian Depredations . . . March 6. 19th Cong., 1st sess., S. Doc. 55. 90 pp.

1826*c*. Letter from the Secretary of War Transmitting Information . . . Respecting the Movement of the Expedition which Lately Ascended the Missouri River. March 6. 19th Cong., 1st sess., H. Doc. 117. 16 pp.

1826*d*. Report of the Secretary of War, 1826. Dec. 5. 19th Cong., 2d sess., S. Doc. 1, pp. 173–516.

1827*a*. Letter of the Secretary of the Treasury on Commerce and Navigation of the . . . United States During the Year Ending . . . Sept. 30, 1826. Feb. 26, 1827. 19th Cong., 2d sess., H. Doc. 120. 296 pp.

1827*b*. Message of the President of the U.S. Dec. 4. 20th Cong., 1st sess., S. Doc. 1. 265 pp.

1827*c*. Report of the Secretary of War, 1827. Dec. 4. 20th Cong., 1st sess., H. Doc. 2, pp. 39–196.

1828. Report of the Secretary of War, 1828. Dec. 2. 20th Cong., 2d sess., H. Doc. 2, pp. 17–110.

1829*a*. Report of the Secretary of War, 1829. Dec. 8. 21st Cong., 1st sess., S. Doc. 1, pp. 21–32, 49–219.

1829*b*. Message of the President of the U.S. Dec. 8. 21st Cong., 1st sess., H. Doc. 2, pp. 1–328.

1830. Report of the Secretary of War, 1830. Dec. 7. 21st Cong., 2d sess., S. Doc. 1, pp. 81–200.

1831*a*. Message from the President of the U.S. . . . Relative to the British Establishments on the Columbia . . . etc. 21st Cong., 2d sess., S. Doc. 39. 36 pp.

1831*b*. Report of the Secretary of War, 1831. Dec. 6. 22d Cong., 1st sess., H. Doc. 2, pp. 25, 153–224.

1832*a*. Message from the President of the U.S. . . . Concerning the Fur Trade and Inland Trade to Mexico. March 5. 22d Cong., 1st sess., S. Doc. 90. 86 pp.

U. S. CONGRESS (*Continued*)

1832*b*. Report of the Secretary of War, 1832. Dec. 4. 22d Cong., 2d sess., H. Doc. 2, pp. 17–201.

1833. Report of the Secretary of War, 1833. Dec. 3. 23d Cong., 1st sess., S. Doc. 1, pp. 51–273.

1834. Report of the Secretary of War, 1834. Dec. 2. 23d Cong., 2d sess., S. Doc. 1, pp. 25–32, 49–298.

1835*a*. Infantry Tactics, by Gen. Winfield Scott. 23d Cong., 2d sess., H. Doc. 121, pp. 3–301. Vol. I, Schools of the Soldier and Company. Vol. II, School of the Battalion, and Instruction for Light Infantry or Rifle. Vol. III, Evolution of the Line.

1835*b*. Report of the Secretary of War, 1835. Dec. 8. 24th Cong., 1st sess., S. Doc. 1, pp. 43–327.

1836*a*. Letter from the Secretary of War in Regard to . . . Ordnance and Ordnance Stores. Jan. 5. 24th Cong., 1st sess., H. Doc. 44. 366 pp.

1836*b*. Col. Dodge's Journal. March 21. 24th Cong., 1st sess., H. Doc. 181. 37 pp., 2 maps.

1836*c*. Report . . . Regarding the Seminole Hostilities and Measures Taken to Suppress Them. June 3. 24th Cong., 1st sess., H. Doc. 271. 272 pp.

1836*d*. Documents in Relation to the Hostilities of the Creek Indians. June 6. 24th Cong., 1st sess., H. Doc. 276. 413 pp.

1836*e*. Report of the Secretary of War, 1836. Dec. 6. 24th Cong., 2d sess., S. Doc. 1, pp. 106–457.

1837*a*. Report of the Secretary of War, 1837. Dec. 5. 25th Cong., 1st sess., S. Doc. 1, pp. 171–713.

1837*b*. Report of a Board of Officers, 1837, Regarding the Examination of Hall, Cochran, Colt, and Baron Hackett Firearms. 25th Cong., 1st sess., S. Doc. 15. 27 pp.

1837*c*. Report of a Board of Officers on the Examination of Certain Firearms. 25th Cong., 1st sess., S. Doc. 29. 15 pp.

1838*a*. Letter from the Secretary of War . . . Proceedings of a Court of Inquiry . . . in Relation to Operations against the Seminole and Creek Indians. Jan. 8. 25th Cong., 2d sess., H. Doc. 78. 832 pp. with app. of 85 pp.

1838*b*. Report of the Secretary of War, 1838. Dec. 4. 25th Cong., 3d sess., S. Doc. 1, pp. 98–593.

1839. Report of the Secretary of War, 1839. Dec. 24. 26th Cong., 1st sess., S. Doc. 1, pp. 41–530.

1840*a*. Report of the Secretary of the Navy [Paulding] in Relation to Adoption of the Improved Boarding Pistols and Rifles Invented by Samuel Colt. May 25. 26th Cong., 1st sess., S. Doc. 503. 14 pp.

1840*b*. Report of a Board of [Navy] Officers to Witness an Exhibition of Mighill Nutting's Patent Cylinder Firearms [10-shot rifle]. June 15. 26th Cong., 1st sess., S. Doc. 558. 2 pp.

1840c. Report of the Secretary of War, 1840. Dec. 9. 26th Cong., 2d sess., S. Doc. 1, pp. 19–402.

1841. Report of the Secretary of War, 1841. Dec. 7. 27th Cong., 2d sess., S. Doc. 1, pp. 59–366.

1842a. Committee on Military Affairs. Report on . . . Military Posts, Council Bluffs to the Pacific Ocean. May 27. 27th Cong., 2d sess., H. Doc. 830. 64 pp. To accompany H. 465.

1842b. Report of the Secretary of War, 1842. Dec. 7. 27th Cong., 3d sess., S. Doc. 1, pp. 177–534.

1843. Report of the Secretary of War, 1843. Dec. 5. 28th Cong., 1st sess., S. Doc. 1, pp. 49–471.

1848. Message of the President of the United States Transmitting Documents in Relation to . . . the War with Mexico. April 28. 30th Cong., 1st Sess., H. Doc. 60, pp. 4–1277.

1852. Committee on Private Land Claims [Regarding] . . . the Petition of . . . James Clamorgan, Deceased, Praying the Confirmation of a Grant of Land . . . Aug. 28. 32d Cong., 1st sess., S. Rept. 354, to accompany S. 551. 25 pp.

U. S. INDIAN TRADE OFFICE

1801–1822. *See* Hopkins, 1842.

1823. "Indian Trade Office, Invoices of Merchandise Purchased and Received as Presents for Indians in the Year 1823, St. Louis." MS. Vol. 2 of Forsyth Papers, Wisconsin State Historical Society, Madison.

U. S. ORDNANCE DEPARTMENT

1841. *Ordnance Manual for the Use of the Officers of the United States Army.* Washington: Gideon. x, 359 pp., 15 pls.

1850. *Ordnance Manual for the Use of the Officers of the United States Army.* Washington: Gideon. xxiii, 475 pp., 19 pls.

1856. *Reports of Experiments with Small Arms.* Washington: A. O. P. Nicholson. (Separate pagination for each of 4 parts.) See also Summary Statement, "New Models for Small Arms," Ordnance Office, June 26, 1856, *in* 34th Cong., 1st sess., H. Doc. 1, pp. 551–553.

U. S. WAR DEPARTMENT

1825. *Infantry Tactics,* Vol. 1. Washington, D.C.: Davis and Force.

1830. *Abstracts of Infantry Tactics; Including Exercises and Maneuvers of Light-Infantrymen and Riflemen; for the Use of the Militia of the U.S.* Boston: Hilliard, Gray, Little and Wilkins. 138 pp.

1861. *Regulations for the Army of the United States.* New York: Harper. xxv, 457 pp., 21 pls.

VAN RENSSELAER, STEPHEN

1947. *American Firearms.* Watkins Glen, N.Y.: Century House. 288 pp.

VICTOR, FRANCES FULLER

1870. *The River of the West.* Hartford, Conn. 602 pp., illus.

VINTON, STALLO (ed.)

1935. *The American Fur Trade of the Far West.* By H. M. Chittenden. New York: Press of the Pioneers. 2 vols. *See also* Chittenden, 1902.

WADSWORTH ATHENEUM

　1940. *Col. Samuel Colt's Collection of His Model Arms and Other Weapons*. Hartford: Privately printed. 8 pp.

WALLACE, WILLIAM STEWART

　1934. *Documents Relating to the North West Company*. Toronto. Publications of the Champlain Society, XXII. xv, 527 pp.

WALLHAUSEN, JOHANN JACOB VON (JACOBI, JOHANN)

　1615. *Kriegskunst su Fuss*. Vol. I. Frankfort on the Main. (In 1815 J. T. de Bry edited and published this as *L'Art Militaire pour l'infanterie*, Oppenheim.)

WARD, CHRISTOPHER

　1930. *The Dutch and Swedes on the Delaware, 1609–64*. Philadelphia: University of Pennsylvania Press. xi, 393 pp.

WARDELL, MAJ. GEN. W. H.

　1888. *Handbook of Gunpowder and Guncotton*. London. 144 pp.

WARNER, J. J.

　1909. "Reminiscences of Early California from 1831 to 1846," Historical Society of Southern California, *Annual Publications*, VII (1907–1908), pp. 176–193.

WEBB, WALTER PRESCOTT

　1927. "The American Revolver and the West," *Scribner's*, Feb., pp. 171–178.

　1931. *The Great Plains*. Boston: Ginn. xv, 525 pp.

WELLER, JAC

　1953. "Confederate-made Infantry Weapons," *Gun and Cartridge Record*, Vol. I, Dec., p. 9.

WESLEY, EDGAR B.

　1931–1932. "The Government Factory System among the Indians, 1795–1822," *Journal of Economic and Business History* (Cambridge, Mass.), IV, 437–511.

WILCOX, LT. C. M.

　1859. *Rifles and Rifle Practice*. New York: D. Van Nostrand. viii, 276 pp.

WILSON, CLIFFORD

　1951. "Battles on Hudson's Bay," *American Heritage*, Winter number, pp. 50–55.

　1955. Personal letter to Carl P. Russell, Oct. 3. MS.

WINANT, LEWIS

　1952. *Pepperbox Firearms*. New York: Greenberg. 186 pp., illus.

WOOD, W. RAYMOND

　1954. *Kipp's Post: Interim Report*. Bismarck, N.D.: State Historical Society. 3 pp. (mimeo.)

WOODWARD, ARTHUR

　1946. "The Metal Tomahawk," Fort Ticonderoga Museum, *Bulletin*, VII (Jan.), 2–42.

1947. "Notes on Gun Flints." 3 typed pp. accompanying letter of Feb. 14, Woodward to Carl P. Russell.

1948*a*. "Notes on the 12-pounder Brass Mountain Howitzer." 3 typed pp. In personal files of Carl P. Russell.

1948*b*. "Trade Goods of 1748," *The Beaver,* Vol. 279, Dec., pp. 3–6.

1953. Personal letter, Woodward to Russell, Jan. 24. MS.

YOUNG, F. G.

1899. *The Correspondence and Journals of Capt. Nathaniel J. Wyeth, 1831–1836.* Eugene, Oregon: University Press. xix, 262 pp.

YOUNG, ROGERS W.

1939. "Kings Mountain, a Hunting Rifle Victory," *The Regional Review* (Richmond, Va.), Vol. III, No. 6 (Dec.), pp. 25–29. Reprinted in National Park Service Popular Studies, *History,* No. 12, 1941, pp. 1–7.

Index

Abert, Col. J. J., quoted, 142

Alger, Cyrus, maker of mountain howitzer, 269, 275

Allen, C. B., maker of Cochran arms, 79, 96

Allen, Ethan, maker of pepperbox revolver, 91, 310 n. 62

American Fur Co., 105, 107–108, 224; Western Dept. of, 59; boat cannon, 265

American Revolution: its effect on gun trade, 49–55; and the Pennsylvania-Kentucky rifle, 175–176, 327–328

American-made trade guns, accepted by Indians, 59

Ames, Nathan P., U.S. pistol M. 1843 made by, 212, 213

Ammunition. *See* Balls, Canister, Cartridge, Fixed ammunition, Grapeshot, Gunpowder, Match, Priming powder, Shell, Shot

Ammunition chest, 277

Arbalest. *See* Crossbow

Archambeau, L., shot by Indians, 260

Arikara: battle of 1823, 261; trade center of, 36

Arquebus: French, 1–4, 7–8; Spanish, 31

Ashley, William H., 241; sent first wheeled cannon over Rocky Mts.,

265–266, 267; quoted, 266, 331–332; owned Hawken rifle, 307 n. 33

Aston, Henry, maker of U.S. pistol M. 1842, 211–212

Astor, John Jacob: established posts on Great Lakes and upper Mississippi, 59; introduced American-made trade guns, 59; attacked Indian factory system, 59; founded American Fur Co., 105

Astorians: musket carried to Columbia by, 66–67; made musket cartridges, 247; cannon used by, 263–265; sold Astoria, 265, 303 n. 84; rifle of, recovered, 306 n. 28

Balls: musket and rifle, 3, 5, 9, 245, 322–323 n. 12; cannon, 254. *See also* Minié ball

Ball screw. *See* Gun worm

Bandolier, 5

Barnett and Sons. *See* Trade muskets

Barrancas, Spanish arsenal, 255

Bate of London, pistol by, 84–86

Battle tactics, in American Revolution, 175

Bayonet, 154, 157

Belgian arms: trade gun, 14, 114–115; pocket pistol, 84

Bernard Pratt and Co., 59